# THE POWER OF THE JURY

Offering an alternative view of the jury process, this book argues that each stage transforms ordinary citizens, who are oftentimes reluctant to serve on juries, into responsible jurors. Jurors, Professor Marder argues, are not found, but rather they are made and shaped by the jury process. This book analyzes each stage of this process, from initial summons to post-verdict interview, and shows how these stages equip jurors with experiences and knowledge that allow them to perform their new role ably. It adopts a holistic approach to the subject of jury reform and suggests reforms that will aid the transformation of citizens into jurors. By studying the jury from the perspective of jurors, it gives readers a better understanding of what takes place during jury trials and allows them to see juries, jurors, and the jury process in a new light.

NANCY S. MARDER is a Professor of Law and Director of the Justice John Paul Stevens Jury Center at Chicago-Kent College of Law, Illinois Institute of Technology. In the fall of 2021, she was a Visiting Professor of Law at Yale Law School. Professor Marder writes about juries, judges, and courts and presents her work in the United States and abroad. She is a coeditor of *Juries, Lay Judges, and Mixed Courts: A Global Perspective* (2021).

CAMBRIDGE STUDIES IN LAW AND SOCIETY

Founded in 1997, Cambridge Studies in Law and Society is a hub for leading scholarship in socio-legal studies. Located at the intersection of law, the humanities, and the social sciences, it publishes empirically innovative and theoretically sophisticated work on law's manifestations in everyday life: from discourses to practices, and from institutions to cultures. The series editors have longstanding expertise in the interdisciplinary study of law, and welcome contributions that place legal phenomena in national, comparative, or international perspective. Series authors come from a range of disciplines, including anthropology, history, law, literature, political science, and sociology.

*Series Editors*



A list of books in the series can be found at the back of this book.

# THE POWER OF THE JURY

*Transforming Citizens into Jurors*

*Nancy S. Marder*

*Chicago-Kent College of Law, Illinois Institute of Technology*

CAMBRIDGE
UNIVERSITY PRESS

**CAMBRIDGE**
**UNIVERSITY PRESS**

University Printing House, Cambridge CB2 8BS, United Kingdom

One Liberty Plaza, 20th Floor, New York, NY 10006, USA

477 Williamstown Road, Port Melbourne, VIC 3207, Australia

314–321, 3rd Floor, Plot 3, Splendor Forum, Jasola District Centre, New Delhi – 110025, India

103 Penang Road, #05–06/07, Visioncrest Commercial, Singapore 238467

Cambridge University Press is part of the University of Cambridge.

It furthers the University's mission by disseminating knowledge in the pursuit of education, learning, and research at the highest international levels of excellence.

www.cambridge.org
Information on this title: www.cambridge.org/9781108483315
DOI: 10.1017/9781108630009



First published 2022

*A catalogue record for this publication is available from the British Library.*

ISBN 978-1-108-48331-5 Hardback
ISBN 978-1-108-70479-3 Paperback

# CONTENTS

# ACKNOWLEDGMENTS

I am extremely fortunate to have had one teacher and two judges who shaped my views of the jury in different ways. I was a student in Professor Owen Fiss's Procedure course at Yale Law School. I remember Professor Fiss made an eloquent defense of judges, and I came to share his view, especially after I had the opportunity to clerk for several judges and to observe firsthand the fine work they did. At the time, though, I wondered why Professor Fiss did not come to the defense of that other judicial decision-maker – the jury. I began to do research and writing on the jury, and Professor Fiss served as my supervisor. If I could persuade him that juries mattered then maybe I could persuade others as well. My interest in the jury began in that Procedure course in my first semester of law school and has continued ever since.

I had the opportunity to watch the jury in action when I clerked for Judge Leonard B. Sand, who was then a federal district court judge in the Southern District of New York. Judge Sand was a great believer in juries. When I clerked for Judge Sand, he had been on the bench for fifteen years. He told me that in those fifteen years, he had presided over many jury trials and he could count on one hand the number of times he had disagreed with a jury's verdict. He treated juries with great respect and took care to explain to jurors what was about to take place in the courtroom, what their role was, and what his role was. He remains my model of a trial judge and his relationship with the jury remains my ideal for the judge–jury relationship.

I also learned about the jury during two years as a law clerk to Justice John Paul Stevens at the US Supreme Court. I was fortunate to have the benefits of Justice Stevens's insights when I clerked for him and in the decades that followed. I had a front-row seat as the Court extended *Batson* v. *Kentucky* in an effort to eliminate discriminatory peremptory challenges. Initially, *Batson* applied just to prosecutors who were intent upon eliminating African-American prospective jurors when the defendant was also African American. However, during the two Terms that I was a law clerk, the Court expanded *Batson*'s reach. In a series of jury cases, the Court decided that *Batson* applied to defense attorneys as well as to lawyers in civil cases and that peremptory challenges could no longer be exercised on the basis of race, gender, or ethnicity. The logic of *Batson* seemed inexorable and held such promise. Justice Stevens, who had been a trial lawyer, had a great appreciation for juries. As a Seventh Circuit judge and then as a Justice, he wanted to make sure that as many citizens as possible could serve as jurors. I admired Justice Stevens and his views on juries, and I was optimistic about *Batson* and its progeny at the time.

These great mentors and these very different vantage points have informed my study of the jury. In my past writing as well as in this book, I seek to describe the experience of jurors in the courtroom, to think about the relationship between judges and jurors, and to make sure that jury service is available to as broad a swath of the population as possible, and that citizens are not excluded from serving as jurors because of discrimination. Each of my early teachers helped to shape my concerns, and their perspectives have guided my study of the jury, from how it works in practice to the challenges it still faces and the ways in which it needs to be reformed to meet an ever-changing society.

Although I have been writing about the jury since law school, and have had the chance to develop many of the ideas in this book in law review articles and book chapters, this book still required more time, feedback, and rewriting than any of my other projects. I could not have written this book without the support of my spouse, Jeremy David Eden. When I explained the idea of the book to him, he embraced it with alacrity. He read and critiqued numerous drafts and when my argument needed clarification, he helped me to sharpen it. He was willing to talk about the book whenever I encountered a problem or needed to test out a new idea. He took on this project with enthusiasm and gave generously of his time, insights, and ideas. He was a partner in this endeavor, as he is in the rest of my life.

This book came to fruition only with the support of several academic communities. My colleagues at Chicago-Kent have been essential to this project. When I first described my book proposal to Christopher Schmidt, who was then Associate Dean for Faculty Development, he was enthusiastic and organized a workshop for it. His own manuscript conference served as a model for mine. He, along with Joan Steinman and Harold Krent, gave me the time to write this book by awarding me the inaugural Freehling Award. Thanks to the generosity of Paul and Sue Freehling, this award gave me a semester free from teaching so that I could focus full time on writing. Paul Freehling, who had been a trial lawyer, continues to have an abiding interest in the jury and I am grateful for our conversations on this subject over the years. My colleagues at Chicago-Kent have given their input at various stages of this project, including the book proposal, a workshop for the first two chapters, and several conference presentations at Chicago-Kent. Now under the leadership of Dean Anita Krug, Chicago-Kent has continued to support my scholarship and to provide summer funding that has allowed me to work on this book.

Another community that has been essential to my work on the jury in general, and to this book in particular, is the Collaborative Research Network (CRN) on Lay Participation that is part of the Law & Society Association. I have been a member of this CRN, organized by Valerie Hans, Sanja Kutnjak Ivković, and Mary Rose, for almost my entire academic career, and in that time I have never missed an annual meeting. These jury scholars, some from the United States and others from around the world, gather every year to share new developments, new methods, and new research on the jury. They have been a source of friendship, collaboration, and knowledge. I have used this group as a sounding board for this project, as well as for my other work on the jury. Indeed, I had the pleasure of collaborating with coeditors Sanja Kutnjak Ivković, Shari Seidman Diamond, and Valerie Hans to publish *Juries, Lay Judges, and Mixed Courts: A Global Perspective* (2021).

Colleagues from Chicago-Kent and the CRN on Lay Participation came together, even with short notice, for a manuscript conference for this book, funded by the Justice John Paul Stevens Jury Center at Chicago-Kent. These colleagues read an early draft of the manuscript and gave me written and oral comments. The participants included: Lori Andrews, Robert Burns, Sonali Chakravarti, Sungjoon Cho, Shari Seidman Diamond, David Erickson, Valerie Hans, Thaddeus Hoffmeister, Sanja Kutnjak Ivković, Richard Lempert, James Matsumoto (a former juror), Barbara O'Brien, Christopher Schmidt, and Carolyn Shapiro. I have also benefited from feedback when I presented chapters of the book at several conferences, including the roundtable organized by Anna Offit as part of the Civil Jury Project created by Stephen Susman at New York University Law School; the jury symposium at Louisiana State University organized by Raff Donelson and the *Louisiana Law Review*; the Midwest Law and Society Retreat; the Association for the Study of Law, Culture, and the Humanities; and the Practicing Law Institute. Carol Lee worked mightily to keep me up to date about jury developments, especially during the pandemic, and I am grateful for her help and friendship.

Another academic community I want to thank is the community at the Baldy Center for Law and Social Policy at the University at Buffalo School of Law in Buffalo, New York. The Baldy Center, then under the directorship of Errol Meidinger, awarded me a Senior Fellowship that allowed me to spend a semester at the Center working on a draft of this book. This fellowship provided me with a community of scholars, as well as uninterrupted time in which to write. The Buffalo winter kept me indoors and free from all distractions.

Most recently, I have benefited from my return to Yale Law School, where I have been a Visiting Professor of Law. Yale, as always, is a vibrant and engaged community and it was a privilege to be a part of it. I benefited enormously from conversations with Judith Resnik, as I have throughout my academic career. I admire her expertise, energy, commitment, and passion. She has been an extraordinary friend and colleague and provided guidance for this project, as well as so many others. Over the decades, Judith and her spouse, Dennis Curtis, have given generously of their time to discuss a wide range of topics, and these conversations occurred even more frequently during my time at Yale. Other colleagues and friends at Yale, including Christopher and Janet Arterton, Owen Fiss, James Forman, and Anthony Kronman, have embraced the subject of this book and have spent time discussing it with me. Yale Law School, under the stewardship of Dean Heather Gerken, has been generous with its resources. I appreciate the tremendous assistance of Research Assistants Justin Cole and Lauren Lin and Faculty Assistant Marilyn Serna.

Throughout this project, Mandy Lee provided excellent library assistance, Sue Jadin and Emily Barney assisted with their technical expertise, Nicole Mszal helped me with conference presentations, and my team at Cambridge University Press helped bring this book to fruition.

Finally, I want to thank my family for always taking an interest in my work. My parents, Ellen R. Marder and Jerome M. Marder, and my siblings, Wendy, Jamie, Scott, and Karen, have always asked about my work and this book was no exception; my in-laws, Judi and Burt Eden, sent me articles pertaining to the jury, and my sister-in-law, Amy Eden, and brother-in-law, Jim Weinrebe, kept me abreast of movies and television programs about the jury. I have been very fortunate to have this support system of family, friends, and colleagues. Without them, I would never have completed this book; with them, I cannot wait to start on the next book.

# INTRODUCTION

Citizens summoned for jury duty usually enter the courtroom with a range of responses from trepidation to dread to even a little awe. These responses are understandable given the power of the jury to decide a party's fate. With such power, however, comes tremendous responsibility. To make matters even more challenging, the jurors will have to decide cases that can be complicated and they will have to reach a unanimous decision, at least in criminal cases in state and federal courts and in civil cases in federal courts.

The question that this book will address is what makes juries work? It does not seem possible that a group of twelve randomly chosen individuals who have no legal training, no expertise in the subject of the trial, no experience adjudicating legal claims, and no real guidance about how to work together as a group, can fairly and correctly decide the fate of the parties on matters about which the group knows little or nothing. It does not help that prospective jurors usually begin by resenting their summons and their jury service when they enter the courtroom, and they bring with them various biases and personality traits as well as a lack of training that make them seem, at first glance, wholly unsuited for the task.

The challenge that the American jury system faces is illustrated by the most famous American jury film, *12 Angry Men*.[1] How does a motley group of jurors, many of whom are unhappy about serving and eager to leave, become a jury that works successfully as a group to

[1] 12 ANGRY MEN (Orion-Nova Films 1957).

reach a unanimous verdict based on the evidence that was presented to them during the trial? In spite of the challenge, the American jury system works reasonably well. What accounts for its success?

The answer lies in the jury process and the way in which it transforms citizens into jurors. The various stages of the jury process, including the summons, *voir dire* (questioning of prospective jurors), instructions, and deliberations, help citizens to step into their role as jurors. The final stage, the post-verdict interview with the judge, helps jurors to leave their role as jurors behind and to resume their lives as private citizens. Even if citizens do not want to be jurors initially or do not think they can perform this task well, the jury process transforms them from citizens who do not want to serve into jurors who perform their role responsibly. Although the jury process carries out this transformation of citizens into jurors reasonably well, there is still room for improvement. Each of the stages of the jury process can be improved upon by looking at the process as a whole rather than at each stage in isolation, and by ensuring that any reforms further the transformation of citizens into jurors.

The traditional view of jurors is that from a pool of citizens it is possible to find those who are jury-ready from the outset. In other words, they are unbiased, competent, and prepared to find the facts and apply the law as presented during the trial. This view assumes that prospective jurors have fixed qualities that can be recognized during *voir dire*. In some cases, prospective jurors are seen as so biased as to make them unable to render a fair verdict and the judge can remove them "for cause." In most cases, however, a juror's subtle biases are not revealed through *voir dire* questions. Lawyers strike a certain number of prospective jurors with peremptory challenges, but they typically know little about these prospective jurors' hidden biases. Once lawyers have exercised their peremptory challenges, they believe that they have removed the biased prospective jurors and that the jurors who remain are impartial and ready to serve. In other words, the traditional view is that jurors who have undergone *voir dire* questioning and survived peremptory challenges start out as ready-made jurors.

I argue that the reverse is true of our jury system: Jurors are made not found. Jurors do not, for the most part, have immutable qualities that lawyers and judges can discern during *voir dire* and that will make them impartial jurors throughout the trial. Rather, jurors are created by transforming citizens into jurors through every stage of the jury process. A dramatic illustration of this transformation is the change in attitude that occurs from when citizens receive their summons to after they complete their jury service. They typically view their summons with irritation, displeasure, and the strong desire to be excused from jury service, whereas after they have served as jurors, they typically feel pride in having ably performed an important role for society. Polls and surveys of those who have served as jurors show that they believe they performed their task as jurors well and that they think more highly of the judiciary after they have served as jurors.[2] A less dramatic, but no less significant, moment that reveals the start of this transformation from citizens to jurors is when citizens, who have entered the courtroom trying to conjure up reasons why they cannot serve, start to experience a change of mind during *voir dire*. There is almost a palpable moment in the courtroom when prospective jurors begin to shift from wanting to be excused to wanting to serve.

The traditional view sees jurors primarily as ready-made problem-solvers. According to the traditional view, lawyers just need to find jurors who have no overt bias. Once these jurors have been found, then the trial will provide them with the facts, and the judge will provide them with the law, so that they can methodically solve the problem of reaching a verdict. According to the traditional view, jurors arrive at the courthouse knowing how to be jurors and the jury process does not have much to teach them.

In contrast, the transformation view accepts that citizens begin their jury service as individuals who might be unprepared for their role as jurors, but who will be transformed into jurors as they go through the stages of the jury process. This book analyzes these stages – from summons to post-verdict interviews – and shows how these stages provide citizens with experiences that change their behavior and their understanding of their role so that they will be transformed into responsible jurors. Everyone in the courtroom – from the jurors who are new to the experience to the judge, lawyers, and press who are all familiar with jury trials – might be unaware of the ways in which

[2] *See, e.g.*, Nancy S. Marder & Valerie P. Hans, *Introduction to Juries and Lay Participation: American Perspectives and Global Trends*, 90 CHI.-KENT L. REV. 789, 789 n.5 (2015) (citing polls and surveys). In addition to myriad recent surveys and polls, there is an extensive literature, going back decades, that shows that those who serve as jurors think highly of their jury experience, and that those who serve leave with positive views of the court system. *See, e.g.*, Brian L. Cutler & Donna M. Hughes, *Judging Jury Service: Results of the North Carolina Administrative Office of the Courts Juror Survey*, 19 BEHAV. SCI. & L. 305, 316, 319 (2001) (surveying 4,654 venirepersons in North Carolina and finding that they had a very positive view of the court system, which became even more positive after jury service).

every stage of the jury process gives jurors experiences that will enable them to assume their role. Prospective jurors enter the courtroom as individuals who are typically reluctant to be there and anxious to leave, but the jury process helps them to become jurors from whom certain behaviors are expected. They develop these behaviors with every stage of the jury process. By the time they reach deliberations, they conceive of themselves as jurors and understand the enormous responsibility that their role entails.

This book analyzes the stages of the jury process and shows how they help to transform ordinary citizens into responsible jurors. The stages that this book describes are the summons, *voir dire*, jury instructions, and jury deliberations. The stages are the same for criminal and civil jury trials. The final stage, the post-verdict interview with the judge, helps jurors leave their role as jurors after the trial and return to their lives as private citizens. It also helps jurors to serve as goodwill ambassadors for the jury system. The exercise of peremptory challenges, which allows lawyers to remove a certain number of prospective jurors from the jury, is another stage of the jury process, but one that I will argue does not help in the transformation of citizens into jurors. In fact, it undermines the process by limiting who can serve as jurors.

The stages of the jury process need to be viewed holistically rather than in isolation because that is how jurors experience them. The traditional view is to look at each stage in isolation, but this is a mistake. It leads to a myopic view of each stage of the jury process, and misses what jurors actually experience when they serve as jurors. I show how each stage of the jury process contributes to a critical, albeit unacknowledged, purpose, which is to transform citizens into jurors. The jury process needs to be viewed in its entirety because it is through this process that citizens who are initially reluctant to serve become jurors who behave responsibly and perform their role ably. It is the jury process, in its entirety, that enables citizens, who are for the most part untrained in the law, to assume their role as jurors.

The judge's interactions with the jury can aid in the process of helping jurors to assume their role. Judge and jury work together throughout the trial process, though they have different roles to perform. Throughout the trial, there is a back-and-forth between the judge and the jury. The jury learns about its role from this ongoing dialogue with the judge.

Because jurors want to do the right thing – they want to perform their role as well as possible – they look to the judge for guidance. In

*Democracy in America*, first published in 1835, the French writer Alexis de Tocqueville recognized the judge–jury relationship as a source of learning when he described the jury as a "free school."[3] Tocqueville suggested that in civil trials jurors would look to the judge for guidance. They would do this more so than in criminal cases, which he thought dealt with easily understandable issues and where the judge was regarded more as an arm of the state. Tocqueville surmised that jurors would learn how to act judiciously and to apply these lessons to their business affairs once they resumed their lives as private citizens. He also described the jury as "above all a political institution" because in a democracy the jury trained citizens to engage in self-governance.[4] Although Tocqueville emphasized that jury service helps jurors to become better citizens, my aim is to show how the jury process helps ordinary citizens to become better jurors.

This holistic view of the jury process also has implications for jury reforms. Rather than assessing a proposed reform in isolation, as the traditional view does, reform needs to be considered in light of how it fits into the entire jury process and whether it aids the transformation of citizens into jurors. Thus, the transformation view is a lens through which any jury reform should be assessed. This understanding of the jury process as transforming citizens into jurors also opens the door for more citizens to serve as jurors because it is the jury process that will help them to become responsible jurors, not an overly simplistic view that they are either unbiased or biased jurors when they walk through the courtroom door.

The power of the transformation view is that it reveals reforms that the traditional view obscures. Accordingly, each chapter in this book explores the reforms suggested by the traditional view and then those revealed by the transformation view.

The book is organized in six chapters that take the reader through every stage of the jury process, as the juror experiences it. Chapter 1 sets the stage for the challenge that the American jury system faces. Citizens receive a jury summons requiring them to appear in court. They are often dismayed when they receive their summons. They might know little or nothing about the jury system. The information they have is probably gleaned from newspaper accounts of jury trials or

[3] Alexis de Tocqueville, Democracy in America 275 (J.P. Mayer ed., George Lawrence trans., Anchor Books 1969) (1835).

[4] *Id.* at 272 (describing the jury as "above all a political institution" and explaining that "it is from that point of view that [the American jury] must always be judged").

movies or television episodes involving a jury, and many of these portrayals are negative.[5] To make matters worse, jury duty inevitably interrupts work and personal lives, so it is not surprising that many citizens view their summons with annoyance if not anxiety.

Those who heed their summons often do so reluctantly. When they enter the courthouse, they are not always treated well. Often they are made to wait and given little explanation as to what will happen next. Those who progress from the Jury Assembly Room to a courtroom usually enter with trepidation. They enter thinking of reasons why they cannot serve.

The traditional view of the summons is that it is just an isolated step designed to bring a sufficient number of prospective jurors to the courthouse to ensure that there will be enough jurors for the scheduled trials. From this point of view, this step is successful as long as enough prospective jurors show up, and it does not matter much how they feel about the experience at this point.

The transformation view is that the experience of receiving a summons and going to the courthouse is an unusual event that begins to transform the outlook and behavior of those who are ultimately selected as jurors. However, from this perspective the summons and introduction to the courthouse can and should be reformed to reinforce the desire of citizens to assume the role of jurors. Even at this early stage of the jury process, there are steps that courts can take to assist in the transformation of citizens into jurors. Courts can design summonses that are written clearly, provide answers to frequently asked questions, and reassure citizens that they do not need any special knowledge to serve as jurors. When citizens heed their summons and go to the courthouse, court staff should answer their questions, and when they enter the courtroom, judges should put them at ease. The summons, which courts view mainly as a vehicle to bring citizens to the courthouse, should instead be viewed as a form of outreach that begins the transformation of citizens into responsible jurors.

Chapter 2 focuses on *voir dire*, which is the questioning of prospective jurors. The traditional view is that this stage is supposed to enable judges and lawyers to determine which prospective jurors are biased and need to be removed and which are unbiased and so can serve on the

[5] For an example of a novel, see JOHN GRISHAM , THE RUNAWAY JURY (1996); for examples of movies, see THE JUROR (Columbia Pictures 1996) and TRIAL BY JURY (Morgan Creek Productions 1994); and for an example of a television episode, see *All in the Family: Edith Has Jury Duty* (CBS television broadcast Mar. 9, 1971).

jury. However, jury scholars, social scientists, and psychologists have conducted numerous empirical studies showing that *voir dire* is not well designed to elicit information about who is biased and who is not.

The transformation view is that *voir dire* has little value as a means of finding jurors who are impartial, but it has a lot of value in helping to transform citizens into impartial jurors. Other than in extreme cases of bias, which can be identified and weeded out for cause, there is little evidence that the kind of biases that everyone has can or should be identified during *voir dire*. The chapter describes the experience of going through *voir dire*, which really begins the process of helping prospective jurors to put aside their private concerns, to understand the crucial need to manage their own biases, and to see themselves as part of a group endeavor. There is a moment during *voir dire* when prospective jurors stop formulating their excuses and start thinking about serving. At that moment, a transformation begins in earnest. It is almost a palpable moment in the courtroom. Citizens who were reluctant to serve now want to be selected for jury service.

Although this stage of the jury process is the beginning of the transformation, the chapter describes how *voir dire* can be reformed to bring about the transformation of citizens into jurors even more effectively than the current practice. For example, the judge–jury relationship can aid in this transformation. *Voir dire* needs to be reformed so that the judge asks different questions of prospective jurors. The judge should devote more of *voir dire* to describing the trial process and the roles of the judge and the jury, rather than trying to uncover hidden biases. If *voir dire* is a crucial stage in helping citizens to step into their role as jurors, as I argue it is, this needs to be made explicit.

Chapter 3 considers peremptory challenges and how they impede the transformation of citizens into jurors. The traditional view of peremptory challenges is that they help to seat an impartial jury. Peremptory challenges permit lawyers to remove a certain number of prospective jurors from the jury without having to give a reason. In this way, lawyers can remove some prospective jurors about whom they have misgivings. Once these prospective jurors have been removed, the parties can have confidence that the jurors seated on the jury will be impartial.

There are several problems with the exercise of peremptory challenges, which the traditional view depends on to reassure the parties that the selected jurors are impartial. One problem is that lawyers are ill-equipped to uncover subtle juror bias during *voir dire*, even though they claim to be able to do so. Another problem is that some lawyers continue to exercise peremptory challenges in a discriminatory manner, particularly in capital cases when the defendant and the prospective juror are African American. This leaves many, particularly African Americans, doubting the impartiality of the jury. The Supreme Court has tried hard to strike a balance so that peremptory challenges could continue, but discriminatory peremptory challenges would end. However, that balance has been difficult to achieve, and peremptory challenges based on race, ethnicity, and gender persist.

According to the transformation view, the jury needs to consist of a diverse group of jurors. They might have some biases, as all people do, but as a group they will be able to learn from each other and challenge each other's biases. As a diverse group, they will have access to a wide range of experiences and perspectives. The transformation view rejects the goal of trying to weed out subtle biases that cannot really be known in favor of the goal of increasing jury diversity.

If a diverse jury is important,[6] as I argue it is, then peremptory challenges, which continue to be exercised in a discriminatory manner, stand in the way of such diversity. Eliminating peremptory challenges is the most effective way of stopping discriminatory peremptory challenges, particularly because other methods have fallen short. Eliminating peremptory challenges would, for example, stop the practice of lawyers who exercise peremptory challenges against African-American prospective jurors in capital cases when the defendant is African American. There are other ways to minimize the harms of peremptory challenges, such as minimizing the number of peremptory challenges allotted to each side or expanding the test of a discriminatory peremptory challenge to include implicit bias and not just discriminatory intent; but, short of eliminating peremptory challenges altogether, these methods are likely to permit lawyers to continue to exclude broad swaths of the population from serving as jurors.

Even with the elimination of peremptory challenges, for cause challenges should remain. For cause challenges, which are decided by the judge and for which a reason must be given in open court, should remain because they allow the judge, *sua sponte* or at the behest of the lawyer, to remove extreme cases of biased jurors, such as those who

[6] Although I see a diverse jury as very important, I recognize that the U.S. Supreme Court has only said that parties have a right to a jury venire, or panel, that is drawn from a fair cross section of the community and not a petit jury that is drawn from a fair cross section of the community. *See* Taylor v. Louisiana, 419 U.S. 522, 537–38 (1975).

admit that they are biased, who have a familial connection to one of the trial participants, or who have a financial stake in the outcome of the trial.

Chapter 4 examines jury instructions, which are given by the judge to provide guidance to the jurors, including an understanding of the relevant law. The traditional view of jury instructions is that jurors are rational problem-solvers who just need to be told the law they must apply. Once they are informed, they will apply the law to the facts as they find them and eventually be able to reach a unanimous verdict. The facts are provided by the parties during the trial and the law is provided by the judge in the jury instructions. The instructions are usually a lengthy monologue that the judge delivers orally at the end of the trial before the jury goes into the jury room to deliberate. The judge assumes that the jurors will understand the instructions and retain everything he or she has told them. According to the traditional view, the carefully written instructions and their oral delivery to the jury are simply a vehicle for making sure that all of the jurors know the law they must apply. The underlying assumption is that they will understand the instructions and use them as the basis for their deliberations.

According to the transformation view, however, the reading of the instructions provides an experience for the jurors that is far more than simply the conveyance of information about the law. As the instructions are read, the jurors have an experience unlike any they would have had in their lives outside of a courtroom, and certainly a different experience than if they had just been handed the instructions to read on their own. The judge's reading of the instructions as the jurors sit together in the jury box ensures that all of the jurors hear the instructions from start to finish, as a group, and that everyone in the courtroom, including the jurors, senses the important role that the instructions play. The jury is being given a very specific task in front of the parties; they are being told to put aside their biases and personal views and to reach a verdict based only on the evidence presented in the courtroom. The reading aloud of the instructions in open court before the jurors, the parties, and the public highlights the importance of the jurors' task, their need to be fair, and the role they are about to play as equals in a group effort to achieve a unanimous verdict.

If jury instructions are understood as part of the jury process of helping jurors to assume their role as jurors, then the oral reading by the judge needs to be supplemented by certain aids so that jurors understand the substance of the instructions. The instructions need to be delivered in a preliminary form at the start of the trial, on a need-to-know basis as the trial proceeds, and in a summary form at the end of the trial. Jurors also need to be given an individual written copy of the instructions, complete with subject headings, so they can follow the instructions as the judge reads them aloud. They should also be permitted to take notes on their written copy of the instructions so that they can highlight words or concepts they want to clarify with their fellow jurors during deliberations. To make jury instructions more of a dialogue than a monologue, jurors should be permitted to submit written questions to the judge after he or she has read them aloud and the judge should answer those questions, to the extent he or she is permitted to do so.

Even when jurors understand the instructions, they might resist following them, as some do with the instruction to refrain from discussing the trial or doing research about it online. However, it is the judge–jury relationship, begun during *voir dire* and developed throughout the trial, as well as their relationship with their fellow jurors and their commitment to the group endeavor, that will ultimately persuade jurors to adhere to the instructions.

Chapter 5 looks at deliberations. The traditional view of jury deliberations is that jurors are capable, from the moment they are selected, to deliberate in a way that yields a fair and just verdict. Moreover, the traditional view is that the jury is an independent body that should be left to its own devices as much as possible. According to this view, it is up to jurors to structure their deliberations as they see fit, and the judge must not intrude in any way. Although jurors are free to structure their deliberations on their own, deliberations should be seen as part of the process of helping jurors to realize fully their role as jurors.

According to the transformation view, jurors are made, not found. The citizens who receive a summons are seemingly quite unprepared for the daunting task ahead of them. They must perform a role for which they have not volunteered; they must be aware of their personal biases and try hard not to be swayed by them; they must deliberate to try to reach a unanimous verdict with a group of strangers; and they must decide the facts and apply the law even though both are new to them and might be quite complicated. However, the experiences they go through from the moment they receive their summons to the moment they are about to enter the jury room help to prepare them to deliberate. In addition, the setting and structure of the deliberations help them to maintain the necessary discipline. The jurors are secluded in the jury room; they are required to vote and to give reasons to each other for their decision; if unanimity is required they must come to an understanding with every other juror; they must make a decision that is far more serious than many have ever had to make; and they cannot discuss this decision with anyone but their fellow jurors. The experience of deliberating might change the very decision that they reach.

Although much of the groundwork will have been laid before jurors deliberate, there are still features of deliberations that help jurors to assume their role as jurors. Having a foreperson means that there is one juror who starts to put the concerns of the group above any individual concerns. Having a diverse jury, made up of jurors from different walks of life, means that jurors will learn from each other. Jurors on a diverse jury are more likely to have a thorough and well-considered deliberation than those on a more homogeneous jury. Having a group deliberation with the requirement of a unanimous verdict means that all jurors' views are needed and every juror's vote counts. Jurors also have the judge's instructions and they help to anchor the jury deliberations to the law. The instructions also give each juror equal access to the law because they have all heard the judge read them aloud from start to finish in open court.

Although judges are reticent to intrude during deliberations, they can provide guidance that will help jurors in their transformation from citizens into jurors. Judges can give jurors advice on how to begin their deliberations, including the suggestion that they wait to take a vote. Another juncture when the deliberating jurors need assistance is when they reach an impasse. Typically, the judge instructs the jurors to keep deliberating and try to reach a verdict; instead, the judge should find out what the point of disagreement is and see if further argument by the lawyers on this point would be helpful. Judges also need to instruct on nullification, which is when the jury decides not to follow the law, so that jurors understand the full power of the jury. If jurors are not told about this power, they might have regrets about their verdict and their jury service when they learn about jury nullification after the trial. Such regrets will interfere with their willingness to serve as ambassadors for the jury system after their jury service has ended.

Chapter 6 explores the final stage of the jury process, the post-verdict interview with the judge, which provides an opportunity for the judge to thank jurors for their service, to answer their remaining questions, to provide them with information about issues that might arise after they leave the courthouse, and to give them an opportunity to share their jury experience with the judge.

The traditional view often overlooks the post-verdict interview. Some judges provide such an interview; others do not. Whether to hold such an interview and what to say during it are usually left to a judge's discretion. Some judges forgo the interview because they do not want to detain jurors any longer than they have to or because they are worried about saying something they should not say or hearing something from the jurors that might require further action.

However, the post-verdict interview can play an important role in the jurors' transformation, helping jurors to leave their public role as jurors and to return to their lives as private citizens. The post-verdict interview with the judge also helps jurors to end their jury service on a positive note. This is important so that when jurors return to their family and friends they will serve as emissaries for the jury system. Finally, the post-verdict interview gives judges the opportunity to learn about the jurors' experience and to discover how the jury process can be improved. The knowledge that judges acquire from hearing jurors speak about their experience, and from collecting their responses to exit questionnaires, can help them to make improvements in the jury process for future jurors.

1

# THE SUMMONS AND THE SETTING: BEGINNING THE TRANSFORMATION OF CITIZENS INTO JURORS

Jury duty begins with a summons. It arrives in the mail; it is official; and it can evoke a range of emotions, including dismay or even dread. Few people are happy to receive a jury summons. One newspaper columnist, trying to describe the terrible reputation of middle school, wrote that it "hovers somewhere between root canal and jury duty."[1] Jury duty, like middle school, does not enjoy a good reputation. It is the obligation that everyone loves to hate. According to John Oliver, "[c]omplaining about jury duty has long been a beloved American pastime."[2] Even the most ardent fans of the jury immediately think about how inconvenient jury duty is. One lawyer who received his jury summons explained: "My first reaction upon getting the [jury] summons was that I was interested but too busy. What happens if it's a long trial?"[3] Jury duty requires one to miss work and to rearrange personal obligations.[4] It is an interruption of one's daily life.

For those who heed their summons, their introduction to the courthouse does not usually make them feel any better about jury duty. Conditions for prospective jurors can be crowded and unpleasant;

[1] Heidi Stevens, *Book Aims to Change Middle School Reputation*, CHI. TRIB., Aug. 28, 2019 (§ 5), at 1.

[2] *Last Week Tonight with John Oliver* (HBO cable television broadcast Aug. 16, 2020).

[3] Phillip H. Hamilton, *Juror Number 10, Attorney at Law*, 98 ILL. B.J. 296, 296 (2010).

[4] Rosie Mullaley, *Newfoundland and Labrador Offers More Supports for Jurors Than Any Other Province in Canada*, WESTERN STAR (Aug. 14, 2019), https://www.thewesternstar.com/news/local/newfoundland-and-labrador-offers-more-supports-for-jurors-than-any-other-province-in-canada-341105/ [https://perma.cc/HN9Z-H34C] ("It can be unsettling for those who worry about lost time from work and family, and the disruption of their daily life, not to mention the added cost of travelling to and parking at court every day.").

information about when they might be assigned to a courtroom is usually not forthcoming. When prospective jurors are sent to a courtroom, the setting is imposing and the procedures are unfamiliar. It is not surprising that citizens think twice about whether to respond to their summons. Yet, even at this early stage, citizens who heed their summons can find that their initial dismay is also tempered by a sense of curiosity or even excitement. They have been asked to perform a service that is out of the ordinary.

The traditional view of the jury summons is that it is mainly a mechanism to bring a pool of prospective jurors to the courthouse. Once inside, these prospective jurors will be randomly assigned to courtrooms. In the courtroom, those who can claim a financial or medical hardship will be excused. The remaining prospective jurors will either be excluded for cause by the judge (for certain identifiable reasons that the judge explains in open court) or considered to be impartial and available to serve, though they might not be selected to serve on the case to which they have been assigned. The traditional view assumes that citizens are capable of working as a member of the jury to apply the law fairly to the facts of the case as long as they are not facing an undue hardship or do not have a specific bias in the specific case to which they have been assigned. The summons, then, is merely a tool to ensure that a sufficient number of prospective jurors show up each day at the courthouse so that judges can seat juries for the trials on their calendar.

According to the transformation view, however, the summons starts the process by which citizens are transformed into jurors through each of the stages of the jury process, beginning with the summons and ending with the post-verdict interview. The transformation view recognizes that most citizens are not ready to work as members of the jury from the outset, but that through the jury process they will be ready by the time they deliberate. The summons begins the transformation; it signals to citizens that they are about to play a role that is out of the ordinary. The setting of the courthouse and courtroom reinforce this sense that what is about to take place is of unusual significance. Citizens, many of whom arrive at the courthouse thinking about the inconvenience of being a juror, begin to consider concerns beyond themselves as they wait as a group in the Jury Assembly Room, walk as a group to a courtroom, and sit as a group in the courtroom, until the moment when twelve of them stand in the jury box to take the oath and are impaneled as a jury.

## WHAT THE SUMMONS AND SETTING ENTAIL

The jury summons usually arrives by US mail;[5] it is a formal document from the court requiring a citizen to appear for jury duty on a certain date, at a certain time, and at a particular courthouse – or suffer the consequences. For example, in Cook County in Chicago, the first sentence of the summons indicates that "failure to obey this summons may be punishable by a fine."[6] Courts need a sufficient number of prospective jurors to appear on a given day so that judges who have scheduled jury trials can seat a jury. The summons is the mechanism by which courts inform citizens that they need to put aside their usual work and family obligations, and instead, they need to appear at the courthouse and be available to serve as jurors.

The summons attempts to get recipients to appear at the designated time and place by being an official document. It uses authoritative language and threats of punishment to try to persuade the recipient to appear. In some jurisdictions, the summons includes a brief questionnaire as to qualifications that the recipient is instructed to bring to court.[7] In other jurisdictions, the qualifications questionnaire will precede the summons.[8] In some jurisdictions, the court will send an order to show cause if the recipient does not appear in court on the designated day.[9] In other jurisdictions, the recipient's failure to respond may result in a sheriff knocking on the door with an order to show cause that requires the recipient to go to court and to explain to a judge why he or she has failed to respond to the jury summons.[10] In some cities, such as Los Angeles and New York, when there were not enough prospective jurors, "court personnel [had to] walk around outside of

[5] Alaska, however, recently started sending jury summonses by email. *See Alaska Starts Summoning Jurors by Email*, JUR-E BULLETIN (Jan. 24, 2020, 8:01 AM), https://www.ncsc.org/newsroom/jure/2020/jan-24.

[6] Summons to Appear for Jury Service, Cook Cnty., Ill. (Aug. 1, 2016) (on file with author) [hereinafter Summons to Appear].

[7] ROBERT G. BOATRIGHT, IMPROVING CITIZEN RESPONSE TO JURY SUMMONSES: A REPORT WITH RECOMMENDATIONS 84 (1998) (describing the process in Maricopa County Superior Court in Phoenix, Arizona, where the court "uses a one-step summoning and questionnaire process").

[8] *Id.* at 93 (describing Montgomery County Court of Common Pleas in Norristown, Pennsylvania, which uses a "two-step questionnaire and summoning process").

[9] *Id.* at 108 (noting that in the U.S. District Court for the Western District of Tennessee show cause warrants are issued to prospective jurors who do not respond to their summonses three months after they have been sent).

[10] *See, e.g.*, Greg Moran, *When Jury Duty Calls: Counties Wrestle with High Evasion Rates*, CAL. LAW., May 2001, at 22 (describing Stanislaus County, California, where a "failure to appear" postcard follows an ignored jury summons, and if that does not elicit a response within ten days, then a uniformed marshal with an order to show cause can appear at the door).

the courthouse looking for citizens willing to volunteer to serve as jurors."[11]

The court needs to send out summonses to as broad a swath of the citizenry as possible. It uses various lists from which to draw names. In the past, courts relied primarily on the voter registration list,[12] perhaps because of convenience or because someone who had registered to vote might be more willing to heed the summons or because voting and jury duty are two responsibilities of citizenship. But, of course, not everyone who could serve as a juror was registered to vote. In fact, some citizens do not register to vote because they think this will enable them to avoid jury duty;[13] others do not register because a past felony conviction precludes them from voting.[14] This practice continues to fall disproportionately on people of color, who had once been explicitly excluded from jury service and voting,[15] and continue to be underrepresented on juries even today.[16]

As states sought to expand the list of people who receive a jury summons, they began to use other lists in addition to the voter registration list, such as those for utilities, taxes, unemployment compensation, state identifications, driver's licenses, and public assistance.[17] The idea was that multiple lists would include a broad array of names that any one list could not provide. Courts need to draw widely from the citizenry because venires or panels of prospective jurors must consist of a fair cross section of the community. Both Congress, through

[11] BOATRIGHT, *supra* note 7, at 4.

[12] *See, e.g.*, David Kairys, Joseph B. Kadane & John P. Lehoczky, *Jury Representativeness: A Mandate for Multiple Source Lists*, 65 CALIF. L. REV. 776, 777 (1977).

[13] *See, e.g.*, Buckley v. Am. Const. L. Found., 525 U.S. 182, 219 (1999) (quoting a witness who explained that some individuals would be willing to circulate petitions but they are not registered voters because they do not want to be called for jury duty and believe the two are connected).

[14] Alexis Hoag, *An Unbroken Thread: African American Exclusion from Jury Service, Past and Present*, 81 LA. L. REV. 55, 75 (2020) (urging states to permit convicted felons to vote and to serve on juries because these exclusions have a disproportionate effect on African Americans and Latinos).

[15] *Id.* at 58 (describing early American jury practices when "[e]very state limited jury service to men, and a few states explicitly conditioned jury service on being white") (footnotes omitted).

[16] *Id.* at 63 ("What started as *de jure* exclusion based on race morphed into *de facto* exclusion with the same result."); *id.* at 73–79 (urging states to summon prospective jurors from multiple lists, not just voter registration lists, and to allow those with felony convictions to vote and to serve on juries because these two practices contribute to the underrepresentation of African Americans on juries today).

[17] *See, e.g.*, ARIZ. SUP. CT. COMM. ON MORE EFFECTIVE USE OF JURIES, JURORS: THE POWER OF 12, at 38–39 (1994), https://azmemory.azlibrary.gov/digital/collection/statepubs/id/17843 [hereinafter THE POWER OF 12] (noting that Arizona uses driver's license and voter registration lists for summoning prospective jurors, but recommending that Arizona also use income tax rolls and federal welfare and assistance program lists).

statutes such as 28 USC §§ 1861 and 1863(b)(3),[18] and the US Supreme Court, through cases such as *Taylor* v. *Louisiana*[19] and *Duren* v. *Missouri*,[20] have indicated that venires must be drawn from a fair cross section of the community.

Citizens who receive a summons have several ways to respond. They can heed their summons and appear at the date, time, and courthouse specified on the summons. They can call the telephone number on the summons if they are ineligible to serve because they do not satisfy a qualification for jury service, such as the age or citizenship requirements. They can ignore the summons and not show up. Or they can call a telephone number on the summons and seek a deferral or an excuse, though the summons does not always make these options clear.[21]

## CITIZENS' RANGE OF RESPONSES TO THEIR SUMMONS

Citizens who receive a summons for jury duty are not blank slates. Although many will not have received a summons or entered a courthouse before, they have most likely watched films and television programs about juries and read about juries in the press. They have formed some views about juries, and for some, these views could well be negative because juries are not usually portrayed in a positive light in popular culture. For example, in two jury films, *Trial by Jury*[22] and *The Juror*,[23] which follow the same story line, the main character is summoned for jury duty. In both films, the main character (Valerie in *Trial by Jury* and Annie in *The Juror*) is initially portrayed as enthusiastic about her jury service, but she is quickly shown to be naive in her views as she is selected for jury duty, targeted by the defendant and his henchman, and her life and the life of her young son are both threatened through violence. In other words, jury duty has turned her life into a nightmare.

18 *See* 28 U.S.C. § 1861 ("[A]ll litigants in Federal courts entitled to trial by jury shall have the right to . . . petit juries selected at random from a fair cross section of the community in the district or division wherein the court convenes."); 28 U.S.C. § 1863(b)(3) (same).

19 419 U.S. 522, 525–26 (1975) (providing that a criminal defendant has a right to an impartial jury, which means a jury drawn from a venire that represents a fair cross section of the community, and a venire that systematically excluded women, even though they made up more than 50% of the community, violated the fair-cross-section requirement of the Sixth and Fourteenth Amendments).

20 439 U.S. 357, 364–67 (1979) (describing a three-part test to establish a fair-cross-section violation).

21 *See, e.g.*, BOATRIGHT, *supra* note 7, at 121–22.

22 TRIAL BY JURY, *supra* note 5 (Intro.).

23 THE JUROR, *supra* note 5 (Intro.).

Given most citizens' lack of familiarity with summonses and courthouses, the jury summons is likely to arouse a mix of responses. There is the dismay that comes with being asked to rearrange one's personal and work obligations. As one newspaper article recounted, "[i]t's a document some people dread finding in their mailbox more than bills."[24] There is also fear when a prospective juror receives "an official and somewhat scary-looking document, in the mail."[25] There is also the apprehension that one feels when confronting a new situation,[26] such as going to a courthouse which might be located far away and even in an unsafe area. According to one empirical study, many citizens understand the importance of jury duty but worry that they do not have the training or skills to be a competent juror.[27] They would like to serve but feel inadequate for the task.[28] And, as described above, there are the negative portrayals of juries that appear in popular movies and television programs.

Yet, in spite of the negative responses that a summons might elicit, the recipient might also feel a tinge of curiosity or even of civic duty. Some citizens will have been called for jury duty before and have had positive experiences. Even those citizens who have not been called may have friends or family who have been called. One study confirmed that "by far the most prevalent source of information about jury service was prior service as a juror or conversations with others who had served."[29] Courthouses can also elicit positive responses because oftentimes they are stately buildings with inspiring words and images of justice. The experience that a citizen has upon entering the courthouse can add either to the positive or to the negative views that the summons might have sparked.

## THE TRADITIONAL VIEW OF SUMMONSES AND COURTHOUSES

According to the traditional view, the summons is the means by which citizens show up at the courthouse so that they can be assigned

[24] Mullaley, *supra* note 4.

[25] Boatright, *supra* note 7, at 110; *see also id.* at 111, 112 (providing observations from the Chief Deputy Clerk and Court Administrator for the United States District Court for the Western District of Tennessee).

[26] *Id.* at 109 (finding that jurors' post-verdict questionnaires in federal district court in Memphis revealed that "they had had apprehensions going in, but had a fairly positive experience").

[27] *Id.* at 111 (noting citizens' "low evaluations of their personal ability to serve competently" in the study of the United States District Court for the Western District of Tennessee).

[28] *Id.* at 117 ("They are uncertain of their ability to serve competently as a juror.").

[29] *Id.* at 119.

to a courtroom and considered for jury service. How citizens feel about the summons is not the courts' main concern, as long as citizens heed their summons. Courts need a sufficient number of citizens so that judges can seat juries. If there were a shortfall, that would be a problem.

Taking a traditional view of the courthouse and courtroom, courts do not give high priority to how citizens might feel upon entering the courthouse or courtroom, possibly for the first time. Rather, it is simply the workplace where cases get decided. Citizens are needed as jurors. They are summoned and then directed to the Jury Assembly Room, where they are sent to wait. In some courthouses, the Jury Assembly Room is not a particularly welcoming environment and the people who staff that room are not particularly helpful. Some courts have made reforms to both the room and the staff, particularly when they needed to address the shortfall in citizens answering their summonses. New York was one such state.[30] Under Chief Judge Judith Kaye, New York courts made a number of improvements to the Jury Assembly Room and the training of the staff so that summoned New Yorkers would respond to their summons and would not be put off by the bad treatment that had become commonplace.

## STRUCTURAL IMPEDIMENTS TO THE TRADITIONAL VIEW OF THE SUMMONS AND THE COURTHOUSE

There are structural impediments to achieving the traditional view of the summons. Citizens who receive a summons do not always heed it; many, for a variety of reasons, just throw it away. Thus, the goal of bringing citizens to the courthouse in sufficient numbers is not always met. There are also structural problems inherent in summoning citizens to serve as jurors. The lists from which citizens are summoned are usually limited so that not everyone who could serve is called. Citizens' addresses are not always up-to-date on these lists so many summonses cannot be delivered. If summonses do not reach a broad swath of the citizenry, then it will be hard to have venires that represent a fair cross section of the community, as required by statute and case law.[31]

[30] *Id.* at 20 ("New York, a state in which juror yield had reached critically low levels by the 1990s, undertook a major overhaul of the jury selection process in 1993, with the guidance and encouragement of new Chief Judge Judith S. Kaye.").

[31] *See supra* notes 18–20 (citing federal statutes and U.S. Supreme Court case law).

**Some Citizens Ignore Their Summons**

A jury summons is a formal notice that arrives in the mail at unpredictable and often inopportune times. The summons itself provides little information. It can be written in intimidating language. As one recipient of a summons to the Old Bailey in London recounted: "I felt a small pop of apprehension . . . . There is no getting away from it: the yellow form is an intimidating document."[32] The summons requires the recipient to appear at the named courthouse at an appointed date and time. The courthouse might not be anywhere near where the recipient lives and the appointed date and time might not be convenient. The summons usually includes some language indicating that a penalty can be imposed, such as "[f]ailure to obey this summons may be punishable by a fine," if the recipient fails to heed the summons.[33] Thus, this official notice, written in formal language, threatens to turn a citizen's life upside down, yet the citizen seems to have little say about when and where this service will take place. Even those citizens who want to perform their jury duty might initially think about how inconvenient the timing is or how hard it will be for them to heed the summons.

There are a variety of reasons why citizens might fail to respond to a summons. They might worry about losing their job if they fail to go to work or worry about losing their income if they get paid only for the days they work. They might also find it impossible to go either because they are taking care of a child, an elderly parent, or an ailing spouse or because they do not have the transportation necessary to get to the courthouse.[34] There are many barriers to heeding a summons, yet the court expects recipients to go to the courthouse to explain their situation even when some recipients cannot manage the trip and are not sure how to proceed. As a result, they simply ignore their summons.

[32] Trevor Grove, The Juryman's Tale 6 (1998) (describing a journalist's experience as a juror in a lengthy trial at the Old Bailey in London).

[33] Summons to Appear, *supra* note 6.

[34] In one unusual case, the judge recognized that some prospective jurors might have to travel over 400 miles from their homes to the courthouse and so she arranged for them to complete a substantive written questionnaire from home so that only qualified prospective jurors would have to make that journey. *How Courts Care for Jurors in High Profile Cases*, U.S. Courts (Jan. 24, 2020, 10:19 AM), https://www.uscourts.gov/news/2020/01/24/how-courts-care-jurors-high-profile-cases [https://perma.cc/UF7K-7CVN] (describing Federal District Court Judge Anna J. Brown's approach to a high-profile case of moving the trial from where the crime occurred to Portland, Oregon and also requiring summonses to be sent to all four of the District of Oregon's federal court divisions for security reasons).

### Summonses Do Not Always Reach a Broad Swath of the Population

Courts might strive to send out summonses to a broad swath of the population, but they need to use multiple lists and to have updated addresses, and even then they might need to take extra steps, though it is not always clear what those steps should be.

The typical list that most courts use to send out summonses is the voter registration list. Many, but not all, states supplement the voter registration list with other lists because the former only draws names from those who have registered to vote, and not all citizens register to vote.[35] One reason courts rely primarily on voter registration lists is because they are readily available. Another reason is the view that these are the people who are most likely to respond to their summons. If they took the trouble to register to vote, then they are likely to take the trouble to go down to the courthouse when they are summoned to do so.

No matter which lists courts use, they still have to worry about outdated addresses. Since people move for a variety of reasons, lists, even multiple lists, are likely to have addresses that are no longer up-to-date. Thus, courts send out the summonses to old addresses, which means they are not delivered to the right person or not delivered at all.

Some judges have asked for additional summonses to be sent to zip codes in which there are a larger number of minority members so that the venires will be more representative of the community.[36] However, at least one appellate court has rejected these individual efforts on the grounds that such plans need to be carried out on a district-wide basis as part of a district's jury selection plan, and not simply at the behest of an individual judge.[37] Some appellate courts have also rejected such methods as violating statutes that require random jury selection because sending out more summonses to certain zip codes appears targeted, and in violation of the US Constitution – such as the Equal Protection Clause – because some groups receive more summonses than

[35] *See, e.g.*, Mary R. Rose, Shari Seidman Diamond & Marc A. Musick, *Selected to Serve: An Analysis of Lifetime Jury Participation*, 9 J. EMPIRICAL LEGAL STUD. 33, 51 (2012) ("[M]ost states ... have moved to expand source lists ... to reach a more diverse group.") (citations omitted).

[36] *See, e.g.*, Nancy Gertner, *12 Angry Men (and Women) in Federal Court*, 82 CHI.-KENT L. REV. 613, 622–23 (2007) (describing one federal judge's efforts to create a venire that represents a fair cross section of the community by ordering the Federal Jury Administrator to send new summonses to residents in the same zip code when summonses were returned to the court as "undeliverable" or as "non responses").

[37] *See, e.g.*, *In re* United States, 426 F.3d 1 (1st Cir. 2005).

other groups, even if this is intended to produce representative venires.[38]

Thus, there are structural impediments that stand in the way of the summons achieving its main purpose, which, according to the traditional view, is to bring a fair cross section of the community to the courthouse in sufficient numbers. Among the impediments are inadequate lists, outdated addresses, and recipients' unwillingness or inability to heed their summons. As a result, courts worry about whether they will have a sufficient number of prospective jurors on any given day so that judges who need to seat a jury can do so. Courts also worry about whether the prospective jurors who heed their summons represent a fair cross section of the population.

**Courts Can Be Forbidding, Uninviting Places**

Even when citizens do heed their summons and go to the courthouse, they are not always treated well once they arrive. Citizens worry about going to a courthouse in an area that they consider unsafe or where they are concerned about how to get there or where to park. Even before they enter the courthouse, the exterior of the building can be off-putting. One former juror described the courthouse on Centre Street in lower Manhattan as "grim and forbidding in a Stalinist sort of way (towering, gray, squint-windowed)."[39]

Once prospective jurors enter the courthouse, they have to go through security before they can proceed any further. Security lines can entail long waits, bellowing security officers, and a lack of signs indicating where prospective jurors need to go next. In one study, defense attorneys noted that members of the public and professionals are treated differently when entering the courthouse, with the latter being treated better than the former.[40] In the same study, which included researchers who observed courtroom proceedings, researchers who were African American or Latino felt that they were not treated with the same respect as those who were white when they went through

[38] *See, e.g.*, United States v. Ovalle, 136 F.3d 1092, 1104-07 (6th Cir. 1998); Hennepin Cnty. v. Perry, 561 N.W.2d 889, 896–97 (Minn. 1997); *see also* Nancy J. King & G. Thomas Munsterman, *Stratified Jury Selection: Cross-Section by Design*, 79 JUDICATURE 273, 276 (1996) (pointing out that one potential challenge to stratified jury selection is based on the Equal Protection Clause).

[39] D. GRAHAM BURNETT, A TRIAL BY JURY 20 (2001).

[40] NICOLE GONZALEZ VAN CLEVE, CROOK COUNTY: RACISM AND INJUSTICE IN AMERICA'S LARGEST CRIMINAL COURT 25 (2016).

the security lines.[41] When prospective jurors enter courthouses they might be subject to security officers' biases, whether explicit or implicit, rather than being treated as citizens who have been summoned to perform their civic duty as jurors.

After prospective jurors find their way to the Jury Assembly Room where they are supposed to wait, they are given little explanation as to what will happen next. In some courthouses, the Jury Assembly Room is cramped and noisy. It is hard to get work done or even just to read when the surroundings are unpleasant and the noise level is high. One journalist summoned for jury duty at the Old Bailey in London was told, along with fellow prospective jurors, to "take the [elevator] to the fifth floor and assemble in the jury restaurant."[42] He described it as "look[ing] like the waiting room of a fogbound provincial airport. It was packed.... There was a distinct feeling of apprehension in the air."[43] In addition, prospective jurors do not know how long they will have to wait in the Jury Assembly Room. They are often informed on a need-to-know basis. For example, an official will tell them they can go to lunch, but that they must return by a set time. Then, when they return, they might be told that they can leave. In some courthouses, like those in New York State before the reforms made by Chief Judge Judith Kaye, prospective jurors were treated as if their time did not matter. They were held for hours in a cramped area with no working toilets nearby. They complained of being treated like cattle in a cattle car. These conditions did not signal that prospective jurors were important and performed an essential role. Rather, as one report acknowledged: "In many counties [in New York], upstate as well as down, the public's picture of the majesty of justice is peeling paint, broken toilets and dirty rooms."[44]

When prospective jurors finally receive a courtroom assignment, they might enter the courtroom with trepidation. For many, this will be their first time in a courtroom. The courtroom can be an intimidating place, especially in federal court, where the courtroom is often large and formal. Everyone has his or her proper place. In a high-profile trial, the courtroom will be filled with people. Typically, they include the

41 *Id.* at 25 ("In contrast to the privileges extended to white researchers, blacks and Latinos – including researchers from this study – were mistaken for defendants and treated like criminals.").

42 Grove, *supra* note 32, at 26.

43 *Id.*

44 The Jury Project, Report to the Chief Judge of the State of New York 92 (1994).

judge, his or her law clerks, the parties and their lawyers, a bailiff, a court reporter, a federal marshal (in federal court), and members of the press and public. As the prospective jurors enter this setting, they might feel like they have joined a theater production in which everyone else knows their lines and they do not. Yet, they are going to be asked to speak in public, before this large audience, and every word they utter will be taken down by a court reporter.

### A Culture of Excuses in the Courtroom

Prospective jurors enter this setting and the initial inclination of many is to be excused. They did not ask to serve on a jury. They did not choose this time or place. Now, when they learn what the case is about and how long the trial will last, their initial response is that they want to be excused.

One of the messages that prospective jurors learn from popular culture is that only the naive and gullible end up serving as jurors. Everyone else figures out how to avoid jury duty. In the two jury films, *Trial by Jury*[45] and *The Juror*[46] mentioned earlier, the main female character embraces jury duty and is portrayed as both naive and gullible. In both films, the character ends up paying for her innocence with threats to her life and the life of her child. These women's lives are turned upside down because they were not savvy enough to recognize that jury duty is only for those who cannot figure out how to avoid it.

The jury box can give rise to "a culture of excuses," according to one anthropologist who was a prospective juror in a high-profile case.[47] He observed that prospective jurors listened to other prospective jurors' requests to be excused and quickly tried to figure out which excuses seemed to be effective with the judge. They then used such excuses on their own behalf.[48] Those prospective jurors who do not manage to be excused may be chastised by family members for not answering questions in a way that would result in an excuse.[49]

[45] TRIAL BY JURY, *supra* note 5 (Intro.).

[46] THE JUROR, *supra* note 5 (Intro.).

[47] Conversation with Kelly McKowen, Co-panelist, Council of Europeanist Studies Conference, Chicago, Illinois (Mar. 29, 2018) (describing his experience as a prospective juror in the "nanny case" in New York).

[48] *Id.*

[49] Conversation with Dr. Julie Levitt, Chicago, Illinois (Apr. 9, 2018) (describing her husband's reaction when she was selected to serve on a jury).

The common understanding seems to be that anyone with a modicum of intelligence will manage to be excused and that only the naive end up actually serving as jurors. As one former juror, Graham Burnett, a history of science professor at Princeton University who wrote a book about his jury experience, acknowledged: "Actually ending up on a jury never crossed my mind."[50] He had been told by a friend that "the magic word was 'philosophy': once the lawyers heard it, you were kindly asked to leave."[51] Burnett assumed that if he described himself as "an intellectual historian," it would have the same effect as describing himself as a philosopher.[52] Burnett was assigned to a courtroom and observed that as soon as the judge announced that the case involved murder, that the trial would take more than a week, that the jury would be sequestered, and that anyone who thought they could not serve should go up to the judge and explain, "80 percent of the room rose."[53] The prospective juror sitting next to Burnett remained seated, but she "was only remaining seated while she thought up an excuse."[54] Across the Atlantic Ocean, Trevor Grove, a journalist summoned for jury duty, had been told that "if you want to get off [jury duty], which of course they assume you do, you must go into court wearing a suit and tie and carrying *The Times* or *Telegraph*."[55]

Judge Whitman Knapp, a federal district court judge who presided over *United States* v. *Torres*,[56] a high-profile case in the Southern District of New York, claimed not to see a culture of excuses as he tried to seat a jury in *Torres*. Rather, he thought that prospective jurors sought to be excused only in instances of genuine hardship. *United States* v. *Torres* involved the bombing of the Mobil Oil Building in Manhattan in which one person died and several bystanders were injured.[57] The *Fuerzas Armada de Liberación Nacional* ("FALN"), a group that advocated independence for Puerto Rico, claimed responsibility for the bombing.[58] The defendant, Ms. Torres, was charged with the bombing. She was not present in the courtroom during jury selection, but was in the courthouse and could

[50] BURNETT, *supra* note 39, at 17.
[51] *Id.* at 17–18.
[52] *Id.* at 18.
[53] *Id.* at 24.
[54] *Id.*
[55] GROVE, *supra* note 32, at 28.
[56] Transcript of Jury Selection, United States v. Torres, No. 77 Cr. 680 (S.D.N.Y. May 19, 1980) [hereinafter *Torres* Transcript] (transcript of jury selection).
[57] Torres v. United States, 140 F.3d 392, 395 (2d Cir. 1998).
[58] *Id.* at 395.

hear the proceedings. She had one "advisor" at this point.[59] She declined to be present in the courtroom during jury selection or to have a lawyer representing her in the courtroom because she rejected the legitimacy of the United States government, including its authority to try her for this crime. Instead, she argued that she was "a prisoner of war" and should be tried by an international court.[60] She declined to participate in the federal district court trial, which Judge Knapp mentioned to the jury at different points during *voir dire*.[61]

After he had seated a jury, the judge thanked the jurors for agreeing to serve. He said that he thought the prospective jurors who had sought an excuse on the grounds of hardship had done so only in instances of genuine hardship that precluded them from serving. He told the jurors who had been seated: "It's very gratifying, there wasn't a single person who applied for an exception who didn't have a perfectly valid reason for applying."[62] However, the transcript of the jury selection reveals that of the thirty-three prospective jurors whose names were called and who were asked to take a seat in the jury box, twenty-one (64 percent) of the prospective jurors sought to be excused on the grounds of hardship.[63] One interpretation of this high percentage seeking excuses (though it was not as high as the percentage in Burnett's venire) is that prospective jurors were looking for reasons not to serve. This was a high-profile trial in which the jury would be sequestered. Another interpretation is that this was a case in which the defendant was not present in the courtroom and had declined to exercise any challenges, so it could be that the federal judge was being particularly circumspect and dismissing all those who sought to be excused to ensure that the jurors who were seated were not resentful about serving. Nevertheless, a high percentage of prospective jurors did seek to be excused from the case. It might be that a high-profile case is more likely to generate a "culture of excuses" than an ordinary case but, in any event, courts do not address this challenge except to try to make sure that enough prospective jurors do show up so that judges can seat a jury.

59 *Torres* Transcript, *supra* note 56, at 43.
60 *Torres*, 149 F.3d at 395–96.
61 *Torres* Transcript, *supra* note 56, at 34, 38–39, 40–41.
62 *Id.* at 68.
63 *Id.* at 55–68.

## HOW THE SUMMONS AND SETTING BEGIN THE TRANSFORMATION OF CITIZENS INTO JURORS

If citizens become responsible jurors through the jury process, as I argue they do, then every stage of the process needs to contribute to this transformation, beginning with the summons and the setting of the courthouse and the courtroom. Every stage has to be understood as part of the entire experience that will enable citizens to be transformed into responsible jurors. They might start out as disinterested, disengaged, or biased but the experience of each stage of the jury process brings them closer to assuming their role as jurors. The summons and setting begin the process. In doing so, they help to counter the negative views that citizens often bring with them when they enter the courtroom.

The summons and the setting begin the transformation by helping prospective jurors to understand that being a juror is an experience that is out of the ordinary and that needs to be taken seriously. The setting augments these feelings because prospective jurors are kept together so that they start to think of themselves as part of a group, rather than as individuals looking to be excused. If they are selected to be on the jury, they will be asked to perform a task that has great consequences for the parties seated before them. The setting of the courtroom, with all of its majesty and formality, contributes to citizens' sense of awe and to their realization that an event of significance is about to take place and that they are being asked to be a part of it. Although the summons and setting, as currently structured, contribute to citizens' transformation into jurors, this initial stage of the jury process can be fine-tuned so that it contributes more effectively.

### The Summons Indicates an Experience Out of the Ordinary

Even though citizens might have misgivings when they receive their summons, there is also another, more positive, response that they are likely to have, and that is a sense that they are being summoned to perform a task that is out of the ordinary. This feeling might be deeply buried within them or it might be missing altogether for some, but it is present for others. Former juror Graham Burnett alluded to it when he wrote: "One sensed a few people [in the Jury Assembly Room] beginning to warm to the prospects, to the idea that they were not in their offices – indeed, that their not being at work was a *civic duty* . . . ."[64] This feeling of jury duty as an out-of-the-ordinary experience needs to be reinforced by the summons so that citizens appreciate the unique role they are being called upon to play.

The jury summons, though it might be met with dismay or even dread, reminds citizens that they are being asked to perform an official role. Even the envelope distinguishes the summons from an ordinary piece of mail. The outside of the envelope indicates that what is inside constitutes official court business. There are only a few times in citizens' lives that they receive an official document that requires them to appear in court. The formal language of the summons, ordering them to appear in a particular court on a particular date and at a particular time, conveys a sense of urgency. They are not being asked if they would like to appear or would be willing to appear; this is not an invitation. Rather, they are being told that they must appear, and if they fail to appear they can be punished by a fine or, in some states, by a sheriff knocking on their door with an order to show cause that requires them to go to court and to explain to a judge why they did not heed their summons.[65]

### The Courthouse as a Setting for Serious Work

Similarly, when citizens heed their summons and enter the courthouse, they might view it as an intimidating building, but they might also view it with respect or even awe. Such a building adds to the sense that the role of a juror is important and imbued with unusual power and responsibility. A courthouse is an official building and there is a sense that something of significance is taking place inside. There are officers, security measures, and throngs of people, but there is also a designated room, the Jury Assembly Room, for citizens with a summons in hand. In some courthouses, such as the Criminal Court at 26th and California Streets in Chicago, prospective jurors are permitted to keep their cell phones while everyone else who enters the courthouse (defendants, family members, members of the press and public) must relinquish them. If a cell phone is a sign of status in our society, this is an indication that in the courthouse, jurors have status.

[64] BURNETT, *supra* note 39, at 20.

[65] *See, e.g.*, Moran, *supra* note 10, at 22 (describing one county's practice of sending a marshal with an order to show cause requiring the prospective juror to appear in court and explain to a judge why he or she did not respond to the summons).

### Moving from the Jury Assembly Room to the Courtroom: Reinforcing Group Identity

As the prospective jurors wait in the Jury Assembly Room, they can look around and see how many other people have been summoned to serve and have heeded their summons. The number of people can be reassuring and even inspiring. Those who have responded to their summons are not gullible, but responsible. They are busy, but have taken time out of their workday to heed their summons. During this waiting period, prospective jurors are kept together with each other and apart from everyone else who enters the courthouse. This is a pattern that will continue if the prospective jurors are seated on a jury.

When thirty or forty prospective jurors are finally called up to the front of the Jury Assembly Room and assigned to a courtroom, they leave as a group, accompanied by a staff member, and they are instructed on where to walk, where to wait, and when to enter the courtroom. There are procedures that they must follow so that they are kept together as a group and apart from everyone else in the courthouse.

### The Courtroom as a Place for Decision-Making

The venire of prospective jurors enters the courtroom together. For many prospective jurors, this will be their first time in a courtroom. Of course, they have seen courtrooms on television and in movies, but they might not have actually been inside a courtroom. Although it is a formal setting that can inspire fear, it can also be an august setting that can inspire awe; the judge can help dispel the former and encourage the latter. There are different styles of courtrooms – modern or traditional, grand or austere – but they display the same symbols of the court's authority, such as the raised bench for the judge, a gavel, flags, an insignia of the jurisdiction, as well as a witness box, tables for the parties and their lawyers, seats for the public and press, seats for the law clerks, a table for the bailiff, and a jury box for the jurors. The courtroom has a particular iconography and this can be found in courtrooms around the world.[66]

The prospective jurors will typically be seated in the front of the public area, and each person whose name is randomly selected will then

[66] *See, e.g.*, Judith Resnik & Dennis Curtis, Representing Justice: Invention, Controversy, and Rights in City-States and Democratic Courtrooms (2011) (studying courthouses around the world).

take a seat in the jury box in the order in which he or she has been called. Prospective jurors are likely to feel a mix of anxiety and excitement with each name that is called. They are likely to feel some nervousness because of the unfamiliar surroundings, procedures, and expectations, as well as excitement or curiosity because the experience is out of the ordinary. They see before them the judge, in his or her black robe, as well as the parties, whose lives will be affected by whatever verdict the jury reaches.

Although at this stage the prospective jurors' overriding feeling might be dread, they are also likely to feel a sense, even if it is inchoate, that what is about to take place in the courtroom has meaning and significance beyond their ordinary activities. Prospective jurors begin to look beyond their own immediate concerns and start to think about the parties before them and their task if they are chosen as jurors. This shift in focus begins the process of transforming citizens into jurors. One juror who tried to capture this sense of gravity reported that when the judge announced to the prospective jurors the name of the criminal defendant and that he was being tried for murder there were "two gravitational centers: the judge and the defendant. This curious feeling was strongest at that moment, but it never entirely vanished. An accused person, standing in a court of law, has, somehow, tremendous weight."[67]

## STEPS COURTS SHOULD TAKE TO FACILITATE THE TRANSFORMATION OF CITIZENS INTO JURORS

### Redesign the Summons to Reinforce Citizens' Sense of Responsibility

The seriousness of purpose that the summons conveys can still be achieved if it is written in plain, clear language with sufficient information so that the recipient understands that a deferral is possible if it is necessary. The goal would be to convey seriousness of purpose without threatening citizens or treating them as disobedient children. Some citizens who heed their summons will end up serving as jurors, which is a role of tremendous responsibility. The summons should treat citizens as the responsible jurors that their role requires them to become.

To start this process, the summons should give jurors some control over the time and place of their jury duty. If it were clear on the front of

[67] BURNETT, *supra* note 39, at 22.

the summons that the recipient could call a telephone number to reschedule the day or to change courthouses, then that would give the recipient some sense of control. As several empirical studies have found, people who can exercise some control over the timing of their jury service are more likely to heed the summons than those who are simply ordered to show up on a particular day and at a particular courthouse under penalty of a fine if they fail to do so.[68] The summons should also provide essential information, such as the availability of child care, food, and parking and what to do when those essential services are not provided by the court.

On the Cook County Summons, the information on the top half of the page is written entirely in capital letters. Although the court might have chosen capital letters to reinforce the seriousness of the summons, the capital letters make the summons difficult to read. Moreover, if all words on the top half are in capital letters, they do not stand out as important. In addition, the information on the bottom half of the page is in a small-size font, perhaps to make up for the large capital letters used on the top half. As a result, those who have trouble reading small print are likely to have difficulty reading the words on the bottom half of the page. Also, every part of the page is filled with words and there are few white spaces, making the document appear cramped and off-putting to all readers.

Although there is limited research on the design of jury summonses, there is variation in how summonses are designed. Courts need not reinvent the wheel, but they should at least choose a design, even if it is borrowed from another state, that is not confusing or difficult to read. One study, albeit done a while ago, recommended the summons used in Massachusetts.[69] At the time, it found the summons in Massachusetts to be "by far the most attractive, the least intimidating, and the easiest to read."[70] Courts in other states could work with a university's design school to create a summons that is clear, easy to read, and conveys the requisite information to a broad array of readers.

68 *See* Susan Carol Losch, Adina W. Wasserman & Michael A. Wasserman, *Reluctant Jurors: What Summons Responses Reveal about Jury Duty Attitudes*, 83 JUDICATURE 304, 310 (2000) ("Our results indicate that commitment, choice, and control distinguish people who tried to postpone current jury duty from those who tried to excuse it."); *see also* BOATRIGHT, *supra* note 7, at 111 (interviewing one jury administrator who observed that summoned jurors do not always understand the language of the summons and do not realize that they can seek a deferral; as a result, they end up ignoring their summons). For a summons that threatens fines, see Summons to Appear, *supra* note 6.

69 BOATRIGHT, *supra* note 7, at xii, 22, 126 app. 1. Although Boatright's study of summonses was published in 1998, *see id.* at ii, it is the most extensive study on this subject that I have found.

70 *Id.* at 22.

This is an area in need of additional research. Although summonses get citizens to courthouses, they do not always get them there in the numbers that are needed, with the diversity that is required by statute, or with a willingness to serve. Courts seem to assume that a summons that is threatening and filled with orders is one that is likely to be most effective, but given the high percentage of people who do not respond to their summons, at least in jurisdictions that have been studied, this assumption needs to be reexamined. For example, Robert Boatright examined responses and nonresponses to summonses in courts in four jurisdictions: a superior court in Maricopa County, Arizona; a state court of common pleas in Montgomery County, Pennsylvania; a superior court in King County, Washington; and the US District Court for the Western District of Tennessee in Memphis, Tennessee. He found that the nonresponse rate was 18.5% in the Maricopa County court, 20% in the Montgomery County court, 15.8% in King County Superior Court, and 18% in the US District Court for the Western District of Tennessee.[71] When the nonresponse rate is high, courts have to summon large numbers of citizens in order to seat juries. Interestingly, Boatright concluded that threats were effective at getting citizens to respond, but that they ran the danger of angering citizens, which could undercut the goal of getting citizens to serve as jurors.[72] This insight led Boatright, as well as some jury administrators and judges, to recommend the use of carrots rather than sticks to entice citizens to respond to the summons.[73]

Courts need to view the summons as the beginning of the jury process in which citizens are transformed into responsible jurors. The summons needs to provide basic information in a clear manner. It also needs to give citizens some control over when and where they serve, not only so that they will heed their summons but also so that they will feel that they are being treated in a respectful manner.

Researchers who have studied why citizens fail to respond to their jury summons have identified several reasons. One reason is the lack of

[71] *Id.* at 85, 93, 101, 107.

[72] *Id.* at xii (suggesting that follow-up mailings, show-cause hearings, and penalties "may produce more jurors, but these jurors may develop negative attitudes toward the court because it has forced them to show up"); *id.* at xi (describing the county with the harshest summons enforcement policy as one explanation for its citizens being "the most hostile towards jury service" of all the citizens in the counties in the study).

[73] *Id.* at 99 ("[I]t is better to have jurors respond to their summonses willingly than to have them report under coercion."); *id.* at 121 ("Many judges and court administrators with whom we spoke were reluctant to coerce reluctant jurors into attending.").

control citizens feel when they receive a summons.[74] The summons dictates the date, time, and place of their service. Citizens who receive a summons are willing to respond to it if they can exercise some control over when they serve. In one study of Connecticut prospective jurors who received summonses, 76 percent of those who postponed their jury service showed up to serve on their new date,[75] leading the author to conclude that jurors who postponed their service were "'committed to serving.'"[76] One problem is that people who receive a jury summons do not always realize that they can call a telephone number on the summons and request a deferral to a more convenient time or an assignment to a courthouse that is closer to home. The summons does not always make this clear, but it should.[77] Otherwise, those who are unaware of this option might instead choose to ignore their summons.

A 2020 report by the Jury Selection Task Force in Connecticut focused in part on the state's summonses, including the official envelopes, and offered ways to redesign them to get recipients' attention, to encourage them to respond to their summons, and to emphasize the contributions that jurors make to the community.[78] The goal was to ensure that the summons drew truly diverse venires into the courthouses of Connecticut. For example, the report suggested ways to make the envelope more personal, such as having the return address be from "Chief Justice Robinson" rather than the anonymous "Jury Administrator."[79] In addition, rather than having the envelope indicate "important court document inside immediate action required," the report suggested using the following, more positive and welcoming, language: "A summons for you to serve your community and ensure equal justice."[80] The report also suggested that the summons highlight two important pieces of information that prospective jurors need to

[74] *See, e.g.*, Losch, Wasserman & Wasserman, *supra* note 68, at 309 ("[Failures to appear] would also benefit from clear, simple prose on the summons directing how to obtain a postponement or excuse.").

[75] Karen A. Berris, *Appearance Rates of Potential Jurors Who Confirm, Postpone, or Fail to Respond to the Jury Summons: Are Postponed Jurors Saying No or Not Now?*, 59 DRAKE L. REV. 649, 657 (2011).

[76] *Id.* at 656.

[77] BOATRIGHT, *supra* note 7, at xii (recommending that courts "establish a toll-free telephone number to discuss summonses with citizens" including deferrals and excuses); *id.* at 79 ("[C]itizens often are not clear on the process of deferring a summons or receiving an excuse from service."); *id.* at 111 ("[C]itizens are scared by the formal language of their summons[;] they do not understand what they should do if they cannot serve.").

[78] JURY SELECTION TASK FORCE, REPORT OF THE JURY SELECTION TASK FORCE TO CHIEF JUSTICE RICHARD A. ROBINSON 9–14 (2020).

[79] *Id.* at 10.

[80] *Id.*

know: Jurors receive payment for their services, including reimbursement for travel and family care, and the summons requires the recipient's appearance in court; it is not an invitation.[81] The report also proposed that the summons include a section that the recipient could tear off and give to his or her employer.[82] That section would explain the employer's responsibility to accommodate the employee's jury service and to pay the employee his or her regular pay for the first five days of jury service.[83] The task force had given thought to what information would be uppermost on the prospective juror's mind and made sure that the summons addressed it. It still remains to be seen whether the Connecticut Supreme Court will adopt these or similar changes and whether they will work, but at least the Jury Selection Task Force is giving thought to these issues and trying to approach them from the perspective of the prospective juror.

### Treat Citizens with Respect in the Courthouse

If court staff, including security officers, were trained to treat prospective jurors with respect, and if courthouses had well-placed signs informing prospective jurors how to find the Jury Assembly Room, that would go a long way toward allaying prospective jurors' initial fears and misgivings when they enter the courthouse.

Once prospective jurors reach the Jury Assembly Room, they should be able to interact with staff who have been trained to treat prospective jurors with respect. In some courthouses, the Jury Assembly Room is a well-designed room where prospective jurors are able to work. It is quiet; the seats are comfortable; and there are restrooms, vending machines, and places for cell phone conversations nearby. The message that this design conveys is that the court recognizes that prospective jurors are busy people who have taken time out of their workday to answer their summons and that the role they will soon be asked to play is significant and worthy of respect. While they wait, the court has ensured that they are able to work. If they do not have work that can be done in the Jury Assembly Room, at least they can use the quiet, comfortable Jury Assembly Room to read or relax until their name is called and they are assigned to a courtroom.

Some state courts have started to focus on the needs of jurors only when the situation becomes so dire that citizens fail to heed their

[81] *Id.*
[82] *Id.* at 10–11.
[83] *Id.*

summonses. For example, before New York State courts made serious strides to improve conditions for prospective jurors, jury duty was falling on a small number of the eligible population, many citizens were automatically exempted due to their professions,[84] and those who did serve mainly complained about the experience.[85] However, Chief Judge Judith Kaye[86] committed her administration to improving conditions for jurors. She convened a blue-ribbon commission, called The Jury Project, and had it explore every aspect of the jury experience. She wanted the commission to look at how prospective jurors were treated and to make recommendations that would improve their experience. Colleen McMahon, the Chair of The Jury Project, described the commission's mission as follows: "The most interesting aspect of our job was putting ourselves in the position of jurors and resolving all doubts about what to recommend in favor of what would be best for the jurors."[87]

Chief Judge Kaye implemented a number of the commission's recommendations. These included improving Jury Assembly Rooms, as well as juror access to working bathrooms and vending machines;[88] training staff so that they treated jurors with respect; implementing "one day, one trial";[89] eliminating automatic sequestration of juries in criminal cases;[90] eliminating automatic exemptions so that almost everyone had

[84] Before Chief Judge Judith Kaye's jury reforms, New York had "the most extensive list of occupational and related exemptions in the United States." THE JURY PROJECT, *supra* note 44, at 31. Many different types of jobs had automatic exemptions from jury duty, including podiatrists, embalmers, and licensed physical therapists. *Id.*

[85] *See, e.g.*, BOATRIGHT, *supra* note 7, at 20 ("The [New York] Jury Project's report cited numerous former jurors who complained bitterly of waiting for long periods of time in cramped, unpleasant conditions, only to be treated poorly and then sent home by lawyers.").

[86] Chief Judge Judith Kaye was Chief Judge for almost sixteen years. *See, e.g.*, Jonathan Lippman, *Chief Judge Judith S.x Kaye: A Visionary Third Branch Leader*, 84 N.Y.U.L. REV. 655 (2009). She began as Chief Judge on March 23, 1993 and served until December 31, 2008. *Id.*

[87] THE JURY PROJECT, *supra* note 44, at vi; *see* BOATRIGHT, *supra* note 7, at 8 ("[W]e call upon court members to put themselves in the shoes of those whom they summon, and to investigate how they can better fulfill their role in this process.").

[88] *See, e.g.*, Jan Hoffman, *Favorable Verdict for Jury Changes; Lawyers Are Unhappy. Other Signs Are Hopeful, Too*, N.Y. TIMES, Apr. 12, 1995, at B1 ("Some deliberating rooms and juror assembly halls have comfortable new chairs, lunch tables, vending machines and work carrels; one Manhattan courthouse now has a television room.").

[89] "One day, one trial" means that citizens are summoned and report to the courthouse for one day. Either they are selected for a jury trial on that day, and serve for the length of the trial, or if they are not selected for a jury on that day, then that one day constitutes their jury duty, and they will not be summoned for another year (or some other period of time depending on the jurisdiction).

[90] Before the elimination of automatic sequestration, all criminal juries in New York were sequestered. *See, e.g.*, Somini Sengupta, *New Law Releases Juries in New York from Sequestering*, N.Y. TIMES, May 31, 2001, at A1. This caused hardship for jurors because it

to serve;[91] and having judges supervise attorneys as they questioned prospective jurors in civil cases so that the questioning did not go on for days as it had when lawyers conducted the questioning on their own.[92]

The reforms of the New York jury system under Chief Judge Kaye went a long way toward helping prospective jurors feel they had greater control when they entered courthouses in New York. Before the reforms, jurors felt that staff treated them in a demeaning way, their time was not valued, and the rooms where they were kept lacked basic amenities. After the reforms, however, jurors felt like the more egregious practices had been eliminated. The hope was that if jurors were treated better, they would obey their summons and not search for excuses when they were assigned to a courtroom. New York's jury reforms were important but they were directed mainly at ensuring that a sufficient number of citizens would show up and be available to serve as jurors.

Although New York's jury reforms were among the most dramatic, other states undertook jury reforms as well. For example, by 2006, 50 percent of US citizens lived in jurisdictions that had adopted "one day, one trial."[93] Citizens in these jurisdictions discovered that if they responded to their summons and went to the courthouse then they would either be assigned to a trial on that day or the day would constitute fulfillment of their jury service and they would not be summoned again for another year (or some other period of time depending on the jurisdiction). In the past, they would have had to appear every day for a number of weeks (depending on the jurisdiction) and would only have completed their jury service once the requisite number of weeks had passed. By making jury duty more respectful of people's time, the view was that more citizens would respond to their summons. At the same time, as states implemented "one day, one trial," they also eliminated automatic exemptions, which had made certain professions exempt from jury service in the past. By making more people eligible to serve, and keeping everyone for a shorter amount of time, jury duty would be less of a burden and one that almost everyone could fulfill. If celebrities such as Oprah Winfrey and former President Barack Obama were called to serve, and if they heeded their summons – as

meant that they had to be away from their families for the length of the trial. However, court officers protected the practice because they received overtime for it. *Id.* The New York State Legislature had to pass legislation to put this reform into effect.

91 *See, e.g.*, Jan Hoffman, *Judges Screen Jurors Faster than Lawyers, Study Says*, N.Y. TIMES, June 24, 1995, at 23.

92 *See, e.g.*, Hoffman, *supra* note 88, at B1.

93 JURY TRIAL INNOVATIONS 25 (G. Thomas Munsterman, Paula L. Hannaford-Agor & G. Marc Whitehead eds., 2d ed. 2006) [hereinafter JURY TRIAL INNOVATIONS (2d ed.)].

they did – that helped to reinforce the powerful message that everyone should do so.[94]

### Tell Citizens in the Summons That They Will Be Given All the Information They Need to Serve

Given that some citizens worry that they will not be able to serve well as jurors, the summons should reassure them that the jury process will provide what they need to know to become a responsible juror. In Boatright's empirical study of responses to summonses in four counties, he found that some citizens, especially those with limited education or economic resources, lacked confidence and did not believe they could serve well as jurors.[95] This finding was particularly pronounced in the federal court that he studied in Memphis, Tennessee.[96] He noted that some court administrators there attributed it to "the rather imposing summons that is standard in all federal courts."[97] Boatright noted that while "[c]ourts are not . . . in the business of raising citizens' self-esteem . . . courts need to demystify the jury, to emphasize that anyone can serve competently as a juror."[98] One step forward is to make sure that the summons is understandable. Another is to make sure that the summons includes a sentence that tells citizens, in effect, that they will be taught what they need to know in order to serve as a juror and that no special expertise or knowledge is needed.

Courts used to send citizens a handbook in the mail that described the role of the juror.[99] Although mailing costs have made this practice

[94] *See, e.g.*, Mike Colias & Anna Johnson, *Oprah Jury Votes to Convict*, ASSOCIATED PRESS (Aug. 17, 2004, 12:11 PM), https://www.cbsnews.com/news/oprah-jury-votes-to-convict [https://perma.cc/CG6L-GSSM] ("When your life intersects with others in this way, it is forever changed.") (quoting Juror Oprah Winfrey); P.J. Huffstutter, *Oprah Is in the Courthouse to Do Civic Duty as a Juror*, L.A. TIMES (Aug. 18, 2004, 12:00 AM), https://www.latimes.com/archives/la-xpm-2004-aug-18-na-oprah18-story.html [https://perma.cc/S3Y9-PV8D]; Patricia Lee Refo, *President's Letter: All Rise for the Jury*, A.B.A. J., June–July 2021, at 6 (recounting ABA President Patricia Lee Refo's experience of serving as a juror); Ellie Silverman, *Barack Obama Has to Report to Jury Duty, Too. (He Didn't Get Picked.)*, WASH. POST (Nov. 8, 2017), https://www.washingtonpost.com/news/politics/wp/2017/11/08/barack-obama-has-to-report-to-jury-duty-too-he-didnt-get-picked/ [https://perma.cc/D5SS-K7RW] (describing former President Obama being called for jury duty in Chicago, and identifying other presidents, as well as Chief Justice Roberts, who have been summoned to serve as jurors).

[95] BOATRIGHT, *supra* note 7, at xi, 61, 68.

[96] *Id.* at xi.

[97] *Id.*

[98] *Id.* at 79–80.

[99] *See, e.g.*, ADMIN. OFF. OF U.S. CTS., HANDBOOK FOR JURORS SERVING IN THE UNITED STATES DISTRICT COURT (1975). This handbook was still sent to jurors in the late 1980s. *See* Nancy S. Marder, Note, *Gender Dynamics and Jury Deliberations*, 96 YALE L.J. 593, 607 nn.69 & 72 (1987).

prohibitively expensive in most jurisdictions, courts could create a juror handbook, posted on their website, that describes the role of the juror and how the jury process enables citizens to assume this role. Some jurisdictions have already done this.[100] The summons could then inform citizens about this resource. Those citizens who do not have a personal computer could use a computer at their public library in order to consult this resource. The handbook, which could be made available online at no cost, would reassure those citizens who worry about their competence that at every stage of the jury process they will be helped to assume their role as a juror.

**Give Citizens Information through Orientation Films**

While prospective jurors wait in the Jury Assembly Room, they can also use their time to learn more about their role and to reduce their anxiety by watching a juror orientation film. Information is one means of reducing the fear of the unknown that some prospective jurors experience from the moment they enter the courthouse. If jurors know what to expect, they will not be so anxious about what will follow. Although some courthouses have long provided juror orientation films, these have tended to be very modest productions, oftentimes done in black and white and consisting of just one figure, usually a judge delivering a lecture about jury duty.[101]

Some of today's jury orientation films are far more informative and well-produced than orientation films in the past and this is a useful development. The best of today's jury orientation films are of course in color; they include famous actors;[102] they show courtrooms and identify the participants and their roles; they explain the dos and don'ts of jury duty; and they might even provide some history about the right to a jury trial and why it is so important for citizens in a democracy to serve as jurors.[103] The more substantive the information that orientation films

[100] *See, e.g.*, Off. of the State Ct. Adm'r, *Answers to Your Questions About Your Colorado Jury System*, COLO. JUD. BRANCH, http://www.courts.state.co.us/userfiles/File/Media/Brochures/jurysystem(1.).pdf (providing brochure).

[101] *See, e.g.*, *Juror Orientation* (Massachusetts Jury Management Advisory Committee 1978) (providing a lecture by Chief Justice James Lynch).

[102] BURNETT, *supra* note 39, at 19 (describing an orientation video narrated by CBS News Reporters Ed Bradley and Diane Sawyer).

[103] Current issues for orientation films now include whether they should discuss implicit bias, as does the orientation film in the Western District of Washington, *see Understanding the Effects of Unconscious Bias*, http://www.wawd.uscourts.gov/jury/unconscious-bias, and the orientation film in New York, *see Jury Service and Fairness: Understanding the Challenge of Implicit Bias*, http://wowza.nycourts.gov/vod/vod.php?source=ucs&video=2021-JuryServiceFairness.mp4, and the need for jurors to abstain from using social media or the Internet to look for information about their trial.

provide in a useful format, the more prepared prospective jurors will be to assume their role as responsible jurors. One former juror described the orientation film he was shown as "a well-put-together account of what jurors are supposed to do and not do."[104] He acknowledged that "all this stuff about juries was alarmingly new" and so he and his fellow prospective jurors "listened intently."[105]

Some juror orientation films provide cutting-edge information about the challenges posed by implicit bias or jurors' use of social media. In some courtrooms, such as in the Western District of Washington, there is a juror orientation film that explains the concept of implicit bias and teaches prospective jurors that everyone, including judges and jurors, has implicit biases.[106] The best that a decision-maker can do is to try to discover his or her own implicit biases and to reach a verdict that is not colored by those biases.[107] In this situation, too, state courts do not have to reinvent the wheel; they can ask the Western District of Washington for permission to show this juror orientation film in their own state courts. As state courts, such as the Illinois Supreme Court, provide justices with seminars about implicit bias,[108] it is equally important for prospective jurors to receive this information, which they can begin to learn about by viewing a juror orientation film on the subject.

In some courthouses, the juror orientation film does a particularly good job of making prospective jurors aware of the dangers of using social media while serving as a juror.[109] The juror orientation film in Colorado raises this subject and explains why it is important for jurors not to post online about their experience while they are serving as jurors. The film explains that jurors can discuss the case only with fellow jurors when the time comes to deliberate and that they need to withhold judgment while the trial is ongoing. Juror orientation films reach prospective jurors early in the process and convey information that is important for them to have.

*See, e.g.*, Ministry of Just. U.K., *Your Role as a Juror*, YOUTUBE (Dec. 1, 2016), http://www.youtube.com/watch?v=yQGekF-72xQ.

104 GROVE, *supra* note 32, at 27.

105 *Id.*

106 *See Understanding the Effects of Unconscious Bias*, *supra* note 103.

107 *See, e.g.*, Jerry Kang et al., *Implicit Bias in the Courtroom*, 59 UCLA L. REV. 1124, 1184 (2012).

108 For example, Illinois Supreme Court Justice Theis, who served as the liaison to the Illinois Supreme Court Committee on Jury Instructions in Civil Cases, mentioned that she and other justices attended a seminar on implicit bias.

109 *See, e.g.*, Colo. Jud. Branch, *Colorado Jury Service: What to Expect*, YOUTUBE (Jan. 9, 2014), http://www.youtube.com/watch?v=zNqt5NStkTY (describing restrictions on using electronic devices and communicating about the trial on social media or doing research online).

## SUMMARY

The transformation view requires looking at the summons, the courthouse, and the courtroom from the perspective of prospective jurors,[110] and considering what would help them to assume their new role. A summons that treats recipients as responsible rather than as childlike, and gives them a choice about when to serve, begins the process of transforming citizens into responsible jurors. A summons that provides recipients with sufficient information about qualifications and deferrals and reassures them that they have the competence to serve also begins the process of enabling citizens who might know little about jury duty to perform their role as jurors. Similarly, a courthouse in which staff treat citizens with respect also helps reinforce the idea that citizens who become jurors will be asked to play a key role in the trial. And a courtroom in which the judge welcomes prospective jurors and tries to put them at ease helps them to assume their role as juror.

Although the formalities of the summons, courthouse, and courtroom are important in instilling a sense in citizens that what is about to take place is of great significance, that sense can still be conveyed by a summons that is well-designed and gives citizens some control over when they serve; by courthouse staff who are knowledgeable and responsive; by a Jury Assembly Room where citizens can work or relax while they wait to be assigned to a courtroom; and by a courtroom in which the presiding judge provides jurors with explanations so that they understand what will happen next. Although each juror might experience the transformation from citizen into juror at a different point in the jury process, the summons, courthouse, and courtroom can facilitate this transformation and certainly should not impede it, as the traditional approach sometimes does.

[110] Even hospitals are beginning to look at the experience of entering a hospital from a patient's point of view. *See, e.g.*, Lisa Schencker, *What Can Appliance Megastore Abt Teach Hospitals about Keeping Patients Happy?*, CHI. TRIB., July 14, 2019 (Business Section), at 1. Hospitals are working with retail stores that are renowned for their service, such as Abt, in order to think about the patient's experience and how to improve it. Hospitals are beginning to recognize that improvement is important not only because patients can choose which hospital to go to and where to spend their money, but also because it is "the right thing" to do. *Id.* at 2. If hospitals can do it, so can courts.

2

# *VOIR DIRE:* INTRODUCING JURORS TO THE JUDGE, THEIR FELLOW JURORS, AND THEIR ROLE

Once twelve names have been randomly selected and called and twelve prospective jurors have been seated in the jury box,[1] the judge, assisted by the lawyers, begins to question them. This process of questioning the prospective jurors is known as "*voir dire*." *Voir dire* is critical to my argument that ordinary citizens become responsible jurors through every stage of the jury process because *voir dire* is the stage at which this transformation takes a big step forward. In fact, there is often a moment during *voir dire* when this shift is almost palpable to those in the courtroom. Prospective jurors stop thinking about their excuses and start thinking about being selected for the jury.

According to the traditional view of *voir dire*, judges (or lawyers in some state courts) question prospective jurors to determine if they can be impartial and serve as jurors in the case. From these fairly basic questions, the judge and lawyers will decide whether the prospective juror can be impartial. The traditional view assumes that jurors who are selected through this questioning will be impartial and will understand their role as jurors from the outset. According to this view, these ready-made jurors just need to be found.

In contrast, the transformation view of *voir dire* recognizes that citizens will become jurors through their participation in the different

[1] There are variations in this process and in the number of jurors who serve on a petit jury, especially in civil jury trials. However, the number in any criminal jury trial cannot go below six jurors. *See* Ballew v. Georgia, 435 U.S. 223, 232–39 (1978) (holding that a state criminal jury trial with only five jurors would reduce the evidence accurately recalled by and available to the jurors, hinder effective deliberation, increase the likelihood of erroneous decisions, weaken the minority's ability to defend its view, and decrease the representation of minorities on the jury).

stages of the jury process and that *voir dire* is a starting point, not an end point. The purpose of *voir dire*, then, is not to try to discern which prospective jurors have biases and which do not because everybody has biases. Rather, the purpose of *voir dire* is to move prospective jurors from thinking solely about their individual excuses to thinking about the needs of the group. Citizens do not have to know how to be jurors when they are first selected because every stage of the jury process will help to transform them from citizens into jurors. By the time the jurors deliberate, they will do so aware of the responsibilities of being a juror, the enormity of the task of judging, the behaviors that they need to strive toward and those they need to resist. *Voir dire* provides a significant step in which citizens go from being disinterested and disengaged individuals thinking mainly about the inconvenience that jury duty entails, to citizens who want to serve and who begin to contemplate the task of the jury. According to the transformation view, then, jurors are made, not found.

## WHAT THE PRACTICE OF *VOIR DIRE* ENTAILS

*Voir dire* is conducted in different ways in different types of courts, but in federal court, the judge typically conducts *voir dire*.[2] A federal district court judge usually asks the prospective jurors, who are seated in the jury box, a series of quotidian questions. These questions typically include the following: Where do you live? What kind of work do you do? Are you married, and if so, what does your spouse do? Do you have children, and if so, what do they do? Have you served on a jury before, and if so, was it criminal or civil and did it reach a verdict? After several questions that are personal but superficial, the judge asks the prospective juror whether there is any reason that he or she cannot be impartial in this case. If the prospective juror says that he or she can be impartial, then that prospective juror has met the impartiality requirement and can serve as a juror, though the prospective juror still might not be selected for that jury.

In federal court, the lawyers can request that the judge ask supplemental questions, but the judge decides whether to ask them.[3]

[2] *See* FED. R. CIV. P. 47(a); FED. R. CRIM. P. 24(a)(1) & (2).

[3] In federal court, the judge does most of the questioning and the lawyers can suggest additional questions, which the judge might or might not ask. *See, e.g.*, FED. R. CIV. P. 47(a); FED. R. CRIM. P. 24(a). State courts can follow federal procedure or deviate from it. Some states, such as New York, deviate from federal *voir dire* procedures. In criminal jury trials in New York,

For example, in the *Torres* case (described in Chapter 1), there were several prospective jurors who were teachers or who had family members who were teachers.[4] The prosecutor wanted the judge to ask them which subjects the teachers taught because he was concerned that they might teach courses that involved politics and that they might have views about political groups engaged in struggles for independence.[5] In *Torres*, the prospective jurors taught apolitical subjects, such as mathematics, so it was not an issue.[6]

In federal court, the judge tries to move the questioning along at a fairly brisk pace. The judge does not want to keep an entire panel of prospective jurors in the courtroom any longer than necessary. The judge also wants to seat a jury as quickly as possible so that the trial can commence. The judge, unlike the lawyers, does not want to intrude too deeply into a prospective juror's personal life. Other than asking for basic background information and asking if there is any reason that the person cannot serve, the judge is willing to accept that prospective juror as a juror. When prospective jurors do raise an issue that they think they should bring to the judge's attention, the judge is usually quick to reassure them that they can still serve. For example, in the *Torres* case, when a prospective juror named James said that he was divorced and was close to a woman who was a parole officer, the judge asked him if the parole officer had any connection to Puerto Ricans. When James said that she did not, the judge thanked him for mentioning his association with the parole office, but said: "I can't see that it makes any difference, but how [would] you know, maybe it would have."[7]

What purpose do the judge's *voir dire* questions serve? They seem too superficial to uncover any deep-seated reason why a prospective juror cannot serve. At best, they might give the prospective juror a chance to articulate a reason why he or she cannot serve, but the judge does not usually probe very deeply when a prospective juror does offer some reason, as the example of James illustrates.

the trial judge "does some (often most) of the questioning." THE JURY PROJECT, *supra* note 44 (Ch. 1), at 46. In contrast, in civil jury trials in New York, lawyers had been allowed to conduct the questioning without a judge being present. However, this arrangement led to many complaints from prospective jurors until the system was changed after *The Jury Project* recommended that a judge should be present. *Id.* at 51.

4 *Torres* Transcript, *supra* note 56 (Ch. 1), at 107.

5 *Id.*

6 *Id.*

7 *Id.* at 74.

## THE TRADITIONAL VIEW OF WHAT *VOIR DIRE* IS SUPPOSED TO ACCOMPLISH

The traditional view of *voir dire* is that the prospective jurors' answers will reveal who has, or appears to have, biases relevant to the case and cannot serve and who does not have, or does not appear to have, biases relevant to the case and can serve. The questioning also gives the lawyers an opportunity to observe the prospective jurors, to hear their responses, and to make a judgment, based on their experience and intuition, about whether this particular prospective juror will be sympathetic to their side. The law requires an impartial jury,[8] and *voir dire* is supposed to be a search for impartial jurors.[9] However, lawyers seek sympathetic jurors, even if they will not always admit it.[10] They are looking for jurors whom they believe will favor their client.

The judge just has to make sure that there is no obvious reason why the prospective juror cannot serve. If there is an obvious reason, the prospective juror can be removed "for cause." A for cause challenge is decided by the judge; it is one for which a reason must be given in open court, and there is no limit to the number of for cause challenges that a judge can grant. The main reasons for granting a for cause challenge are: a familial connection between the prospective juror and one of the trial participants; the prospective juror has a financial stake in the outcome of the case; or the prospective juror says that he or she cannot be impartial.[11] These reasons are understood to preclude a prospective juror from being impartial or from satisfying the appearance of impartiality in a particular case.

[8] U.S. CONST. amend. VI, § 1 (providing for the right to "an impartial jury" in all criminal prosecutions); Thiel v. S. Pac. Co., 328 U.S. 217, 220 (1946) (interpreting an impartial jury as a requirement under the Seventh Amendment right to a jury trial in civil cases). Although the Sixth Amendment has been applied to the states, *see* Duncan v. Louisiana, 391 U.S. 145, 149 (1968), and therefore, states must also provide an impartial jury in criminal jury trials, the Seventh Amendment has not been similarly applied to the states; however, the Due Process Clause of the Fourteenth Amendment, which does apply to the states, requires an impartial decision-maker even in civil cases. *See* Morrissey v. Brewer, 408 U.S. 471, 488–89 (1972) (noting that "the minimum requirements of due process" in parole violation hearings include "a 'neutral and detached' hearing body").

[9] SAUL M. KASSIN & LAWRENCE S. WRIGHTSMAN, THE AMERICAN JURY ON TRIAL: PSYCHOLOGICAL PERSPECTIVES 50 (1988) ("The *voir dire* is designed by law to serve only one purpose: to enable counsel to probe jurors for information about their state of mind that might provide grounds for their removal.").

[10] Barbara Allen Babcock, *Voir Dire: Preserving 'Its Wonderful Power,'* 27 STAN. L. REV. 545, 551 (1975) ("Of course, neither litigant is trying to choose 'impartial' jurors, but rather to eliminate those who are sympathetic to the other side, hopefully leaving only those biased *for* him.").

[11] Hopt v. Utah, 120 U.S. 430, 433 (1887) (providing instances when it is appropriate for a judge to grant a for cause challenge).

The mundane questions that a federal judge asks during *voir dire* do help him or her to recognize whether a for cause challenge needs to be granted. The judge, in the course of asking about the prospective juror's family members and their jobs, even in a very abbreviated fashion, can elicit information that might reveal a familial or financial connection to the case. The judge also asks each prospective juror whether he or she can be impartial, or in the words of one judge, whether each has a "slant one way or another in this case."[12] Although the prospective juror might be in the best position, compared to the judge or lawyers, to know whether he or she has biases that prevent him or her from serving, it is nevertheless difficult for a person to do any real soul-searching in the midst of this quick questioning in open court.[13] Moreover, the tendency, as psychologists have long recognized, is for people to say that they can be impartial, whether or not this is true, because they know that it is the "socially desirable" answer and thus it is the answer they give.[14]

Lawyers want as much information as possible about the prospective jurors, if they are permitted to ask questions on their own or even if they are just given the opportunity to request that the judge ask supplemental questions – unless the information would help the other side. They are not worried about being overly intrusive or veering into territory that has nothing to do with the case at hand. Their search for sympathetic jurors sometimes leads them to ask idiosyncratic *voir dire* questions such as: "What baseball team do you root for?"[15] Perhaps they believe that if the juror and their client both root for the Cubs, they might share other traits as well. In general, lawyers believe the more information, the better because what they are trying to discern is not whether this prospective juror can be impartial, but whether this prospective juror is likely to favor their client,[16] or at least not to harbor

[12] *Torres* Transcript, *supra* note 56 (Ch. 1), at 74.

[13] Regina A. Schuller & Caroline Erentzen, *The Challenge for Cause Procedure in Canadian Criminal Law*, 6 OÑATI SOCIO-LEGAL SERIES 315, 321 (2016) (noting that it is difficult for a person to recognize his or her own biases).

[14] Neil Vidmar, *When All of Us Are Victims: Juror Prejudice and Terrorist Trials*, 78 CHI.-KENT L. REV. 1143, 1150 (2003); Schuller & Erentzen, *supra* note 13, at 327, 329.

[15] KASSIN & WRIGHTSMAN, *supra* note 9, at 53.

[16] *See, e.g.*, Matthew Clair & Alix S. Winter, Jury Selection in the Age of Mass Criminalization: Who Is Impartial? 7 (June 7, 2018) (unpublished paper presented at the Law & Society Annual Meeting, Toronto, Canada) (describing a study in which 103 lawyers and judges in a Northeast state court system were interviewed and quoting a number of public defenders and prosecutors who admitted that they sought sympathetic rather than impartial jurors); *id.* ("[L]awyers – especially public defenders – often interpreted jury selection as a process meant to identify and seat jurors who were biased in their favor.").

any resentment toward their client. Lawyers believe that they can discern prospective jurors' biases for or against their client. As one public defender who was interviewed as part of a study on impartial jurors explained: "My goal during [the] jury selection process is to get a jury that would be most sympathetic or able to identify the most with my client."[17] According to another public defender in the same study: "I mean, you're not looking for an impartial jury, you're looking for a partial jury toward your side."[18] Moreover, that view is not limited to public defenders. According to one prosecutor: "[My goal is] [t]o obtain a fair and impartial fact finder . . . that . . . officially, legally is the goal. I would say personally I want someone that I think is going to listen to me . . . ."[19]

Lawyers point to their years of experience and believe that they have honed their skills at uncovering prospective jurors' biases. However, they cannot point to any evidence that they have done this. They might have rules of thumb, stereotypes, or gut feelings, but they do not have any way of knowing whether they have picked jurors who will end up voting in favor of their client for the reasons the lawyer believed would motivate that prospective juror. As trial lawyer and law professor Alan Dershowitz once observed: "Lawyers' instincts are often the *least* trustworthy basis on which to pick jurors. All those neat rules of thumb, but no feedback. Ten years of accumulated experiences may be 10 years of being wrong."[20] Professor Dershowitz is not alone in this view. According to one commentator, "[s]ome of the most experienced trial lawyers in the country have concluded that a minutely investigated jury, vetted by leading trial consultants at tremendous financial cost, is not likely to perform substantially differently from a jury picked at random."[21]

There is little in lawyers' legal training that prepares them to perform the task of uncovering prospective jurors' biases during *voir dire*. In fact, the empirical evidence suggests that lawyers do not have any particular skill at performing this task. In several empirical studies, lawyers fared no better than chance at identifying prospective jurors' biases. In one study using mock jurors, researchers showed prosecutors, defense attorneys, and judges a taped *voir dire* and asked them which jurors they

[17] *Id.* (quoting Public Defender 99).
[18] *Id.* (quoting Public Defender 130).
[19] *Id.*
[20] Morton Hunt, *Putting Juries on the Couch*, N.Y. Times, Nov. 28, 1982 (§ 6 Magazine), at 70, 82 (emphasis added).
[21] Caren Myers Morrison, *Investigating Jurors on Social Media*, 35 Pace L. Rev. 285, 302 (2014).

would have excused.[22] The researchers found that those who were excused "were no more or no less likely to convict than those who were acceptable to judges and defense attorneys."[23] Although the attorneys believed they would be correct in their predictions about how prospective jurors would vote 71.9% of the time, in fact, they were correct only 45.4% of the time.[24] The researchers noted that the lawyers did "about as well as one might do by flipping a coin."[25] These researchers noted that "[t]hose charged with making juror selection decisions receive little formal training for the task, and what little is provided is largely anecdotal or based on folklore or stereotypes."[26] They added that it is difficult for lawyers to "'learn on the job'" because "there is no effective feedback of how good one's decisions have been."[27] In another study, the researchers noted: "It is difficult to recognize one's own prejudice, and even more difficult to admit to it in open court. It is perhaps more difficult yet to recognize it in another person . . . ."[28] These same researchers noted that "there exists a wealth of research suggesting that people (whether trained or untrained) are not much better than chance in assessing whether someone is truthful or not."[29]

In three other experiments, another group of researchers found that lawyers tended to rely on just a few characteristics when deciding whether a prospective juror was biased.[30] In the first experiment, the researchers found that there was some agreement among trial lawyers about which characteristics revealed bias among jurors.[31] In the second experiment, the researchers found that the trial lawyers' use of these two or three characteristics, for which there was agreement, was no more sophisticated than characteristics used by college sophomores in selecting jurors.[32] In the third experiment, when the researchers asked

22 Norbert L. Kerr, *The Effects of Pretrial Publicity on Jurors*, 78 JUDICATURE 120, 126 (1994). *See generally* Norbert L. Kerr, Geoffrey P. Kramer, John S. Carroll & James J. Alfini, *On the Effectiveness of Voir Dire in Criminal Cases with Prejudicial Pretrial Publicity: An Empirical Study*, 40 AM. U. L. REV. 665, 699 (1991).

23 Kerr, *supra* note 22, at 126.

24 *Id.*

25 *Id.*

26 *Id.*

27 *Id.*

28 Schuller & Erentzen, *supra* note 13, at 329.

29 *Id.* at 329 & n.33 (citing a meta-analysis of 384 studies in which the overall accuracy rate in detecting deception was only 54%).

30 Paul V. Olczak et al., *Attorneys' Lay Psychology and Its Effectiveness in Selecting Jurors: Three Empirical Studies*, 6 J. SOC. BEHAV. & PERSONALITY 431, 438 (1991) (finding that lawyers have "a tendency to emphasize only a few characteristics when forming judgments of bias").

31 *Id.* at 435, 440.

32 *Id.* at 442.

trial lawyers and students whether to accept or reject a juror, both groups exhibited the same pattern of errors: "Both attorneys and students made more incorrect acceptance and rejection choices than corresponding correct choices . . . ."[33]

Although these empirical studies suggest that it is difficult for lawyers to identify prospective jurors who are biased, lawyers and judges continue to believe that they can identify such prospective jurors. They take the traditional view that impartial jurors are found, not made. They believe that they can make these determinations after hearing *voir dire* questions that elicit very basic background information – the kind of information that one gleans at a cocktail party.

## STRUCTURAL IMPEDIMENTS TO THE TRADITIONAL VIEW OF *VOIR DIRE*

The raison d'être of *voir dire*, according to the traditional view, is to uncover prospective jurors' biases so that these prospective jurors are not seated on the jury. Although it is hard for a person to uncover another person's subtle biases, it is particularly hard to do so given the way that *voir dire* is structured. One difficulty is that *voir dire* is conducted in a group. Another difficulty is that it is conducted orally and prospective jurors must respond immediately. Yet another difficulty is that attorneys, at least in federal court, do not have the opportunity to ask many questions, and yet they are more familiar with the facts of the case and the types of bias that might be relevant to the case than the judge.

The way that *voir dire* is typically conducted in federal court, and even in most state courts, is that the prospective jurors are questioned while they are sitting together as a group.[34] As psychologists have noted, there is pressure in a group setting to give the socially desirable response when asked if one can be impartial.[35] There might also be pressure not to volunteer information that will show oneself in a bad light. The group

33 *Id.* at 446.

34 *See, e.g.*, JURY TRIAL INNOVATIONS (2d ed.), *supra* note 93 (Ch. 1), at 66 ("Voir dire typically takes place in a group setting in which the panel members respond to questions posed by the trial judge or attorneys in the presence of other panel members.").

35 *See, e.g.*, Schuller & Erentzen, *supra* note 13, at 327 (describing prospective jurors' propensity to give "a socially desirable response" to a question about bias); Regina Schuller & Neil Vidmar, *The Canadian Criminal Jury*, 86 CHI.-KENT L. REV. 497, 522 (2011) (finding that "people may be unaware of existing biases and often maintain that they are personally fair and egalitarian"); Vidmar, *supra* note 14, at 1150 ("Some prospective jurors who hold biases are likely to state that they can be impartial solely because that answer is consistent with socially

setting of *voir dire*, exacerbated by the public setting of the courtroom, is likely to inhibit candor by prospective jurors. When the judge asks prospective jurors to think about whether there is any reason why they cannot be impartial, they might not think very hard. They might just respond with the socially acceptable answer that they can be impartial.

Judge Gregory Mize, a former trial judge in the District of Columbia, urged fellow judges to conduct individual *voir dire* in addition to group *voir dire*.[36] He encouraged judges to conduct a group *voir dire*, as is the common practice, but also to conduct an individual *voir dire* because it is more likely to elicit candid and relevant information from prospective jurors than a group *voir dire*. The individual *voir dire*, typically conducted in a more intimate setting, such as the jury room or the judge's robing room, with only the judge, the attorneys, the court reporter, and the prospective juror present, is more likely to yield useful information. At the very least, an individual *voir dire* means that the prospective juror could not remain silent in the face of a question; he or she has to respond.

Judge Mize supplemented group *voir dire* with an individual *voir dire* in his own courtroom and reported that an individual *voir dire* did not add very much time to the trial and did reveal useful information.[37] In some instances, it produced information that led him to grant a for cause challenge. For example, he granted a for cause challenge when one prospective juror admitted during the individual *voir dire* that she was the defendant's fiancée.[38] She had not responded during the group *voir dire* when Judge Mize asked the prospective jurors if they knew any of the trial participants. When another prospective juror revealed during the individual *voir dire* that he did not want to be a juror and that he had already lied in response to *voir dire* questions, Judge Mize removed him for cause as well.[39]

Another structural problem that makes it difficult to identify which prospective jurors have biases is that *voir dire* is conducted orally by the judge and calls for a quick response by the prospective juror. There is little time for reflection. If *voir dire* were conducted not only orally in

learned values that people should be impartial, a phenomenon that psychologists call 'socially desirable' responses.").

36 Gregory E. Mize, *On Better Jury Selection: Spotting UFO Jurors Before They Enter the Jury Room*, CT. REV., Spring 1999, at 10.

37 *Id.* at 12, 15.

38 *Id.* at 12.

39 *Id.*

court, but also by questionnaire prior to court, then prospective jurors would have more time to reflect upon their responses and those who may be reluctant to speak in public could be more forthcoming in writing. In some cases today, prospective jurors do complete a written questionnaire in advance of the in-court *voir dire*, but such cases tend to be high-profile or involve extensive pretrial publicity.[40] Run-of-the-mill cases do not typically include a written questionnaire. This is because written questionnaires add time and expense to the case. However, written questionnaires give prospective jurors a chance to think about their responses. Such questionnaires also allow the same question to be asked in more than one way. When a prospective juror gives different answers to similar questions phrased in different ways such inconsistencies point to the need for follow-up questions during the in-court *voir dire*.[41] Also, while prospective jurors who are extroverts might not have a problem responding to questions in open court, prospective jurors who are introverts might be more reticent.[42] In addition, some people express themselves more effectively in writing while others do so in conversation. A written questionnaire, when coupled with in-court oral questions, allows the court to reach prospective jurors who favor different styles of expression.

Another structural problem in federal court, and in some state courts, is that the judge, rather than the lawyers, conducts *voir dire*. Federal judges are authorized to do so under the *Federal Rules*.[43] Even though there are many reasons to have the judge conduct *voir dire*, such as speed, efficiency, and respect for the prospective jurors' privacy, if the lawyers conduct it, even under the supervision of the judge, they would be able to elicit more information from the prospective jurors. They can do this because they are willing to be intrusive, unlike the judge who is supposed to be a neutral arbiter. If lawyers become too aggressive in their questioning, they know they can always use a peremptory

[40] *See, e.g.*, Robert M. Takasugi, Commentary, *Jury Selection in a High-Profile Case:* United States v. DeLorean, 40 AM. U. L. REV. 837, 839 (1991) ("With the cooperation of counsel, the court prepared an extensive jury questionnaire, principally aimed at the prospective jurors' media exposure [in the case of *United States v. DeLorean*, CR 82–910-RMT (C.D. Cal. 1983)].").

[41] *See also* Vidmar, *supra* note 14, at 1145, 1168–70 (describing inconsistent responses to similarly worded questions in a survey questionnaire designed in support of a change of venue motion in the trial of John Phillip Walker Lindh, "the so-called 'American Taliban'").

[42] *See generally* SUSAN CAIN, QUIET (2012) (describing differences between introverts and extroverts and how introverts' strengths are often missed because so many environments are designed for extroverts).

[43] *See* FED. R. CIV. P. 47(a); FED. R. CRIM. P. 24(a)(1) & (2).

challenge to remove a prospective juror whom they have offended; judges do not have that option. Lawyers are also more familiar with the case than the judge and can ask follow-up questions that a judge might not know to ask. Also, prospective jurors might be more forthcoming with a lawyer than a judge because the judge is the authority figure in the courtroom and they might try to give answers they think the judge is looking for in an effort to please him or her.[44] They might not feel this same compunction with the lawyers.

However, removing these structural impediments to *voir dire* would only be useful if one subscribes to the traditional view. The traditional view of *voir dire*, as described earlier, is to determine which prospective jurors have biases or the appearance of biases and should not be permitted to serve as jurors. Although the basic questions that a judge asks prospective jurors will allow him or her to figure out which prospective jurors need to be removed for cause, the basic questions do not reveal more subtle biases, which we all have. Lawyers claim that they can recognize prospective jurors about whom they have misgivings and remove them with their peremptory challenges. The problem, as described earlier, is that there is no evidence that lawyers can do this. In fact, there is some empirical evidence, especially work conducted by social psychologists, suggesting that lawyers and judges cannot do this, nor can prospective jurors. If lawyers, judges, and even prospective jurors cannot identify who has biases, much less implicit or unconscious biases, then should *voir dire* be abandoned altogether? In the next section, I explain why *voir dire* should not be abandoned or restructured to help achieve the traditional goal of removing prospective jurors with hidden biases. Instead, *voir dire* needs to be recognized as serving a different purpose, which is to help citizens to become jurors.

## WHAT *VOIR DIRE* ACTUALLY ACCOMPLISHES: HELPING CITIZENS TO BECOME JURORS

The traditional view of prospective jurors is that either they are biased and cannot serve or they are unbiased and can serve. It is a black-or-white conception of jurors, with no shades of gray. It is a view that assumes that prospective jurors have fixed qualities that can be recognized during *voir dire* and that will affect them during deliberations in

[44] *See* Vidmar, *supra* note 14, at 1150 ("The tendency to provide such [socially desirable] answers can be enhanced by the authoritative presence of the judge.").

ways that can be predicted. Of course, in some cases, prospective jurors are seen as so biased as to make them unable to render a fair verdict. For example, those prospective jurors who say they cannot be impartial should not serve. In such cases, the judge can remove them for cause.

In most cases, however, jurors do not have immutable qualities that lawyers and judges can discern during *voir dire* and that will make them biased or unbiased jurors during the course of the trial and deliberations. Lawyers might believe they can discern these qualities, but social psychologists suggest otherwise. They explain that we cannot discern these qualities in ourselves, much less in another person. Moreover, everyone has biases of one kind or another, particularly implicit or unconscious biases. No one is free of these biases, including the judge.[45] So, the question becomes: How can ordinary citizens work toward achieving the impartiality necessary to serve as jurors on a jury?

The answer is that such jurors are made, not found. Every stage of the jury process, with great strides made during *voir dire*, helps citizens to assume their role as jurors. *Voir dire* provides prospective jurors with new experiences that begin to alter their perspective. They might come into the courtroom thinking about their individual concerns and why they cannot serve, but once they are seated together in the jury box their perspective starts to shift. They think less about how to get excused from jury duty and more about how to get seated on the jury.

*Voir dire* entails a number of experiences that are likely to be new to the prospective jurors, including sitting in a jury box together and being watched by everyone else in the courtroom; having the judge ask them questions and having to answer these questions in front of everyone in the courtroom, including their fellow prospective jurors; and standing up and taking an oath together in open court. These new experiences help them to begin the transformation from citizens focused on individual concerns to jurors focused on the group task.

### The Setting of the Jury Box

The *voir dire* typically takes place when the prospective jurors are seated in the jury box. Not all of them will end up serving as jurors. Some will be excused and replaced by others. Some will be removed for cause or

[45] There is much scholarship on judges' implicit bias. *See, e.g.*, Chris Guthrie, Jeffrey J. Rachlinski & Andrew J. Wistrich, *Blinking on the Bench: How Judges Decide Cases*, 93 CORNELL L. REV. 1 (2007); Kang et al., *supra* note 107 (Ch. 1), at 1124; Andrew J. Wistrich & Jeffrey J. Rachlinski, *Implicit Bias in Judicial Decision Making: How It Affects Judgment and What Judges Can Do About It*, *in* ENHANCING JUSTICE: REDUCING BIAS 187 (2017).

with peremptory challenges. However, it is important that they are seated together for the *voir dire*. The jury box is usually off to one side, the side closest to the witness box,[46] so that the jurors will be able to observe the witnesses' demeanor as an aid to judging their credibility.

The prospective jurors are seated together in the jury box, and yet, the jury box is set apart from others in the courtroom. This arrangement, in which the jurors are seated together and yet separated from others in the courtroom, is one that began when they were assigned to a courtroom and when they went from the Jury Assembly Room to that courtroom. This arrangement is also a manifestation of their role throughout the trial. Once they are selected and sworn in as jurors, they can talk to each other, but not to anyone else in the courtroom. As one former juror described the oddity of the experience after his jury was impaneled: "From this moment on, no member of the jury would be required or allowed to speak in court again. We would be a silent tribunal, giving away nothing except what could be read on our faces."[47]

Another distinctive feature about the jury box is that the prospective jurors who sit in it can easily observe everyone in the courtroom but, at the same time, they, too, are easily observed. The prospective jurors can see all of the trial participants before them: the judge, the lawyers, the parties, the witness, the court reporter, the bailiff, the law clerks, and the members of the press and public. Indeed, those in the jury box command one of the best views in the courtroom, like having orchestra seats in a theater. They also see all the symbols of the court's authority, including the raised bench of the judge, the judge in his or her robe, the gavel, the flags, and the court's insignia. In some federal courtrooms, there will also be an armed federal marshal. As jurors, they will watch others in the courtroom and note their performances. For example, they will watch the judge and see how he or she responds to the lawyers and the parties, whether through the judge's tone of voice or body language.[48] They will also observe the parties and their lawyers when

[46] *But see* GROVE, *supra* note 32 (Ch. 1), at 118 ("But a jury cannot always get a decent look at whoever is giving evidence: in Court 3 at the Old Bailey, for example, the witness box is alongside the jury, not facing it.").

[47] *Id.* at 34.

[48] *See, e.g.*, Peter David Blanck, Robert Rosenthal & LaDoris Hazzard Cordell, Note, *The Appearance of Justice: Judges' Verbal and Nonverbal Behavior in Criminal Jury Trials*, 38 STAN. L. REV. 89, 123–24 (1985) (finding that jurors are influenced not only by what a judge says, but also by the way in which he or she says it); Note, *Judges' Nonverbal Behavior in Jury Trials: A Threat to Judicial Impartiality*, 61 VA. L. REV. 1266, 1278 (1975) (finding that jurors look to judges for guidance because they are uncertain how to perform their role); Robert J. Hirsh, Jan Mills Spaeth & Thomas G. Hippert, *Attorney Voir Dire and Arizona's Jury Reform Package*,

they are performing and even when they are "offstage" but still present in the courtroom.[49]

However, at the same time that the prospective jurors can see all those present in the courtroom, those present in the courtroom can also see the prospective jurors. It is an early indication that the prospective jurors are stepping into a unique role as jurors. They had been private citizens but as jurors they will have a public role to play. In that role, they are subject to others' gaze and scrutiny in the courtroom. They will be under intense observation, not just by the lawyers and parties and in some cases jury consultants, but also by members of the press, and even by the courtroom artist. As one thoughtful juror observed: "[Y]ou are immediately aware that you are very much part of the 'show' as you are watched by the principals in the case while being scrutinized by the attorneys so they can get a 'read' on how their case is being accepted . . . ."[50] Some judges will warn the jurors, once they are impaneled, that they will be under intense observation and that lawyers and parties will try to glean as much information as possible from their facial expressions and body language. Judges may tell the jurors that part of their role is to remain as impassive as possible, just as the judge tries to do.[51] Those in the courtroom should not be able to read agreement or disagreement on the faces of the jurors. As one juror described their affect: "[Y]ou try to be neutral in your responses, which effectively eliminates all avenues of expression since we are not permitted to discuss [the case]."[52] Jurors need to sit in the jury box in a manner that expresses that they are keeping an open mind; they need to satisfy impartiality, as well as the appearance of impartiality.

ARIZ. ATT'Y, Apr. 1996, at 24, 32 ("Jurors very quickly pick up on judges' expectations and mannerisms . . . .").

49 *See, e.g.*, Mary R. Rose, Shari Seidman Diamond & Kimberly M. Baker, *Goffman on the Jury: Real Jurors' Attention to the "Offstage" of Trials*, 34 LAW & HUM. BEHAV. 310, 322 (2010) (finding that jurors do pay attention to trial actors' behavior when they are not engaged in the formal presentation of the trial, but that these observations do not play much of a role during the jury's deliberations); Amy J. St. Eve & Gretchen Scavo, *What Juries Really Think: Practical Guidance for Trial Lawyers*, 103 CORNELL L. REV. ONLINE 149, 159 (2018) (describing a juror questionnaire completed by 500 jurors in approximately 50 trials and finding that "jurors do not like unprofessional lawyers, and they pay close attention to how lawyers treat opposing counsel, witnesses (including parties), the judge, courtroom staff, members of the jury, and even their own co-counsel").

50 JURY TRIAL INNOVATIONS 305 (G. Thomas Munsterman, Paula L. Hannaford & G. Marc Whitehead eds., 1997) (quoting from Letter from a Juror in a High-Profile Case) (app. 13).

51 *See, e.g.*, *id.* at 264 ("It is your job and no one else's to decide what the facts are. I intend to preside impartially and not express any opinion concerning the facts. Any views of mine on the facts are totally irrelevant.") (sample preliminary jury instructions) (app. 8).

52 *Id.* at 305 (app. 13).

During *voir dire*, the prospective jurors are seated together in the jury box, which is separated from the other seats in the courtroom. The jury box is a physical reminder of the new role they will assume if they are selected for the jury: They sit together, marked off from everyone else. They will be expected to observe carefully what is happening in the courtroom, while knowing that they are being watched by everyone else in the courtroom. They know that they are supposed to appear neutral and impassive when they are in the jury box, as a way of showing that they have an open mind and are not making any early judgments. In a sense, they are being asked to perform their role even before they have fully understood it. This new experience of sitting together in the jury box teaches them during *voir dire*, and at every point throughout the trial if they are selected to serve on the jury, that whenever they are in the courtroom they need to pay attention, to listen carefully, and to sit impassively because it is important to their role – and that everyone in the courtroom will be scrutinizing them and seeing how they play their role.

**Group *Voir Dire* and Oral Questioning**

Group *voir dire* is important for the making of jurors and the formation of the jury. To begin with, it allows the prospective jurors to learn basic information about each other. It also means that all the members of the jury will have answered the same questions and will have begun to think about the same issues. It also ensures that the judge provides all the jurors with the same information about the trial and their role in it. Finally, the repetition, as each prospective juror answers the same series of questions, reinforces the lesson about impartiality. It also changes the dynamic in the courtroom. The group nature of the *voir dire* leads prospective jurors to think about serving as jurors and wanting to be considered fair-minded and impartial rather than seeking to be excused, which is what they might have thought about when they entered the courtroom.

At the most basic level, a group *voir dire*, even one that involves superficial questions, enables prospective jurors, who are strangers, to learn about each other. The kinds of questions the judge asks the prospective jurors are similar to questions one might ask a stranger at a cocktail party: Where do you live? What do you do? Are you married? What does your spouse do? Do you have children? How old are they and what do they do? Although the ostensible purpose of such questions is to reveal whether a for cause challenge is appropriate, these basic questions help break the ice for jurors. When they go into the jury room, they will already know something about each other. This basic background information will help them to talk to each other; it will give them a starting point. Even though they come from different walks of life, they might have the same number of children or a child of the same age. These connections will help them to feel more comfortable with each other in this unfamiliar setting and to lay the foundation for working with each other later on.

At a deeper level, the group *voir dire* gives the jurors a shared group experience. It allows them to hear the same questions over and over again, to listen to others' responses, and to think about their own responses before they must answer the same questions. Not only do they learn details about other prospective jurors' lives, but also they hear others say that they can be impartial and that they do not have a fixed view of the case one way or the other. Although some of the prospective jurors might have entered the courtroom thinking about their excuses, when they hear one prospective juror after another say they can serve, it becomes harder for them to say that they cannot. It becomes particularly hard for them to say that they cannot be impartial. Not only is impartiality the socially acceptable answer, as social psychologists have explained, but also there is the added pressure that other prospective jurors have said that they can be impartial. There is a tendency to conform to the group.[53]

Peer pressure is a powerful force. Over sixty-five years ago, Solomon E. Asch conducted experiments in which college students were asked to say which one of two lines was longer.[54] A subject gave the same answers that he had heard others in the group give (all of whom were confederates), even when the others' answers were contrary to what the subject saw with his own eyes.[55] The subject had to decide between "the evidence of his senses" and "the unanimous opinion of a group of his peers."[56] The pressure was heightened because the subject had to "declare his judgments in public, before a majority which has also stated its position publicly."[57]

During *voir dire*, those in the courtroom (except for the lawyers) might find the asking and answering of the same questions to be

[53] *See* Robert Buckhout, *Eyewitness Testimony*, SCI. AM., Dec. 1974, at 23, 28.
[54] Solomon E. Asch, *Opinions and Social Pressure*, SCI. AM., Nov. 1955, at 2, 3.
[55] *Id.* at 3.
[56] *Id.*
[57] *Id.*

monotonous, but it is important that the prospective jurors hear this litany of questions over and over again. The repetition operates almost like a catechism that everyone is asked to repeat in the hope that everyone will start to believe it. If prospective jurors are asked, one after another, to say whether they can be impartial and to think carefully about whether there is any reason that they cannot hear the case without "a slant one way or another,"[58] they start to believe that they can be impartial. If there is any reason that causes them concern, they can bring it to the attention of the judge, and the judge will usually reassure prospective jurors that the reason will not stand in the way of their service.

The group *voir dire* is also important because it means that the judge imparts information to all the prospective jurors at the same time. They are treated equally from the outset, which conveys a powerful message about how they are to treat each other during the deliberations. As the judge explains to the prospective jurors the type of case that they will hear, how long the trial is likely to last, and asks them whether they know any of the trial participants, the judge is already treating the prospective jurors as a group.

### Questioning by the Judge

It is also important that the judge conducts the questioning of prospective jurors during *voir dire*, even though this is not how *voir dire* is conducted in every courtroom. Although the lawyers might elicit more information from prospective jurors if they did the questioning, the judge's questioning marks the starting point of the judge–jury relationship. The jurors tend to look to the judge as an authority figure in the courtroom.[59] Although judge and jury each have their own role to play, the judge helps the jury to understand its role as the trial proceeds. The back-and-forth between judge and jury begins primarily during *voir dire*, continues throughout the trial, and ends when the jury is dismissed, or in some courtrooms, after the judge and jury meet for a post-verdict interview.

One of the concepts that the judge has to explain during *voir dire* is that of "impartiality" because the prospective jurors will be asked whether they can be impartial. Judges try to keep their explanation brief and practical. In the *Torres* case, Judge Knapp explained

[58] *Torres* Transcript, *supra* note 56 (Ch. 1), at 89 (quoting Judge Knapp).
[59] *See, e.g.*, Blanck, Rosenthal & Cordell, *supra* note 48, at 123–24, 151.

impartiality as not having any "slant one way or another."[60] He also told the prospective jurors that everyone, including the judge,[61] has biases of one kind or another, but that just because one has biases that are relevant in one case does not mean that one cannot serve in another case in which those particular biases are irrelevant. Thus, Judge Knapp tried to ensure that prospective jurors would not feel any stigma by admitting to having biases and being unable to serve in that particular case.[62]

The questions that the judge asks prospective jurors during *voir dire* – the basic background questions that culminate with the question whether they can be impartial – push prospective jurors to think beyond their own personal concerns and to ask themselves whether they can serve. They become aware of the enormity of the task they will be asked to perform as jurors. They will be asked to make a judgment that will affect other people's lives. They might also be intrigued by the judge's brief description of the case or by the role the jury will play.

At some point during *voir dire*, some of the prospective jurors begin to hope, perhaps for the first time that day, that they will be selected for the jury. They have the opportunity to participate in an event of public note. Psychologists have observed that people have a tendency "to maintain they were present when a significant historical event took place . . . even though they were not there at all."[63] They do it not only "to sound interesting," but also "to be a small part of history."[64] For example, Juror #9 in the American jury film *12 Angry Men* was able to explain to his fellow jurors why an elderly witness might have said he heard the defendant shout "'I'm going to kill you,'" "heard the body hit the floor," and then saw the defendant run out of the apartment, even though the elderly witness might not have actually heard or seen what he described in his testimony.[65] Juror #9, also an elderly man, was able to understand why the elderly witness might have needed to feel important, just once in his life, and he tried to explain this to his fellow jurors: "A man like this needs to be recognized, to be listened to, to be quoted just once. This is very important."[66] The witness was a poor,

60 *Torres* Transcript, *supra* note 56 (Ch. 1), at 70, 74, 83, 98 (quoting Judge Knapp).
61 *Id.* at 35–36.
62 *Id.* at 38.
63 Buckhout, *supra* note 53, at 26.
64 *Id.*
65 Reginald Rose, *Twelve Angry Men*, *in* FILM SCRIPTS TWO 156, 229–31 (George P. Garrett, O. B. Hardison, Jr. & Jane R. Gelfman eds., 2013).
66 *Id.* at 241 (quoting Juror #9).

meek man who now had an opportunity to contribute to an important trial. This was his moment to be a small part of history. The opportunity to be a juror in a jury trial might work in a similar fashion. Citizens who are selected to serve on the jury will have the opportunity to be present at an important event, and not only to be present as an observer, but also to play an integral role as a key participant.

The formal questioning of prospective jurors by the judge, the authority figure in the courtroom, signals that what they are being asked to do as jurors has significance outside of their daily lives. The questioning reminds them to put aside their own personal inconveniences and to think about what it would mean to participate as a juror in this trial. This transformation – from ordinary citizen to responsible juror – is not carried out just during *voir dire*, but *voir dire* marks a significant step forward in the process. The seeds were planted when the citizen received his or her official summons, entered the courthouse, and was assigned to a courtroom, but they begin to bloom when the prospective juror is being questioned during *voir dire*.

Those who are present in the courtroom during *voir dire* can almost feel the change that occurs in the prospective jurors when they shift from wanting to be excused to wanting to serve. Although this shift is difficult to document, perhaps the best sources are the individual accounts of jurors or prospective jurors who have written about their jury experiences and who have alluded to the change they experienced during *voir dire*. Graham Burnett, the professor who served as foreperson on a jury in a murder trial in New York City, experienced this transformation.[67] In *A Trial by Jury*, he described his initial response to reporting for jury duty as follows: "I decided to treat the *unwelcome interruption* ... as something like a vacation, a brief visit to a foreign country of bureaucratic languor and vast waiting rooms . . . ."[68] Yet, by the time of *voir dire*, he "was completely absorbed – aware that this was a rare opportunity to participate in something important, weighty, real, something very different from my academic life."[69] Indeed, it became such "a deeply affecting experience" in his life that he chose to write a book about it.[70] Trevor Grove, a journalist who served as foreperson in a kidnaping case and also wrote a book, *The Juryman's Tale*, about the

[67] BURNETT, *supra* note 39 (Ch. 1), at 17–32.
[68] *Id.* at 17 (emphasis added).
[69] *Id.* at 29.
[70] D. Graham Burnett, *Foreword to the 50th Anniversary of* 12 Angry Men, 82 CHI.-KENT L. REV. 551, 552 (2007).

experience, underwent a similar shift from uncertainty about serving to an eagerness to serve. After the judge told Grove and several other prospective jurors to go home and spend the weekend thinking about whether they could serve on a lengthy trial, Grove realized he "was suddenly rather keen to be on [the jury]."[71]

Other prospective jurors felt regret when they were not selected as jurors. One recounted: "Surprisingly, that [excuse] was a bittersweet moment for me. I had gone from wanting to get out of this [jury service], to a heartfelt obligation to serve."[72] This response is not unusual. The nurse who could have sought a deferral but who chose not to because she saw jury duty as "just as important as working as an emergency nurse at a large city hospital," was both "relieved" when she was not chosen to sit on a criminal jury but also "disappointed."[73] So, too, was another prospective juror, a high school teacher, who was excused from a jury and responded: "[A] part of me was a little disappointed."[74]

As the judge conducts the *voir dire*, he or she becomes the figure in the courtroom that the prospective jurors begin to trust. The judge is the jury's source of information about the trial and the jurors begin to turn to the judge for an understanding about what is taking place in the courtroom. The jurors recognize that the judge is supposed to be neutral, whereas the lawyers are advocates for their respective sides. The French writer Alexis de Tocqueville recognized this special relationship between the judge and the jury when he visited America in the 1830s, examined many of its institutions, and published his observations in *Democracy in America* in 1835. He wrote that the judge, particularly in civil cases, "appears as a disinterested arbitrator between the litigants' passions. The jurors feel confidence in him and listen to him with respect . . . ."[75]

One way of viewing the judge–jury relationship is as a partnership that begins with *voir dire* and continues throughout the trial. Although judge and jury each have their own roles to perform, they need to work together. This partnership is characterized by an ongoing dialogue. The dialogue begins during *voir dire* and continues throughout the trial. During *voir dire*, the judge asks the questions and the jurors try to answer them. However, later in the trial, the jurors will ask the

[71] GROVE, *supra* note 32 (Ch. 1), at 33.
[72] Dan Hatfield, *Jury Service an Engaging Adventure*, JUDGES J., Fall 2004, at 34, 36.
[73] Deborah J. Golder, *Reflections: A Different Duty*, 90 AM. J. NURSING 92 (1990).
[74] *My Day in Court. Reflections on Jury Duty*, STEPHEN J. STIRLING (May 11, 2014), https://stephenjstirling.org/my-day-in-court-reflections-on-jury-duty/.
[75] TOCQUEVILLE, *supra* note 3 (Intro.), at 275.

questions and the judge will try to answer them. Throughout the trial, it is important that the judge is responsive to the jurors. Even if the judge is not permitted to answer some of the jury's questions, the judge needs to explain why that is the case.

**The Oath: Another Connection between Judge and Jurors**

Another connection between judge and jury and the roles they perform is that they are required to take an oath. The oath that the jurors take is similar to the oath that the judge takes. In both cases, they take an oath that reinforces the enormous responsibility they have been entrusted with to decide a case fairly. Prospective jurors take their oath together as a group after *voir dire* and the selection of jurors. Once they have taken their oath, they officially become jurors. The oath-taking instructs them about their role in a formal way and distinguishes their work as jurors from whatever work they do in their daily lives.[76] Judges remind jurors of their oath throughout the course of the trial.

Jurors take their oath as soon as all of the jurors have been selected. A typical oath is the one used in California, in which jurors in criminal trials swear to the following: "You and each of you, do solemnly swear that you will well and truly try the cause now pending before this Court, and a true verdict render therein, according to the evidence and the instructions of the Court, so help you God?"[77] This is similar to the oath that a federal judge takes when he or she is sworn into office:

> I, ____, do solemnly swear (or affirm) that I will administer justice without respect to persons, and do equal right to the poor and to the rich, and that I will faithfully and impartially discharge and perform all the duties incumbent upon me as _____ under the Constitution and laws of the United States. So help me God.[78]

When jurors take their oath, they are asked to stand together in the jury box. The oath is administered by the bailiff in the presence of the public, parties, press, and judge. Once the jurors have taken the oath, the jury is said to be "impaneled." At this point, the prospective jurors become jurors and the jury trial has commenced.

[76] Of course, some professions do require an oath. Doctors take an oath, as do lawyers. Politicians are also sworn into office. However, most jobs do not require an oath, even though they might entail a lot of responsibility or trust. For example, teachers and caregivers perform invaluable work, and yet they are not required to take an oath.

[77] California Superior Court Criminal Trial Judges' Deskbook 356 (Ronald M. George ed., 1988 ed.).

[78] 28 U.S.C. § 453 (2018).

The group oath-taking is important in marking the transformation from citizens into jurors. All of the prospective jurors are required to take the same oath, and to take it in public, but it is administered to them as a group. They are required to say the oath aloud before everyone in the courtroom and the oath requires them to decide the case based on the evidence and the judge's instructions (which contain the law). Even though they individually swear or affirm to do this, they do so in the context of the group. They acknowledge their individual responsibility, but they do so as part of a group ceremony and will exercise this responsibility as a member of this group. The experience of taking an oath is a new one for most jurors. As one former juror observed, "[t]he only other occasions on which such solemn undertakings [as an oath] are pronounced in public are weddings and christenings."[79]

Although the public oath-taking occurs at the beginning of the trial, both the judge and jurors might refer back to the oath later on. The oath is a commitment that the jurors make to follow the law and to decide the case based only on the evidence presented in the courtroom. During the trial, judges will remind jurors of the oath they took to ensure that they decide the case based only on the law and evidence. Given the omnipresence of social media, and the jurors' temptation to do online research or to express their views about the trial on social media, judges instruct them to refrain from doing so and remind them that doing so would be a violation of their oath. Judges' instructions to the jury at the end of the trial, before the jury begins its deliberations, also remind jurors of their oath and that they need to decide the case based only on the law and evidence. Some jurors will remind each other during deliberations that they took an oath to decide the case based only on the law and evidence. When some jurors introduce extraneous arguments, other jurors will remind them of their oath and try to limit their arguments to those that pertain to the law or evidence. Thus, the oath attempts to impose a constraint on jurors. The words they swore to, and the public nature of the oath-taking, try to limit the jury's power. However, the jury does have power beyond what the oath specifies. In rare instances, some juries recognize this power and make use of it.

[79] GROVE, *supra* note 32 (Ch. 1), at 33.

## STEPS JUDGES CAN TAKE DURING *VOIR DIRE* TO HELP CITIZENS BECOME JURORS

Although judges already take some steps to help citizens become jurors, there is more they can do. One step they could take is to use their questions and remarks during *voir dire* to teach prospective jurors about the roles of the judge and the jury and the ways they need to work together. Judges could also take judicial training programs that teach them ways to foster a good judge–jury relationship. A more radical step to help jurors assume their role is to have them wear a robe, just as the judge does when he or she is in the courtroom. Those prospective jurors who are selected for the jury could don a robe when the jury is impaneled. Admittedly, having jurors wear robes is a break with tradition, but it could be tried as a pilot program to see whether jurors find it helpful.

### Revising Judges' Questions and Remarks to Jurors

Judges should continue to ask prospective jurors a few questions about their background, as they do now, to decide if a for cause challenge is appropriate, but they should not stop there; instead, they should ask questions and provide information about the roles of the judge and the jury, and the challenges of judging. The background questions are useful for helping the judge to discern whether a challenge for cause is appropriate and they provide jurors with some basic information about their fellow jurors. However, most of the judges' questions should not attempt to uncover subtle biases, as lawyers would like them to do, but should help prospective jurors to understand their role as jurors.

Judges could begin by asking prospective jurors which roles they play in their everyday lives. Everybody plays multiple roles, whether in the workplace or the home. People understand that there are different behaviors suitable for different roles, and they are accustomed to switching back and forth. The judge could explain to prospective jurors that the role of juror entails a number of behaviors. During the trial, jurors need do the following: listen carefully to everything that is said and done in the courtroom; think critically about everything they have heard in court; refrain from forming a judgment in favor of one side or against the other until deliberations; maintain an impassive expression in the courtroom; be civil toward fellow jurors when they are together; follow the judge's instructions, including the need to avoid any online communication about the trial; and be aware of and challenge their own implicit biases and those of their fellow jurors.[80] During deliberations, jurors need to be willing to speak and to listen to each other, and to give reasons for their views. They need to be open to each other's views, but they do not have to change their views simply to conform with others.

Judges also need to explain their role to jurors and how the judge and jurors perform different roles but work together. Judges could ask jurors for examples outside the courtroom where people work together but have different functions, such as in sports or families. Judges could describe some of their responsibilities, such as presiding over the courtroom, making sure the lawyers follow courtroom procedures, ruling on objections, ruling on the admissibility of evidence, making sure that lawyers treat each other and the witnesses with respect, protecting the jury from an exhibit or testimony that is more prejudicial than probative, protecting the jury from outside influences, having occasional sidebars with the attorneys to discuss issues that arise, and making sure that the trial runs smoothly. Judges can also describe some of the challenges that they face, like making sure that they let lawyers conduct their case, being fair and evenhanded in their rulings, ruling on objections and motions even in the face of limited information, respecting jurors' time by limiting sidebars, and keeping jurors apprised of the schedule even when there are many unknowns.

Judges can also describe what judges' and jurors' roles have in common, and make sure that jurors know that judges and jurors face some of the same challenges. For example, both need to listen in court, to think critically about the evidence and arguments, and to avoid siding with one party or the other until the end of the trial. Judges decide the law and juries decide the facts and apply the law to those facts,[81] but they have to engage in similar behavior to perform these tasks. Of course, jurors have the added challenge of working with fellow jurors and reaching a group decision. Judges also need to make clear that they are a source of information for the jury during the trial, and if jurors have a problem they can turn to the judge for assistance by sending a note to the judge through the bailiff. Judges can also admit that they

[80] *See infra* Chapter 4.

[81] Judges distinguish the judge's task from the jurors' task in this way and typically instruct jurors as follows: "I instruct you that the law as given by the Court in these and other instructions constitute the only law for your guidance. It is your duty to accept and to follow the law as I give it to you even though you may disagree with the law." 1A KEVIN P. O'MALLEY ET AL., FEDERAL JURY PRACTICE AND INSTRUCTIONS § 10.01, at 5 (5th ed. 2000).

have to be as restrained as jurors in their use of the Internet or social media while the trial is underway.[82]

Another challenge that judges and jurors both face is the need to be impartial, but this is not a state of being, but of becoming. The challenge is made more difficult by implicit biases, which everyone has. Judges can explain implicit bias to the jury during *voir dire*, or wait until the jury has been impaneled.[83] The judge can explain that every person has implicit or unconscious biases, and the nature of these biases means that one is not fully aware of them. Although it is unclear how best to combat implicit biases, whether for a judge or a juror, there is general agreement that the first step is awareness, to the extent that this is possible.[84] Judges can attend judicial training seminars on implicit biases, but jurors do not have that opportunity as jurors.[85] They depend on the judge for their information. In jurisdictions that have addressed this issue, such as California, Illinois, and the Western District of Washington, they have relied on a preliminary instruction that can be repeated before the jury begins its deliberations. Federal courts in the Western District of Washington and state courts in New York have also added their own film, which they show to prospective jurors while they are waiting in the Jury Assembly Room.[86]

The approach of the federal courts in the Western District of Washington is to build on the film by having the judge instruct on implicit bias as a preliminary instruction, as part of a witness credibility

[82] For example, Judge Virginia Kendall, a federal district court judge in the Northern District of Illinois, explains to jurors in her courtroom that judge and jury alike face temptations when it comes to the use of social media, but that it is essential for judges and jurors to refrain from using social media to learn more about the case. *See, e.g.*, Virginia Kendall, Panelist, Social Media's Effect on Litigation, Second Circuit Judicial Conference (June 8, 2017) (notes on file with author).

[83] In some courthouses, prospective jurors are introduced to the concept of implicit bias by watching a brief orientation film on the subject while they are still in the Jury Assembly Room. *See, e.g.*, *Understanding the Effects of Unconscious Bias*, *supra* note 103 (Ch. 1) (providing the film used in federal district court in the Western District of Washington); *Jury Service and Fairness: Understanding the Challenge of Implicit Bias*, *supra* note 103 (Ch. 1) (providing the film used in New York).

[84] *See, e.g.*, Kang et al., *supra* note 107 (Ch. 1), at 1184; W. Dist. of Wash., *Criminal Jury Instructions – Implicit Bias*, https://www.wawd.uscourts.gov/sites/wawd/files/CriminalJuryInstructions-ImplicitBias.pdf [https://perma.cc/9HUN-3RTA].

[85] *See, e.g.*, Chief Justice Lloyd A. Karmeier, *Another Step toward Equal Justice: Identifying Implicit Bias*, ILL. CTS. CONNECT (Nov. 29, 2017), http://www.illinoiscourts.gov/Media/enews/2017/112917_chief_message.asp (choose "Illinois Courts Connect"; then choose "archive" and "2017"); Press Release, Ill. Sup. Ct., Illinois Supreme Court Announces Findings, Next Steps Following Judicial Decision-Making Study (Nov. 6, 2017).

[86] *See Understanding the Effects of Unconscious Bias*, *supra* note 103 (Ch. 1) (Western District of Washington); *Jury Service and Fairness: Understanding the Challenge of Implicit Bias*, *supra* note 103 (Ch. 1) (New York).

instruction, as part of closing instructions, and during *voir dire* if the parties are going to ask about bias, including implicit bias.[87] Federal courts in the Western District of Washington recognize that prospective jurors, or even newly impaneled jurors, will not necessarily be aware of their implicit biases, and that they need to strive toward greater awareness. During deliberations, fellow jurors can also help each other to recognize implicit biases and how they might shape what different jurors see. For example, the implicit bias instruction in civil cases in Illinois asks jurors to help each other to recognize and to resist their implicit biases.[88]

### Training Judges to Foster the Judge–Jury Relationship

Although new judges can attend judicial training programs, these programs do not typically include a section on fostering the judge–jury relationship. In general, these programs aim to teach new judges about developments in a variety of areas of law and they might also include units on case management and maintaining control over one's docket. In this age of settlements, they can also include techniques on helping the parties to reach a settlement, but what about the techniques for helping jurors to understand their role?

There are several organizations and law schools that offer judicial training programs, but the programs tend to focus on subject areas of the law. Many of these programs are directed toward new judges. For example, the Federal Judicial Center (FJC) offers training for new federal district court judges (among other types of new judges).[89] The FJC program consists of "two one-week programs" so there is limited time and the program covers many topics in that two-week period.[90] The first phase includes ethical issues, *voir dire* methods, caseload

[87] W. Dist. of Wash., *supra* note 84.

[88] *See, e.g.*, Ill. Sup. Ct. Comm. on Jury Instructions in Civil Cases, Illinois Pattern Jury Instructions – Civil § 1.08 (2019–2020 ed.) [hereinafter IPI] (instructing jurors to "help each other to resist[] any urge to reach a verdict that is influenced by bias for or against any party or witness").

[89] Fed. Jud. Ctr., Education for the Courts: Programs and Resources for Judges, http://www.fjc.gov/education/programs-and-resources-judges [https://perma.cc/JWA7-FWLM] [hereinafter FJC Education for the Courts]. The National Center for State Courts (NCSC) offers judicial training for state court judges, including new trial judges. Its website includes the areas covered as well as numerous role-playing exercises and some hypothetical examples. *See* http://www.ncsc.org. A number of the lessons deal with the jury, and would lend themselves well to teaching judges how to put themselves in the place of jurors or prospective jurors. The New York State Judicial Institute offers training for new state court judges in New York. In 2021, the Judicial Institute provided several days of lectures, including one on bias in civil jurors. *See* New York State Judicial Institute, Agenda (Jan. 29, 2021).

[90] FJC Education for the Courts, *supra* note 89.

management, settlement, criminal trials, the workings of federal prison, evidentiary decisions, sentencing using the *United States Sentencing Guidelines*, and judicial security issues.[91] The second phase focuses on case management, federal jurisdiction, sentencing, civil rights law, *habeas corpus*, employment law, media relations, and ethics.[92] The section on *voir dire* considers different methods of *voir dire*, but could be expanded to include the judge–jury relationship and how the judge can create a good working relationship with the jury.

Not all judges see a good judge–jury relationship as a goal,[93] and yet, this relationship is important to helping citizens become responsible jurors. Judicial training programs need to get judges in the habit of asking themselves at every stage of the jury process, beginning with *voir dire*: If I were a juror, what would I want to know at this point? In other words, judges need to put themselves in the shoes of a juror and to see the trial from their perspective. They need to be able to take a jury-centric approach.[94] This is not easy to do because judges have been to law school and, typically, have practiced law before becoming a judge. It is hard to remember what it is like to be untrained in the law, and yet, that is precisely the imaginative leap that judges need to take because that is the situation in which most jurors find themselves.

Judicial training programs intent on helping a judge to foster good judge–jury relationships would ask judges to consider what they would want to know during *voir dire* if they were jurors. Such a focus might lead the judge to explain to the prospective jurors who the trial participants are and what their role is during the trial; what the case is about (in brief); the types of questions the judge will ask during *voir dire* and what the purpose of such questions is; what the prospective jurors should do if they are embarrassed to answer a question; and why impartiality is important and that it is not a fixed quality but a goal toward which jurors should work throughout the trial.

A judicial training program that strives to help judges develop a good judge–jury relationship also needs to focus on the interactions between

91 *Id.*

92 *Id.*

93 *See, e.g.*, BURNETT, *supra* note 39 (Ch. 1), at 81 ("The judge ... liked his juries as out of it as possible. This became clear early [on] ....").

94 *See, e.g.*, Judge B. Michael Dann (ret.), *Jurors and the Future of "Tort Reform,"* 78 CHI.-KENT L. REV. 1127, 1136 (2003) (describing himself as a "juror-centric observer"); Nancy S. Marder, *Introduction to the Jury at a Crossroad: The American Experience*, 78 CHI.-KENT L. REV. 909, 918 (2003) (describing a "jury-centric" perspective as one that asks: "What tools do jurors need in order to perform more effectively the tasks with which they have been charged?").

judge and jury that will build respect between them. For example, when the judge enters and leaves the courtroom, everyone in the courtroom stands as a sign of respect. In some courtrooms, such as that of Judge Leonard B. Sand in the Southern District of New York, Judge Sand stood, and so did everyone in the courtroom, when the jury entered and exited the courtroom. It is a show of respect for the jury and also a recognition that the jury performs as a decision-maker, just as the judge does. Similarly, the judge is tasked with controlling the trial, and one of the ways of showing respect for the jury is by being respectful of the jury's time. When the questioning of a witness becomes repetitious,[95] or the objections of one side or the other seem designed just to be disruptive,[96] it is up to the trial judge to ensure that these questions are not permitted and that the trial moves along as seamlessly as possible. At the same time, if the judge senses that the jury needs a break in order to maintain its focus, the judge needs to provide a recess.

The judicial training program needs to teach judges to be self-aware about their own behavior because jurors will be watching that behavior and attempting to mirror it. As Tocqueville noted, the judge is the authority figure to which the jurors turn in order to know what is expected of them.[97] If the judge is attentive to those in the courtroom, that signals to the jurors that they must be attentive. If the judge maintains a neutral facial expression, that serves as an example to the jurors. If the judge is an active listener and takes notes and pays attention, the jurors are likely to follow that example. If the judge treats the parties fairly and evenhandedly, that reminds the jurors they must do the same. Although everyone in the courtroom watches the judge, the jurors in particular are attuned to the judge because they take their cues from him or her. Perhaps the judicial training programs could have a segment for judges on how to treat everyone in the courtroom with respect, including the jurors; it is not clear from any of the online syllabi that this is covered. If it is not covered, then it needs to be. This seems like a lesson that experienced, well-regarded judges could teach, as guest lecturers, to new judges attending judicial education programs.

[95] *See, e.g.*, St. Eve & Scavo, *supra* note 49, at 165 (reporting the results of a survey given to 500 jurors and finding that 169 jurors (33.7%) disliked attorneys repeating questions or concepts).

[96] *Id.* at 160 ("Jurors like when opposing counsel get along and treat each other with respect during trial.").

[97] *See* TOCQUEVILLE, *supra* note 3 (Intro.), at 275 (describing how jurors in civil cases "feel confidence in [the judge] and listen to him with respect").

### Having Jurors Wear Robes or Badges

One way in which courts can help citizens to assume their role as jurors is to have them literally slip into that role by putting on a plain black robe. It could be a robe similar to the ones that American judges wear or it could be even more basic, like the plain robe that students and fellows wear when they eat dinner in Hall at Cambridge or Oxford.[98] The robe would be a reminder to jurors, and to the people in the courtroom observing them, that they have left behind their role as private citizens and have assumed a new public role as jurors. They are decision-makers in the courtroom, just like the judge. They could don a robe, just as the judge does. Admittedly, having jurors in robes is not part of our jury tradition, but we could try it as a pilot program and see if its upsides outweigh its downsides. Many positions, especially those performed in the service of others, such as doctors, nurses, dentists, firefighters, police officers, religious leaders, members of the military, pilots, and flight attendants, include the wearing of uniforms. The uniforms enable everyone to recognize instantly the nature of that person's work. If jurors wore robes, these could serve as a reminder to them, and to others in the courtroom, of the nature of their role.

The main reason to have jurors wear robes is that it would remind them of their role as jurors every day that they serve. They could be given their robes once the jury has been selected and they could put them on before they stand to take their oath and the jury is impaneled. At the end of every day in court, they would leave their robe in the jury room, and when they return the next day, they would put their robe on before entering the courtroom. It would be a tangible reminder that they have left behind their role as private citizen and assumed a new public role as juror. One tradition that they could borrow from the US Supreme Court is to shake hands with each other after they put on their robes in the jury room and before they enter the courtroom and go to the jury box. The Supreme Court Justices follow this ritual because it fosters collegiality.[99] It signals to the Justices that whatever their

[98] I thank Renée Lerner, Professor of Law at The George Washington University Law School, for reminding me at the Civil Jury Project's Academic Roundtable, held at New York University Law School on April 24, 2019, about the plain black robes that students and fellows wear at Cambridge and Oxford.

[99] *See* Justice John Paul Stevens, Five Chiefs: A Supreme Court Memoir 152 (2011) ("Like the practice of shaking hands with every member of the Court before going on the bench to hear oral argument, that custom [of celebrating each Justice's birthday with a glass of wine] played an important role in maintaining the cordial relations among the nine individuals who sometimes used pretty strong language when expressing disagreement with the views of the majority on more important issues.").

differences in any given case or during any given oral argument, they are colleagues. This would be a good message to convey to jurors as well, especially when they begin their deliberations.

Another reason for jurors to wear robes is that it would remind them and others in the courtroom that jurors are decision-makers in a jury trial. As former juror Trevor Grove explained, the reason that everyone in the courtroom watched his jury so intently was because they knew "it was we twelve [jurors] who had ultimate power in this court."[100] Although a judge has many decisions to make in the course of a jury trial, from motions to rulings on objections to jury instructions, the jury makes the key decision in a jury trial – it reaches a verdict. The robe highlights this connection between judge and jury. The robe also highlights the attributes that judicial decision-makers – judge and jury alike – must strive for, including impartiality.

Wearing robes would also reinforce the equality among jurors by obscuring many of their differences. They might dress differently and come from different socioeconomic classes and have different genders and body types, but when they put on a robe they mask many of those differences. The viewer sees what they have in common – the robe and the role that it signifies – rather than all the ways in which they differ from each other. Of course, differences still come through based on gender, race, age, ethnicity, and perhaps even religion. The masking is not complete, nor is it meant to be. Rather, it simply shifts the focus from all the ways in which these citizens are different from each other to the one respect in which they are all the same: They are all jurors.

In other roles in which people wear a uniform, the uniform highlights the role over the individual. A person who wears a doctor's white coat or an airline pilot's uniform is seen primarily in that capacity. Perhaps it is because the public needs to trust that person and the uniform is the first sign that the person can be trusted to play that role. Or perhaps it is because a uniform allows everyone to make an immediate identification of the role the person plays. In some instances, the uniform is protective, such as in the case of the firefighter or the member of the military, and other times it is just an indication of the role that person plays in the community, for example, the religious leader or the judge.

Although American judges wear robes and jurors do not, that does not mean that these practices are fixed in stone. For example, in England, the judge wears a robe, as do the clerk and the barristers.

[100] GROVE, *supra* note 32 (Ch. 1), at 34.

The robe (called a gown) is not limited to the judge. Of course, in England the judge, clerk, and barristers also wear wigs, which would not be widely embraced in the United States. In England, "[w]igs are said to provide the lawyers and judges not merely with an aura of impersonal authority but also a degree of anonymity, which is useful for their own protection."[101] However, in the United States, wigs would be seen as a relic of a bygone era, in a way that a plain black robe is not. In Canada, the judge, clerk, and barristers wear a robe, as well as white collars, but no wigs. Although these countries do not have jurors donning robes, they do have other legal actors, in addition to the judge, wearing a robe. These other countries' use of robes for judges, barristers, and clerks suggests that the robe need not be limited to judges.

Although robes would help jurors to slip into their role and help others to recognize their role, they could have possible downsides. One is that robes would make jurors look more like judges than ordinary citizens and one of the reasons that jurors are so well-regarded is that they are ordinary citizens who have been summoned to serve. They serve for one trial and then return to their private lives. They are not professionals, and thus, there is less risk that they would become hardened in the way that a professional judge might over time.[102] Another possible downside is that a jury is supposed to be drawn from a fair cross section of the community.[103] A jury that is made up of a broad swath of the community, and that "looks like America," is more likely to command the public's respect, even if members of the public disagree with the jury's verdict. To the extent that robes mask jurors' differences, the public might be less aware of how diverse that jury is and more willing to question its legitimacy. Of course, judges wear robes and that has not stopped members of the public, press, and legal community from noting judges' gender and race and the need for greater diversity in both federal and state judiciaries.[104]

101 *Id.* at 99.

102 Taylor v. Louisiana, 419 U.S. 522, 530 (1975) (describing the jury as a "hedge against the overzealous or mistaken prosecutor and in preference to the professional or perhaps over-conditioned or biased response of a judge"); Duncan v. Louisiana, 391 U.S. 145, 156 (1968) (describing the criminal jury as providing "an inestimable safeguard against the corrupt or overzealous prosecutor and against the compliant, biased, or eccentric judge").

103 The venire or jury panel must be drawn from a fair cross section of the community. This is required by the Sixth Amendment to the U.S. Constitution, *see Taylor*, 419 U.S. at 530–31, and is made applicable to the states by the Fourteenth Amendment. *See Duncan*, 391 U.S. at 149. There are also federal statutes that require prospective jurors to be drawn from a fair cross section of the community. *See, e.g.*, 28 U.S.C. §§ 1861, 1863(b)(3) (2020).

104 *See, e.g.*, Suja A. Thomas, The Missing American Jury: Restoring the Fundamental Role of the Criminal, Civil, and Grand Juries 225–26 (2016) (providing statistics from 2009–10 showing that state and federal judiciaries were not as

Another potential downside is that jurors attired in robes might feel greater anonymity and there is some social psychology research suggesting that those protected by anonymity are more willing to engage in bad actions.[105] However, jurors already serve anonymously in cases in which there is a danger of jury tampering or a threat to jurors' safety, such as cases involving gangs or organized crime. In those cases, jurors' names and addresses are withheld from public disclosure until after the trial, whereas jurors who wear robes would still be identified by name and their responses during *voir dire* would still be public. Thus, even if jurors wore robes, they would not be cloaked in anonymity, as some jurors are in certain kinds of cases.

One way to see if the upsides outweigh the downsides of robes for jurors is to try this as a pilot program and to see how it works. Many trial practices have been tried on an experimental basis, and if judges, lawyers, and jurors are happy with the practice, it can be implemented more broadly. For example, a number of federal district court judges in the Seventh Circuit participated in a study in which they experimented with different trial practices, from limiting the time for the trial, to allowing jurors to submit written questions to witnesses via the judge, to having the lawyers provide summaries before the jurors began their deliberations.[106] Some judges, such as Chief Judge Holderman (now retired), liked some of the practices so much that they decided to continue them in their own courtrooms even after the pilot program ended.[107] State courts are free to experiment as well and to learn from each other. As Justice Louis D. Brandeis once observed: "[A] single courageous State may, if its citizens choose, serve as a laboratory; and try novel social and economic experiments without risk to the rest of the country."[108]

Perhaps a less radical approach would be to have jurors wear juror badges, rather than robes. In some courts, jurors already wear badges, such as when the jurors remain anonymous and are known only by

diverse by race or gender as the general population). For example, women constituted 18% of the federal judiciary in 2009, whereas, according to the census in 2010, they constituted 51% of the general population. *Id.* at 226.

105 *See, e.g.*, Leonardo Mangat, Note, *A Jury of Your [Redacted]: The Rise and Implications of Anonymous Juries*, 103 CORNELL L. REV. 1621 (2018).

106 *See* SEVENTH CIR. AM. JURY PROJECT COMM., SEVENTH CIRCUIT AMERICAN JURY PROJECT FINAL REPORT (2008).

107 *See* James F. Holderman, *Foreword to Juries and Lay Participation: American Perspectives and Global Trends*, 90 CHI.-KENT L. REV. 785, 787 (2015).

108 New State Ice Co. v. Liebmann, 285 U.S. 262, 311 (1932) (Brandeis, J., dissenting).

a number[109] or by their first name and initial of their last name.[110] Juror badges might seem less radical because they are already used in certain types of cases. In addition, a juror badge is distinctive, but does not share the potential downsides of a robe; a badge does not obscure juror differences nor make jurors look more like professionals than like ordinary citizens. Yet, juror badges are tangible and could provide a physical reminder that helps citizens assume their role as jurors. In England and Wales, the court system considered giving jurors a laminated card that would remind them of their rights and responsibilities (and in particular their responsibility to refrain from making any online comments about the trial).[111] Although the laminated card was not adopted, it would have provided a tangible reminder to jurors, similar to the badge, of the need to act in accordance with their role as jurors.

However, a juror badge also has its limitations. It does not provide the dignity that a robe does; nor does it have the connection to the judge and the activity of judging. In fact, wearing a badge with a juror number might make a juror feel more like a prisoner, especially after being summoned to court. Of course, the juror badge does not have to include a number, and it should not include the juror's name or any other personal information.[112] The badge could consist of the word "juror" and a symbol of the court, such as its insignia. The badge would be issued by the court, include the court's name and insignia, and identify the wearer as a juror. The goal would be simply for jurors to wear a badge, just as conference attendees wear a badge, so that they feel that they belong, and others recognize that they belong. Jurors could put on the badge before they enter the courtroom each day of the trial and leave their badge in the jury room at the end of the day.

109 *See, e.g.*, *How Courts Care for Jurors in High Profile Cases*, *supra* note 34 (Ch. 1) (describing a jury trial in which the jurors were anonymous and were "assign[ed] badges with numbers that corresponded with seats in the jury box").

110 *See Torres* Transcript, *supra* note 56 (Ch. 1), at 48–49 ("I am just going to keep your identities secret from anybody but you and me . . . . All that will be known will be your first name and the initial of your last name.") (quoting Judge Knapp).

111 *See* Cheryl Thomas, Are Juries Fair?, Ministry of Justice 50 (Feb. 2010), https://www.justice.gov.uk/downloads/publications/research-and-analysis/moj-research/are-juries-fair-research.pdf [https://perma.cc/V8Q3-LP3U] (recommending that jurors receive written guidelines that outline their responsibilities as jurors).

112 *Cf.* Buckley v. Am. Const. L. Found., 525 U.S. 182, 198–200 (1999) (invalidating a state statute that required paid circulators, seeking to collect signatures from passersby, to wear identification badges that displayed their names; the Supreme Court held that such a requirement would chill political speech at a critical moment).

The act of putting on and wearing a badge or robe would remind jurors of their role and their need to act in accordance with it. The jury process, initiated by the summons and facilitated by *voir dire*, helps jurors with this shift from citizen to juror, but the robe or badge would provide them with a physical reminder, especially at the beginning when everything seems so foreign. The robe or badge would also remind others in the courtroom of the role that these citizens must now play. Sometimes it is easier to assume a role when everyone around you recognizes it. The jury box, which separates jurors from everyone else in the courtroom, conveys the message to jurors and others in the courtroom that these citizens are stepping away from their private roles and assuming a new public role, but it would be useful for jurors to have some other indicia of this role change, especially at the beginning of the trial.

## SUMMARY

Although robes or badges would provide jurors with tactile reminders of their new role, *voir dire* helps to bring about citizens' transformation into jurors even without these reminders. One way in which *voir dire* does this is that prospective jurors sit as a group in the jury box. They can observe all the other participants in the trial, but they are also keenly aware that they are being observed. They start to think more about the group role they are being asked to play and less about the individual reasons why they cannot serve. In addition, the judge questions the prospective jurors as a group. This group questioning is important – not for revealing subtle biases as the traditional view suggests – but because the group questioning helps prospective jurors to focus on their group role. As one prospective juror after another says that he or she can be impartial and can serve, others begin to believe that they too can be impartial and can serve.

Jurors do not start out as either impartial or partial, but work toward becoming impartial jurors through every stage of the jury process. Although the traditional view holds that jurors are either impartial or partial from the start, and the partial ones just need to be weeded out, the transformation view recognizes that all jurors have subtle biases and they need to hold these in check, just as a judge strives to do. *Voir dire* helps jurors to start thinking in terms of their group responsibilities rather than their individual inconveniences.

Thus, *voir dire* helps citizens become jurors who will ultimately be able to work together and put aside their own biases and participate as equals in a group task. The judge can help prospective jurors with this transformation by using *voir dire* to explain to them the responsibilities of being a juror. Although judge and jury have different roles to play, they also work together throughout the trial and jurors look to the judge for guidance in their role as jurors.

3

# PEREMPTORY CHALLENGES: A BARRIER THAT UNNECESSARILY LIMITS WHO CAN SERVE AS JURORS

After prospective jurors have been questioned during *voir dire*, but before they are seated as jurors on a jury, the lawyer on each side has the opportunity to exercise a certain number of peremptory challenges. In doing so, each side's lawyer has an opportunity to remove a certain number of prospective jurors so that they will not serve on that particular jury. The lawyers do not have to offer any explanation for how they exercise their peremptory challenges, except in certain limited circumstances.

The traditional view of the peremptory challenge is that it allows lawyers to remove prospective jurors they think are biased. Lawyers believe that these prospective jurors have implicit or unconscious[1] biases that the lawyers have been able to discern, even though the prospective jurors have said they could be impartial and have not been removed for cause. To discern these subtle biases, lawyers rely on their intuition, rules of thumb, or even the way the prospective juror looks at them, though there is no evidence that lawyers can detect these biases. Social psychologists have said that it is hard for people to identify such biases in themselves, much less in others.

The only limitation on lawyers' exercise of their peremptory challenges is that they cannot be based on the prospective juror's race, ethnicity, or gender.[2] The Supreme Court devised a test in *Batson*

[1] The terms implicit bias or unconscious bias are used interchangeably. *See, e.g.*, AM. BAR ASS'N, *Achieving an Impartial Jury (AIJ) Toolbox 12*, https://www.americanbar.org/content/dam/aba/publications/criminaljustice/voirdire_toolchest.authcheckdam.pdf [https://perma.cc/9TEN-5C2A]. I also use the phrases "subtle biases" or "hidden biases" to indicate implicit or unconscious biases.

[2] *See* Batson v. Kentucky, 476 U.S. 79 (1986) (prohibiting peremptory challenges based on race); Powers v. Ohio, 499 U.S. 400 (1991) (prohibiting peremptory challenges based on race or

v. *Kentucky*, and extended it in other cases,[3] which was supposed to stop discriminatory peremptory challenges while still preserving the peremptory challenge. However, the test has been ineffective and discriminatory peremptory challenges continue.[4]

When lawyers exercise peremptory challenges based on race, gender, or ethnicity, it becomes more difficult for members of certain groups, such as African-American men or all women, to serve in certain kinds of cases, such as capital cases.[5] As a result, juries are less diverse than they otherwise would be, and diverse juries are important to the transformation of citizens into jurors. With diverse juries, jurors can challenge each other's assumptions and engage in a more thorough and careful deliberation based on reasons rather than stereotypes.

The exclusion of qualified prospective jurors who have said that they can be impartial means that citizens who are willing to serve are not being given the opportunity to do so; instead, they are removed from the petit jury by peremptory challenges. They are struck based on impermissible prejudices or personal idiosyncrasies of lawyers and, unfortunately, the latter serves as a mask for the former. In either case, peremptory challenges stand in the way of qualified citizens serving as jurors.

If citizens step into their role as jurors through the jury process, as I argue they do, then there is no role for peremptory challenges, and more incremental remedies, such as reducing the number of peremptory challenges, fall short. Peremptory challenges do not rid juries of jurors with implicit biases, which we all have. But discriminatory peremptory challenges do reduce juries' diversity, with the result that jurors are less able to challenge each other's assumptions during deliberations. Discriminatory peremptory challenges also leave the prospective jurors

ethnicity); J. E. B. v. Alabama *ex rel.* T.B., 511 U.S. 127 (1994) (prohibiting peremptory challenges based on gender).

3 *See* Edmonson v. Leesville Concrete Co., 500 U.S. 614 (1991) (extending *Batson* to civil cases); Georgia v. McCollum, 505 U.S. 42 (1992) (extending *Batson* to defense attorneys, in addition to prosecutors).

4 *See, e.g.*, Nancy S. Marder, Batson *Revisited*, 97 Iowa L. Rev. 1585, 1588–95 (2012) (arguing that *Batson* and the cases that followed tried to limit discriminatory peremptory challenges, but the *Batson* test, which is supposed to help lawyers and judges to distinguish discriminatory peremptory challenges from permissible peremptory challenges, is easy to circumvent).

5 *See, e.g.*, Foster v. Chatman, 578 U.S. 488 (2016) (holding that prosecutors used peremptory challenges to exclude African-American prospective jurors in violation of *Batson*); Equal Just. Initiative, Illegal Racial Discrimination in Jury Selection: A Continuing Legacy 28–34 (2010), http://eji.org/sites/default/files/illegal-racial-discrimination-in-jury-selection.pdf [https://perma.cc/WG4M-TK5R] (recounting numerous instances in which African-American prospective jurors were removed through prosecutors' peremptory challenges).

who have been subjected to them with negative views of the jury system, instead of the positive views that they might otherwise have if they were permitted to serve. Although there is a role for juror qualifications (such as to ensure that jurors meet a minimum age threshold) and for cause challenges (such as to remove prospective jurors who say they cannot be impartial), peremptory challenges do not serve such roles. Instead, they interfere with the transformation of citizens into responsible jurors.

## HOW PEREMPTORY CHALLENGES WORK

In general, peremptory challenges permit lawyers to remove a certain number of prospective jurors from the jury without having to give a reason. The number of peremptory challenges varies depending on the court (state or federal), whether it is a civil or criminal case, and, in a criminal case, the type of crime. In federal court, for example, each side is given three peremptory challenges in civil cases,[6] and varying numbers in criminal cases, depending on the seriousness of the crime.[7] In criminal cases in federal court, the criminal defendant is allotted more peremptory challenges than the prosecution in felony cases,[8] but the same number as the prosecution in misdemeanor cases,[9] as well as in cases in which the prosecutor seeks the death penalty.[10] For example, in a capital case in federal court, the prosecutor has twenty peremptory challenges, as does the criminal defendant.[11] In state courts, each state decides how many peremptory challenges to allot in civil and criminal trials. One state, Arizona, has recently eliminated peremptory challenges[12] and two other states, Washington and California, have established a new standard ("an objective observer's" standard) for

[6] *See* 28 U.S.C. § 1870 ("In civil cases, each party shall be entitled to three peremptory challenges."); FED. R. CIV. P. 47(b) ("The court must allow the number of peremptory challenges provided by 28 U.S.C. § 1870.").

[7] *See* FED. R. CRIM. P. 24(b)(1)–(3).

[8] *See id.* at 24(b)(2) (providing the government six peremptory challenges and the defendant or defendants together ten peremptory challenges if the offense is punishable by more than one year in prison).

[9] *See id.* at 24(b)(3) (providing the government and the defendant each with three peremptory challenges if the offense charged is punishable by imprisonment of not more than one year or by a fine).

[10] *Id.* at 24(b)(1).

[11] *Id.*

[12] Hassan Kanu, *Arizona Breaks New Ground in Nixing Peremptory Challenges*, REUTERS (Sept. 1, 2021), https://www.reuters.com/legal/legalindustry/arizona-breaks-new-ground-nixing-peremptory-challenges-2021-09-01/.

judging whether a lawyer has exercised a discriminatory peremptory challenge.[13] Each state sets the number of peremptory challenges by statute, rule, or both.

One common method of exercising peremptory challenges, known as the "struck method,"[14] is to have the lawyers exercise their peremptory challenges at the end of the *voir dire*. This approach allows the lawyers to see the complete set of prospective jurors from which the petit jury will be drawn before they exercise their peremptory challenges. It also allows jury selection to proceed efficiently because all the prospective jurors removed by peremptory challenges will be eliminated at once, and it allows lawyers to exercise their peremptory challenges without the prospective jurors knowing which lawyer struck which prospective juror. This method requires that if, for example, twelve jurors need to be seated and each side has three peremptory challenges, then eighteen prospective jurors need to be called randomly to the jury box, plus the number of alternate jurors and the number of peremptory challenges available to be exercised for the selection of alternates.[15]

The other common method, called "strike-and-replace," involves questioning small groups of prospective jurors (six to eight at a time) and replacing those who are removed for cause or with a peremptory challenge with others on the panel until a jury is formed.[16] When a prospective juror is removed for cause or with a peremptory challenge, he or she is replaced with another prospective juror from the venire. Alternate jurors are selected at the end of jury selection, and each lawyer has additional peremptory challenges for the alternates.[17] The trend is toward the "struck" method rather than the "strike-and-replace" method.[18]

13 WASH. ST. SUP. CT. GEN. R. 37(f) (2018) (containing Washington's new standard); AB 3070, Juries: peremptory challenges (Sept. 30, 2020) (amending CAL. CIV. PROC. CODE § 231.7) (containing California's new standard); *see infra* text accompanying notes 136–43 for a discussion of both.

14 *See, e.g.*, JURY TRIAL INNOVATIONS (2d ed.), *supra* note 93 (Ch. 1), at 80–81 (describing "struck" method of jury selection); AM. BAR ASS'N, PRINCIPLES FOR JURIES & JURY TRIALS 78 (2005) (Comment, Subdivision D) (advocating the use of the "struck jury system").

15 Some states do not tell jurors who the alternates are until the jury is ready to deliberate. *See, e.g.*, AM. BAR ASS'N, *supra* note 14, at 69 (Principle 11, G(2)) ("The status of jurors as regular jurors or as alternates should be determined through random selection at the time for jury deliberation."). The rationale is that all jurors should pay attention throughout the trial and the concern is that alternate jurors might think that they do not have to pay as much attention as jurors even though they could end up as a juror if one of the other jurors is unable to complete his or her service.

16 *See* JURY TRIAL INNOVATIONS (2d ed.), *supra* note 93 (Ch. 1), at 80.

17 *See* FED. R. CRIM. P. 24(c)(4).

18 JURY TRIAL INNOVATIONS (2d ed.), *supra* note 93 (Ch. 1), at 80.

The US Supreme Court has explained that although peremptory challenges have always been part of the country's jury tradition, they are not guaranteed by the US Constitution.[19] When peremptory challenges are exercised in a discriminatory manner, such as those based on race, gender, or ethnicity, they violate the Equal Protection Clause of the Fourteenth Amendment, which provides that no "citizen shall be denied the equal protection of the laws."[20] Since peremptory challenges are not guaranteed by the US Constitution, and equal protection is guaranteed by the Fourteenth Amendment, discriminatory peremptory challenges are not permitted. However, the Court has taken an incremental approach, and has expanded the groups protected from discriminatory peremptory challenges slowly over time.

The US Supreme Court has struggled with the problem of discriminatory peremptory challenges. It wanted to preserve the peremptory challenge, which allows parties to strike a certain number of prospective jurors without giving any reason, yet it wanted to eliminate discriminatory peremptory challenges, which it had recognized as violating the Equal Protection Clause. The two goals were in tension. In 1986, the Court in *Batson* v. *Kentucky*[21] devised a test that was essentially a compromise.[22] It established that prosecutors could not exercise peremptory challenges against African-American prospective jurors when the criminal defendant was an African American.[23] The Court explained that even though peremptory challenges had always been part of the American jury tradition, they could not be exercised based on race because that violated a criminal defendant's right to be tried by a jury that included members of his or her own race.[24] After *Batson*, an African-American criminal defendant could raise a *Batson* challenge when the prosecutor attempted to use peremptory challenges to remove African-American prospective jurors from the petit jury. If the defense

[19] *See, e.g.*, Batson v. Kentucky, 476 U.S. 79, 98–99 (1986).

[20] U.S. Const. amend. XIV, § 1. The U.S. Supreme Court held that peremptory challenges based on race, ethnicity, or gender were a violation of the Equal Protection Clause of the Fourteenth Amendment to the U.S. Constitution. *See, e.g.*, Swain v. Alabama, 380 U.S. 202 (1965) (race); *Batson*, 476 U.S. at 79 (race); Powers v. Ohio, 499 U.S. 400 (1991) (race and ethnicity); J. E. B. v. Alabama *ex rel.* T.B., 511 U.S. 127 (1994) (gender). They were not a violation of the Sixth Amendment, *see, e.g.*, Holland v. Illinois, 493 U.S. 474 (1990), or of the Due Process Clause of the Fourteenth Amendment. *See* Peters v. Kiff, 407 U.S. 493 (1972) (only three members of the Court took this view).

[21] 476 U.S. at 89 (1986) (holding that a prosecutor's use of a peremptory challenge based on race violates the Equal Protection Clause of the Fourteenth Amendment to the U.S. Constitution).

[22] *Id.* at 126 (Burger, C.J., dissenting) (describing *Batson* as a "curious hybrid").

[23] *Id.* at 89.

[24] *Id.* at 86.

established a prima facie case of a race-based peremptory challenge,[25] the prosecutor had to give a reason for the exercise of the peremptory challenge.[26] As long as the prosecutor gave a race-neutral reason, the peremptory challenge would be permitted. Prosecutors quickly learned to give race-neutral reasons to explain their peremptory challenges when they were challenged.

Over the next decade, the Supreme Court expanded the reach of *Batson*. In *Powers* v. *Ohio*, the Court held that a prosecutor could not exercise a peremptory challenge based on race or ethnicity even when the defendant was white and the prosecutor used a peremptory challenge to strike an African-American prospective juror.[27] In *Edmonson* v. *Leesville Concrete Co., Inc.*,[28] the Court extended *Batson* to civil cases and in *Georgia* v. *McCollum*,[29] it extended *Batson* to criminal defendants as well. In *J.E.B.* v. *Alabama* ex rel. *T.B.*,[30] the Court held that peremptory challenges could not be exercised based on gender. However, in *Purkett* v. *Elem*,[31] a *per curiam* opinion, the Court retreated somewhat from *Batson* and held that as long as the reason was race-neutral, even if it had no relevance to the particular case, as *Batson* had required,[32] the peremptory challenge would be allowed.

Although the Supreme Court appeared to be taking action to root out discriminatory peremptory challenges with this line of cases, at least until *Purkett* v. *Elem*, the *Batson* prohibitions were, in fact, easy to evade. The Court left trial judges to decide how to implement *Batson*[33] and trial judges did not question reasons that appeared, on the surface, to be race-neutral. Appellate judges tended to defer to trial judges because appellate judges had only the written record

25 *Id.* at 93–97 (identifying the requirements for the defendant's prima facie case).

26 *Id.* at 97–98 (describing the three-step *Batson* test).

27 Powers v. Ohio, 499 U.S. 400, 402 (1991) (holding that a *Batson* challenge can be made by a defendant of any race whenever the prosecutor exercises a peremptory challenge based on race).

28 Edmonson v. Leesville Concrete Co., 500 U.S. 614, 616 (1991) (extending *Batson* to parties in civil cases).

29 Georgia v. McCollum, 505 U.S. 42, 59 (1992) (extending *Batson* to defense attorneys).

30 J. E. B. v. Alabama *ex rel.* T.B., 511 U.S. 127, 129 (1994) (holding that gender-based peremptory challenges violate the Equal Protection Clause of the Fourteenth Amendment).

31 Purkett v. Elem, 514 U.S. 765, 768 (1995) (holding that it is not until the third step of the three-step test that a trial court determines whether the opponent of a peremptory strike has met its burden of proving purposeful discrimination, and that the reason given by the proponent of the strike at step two can be silly or frivolous as long as it is race neutral).

32 Batson v. Kentucky, 476 U.S. 79, 98 (1986) (requiring the prosecutor to "articulate a neutral explanation related to the particular case to be tried").

33 *Id.* at 99 n.24 (leaving it to trial judges to work out the implementation of *Batson* and the appropriate remedy in case of a *Batson* violation).

before them, whereas trial judges were in the courtroom and ostensibly in a better position to gauge the sincerity of the reasons being offered for peremptory challenges.[34] Meanwhile, lawyers quickly learned which reasons to give and assiduously avoided reasons that suggested race, gender, or ethnicity as the basis for a peremptory challenge. The *Batson* test made it look like discriminatory peremptory challenges would not be permitted, but in practice they continued.[35] The *Batson* test allowed courts to appear as if they were taking action against discriminatory peremptory challenges when, in fact, lawyers had figured out ways to circumvent the test; trial judges did not press them on their reasons and appellate judges deferred to trial judges' rulings on *Batson* challenges.[36]

## THE TRADITIONAL VIEW OF PEREMPTORY CHALLENGES

The traditional view of the peremptory challenge is that it is supposed to ensure that jurors who are seated on the jury are impartial.[37] According to the traditional view, prospective jurors are either biased or not biased with respect to the case when they enter the courtroom and so it is critical to weed out those who are biased. There are two mechanisms to remove prospective jurors who are biased. One mechanism is the for cause challenge. It allows the judge to remove those

[34] *See, e.g.*, Tinner v. United Ins. Co. of Am., 308 F.3d 697, 703 (7th Cir. 2002) (explaining that the appellate court would accept a trial judge's rulings in a *Batson* challenge unless they were "completely outlandish" or their "falsity" was readily apparent); United States v. Chinchilla, 874 F.2d 695, 697–98 (9th Cir. 1989) ("Since the district court's determination of whether a peremptory challenge constituted purposeful discrimination turns on an evaluation of credibility of the prosecutor's explanation, we should give those findings great deference.").

[35] *See, e.g.*, Ronald F. Wright, Kami Chavis & Gregory S. Parks, *The Jury Sunshine Project: Jury Selection Data as a Political Issue*, 2018 U. ILL. L. REV. 1407, 1423 (studying felony trial records in 2011 in North Carolina and finding "evidence related to racial disparities in jury service"); EQUAL JUST. INITIATIVE, *supra* note 5, at 18 (describing the efforts of numerous African Americans to serve as jurors only to find that they were removed by the prosecution's exercise of its peremptory challenges).

[36] *See, e.g.*, Catherine M. Grosso & Barbara O'Brien, *A Stubborn Legacy: The Overwhelming Importance of Race in Jury Selection in 173 Post-*Batson *North Carolina Capital Cases*, 97 IOWA L. REV. 1531, 1557 (2012) ("In the past, North Carolina trial courts have not been especially willing to sustain *Batson* objections, and reviewing courts have shown almost complete deference to those rulings."); Marder, *supra* note 4, at 1592; Nancy S. Marder, *Justice Stevens, the Peremptory Challenge, and the Jury*, 74 FORDHAM L. REV. 1683, 1708–09 (2006).

[37] *See, e.g.*, KASSIN & WRIGHTSMAN, *supra* note 9 (Ch. 2), at 50 (observing that a legitimate purpose of *voir dire* is so that lawyers can use the peremptory challenge to remove biased prospective jurors, but noting that lawyers are motivated to find sympathetic jurors, not impartial jurors).

prospective jurors who have an obvious bias.[38] Another mechanism is the peremptory challenge. This allows lawyers to remove those prospective jurors who might have hidden biases that are hard to discern, but that lawyers, using whatever rules of thumb or approaches they have honed over the years, will be able to recognize. Both the for cause challenge and the peremptory challenge are supposed to enable both sides to trust that the jury is impartial. Although the for cause challenge does provide for the removal of those prospective jurors with an obvious bias, it is unlikely that the peremptory challenge provides for the removal of prospective jurors with hidden biases. However, it does allow for the removal of prospective jurors about whom one side or the other has misgivings, even if the prospective juror says he or she is impartial and able to serve.

Lawyers have explained the doubts they harbor about prospective jurors in a variety of ways. In some instances, lawyers believe that the prospective juror cannot be impartial, even though the person has said he or she can be impartial and survived a challenge for cause. Another understanding the lawyer might have is that the prospective juror will be unsympathetic to the lawyer's client.[39] Alternatively, lawyers have said that the prospective juror will not work well with the other jurors,[40] will not understand the case,[41] will not pay attention during the trial,[42] or will simply be an unreliable juror.[43] Sometimes they just do not like the look of the prospective juror. One lawyer who was required to give a reason to justify two of his peremptory challenges said that he struck one prospective juror because he had "long curly hair"

[38] The for cause challenge is supposed to be used to remove prospective jurors for limited reasons, such as having a familial relationship with one of the trial participants, a financial stake in the outcome of the case, or saying they cannot be impartial. *See* Hopt v. Utah, 120 U.S. 430, 433 (1887). For further discussion of the for cause challenge, see *infra* text accompanying notes 177–84.

[39] *See, e.g.*, KASSIN & WRIGHTSMAN, *supra* note 9 (Ch. 2), at 50 (describing lawyers as seeking sympathetic jurors rather than impartial jurors); JAMES P. LEVINE, JURIES AND POLITICS 51 (1992) ("The use of peremptory challenges is supposed to eliminate people who are biased and leave a batch of open-minded jurors. But lawyers use their prerogatives to try to accomplish just the opposite – a jury packed with sympathizers or at least devoid of antagonists."); Babcock, *supra* note 10 (Ch. 2), at 551.

[40] *See, e.g.*, Jay Schulman, Phillip Shaver, Robert Colman, Barbara Emrich & Richard Christie, *Recipe for a Jury*, PSYCH. TODAY, May 1973, at 37, 44 (describing social scientists' efforts to predict which jurors would befriend each other).

[41] *See, e.g.*, STEPHEN J. ADLER, THE JURY: TRIAL AND ERROR IN THE AMERICAN COURTROOM 118–22 (1994).

[42] *See, e.g.*, Transcript of Argument on Objection Pursuant to *Batson v. Kentucky*, in 1 Joint App. at 52–53, Foster v. Chatman, 578 U.S. 488 (2016) (No. 14-8349).

[43] *See, e.g.*, *id.* at 49–51.

and he struck another prospective juror because he had a "mustache and a goatee type beard."[44] The lawyer did not "like the way they looked" and their hair "look[ed] suspicious" to him.[45] In another case, a lawyer who was required to explain his exercise of a peremptory challenge said that he did not like the way the prospective juror dressed; the lawyer thought the person "looked like a rock star."[46]

Lawyers have defended the peremptory challenge because it gives them some control, albeit limited, as to who sits on the jury.[47] They view the selection of the jury as a right that belongs to their client and peremptory challenges give them a tool to shape the jury, at least to a limited extent. They do not trust the judge to decide who sits on the jury because the judge has different priorities, such as having jury selection move quickly and efficiently and not prying too deeply into a prospective juror's private life. In addition, lawyers explain that it is their job to provide zealous advocacy on behalf of their client, and removing prospective jurors who they believe will be unfavorable to their client is part of that job. Some lawyers believe they are particularly adept at jury selection and that peremptory challenges give them the opportunity to use their skill to their client's advantage.

Peremptory challenges might also assuage a criminal defendant's concerns. In a criminal case, the criminal defendant confronts the power of the state. To the extent that a criminal defendant gets to remove a certain number of prospective jurors about whom he has misgivings, he might be reassured that the jury is open to his point of view and will not necessarily side with the government. If either party forms a negative view of a prospective juror – no matter how irrational that view might be – the party can use a peremptory challenge to remove that prospective juror, thus reassuring the party that he or she will receive a fair trial by an impartial jury. Peremptory challenges provide some wiggle room. They allow parties to remove a fixed number of prospective jurors to ensure that the jury that is seated is viewed as fair by both parties.

[44] Purkett v. Elem, 514 U.S. 765, 766 (1995) (per curiam) (quoting App. to Petition for Writ of Certiorari, at A-41).

[45] *Id.* at 766 (quoting App. to Petition for Writ of Certiorari).

[46] United States v. Clemons, 941 F.2d 321, 323 (5th Cir. 1991).

[47] The prosecutor in *Foster v. Chatman* described jury selection, not as the opportunity to select those whom he wanted on the jury, but rather as the limited opportunity to remove those whom he thought would be least sympathetic to his side. *See* Transcript of Hearing on Motion for New Trial (Nov. 24, 1987), in 1 Joint App. at 96, Foster v. Chatman, 578 U.S. 488 (2016) (No. 14-8349).

Viewed in the best light according to the traditional view, peremptory challenges allow lawyers to remove those prospective jurors about whom they have misgivings without having to give a reason. The lawyer is not able to give a reason that would satisfy a for cause challenge, but the lawyer nevertheless has doubts – whether based on permissible or impermissible reasons – about that prospective juror. A peremptory challenge allows the lawyer to act upon his or her doubts and to remove that prospective juror without having to give a reason, at least in most cases.

## PEREMPTORY CHALLENGES FALL SHORT OF THE TRADITIONAL VIEW'S PURPOSE

Peremptory challenges fail to accomplish the traditional view's purpose because lawyers think they can identify prospective jurors with hidden biases, even though this is hard to do. Biases are hard for individuals to recognize in themselves,[48] and even harder for a person to recognize in another.[49]

As psychologists have demonstrated, implicit biases are hard to uncover. We keep them hidden from ourselves. They are also hidden from other people. It is all too easy for people to give socially acceptable answers in response to superficial questions during *voir dire*,[50] and so it becomes even more difficult to discover who holds biases, particularly implicit biases. Given the public setting of *voir dire* and the quotidian nature of the questions that are asked, lawyers have little to go on when deciding whether a prospective juror has implicit biases.[51] Implicit

[48] *See, e.g.*, Valerie P. Hans & Alayna Jehle, *Avoid Bald Men and People with Green Socks? Other Ways to Improve the Voir Dire Process in Jury Selection*, 78 CHI.-KENT L. REV. 1179, 1196 (2003) ("Even if prospective jurors are willing to reveal all, they may be unaware of their own biases."); Schuller & Erentzen, *supra* note 13 (Ch. 2), at 329 ("Much psychological research, however, suggests that people are quite unable to predict or recognize the ways that racial bias can affect them.").

[49] *See, e.g.*, Mary R. Rose, *A Voir Dire of Voir Dire: Listening to Jurors' Views Regarding the Peremptory Challenge*, 78 CHI.-KENT L. REV. 1061, 1063 (2003) ("The little empirical research available does indeed show that attorneys are poor at assessing bias and predicting its effects."); Schuller & Erentzen, *supra* note 13 (Ch. 2), at 329 ("It is difficult to recognize one's own prejudice . . . . It is perhaps more difficult yet to recognize it in another person.").

[50] *See, e.g.*, Schuller & Erentzen, *supra* note 13 (Ch. 2), at 329 ("[I]t is possible that many [jurors] felt pressure to report impartiality due to social desirability."); Hans & Jehle, *supra* note 48, at 1195 ("Social psychologists have documented a phenomenon they label the 'social desirability effect.' People are motivated to present themselves in a positive, socially desirable light.") (footnote omitted); Vidmar, *supra* note 14 (Ch. 2), at 1150 (describing the tendency to say one can be impartial because that is the "socially desirable" response).

[51] *See supra* Chapter 2.

biases remain hidden and neither lawyers nor judges can uncover them very readily in prospective jurors.

To make matters even more challenging, lawyers have their own biases, which they might or might not recognize as they exercise peremptory challenges.[52] Nobody is entirely objective or neutral, even if their role – such as that of judge or juror – requires them to aspire to be so.[53] As lawyers view prospective jurors, they view them through the lens of their own biases. Although the US Supreme Court has said that peremptory challenges cannot be exercised based on the race, gender, or ethnicity of a prospective juror, a lawyer might be unaware that he or she is exercising a peremptory challenge based on these characteristics.[54] In effect, lawyers who are guided by their own biases might end up with a jury that reflects those biases. This is contrary to the traditional view of the peremptory challenge, which is, ostensibly, to seat an impartial jury.

For example, the lawyer who said that he was "suspicious" of "long curly hair" might have thought it was the hair that was suspicious to him;[55] he might have been unaware that it was actually the man's race. If a white man had long, curly hair, the lawyer would probably not have said he found it "suspicious," though there was a time when men who wore their hair long were viewed with suspicion by an older generation.[56] However, the lawyer was "suspicious" when an African-American man had long, curly hair. The lawyer said that the man's "hair" was the reason for exercising a peremptory challenge. "Hair" seemed like a race-neutral reason to the trial judge (even though people of different races have different types of hair),[57] so the judge permitted

[52] Justice Thurgood Marshall recognized that prosecutors might or might not recognize their own biases when exercising their peremptory challenges. *See* Batson v. Kentucky, 476 U.S. 79, 106 (1986). This was one of the reasons he recommended the elimination of peremptory challenges in his concurring opinion in *Batson*. *See id.* at 107–08.

[53] Judges strive to be impartial as their role requires, yet they, like all human beings, hold a variety of biases. *See, e.g.*, Guthrie, Rachlinski & Wistrich, *supra* note 45 (Ch. 2), at 1; Kang et al., *supra* note 107 (Ch. 1), at 1124; Wistrich & Rachlinski, *supra* note 45 (Ch. 2), at 88.

[54] *See, e.g.*, *Batson*, 476 U.S. at 107–08 (Marshall, J., concurring); Mark W. Bennett, *Unraveling the Gordian Knot of Implicit Bias in Jury Selection: The Problems of Judge-Dominated Voir Dire, the Failed Promise of* Batson, *and Proposed Solutions*, 4 HARV. L. & POL'Y REV. 149, 152 (2010) (explaining that implicit biases "operate outside of conscious awareness").

[55] Purkett v. Elem, 514 U.S. 765, 766 (1995) (quoting App. to Petition for Writ of Certiorari).

[56] *See* Ham v. South Carolina, 409 U.S. 524, 529–30 (1973) (Douglas, J., concurring in part and dissenting in part) ("Hair growth is symbolic to many of rebellion against traditional society and disapproval of the way the current power structure handles social problems.").

[57] Consider the ways in which "hair" is associated with race. Caucasians' hair is viewed as the norm and African-Americans' hair is seen as "other," suggesting that hair is not viewed in a race-neutral manner. For example, there was a backlash when the U.S. military specified ways in which women in the military could wear their hair, but it was a policy based on the kind of

the peremptory challenge. The lawyer did not have to delve deeply into his reason for exercising a peremptory challenge, nor did the trial judge. The lawyer could say "hair" and not examine what about the hair made him view it with "suspicion." One problem, then, with peremptory challenges is that lawyers have their own biases through which they view prospective jurors, even if they are unaware of them. As in the case cited, they might say they are removing a prospective juror because of his hair but actually be motivated by his race.

Another problem is that lawyers could have explicit biases, of which they are aware, and they can exercise peremptory challenges based on these explicit biases but mask them with neutral-sounding reasons. So, with the hair example, the lawyer could be suspicious of African-American men and exclude them based on their race. If challenged, as this lawyer was, he knew not to give race as a reason, even if it were the real reason, and he knew it was. Instead, the lawyer could comply with *Batson*[58] and give any other reason, no matter how "silly or superstitious,"[59] just as long as it appears race-neutral. So, the lawyer explained that the peremptory challenge was based on the prospective juror's "hair."

To make matters worse, lawyers often use their peremptory challenges against African-American men and women, particularly in capital cases.[60] In such cases, lawyers' exercise of their peremptory challenges is not random; they remove citizens from serving on a particular jury because of their race and/or gender. In one case that reached the US Supreme Court, the prosecutor tried the criminal defendant six times, and each time he tried to remove all the African-American prospective jurors on the venire.[61] *Batson* and subsequent cases attempted to correct for this problem of discriminatory peremptory challenges, but lawyers

styles that worked for white women's hair, but not African-American women's hair. For a humorous critique of the military's limited perspective, see Jessica Williams, Operation Black Hair, *The Daily Show with Jon Stewart* (Comedy Central television broadcast July 17, 2014). The military has since revised its policy, particularly in light of the growing numbers of African-American women in the military. *See, e.g.*, Dave Phillips, *In a Changing Military, Army Eases Its Restrictions for Women's Hair*, N.Y. TIMES, Feb. 26, 2021, at A16.

58 *Batson*, 476 U.S. at 98.

59 *Elem*, 514 U.S. at 768.

60 *See, e.g.*, EQUAL JUST. INITIATIVE, *supra* note 5, at 5 ("Racially biased use of peremptory strikes and illegal racial discrimination in jury selection remains widespread, particularly in serious criminal cases and capital cases."); Henry R. Chalmers, *A Long Way to Go: Report Finds Lingering, Hard-to-Eradicate Discrimination in Jury Selection*, LITIG. NEWS, Fall 2010, at 6, 7 ("In death penalty cases from 2005 to 2009 in one Alabama county, prosecutors used peremptory strikes to remove 80 percent of the qualified African Americans in the jury venires, according to the [EQUAL JUST. INITIATIVE] report.").

61 *See* Flowers v. Mississippi, 139 S. Ct. 2228 (2019).

learned to give reasons that sounded race-neutral and judges felt they had little choice but to accept them.

In sum, the traditional view of peremptory challenges is that prospective jurors enter the courtroom as either biased or unbiased and that lawyers can distinguish between the two and use peremptory challenges to remove those who are biased. This is an overly simplistic view of human beings. It assumes that lawyers can recognize subtle biases and that these subtle biases are fixed in stone. The traditional view also assumes that lawyers are not exercising discriminatory peremptory challenges for the most part, and that when they are, the *Batson* test will address the problem, even though it has failed to do so for the past thirty-six years.

## PEREMPTORY CHALLENGES INTERFERE WITH THE TRANSFORMATION OF CITIZENS INTO JURORS

The transformation view recognizes that everyone has biases but that the various stages of the jury process will transform a disparate group of citizens, each with his or her own biases, experiences, and skills, into a jury that usually works together in a fair and impartial way to reach a verdict. According to this view, for cause challenges still make sense because there might be some citizens who are not open to transformation or who will be perceived as not able to be transformed. However, peremptory challenges do not make sense. Even the jurors who are seated after lawyers have exercised their peremptory challenges still have biases of various kinds, and if lawyers exercise discriminatory peremptory challenges they interfere with the creation of diverse juries. This then calls into question the integrity of the jury process for the parties and the community, and excludes prospective jurors who would have served responsibly, but instead leave with a loss of dignity and a sense that they have been betrayed by the jury system.

The antidote to jurors with subtle biases is not the peremptory challenge, but a jury process that takes a diverse group of jurors, who will necessarily have biases as all human beings do, and transforms them into a jury that understands its role and can work together for the particular purpose of reaching a fair verdict.

### The Need for Diverse Juries

The goal of the jury process is to ensure that jurors will act in a fair and impartial way by the time they deliberate and reach a verdict. The more diverse the group, the more likely they will be able to recognize and question each other's subtle biases.[62] Peremptory challenges interfere with the creation of diverse juries. The all-white juries in the South in the United States that heard cases against white men charged with the murder of civil rights workers were seated after the exercise of peremptory challenges.

More recently, in one study of prosecutors' exercise of peremptory challenges in capital cases over a twenty-year period in North Carolina, the researchers found that prosecutors struck eligible African-American prospective jurors at about twice the rate that they struck eligible prospective jurors who were not African Americans.[63] When the defendant was African American, prosecutors struck eligible African-American prospective jurors at 2.5 times the rate that they struck eligible prospective jurors who were not African Americans.[64] Thus, peremptory challenges can produce juries that are less diverse than juries would be if there were only for cause challenges.

Diverse juries are important because when jurors come from different backgrounds, perspectives, and life experiences, they are likely to bring different ways of viewing the case into the jury room.[65] During the deliberations, they engage in group discussion and try to reach a common understanding. Through this process, they can correct each other's mistaken notions, broaden each other's perspectives, and suggest different ways of looking at the evidence. A racially diverse jury allows jurors to challenge each other's biases[66] and can even lead white jurors to engage in a more thorough and careful deliberation than they would on a racially homogeneous jury by becoming more willing to discuss race-related issues.[67] As Samuel Sommers concluded after observing deliberations of mock juries that were racially diverse and

[62] *See infra* notes 65–68 and accompanying text.

[63] Grosso & O'Brien, *supra* note 36, at 1548–49.

[64] *Id.* at 1549–50.

[65] *See* Peters v. Kiff, 407 U.S. 493, 503–04 (1972); VALERIE P. HANS & NEIL VIDMAR, JUDGING THE JURY 50 (1986) ("[A] jury composed of individuals with a wide range of experiences, backgrounds, and knowledge is more likely to perceive the facts from different perspectives and thus engage in a vigorous and thorough debate.").

[66] HANS & VIDMAR, *supra* note 65, at 50 ("The jury's heterogeneous makeup may also lessen the power of prejudice.").

[67] Samuel R. Sommers, *On Racial Diversity and Group Decision Making: Identifying Multiple Effects of Racial Composition on Jury Deliberations*, 90 J. PERSONALITY & SOC. PSYCH. 597, 605–06 (2006) (describing the findings of an empirical study using mock jurors in which white jurors on racially diverse juries discussed more facts, made fewer inaccurate statements, and considered more race-related topics than white jurors on homogeneous juries); *see also* Samuel R. Sommers & Phoebe C. Ellsworth, *How Much Do We Really Know About Race and Juries? A Review of Social Science Theory and Research*, 78 CHI.-KENT L. REV. 997, 1025 (2003)

comparing them to those that were racially homogeneous, the diverse juries "raised more facts from the trial; they discussed a broader range of information; they discussed the information more accurately; . . . [and they] were more willing to have uncomfortable conversations about controversial issues like those involving race and racial profiling."[68] For a diverse jury to agree on a verdict means that the evidence was strong enough that jurors came to view the case in the same way even though they might have started out from very different positions.

*Importance to the Community*

A diverse jury will also reassure those in the community as to the fairness of the verdict. If jury selection begins with discriminatory peremptory challenges, that can make the entire trial open to question. Justice Anthony Kennedy described discriminatory peremptory challenges' harm to the community in *Powers* v. *Ohio*.[69] He observed that jury selection marks the beginning of the trial and if it is marred by discriminatory peremptory challenges, this will cast doubt on the integrity of the entire trial.[70] The harm that is done during jury selection taints the entire proceeding and reaches beyond those in the courtroom. If the larger community is going to accept the verdict, even if it disagrees with the verdict, then it needs to be convinced of the fairness of the process. Discriminatory peremptory challenges, which interfere with diverse juries, undercut that fairness.

When a community is already distrustful of the criminal justice system, discriminatory peremptory challenges only add to that distrust. If a community includes African Americans, and yet discriminatory peremptory challenges are used by the prosecutor to strike the few African-American prospective jurors from the venire, leaving an all-white jury, it will be hard for African Americans in that community to accept that the process was fair and that the verdict is legitimate. Instead, the practice contributes to widespread skepticism about the fairness of the criminal justice system.

*Importance to the Criminal Defendant*

A diverse jury is also important for the criminal defendant's trust in the fairness of the trial, and discriminatory peremptory challenges

("[M]embership on a racially heterogeneous jury might also influence White jurors' behavior during deliberations."); *id.* at 1028–29.

68 *Last Week Tonight with John Oliver*, *supra* note 2 (Ch. 1).

69 499 U.S. 400, 412–13 (1991).

70 *Id.*

undermine that trust. If peremptory challenges are exercised in a discriminatory manner, then it appears that the deck is being stacked against the criminal defendant. The jury in a criminal trial stands as a buffer between the individual defendant and the powerful government, including the "corrupt or overzealous prosecutor" or the "compliant, biased, or eccentric judge";[71] however, the jury will be unable to play this key role if it is compromised from the start. For example, James Batson, the defendant in *Batson* v. *Kentucky*, had to sit in the courtroom during jury selection and watch as the prosecutor stuck each of the four African-American prospective jurors from his jury. His initial reaction was: "[The prosecutors] struck all the blacks off the jury pool. It ain't right."[72] Batson was not a lawyer, but he knew that the practice of discriminatory peremptory challenges was wrong. This intuition spurred him to tell his lawyer to "object anyway!" even if there was no basis in law at the time for such an objection.[73] All James Batson had to do, though, was look around the courtroom and see that "[e]verybody in the courtroom was white," except for Batson.[74] Batson's lawyer was white; the prosecutor was white; the judge was white, and after the peremptory challenges, all twelve jurors on his jury were white.[75] Discriminatory peremptory challenges take place in the courtroom and the results are visual and perhaps visceral, as they were for defendant James Batson.

### *Importance to the Excluded Prospective Juror*

The targeted use of peremptory challenges often leaves those who are subject to them feeling that they are being kept from the jury for improper reasons. Although one study found that prospective jurors who were removed by peremptory challenges understood that it was part of the process and they should not take it personally,[76] other prospective jurors, particularly those who have been removed by what they viewed as a discriminatory peremptory challenge, see it as an

[71] Duncan v. Louisiana, 391 U.S. 145, 156 (1968).

[72] Transcript: *Object Anyway* at 13 (RadioLab July 16, 2016) (copy on file with author) (quoting James Batson).

[73] *Id.* (quoting James Batson).

[74] *Id.*

[75] *Id.* at 12–13.

[76] *See* Rose, *supra* note 49, at 1067 (finding that "the data are more consistent with what has been described as a 'generally accepting attitude' toward voir dire and its practices") (quoting Shari Seidman Diamond, *What Jurors Think: Expectations and Reactions of Citizens Who Serve As Jurors*, *in* VERDICT: ASSESSING THE CIVIL JURY SYSTEM 282, 289 (Robert E. Litan ed., 1993)).

affront to their dignity.[77] They understand that they have been removed because of their race. Even though they said that they could be impartial and wanted to serve, they were nonetheless removed. As they sat in the courtroom and watched who else was removed, they concluded that they were eliminated on the basis of their race. They did not think that their race should have anything to do with serving as a juror.[78] Such citizens leave thinking that the jury system is rigged and that they have been treated poorly.

In the case of discriminatory peremptory challenges, those who are removed from the petit jury are not only excluded from jury service but stigmatized as well. African-American men and all women were originally excluded from jury service. State statutes kept African-American men from serving on juries until 1880 when the US Supreme Court held in *Strauder* v. *West Virginia* that such statutes violated the Equal Protection Clause of the Fourteenth Amendment.[79] After *Strauder*, states could not use statutes to keep African-American men from serving on the jury, but lawyers were able to use peremptory challenges for that purpose. In 1965, the Supreme Court decided *Swain* v. *Alabama*.[80] Although it held that peremptory challenges could not be used to keep African-American men from serving on the jury, it created a test that was exceedingly difficult to meet. An African-American defendant who wanted to challenge the exclusion of an African-American prospective juror based on race had to show that the prosecutor had a history of using peremptory challenges in a discriminatory manner. It was not until twenty years later, in *Batson*, that the Court created a test that imposed a less "crippling burden of proof"[81] than the test in *Swain*. After *Batson*, an African-American defendant could challenge the prosecutor's use of a peremptory challenge to strike an African-American prospective juror based only on the use of that particular peremptory challenge, but the defendant had to show purposeful discrimination on the part of the prosecutor. This test, too, proved exceedingly difficult to satisfy, particularly when prosecutors learned to give race-neutral reasons for their peremptory challenges whenever they were challenged.

77 *See, e.g.*, EQUAL JUST. INITIATIVE, *supra* note 5, at 28–34; Dale W. Broeder, *The Negro in Court*, 1965 DUKE L.J. 19, 26.
78 *See, e.g.*, Broeder, *supra* note 77, at 26; EQUAL JUST. INITIATIVE, *supra* note 5, at 28–34.
79 Strauder v. West Virginia, 100 U.S. 303, 304 (1880).
80 Swain v. Alabama, 380 U.S. 202 (1965).
81 Batson v. Kentucky, 476 U.S. 79, 92 (1986).

Women were kept from serving on juries through statutes, and later through practices like affirmative registration and gender-based peremptory challenges. Women did not uniformly have the right to serve as jurors in federal court until the Civil Rights Act of 1957.[82] Before then, some states allowed women to serve as jurors and others did not, but federal courts excluded or included women as jurors depending on what the practice in the state was. Even after all federal courts had to include women as jurors, some states, for example, Florida and Louisiana,[83] maintained practices such as affirmative registration that kept women from actually being called for jury duty in those state courts. Affirmative registration required a woman to take the additional step of going to the courthouse and registering for jury service in order to be summoned even though a man did not have to take that additional step. Finally, in 1975, the Court held in *Taylor* v. *Louisiana* that affirmative registration for women violated a defendant's Sixth Amendment right to a venire drawn from a fair cross section of the community.[84] With the elimination of affirmative registration, women could be called to serve as jurors in equal numbers as men. However, lawyers then used peremptory challenges to keep women from serving on juries. Although some states, such as California[85] and Massachusetts,[86] prohibited gender-based peremptory challenges, it was not until 1994 that the US Supreme Court held in *J.E.B.* v. *Alabama* ex rel. *T.B.* that gender-based peremptory challenges violated the Equal Protection Clause of the US Constitution.[87] Even after *J.E.B.*, however, lawyers still manage to use peremptory challenges to exclude women from serving on juries because they know to give gender-neutral reasons if they are required to give a reason. Thus, discriminatory peremptory challenges, which kept and continue to keep African-American men and all women from serving on juries, need to be understood in light of a history of exclusion.

Although many citizens who receive a jury summons see it initially as an inconvenience to be avoided, many others, especially those who

[82] Civil Rights Act of 1957, Pub. L. No. 85–315, § 152, 71 Stat. 634, 638 (codified as amended at 28 U.S.C. § 1861).

[83] *See* Hoyt v. Florida, 368 U.S. 57, 62–63 (1961) (upholding the constitutionality of affirmative registration based on women's role in the home, and noting that several other states, including Louisiana, adhered to the practice).

[84] Taylor v. Louisiana, 419 U.S. 522, 523, 525 (1975).

[85] *See, e.g.*, Di Donato v. Santini, 283 Cal. Rptr. 751, 762 (Ct. App. 1991).

[86] *See, e.g.*, Commonwealth v. Hyatt, 568 N.E.2d 1148, 1150 (Mass. 1991).

[87] *See* J.E.B. v. Alabama *ex rel.* T.B., 511 U.S. 127, 129 (1994).

have been historically excluded from jury service, regard it as a badge of full citizenship. They feel pride upon receiving a summons and in going down to the courthouse in order to serve as a juror. As one African American, Mr. Cox, a sanitation worker, explained:

> [It was] one of the proudest moments of my life. Ever since I was a little kid . . . I've had a desire to serve. . . . I've read many books on the jury and when I was first called to serve I went to the library and read up on the jury system and what a fine institution it is. . . . When I got my summons . . . I got a sense of really belonging to the American community.[88]

A more recent example, in 2016, was the exclusion of prospective juror Crishala Reed. She was being considered to be a juror in a double-murder trial. When the prosecutor asked her if she agreed with Black Lives Matter, she indicated that she supported the cause, though not any illegal behavior. Nonetheless, the prosecutor removed her with a peremptory challenge. Reed said she felt "targeted" and found it to be "a life-changing experience" and one that she "would never want [her] kids to go and do."[89] In another case, prospective juror Sharon "Nichole" Young, an African-American woman, was struck from the petit jury in one of the six times that Curtis Flowers was tried by the State of Mississippi. She explained why she thought she was excluded: "I think they might have assumed that because I was black I was going to agree that [the defendant] was innocent just by the color of his skin but I actually would have listened to the evidence and had an open ear. I actually was looking forward to serving."[90]

A report issued by the Equal Justice Initiative provides a number of accounts of African-American prospective jurors in Southern states who were struck for reasons that they knew to be false and that they viewed as a cover for racial discrimination.[91] The experience left them feeling "unworthy,"[92] "false[ly] accus[ed],"[93] and convinced of the unfairness of the system, even years afterward.[94] Melodie Harris,

[88] Broeder, *supra* note 77, at 26. For more recent accounts of the harm suffered by excluded jurors, see EQUAL JUST. INITIATIVE, *supra* note 5, at 28–30.

[89] Abbie Vansickle, *You Can Get Kicked Out of a Jury Pool for Supporting Black Lives Matter: But Is It Legal? A California Appeals Court Is Going to Decide*, THE MARSHALL PROJECT (July 7, 2020), https://www.themarshallproject.org/2020/07/07/you-can-get-kicked-out-of-a-jury-pool-for-supporting-black-lives-matter [https://perma.cc/X97R-LYD9].

[90] *Last Week Tonight with John Oliver*, *supra* note 2 (Ch. 1).

[91] EQUAL JUST. INITIATIVE, *supra* note 5, at 28–34.

[92] *Id.* at 30 (describing excluded prospective juror Allen Mason).

[93] *Id.* at 29 (describing excluded prospective juror Brenda Greene).

[94] *Id.* ("Mrs. Greene desperately wanted to clear her family's name, even though the statements were made in 1992."); *id.* at 30 ("Nearly 20 years later, Mr. Mason grew emotional as he recalled how the prosecutor's racist actions made him feel unworthy.").

a prospective juror, described her exclusion and that of other African Americans in the trial of Alvin Robinson, an African-American defendant, as "just so blatant."[95] In her eyes, jury selection, in which the prosecution used its peremptory challenges to remove African-American prospective jurors, was not operating fairly. As prospective juror Gerald Mercer described his experience, there was "unequal justice."[96]

Against this backdrop, discriminatory peremptory challenges are an affront to the African-American man or any woman who has been called to serve but is kept from service because of their race or gender.[97] Whereas the summons serves as a badge of full citizenship, the discriminatory peremptory challenge is a reminder that African-American men and all women were once second-class citizens and that they have not fully overcome that status. The lawyer who exercises a discriminatory peremptory challenge is judging them to be unsuitable for the particular case, not on the basis of any individual characteristic, but solely on the grounds of group membership.

The visibility of race and gender, unlike many other characteristics, means that everyone in the courtroom is aware that the excluded prospective juror is being struck because of race or gender. For example, when one African American after another is struck by a lawyer exercising peremptory challenges, it is clear to those in the courtroom that these prospective jurors are being removed because of their race.[98] Even if all the peremptory strikes are exercised at once, rather than one at a time, it is still apparent when an all-white jury is seated that the prosecutor has used his or her peremptory challenges to remove all of the African-American prospective jurors because of their race.[99] After the prosecutor exercised a peremptory challenge to remove Crishala Reed from the jury, she looked over to the jury box and "didn't see any other Black people."[100]

Jurors excluded by discriminatory peremptory challenges are likely to experience a range of feelings and these are likely to be negative. Such

[95] *Id.* at 28 (quoting excluded prospective juror Melodie Harris).

[96] *Id.* at 29 (quoting excluded prospective juror Gerald Mercer).

[97] *See, e.g.*, *id.* at 28–30 (describing the stigma that African-American prospective jurors felt when they were struck from the jury).

[98] *See, e.g.*, Foster v. Chatman, 578 U.S. 488, 513–14 (2016).

[99] Nancy S. Marder, Foster v. Chatman: *A Missed Opportunity for* Batson *and the Peremptory Challenge*, 49 CONN. L. REV. 1137, 1144–46 (2017) (describing the prosecutors' exercise of peremptory challenges against the remaining four African-American prospective jurors in *Foster*).

[100] Vansickle, *supra* note 89 (quoting prospective juror Crishala Reed).

prospective jurors might feel stigmatized that they are being judged deficient because of their race, or angry that they are still not being treated as full citizens, or annoyed that they have been summoned to the courthouse and have taken time away from work only to find that their race is being used against them. Mr. Cox described how he felt as follows: "I was excused seemingly just because my skin was black. There was no other reason why I should have been challenged. I was very irritated and extremely disappointed that such a practice should be allowed."[101] After the prosecutor exercised a peremptory challenge against Crishala Reed for supporting Black Lives Matter, she felt like she "'wanted to cry, but [she] held it, ... [she] didn't want to look weak.'"[102]

Typically, judges explain that peremptory challenges are part of the selection process and that they do not mean that the prospective juror cannot serve but only that he or she cannot serve in that particular case. Judges also tell excluded prospective jurors not to take their exclusion personally, and most try to follow the judge's words. However, it is hard to accept that a discriminatory peremptory challenge is part of the selection process and prospective jurors excluded on this basis are likely to leave the courthouse feeling dissatisfied with their jury experience. Not only are they harmed by the exercise of a discriminatory peremptory challenge, but so is the party that wanted them to serve. Their elimination means that the jury is less likely to have available to it as wide a range of perspectives from which to judge the evidence as it would if there had been no discriminatory peremptory challenges.[103]

Those eliminated through discriminatory peremptory challenges also return to their communities, not as goodwill ambassadors for the jury system, but as disillusioned citizens who had wanted to serve as jurors but who were denied the opportunity.[104] Crishala Reed's experience led her to conclude that "she doesn't want to go through jury duty again."[105] In

[101] Broeder, *supra* note 77, at 28 (internal quotation marks omitted).

[102] Vansickle, *supra* note 89 (quoting prospective juror Crishala Reed).

[103] *See, e.g.*, HANS & VIDMAR, *supra* note 65, at 50; Jeffrey Abramson, *Two Ideals of Jury Deliberation*, 1998 U. CHI. LEGAL F. 125, 133; Deborah Ramirez, *Affirmative Jury Selection: A Proposal to Advance Both the Deliberative Ideal and Jury Diversity*, 1998 U. CHI. LEGAL F. 161, 165; Jeannie O'Sullivan, *Will Spotlight on Racial Justice Force More Diverse Juries?*, LAW360 (June 28, 2020, 10:02 PM), https://www.law360.com/articles/1287048 [https://perma.cc/GU7F-6CR4] ("'Jurors from a cross-section of the community bring different life experiences and perspectives to jury deliberations, leading to more informed discussions and greater public confidence in the judicial process.'") (quoting Chief Judge Juan R. Sanchez (E.D.Pa.)).

[104] *See, e.g.*, Broeder, *supra* note 77, at 26; EQUAL JUST. INITIATIVE, *supra* note 5, at 28–30.

[105] Vansickle, *supra* note 89 (quoting prospective juror Crishala Reed).

contrast, the citizen who might have been reluctant to serve initially, having served, understands from firsthand experience the benefits of the jury system. Polls and surveys of former jurors show that they believe their jury performed responsibly and did the best job it could.[106] Jurors also leave their jury service with faith in the jury and the judiciary.[107] Thus, the jury process not only helps to transform citizens into responsible jurors, but also produces former jurors who leave their service convinced of the merits of their job performance and of the importance of the jury in the judicial system.

Discriminatory peremptory challenges deny excluded prospective jurors this opportunity to be transformed by the jury process and to serve as emissaries for the jury system. They lead to the removal of willing and able citizens, leaving juries less diverse and with a narrower range of views from which to assess the evidence and testimony. Discriminatory peremptory challenges also leave prospective jurors who were removed disillusioned about the jury system.[108] If these citizens had been permitted to serve, they would have likely left their jury service convinced of the merits of the jury system and willing to share their positive experiences with friends and family after their jury duty had ended. Instead, they leave the courtroom disheartened because they were denied the opportunity to serve, particularly those who are members of groups that had once been excluded from citizenship and the concomitant right to serve on a jury.

## Harms of Idiosyncratic Peremptory Challenges

Whether peremptory challenges are based on lawyers' idiosyncrasies or biases they exclude qualified jurors who have said they can be impartial. The US Supreme Court has attempted to allow lawyers to exercise peremptory challenges based on their idiosyncrasies but not based on discrimination; however, the distinction has proven difficult to make in practice. Since both types of peremptory challenges keep qualified

[106] *See, e.g.*, Marder & Hans, *supra* note 2 (Intro.), at 789 n.5.

[107] *See, e.g.*, Diamond, *supra* note 76, at 285–86; John Gastil, Hiroshi Fukurai, Kent Anderson & Mark Nolan, *Seeing Is Believing: The Impact of Jury Service on Attitudes Toward Legal Institutions and the Implications for International Jury Reform*, 48 CT. REV. 124 (2012).

[108] *See, e.g.*, Broeder, *supra* note 77, at 26 (describing Mr. Cox's disillusionment); EQUAL JUST. INITIATIVE, *supra* note 5, at 29 (recounting negative experiences with jury selection and leading to the view that it was unfair); Vansickle, *supra* note 89 (describing Crishala Reed's negative jury selection experience as one that she "would never want [her] kids to go and do").

prospective jurors from serving and the peremptory challenge continues to serve as a mask for discrimination during jury selection, the most effective remedy is to eliminate peremptory challenges altogether.

Even idiosyncratic peremptory challenges limit who can serve as jurors. The prospective juror who has heeded his or her summons, appeared in court, satisfied the juror qualifications, and withstood challenges for cause should be permitted to serve. Although such prospective jurors might never find out why a lawyer used a peremptory challenge to strike them, in some cases they will hear the reason. To learn that they were struck for a "silly" or fanciful reason,[109] such as wearing a green shirt or a plaid tie, demeans the process of jury selection. A citizen who meets the qualifications for service[110] should not be denied the opportunity to serve because of the idiosyncratic likes or dislikes of a lawyer. In other cases, lawyers will rely on stereotypes, such as avoiding a businessman because he is likely to be conservative or pro-government, when in fact, the prospective juror, though a businessman, may be liberal or likely to see the case from the criminal defendant's point of view. Such faulty assumptions should not be the basis for excluding a citizen from jury service. But lawyers' idiosyncrasies can form the basis of a peremptory challenge without running afoul of *Batson*. The Supreme Court has permitted lawyers to continue to exercise peremptory challenges based on their idiosyncrasies, even though they are not permitted to exercise peremptory challenges based on a prospective juror's race, ethnicity, or gender. This approach permits lawyers to exclude prospective jurors based on their idiosyncrasies, and it also permits idiosyncrasies to be used as a mask for discrimination.

## LEARNING FROM THE ELIMINATION OF PEREMPTORY CHALLENGES ABROAD

Even though eliminating peremptory challenges in the United States has met with opposition, other countries have taken this step and their

[109] Purkett v. Elem, 514 U.S. 765, 768 (1995) (per curiam).

[110] The qualifications for jury service are fairly minimal. For example, to be a juror in federal court, a person needs to be: a citizen of the United States, at least eighteen years old, and a resident in the judicial district for at least one year; able to read, write, and understand English sufficiently to complete the juror qualification form; able to speak English; not have a physical or mental infirmity that interferes with jury service; and not have a charge pending or a conviction for a crime punishable by imprisonment for more than one year, with one's civil rights not having been restored. *See* 28 U.S.C. § 1865 (b)(1)–(5) (2018). For additional discussion of juror qualifications, see *infra* text accompanying notes 156–76.

experiences show that peremptory challenges are not integral to a fair jury trial. Countries such as England and Wales, which share the same legal system, eliminated peremptory challenges and their citizens continue to think that their trials are fair. Canada recently eliminated peremptory challenges in order to have petit juries that are more representative of the citizenry, including Indigenous people. Other countries' experience with eliminating peremptory challenges suggests that it is a reasonable way to produce more diverse juries even though many lawyers, judges, and academics in the United States resist it.

England and Wales eliminated peremptory challenges as of 1989,[111] and did so in order to have more representative juries. As one report in the United Kingdom explained: "A jury should represent a cross-section drawn at random from the community, and should be the means of bringing to bear on the issues the corporate good sense of that community."[112] English barristers and judges also took the view that jurors will rise to the occasion and put aside biases and perform their role as impartial jurors. When questioned about this, they suggested that most jurors can serve because they take their responsibilities seriously and will step into their role as "impartial jurors."[113] As one barrister explained to another researcher: "I happen to take the view that whatever one's personal prejudices, the chances are that a juror called to jury service and knowing the weight of responsibility upon him will do his utmost to discard prejudice."[114]

Jury selection in England and Wales proceeds quickly, mainly because these countries do not have *voir dire* or peremptory challenges. Instead, twelve jurors are randomly selected and seated. They are asked whether they know the parties, and which holy book they would like to take their juror oath on, but other than those questions, they are not

[111] As a result of the Criminal Justice Act of 1988, which took effect on January 5, 1989, criminal defendants in England and Wales no longer exercise peremptory challenges. *See* Criminal Justice Act, 1988, c. 33, § 118(1) (Eng. & Wales). The Crown does not generally exercise standbys (in which the Crown can reserve judgment on a prospective juror until all other prospective jurors are considered), except in "a small number of cases." John F. McEldowney, *Stand By for the Crown: An Historical Analysis*, 1979 CRIM. L. REV. 272, 281 (internal quotation marks omitted) (quoting the Attorney-General).

[112] Laura K. Donohue, *Terrorism and Trial by Jury: The Vices and Virtues of British and American Criminal Law*, 59 STAN. L. REV. 1321, 1345 (2007) (quoting DEPARTMENTAL COMM. ON JURY SERV., REPORT, 1965, Cmnd. 2627, ¶ 53).

[113] Nancy S. Marder, *Two Weeks at the Old Bailey: Jury Lessons from England*, 86 CHI.-KENT L. REV. 537, 553 (2011); Interview with Judge Brian Barker, The Common Serjeant of London and Deputy Senior Judge at the Cent. Crim. Ct., Old Bailey, London, in Chi., Ill. (Sept. 7, 2011) (confirming this view).

[114] HANS & VIDMAR, *supra* note 65, at 49 (quoting Valerie P. Hans (1983), unpublished data).

asked anything else.[115] Occasionally, there is some reason why a particular juror cannot serve, such as logistical reasons or lack of basic skills, but otherwise those whose names are randomly selected and called are seated on the jury. As a result, jury selection not only proceeds quickly, but also the jury that is impaneled tends to be diverse. According to one empirical study that was done at the request of the UK Ministry of Justice, respondents believed that jury trials in England and Wales are fair, and that they are fair for defendants who are members of a minority group.[116]

In 2019, the Parliament of Canada enacted legislation to eliminate peremptory challenges.[117] The catalyst for this statute was the acquittal of Gerald Stanley, a white criminal defendant, charged with killing a man named Colten Boushie, who was a member of the Cree tribe. The defendant was tried by a jury that included no jurors who were Indigenous.[118] In 2020, the Supreme Court of Canada upheld the constitutionality of this legislation from the bench,[119] and in 2021, it issued an opinion giving its reasons.[120] Prior to this and similar cases, a former Canadian Supreme Court Justice was asked to undertake a study and write a report on whether Canadian trials were fair, including for Indigenous people.[121] The report identified a number of reasons why there are so few Indigenous people on Canadian juries and the use of peremptory challenges was one of the contributing factors. Parliament eliminated peremptory challenges by passing Bill C-75, An Act to Amend the Criminal Code, and it became effective on September 19, 2019.[122] The Supreme Court of Canada held that the

[115] *See, e.g.*, Marder, *supra* note 113, at 552 (observing jury selection in several cases at the Old Bailey, London, in Dec. 2010 and describing one of the cases).

[116] *See* Thomas, *supra* note 111 (Ch. 2), at 46.

[117] *See* Bill C-75, § 2.1.6 (Peremptory Challenges in Jury Selection), S.C. 2019, c. 25 (Can.).

[118] *See, e.g.*, Jason Warick, *Stanley Trial Exposes Problems with Jury Selection, Say Legal Experts*, CBC NEWS (Feb. 4, 2018, 3:00 AM CT), https://www.cbc.ca/news/Canada/saskatoon/jurors-indigenous-representation-1.4517610.

[119] *See, e.g.*, Brian Platt, *Supreme Court Upholds Ban on Peremptory Challenges for Jury Selection*, NAT'L POST (Oct. 7, 2020), https://nationalpost.com/news/colten-boushie-case-again-in-spotlight-as-supreme-court-hears-arguments-on-jury-selection-rules [https://perma.cc/GD5R-9SFN].

[120] *See* R. v. Chouhan, 2021 S.C.C. 26 (Can.).

[121] FRANK IACOBUCCI, FIRST NATIONS REPRESENTATION ON ONTARIO JURIES: REPORT OF THE INDEPENDENT REVIEW CONDUCTED BY THE HONOURABLE FRANK IACOBUCCI 91 (2018) (Recommendation 15).

[122] Olivia Stefanovich, *Supreme Court Says Government's Jury Reforms Are Constitutional*, CBC NEWS (Oct. 7, 2020 4:00 AM ET), https://www.cbc.ca/news/politics/stefanovich-supreme-court-hearing-peremptory-challenges-1.5752251.

elimination of peremptory challenges was constitutional and could be applied retroactively.[123]

The example of England and Wales suggests that jury systems, such as the American jury system, that have a tradition of peremptory challenges can eliminate peremptory challenges and still be seen as fair. The recent decision to eliminate peremptory challenges in Canada because they are exercised in a discriminatory manner that undermines the representativeness of juries could also serve as a model for the United States. Although Canada has an unusual method of *voir dire*,[124] which the United States should not emulate, Canada's jury selection without peremptory challenges could serve as a model for the United States, particularly if the Canadian experience leads to more diverse juries.

## REMEDIES OTHER THAN ELIMINATING PEREMPTORY CHALLENGES FALL SHORT

Eliminating peremptory challenges is important to the transformation view because peremptory challenges interfere with the creation of diverse juries, particularly when lawyers exercise them based on race, gender, or ethnicity. Discriminatory peremptory challenges also undermine the integrity of jury selection, leaving the criminal defendant and the community with doubts about the fairness of the trial. They also cause prospective jurors, who have been subjected to them, to have negative views of the jury system. Justice Thurgood Marshall, in his concurrence in *Batson* v. *Kentucky* in 1986,[125] recognized that discriminatory peremptory challenges could not be stopped except by eliminating peremptory challenges altogether. He explained that the *Batson* test would not be able to eliminate discriminatory peremptory challenges because prosecutors could be acting as a result of biases of which they were aware or unaware. In either case, they could give reasons that had nothing to do with race.

Although academics, judges, and lawyers have suggested several ways of trying to reduce the effects of discriminatory peremptory challenges

[123] R. v. Chouhan, 2021 S.C.C. 26 (Can.).

[124] *See, e.g.*, Schuller & Vidmar, *supra* note 35 (Ch. 2), at 516–17 (describing the "unique" way that *voir dire* is conducted in Canada whereby two "triers," who are individuals from the jury panel, begin the process of deciding whether the next person called can be impartial); Schuller & Erentzen, *supra* note 13 (Ch. 2), at 321–23 (describing the limitations of the challenge question that is asked during Canadian *voir dire* when race might be an issue in the case).

[125] 476 U.S. 79, 102 (1986) (Marshall, J., concurring).

without eliminating peremptory challenges altogether, these remedies are unlikely to stop peremptories that are discriminatory in nature. The alternatives include reducing the number of peremptory challenges,[126] revising the *Batson* test,[127] and reducing death sentences to life imprisonment without parole whenever prosecutors use discriminatory peremptory challenges in capital cases.[128] Indeed, there is an extensive academic literature on *Batson*, in which most writers are critical of the *Batson* test.[129] Although some *Batson* commentators want to eliminate the peremptory challenge, and are joined by some judges and lawyers,[130] this remains a minority point of view.

One of the proposed alternatives is to limit the number of peremptory challenges. The idea is that peremptory challenges might still do harm, but they would do less harm. Admittedly, three peremptory challenges would do less harm than ten, but peremptory challenges, even a limited number, would still do harm. Even a limited number would mean that qualified prospective jurors will still be struck from the petit jury. The harm remains pronounced in the case of discriminatory peremptory challenges. The prospective juror who is struck because he is African American will still feel bad about having been struck because of his skin color, as Mr. Cox did, and the message that such a peremptory challenge conveys is no less demeaning because the number of peremptory challenges is limited. Moreover, since the US Supreme Court has said that even one discriminatory peremptory challenge is a violation of the US Constitution,[131] it is hard to justify simply reducing the number of peremptory challenges as long as

126 *See, e.g.*, Shari Seidman Diamond, Judicial Rulemaking for Jury Trial Fairness, Presentation at the 2021 Forum for State Appellate Court Judges, Pound Civil Justice Institute (July 17, 2021); Jean Montoya, *The Future of the Post-*Batson *Peremptory Challenge: Voir Dire by Questionnaire and the Blind Peremptory*, 29 U. Mich. J.L. Reform 981, 1011 & n.144 (1996) (citing scholars and commentators who have made this proposal).

127 *See, e.g.*, Wash. St. Sup. Ct. Gen. R. 37 (2018).

128 *See, e.g.*, North Carolina Racial Justice Act of 2009 (RJA), 2009 N.C. Sess. Laws § 15A-2011(b)(2) (codified as amended at N.C. Gen. Stat. § 15A-2011(b)(2)(2012)) (repealed 2013) (trying to deter race-based peremptory challenges by prosecutors in North Carolina by providing that the remedy for a *Batson* violation in a death penalty case would be life imprisonment without the possibility of parole rather than death).

129 *See* Marder, *supra* note 99, at 1140 n.9 (providing citations of recent articles). For an extensive collection of early articles critical of *Batson*, see People v. Bolling, 591 N.E.2d 1136, 1144–45 (N. Y. 1992) (Bellacosa, J., concurring) (providing citations).

130 *See, e.g.*, Marder, *supra* note 99, at 1194–99 (identifying judges who have urged the elimination of the peremptory challenge and some lawyers who have agreed); Marder, *supra* note 36, at 1713–15 (noting judges who have recommended the elimination of peremptory challenges).

131 Foster v. Chatman, 578 U.S. 488, 499 (2016) (quoting Snyder v. Louisiana, 552 U.S. 472, 478 (2008)).

discriminatory peremptory challenges persist. Finally, race-based peremptory challenges are prevalent in capital cases where the defendant is African American.

Another alternative is to revise the *Batson* test in some way so that it is more effective than it currently is at stopping discriminatory peremptory challenges. The problem with this remedy is that it is unclear how to make the *Batson* test more effective. The US Supreme Court has declined to try to do this, even though it has had the opportunity in two recent cases that raised the issue of *Batson* violations. Instead, the Court decided both cases, *Foster* v. *Chatman*[132] and *Flowers* v. *Mississippi*,[133] on narrow grounds by simply holding in each that the prosecutor had exercised discriminatory peremptory challenges in violation of *Batson*.[134] Admittedly, the criminal defendant in each case had only asked the Court to decide the narrow question whether *Batson* had been violated,[135] and not whether *Batson* should be revised or rejected.

The state of Washington has altered the *Batson* test in an effort to make it harder for lawyers to exercise discriminatory peremptory challenges. A new state rule, General Rule 37 (GR37), provides that if "an objective observer" would view the peremptory as discriminatory then it will not be allowed.[136] The rule describes this objective observer as one who "is aware that implicit, institutional, and unconscious biases, in addition to purposeful discrimination, have resulted in the unfair exclusion of potential jurors in Washington State."[137] The rule addresses peremptory challenges based on "race or ethnicity," but does not include gender.[138] The rule also provides that some of the reasons that were accepted as race-neutral in the past will now be regarded as "presumptively invalid" because they have long been used to mask discriminatory peremptory challenges.[139] Courts in Washington have had limited experience

[132] *Id.* at 488.

[133] Flowers v. Mississippi, 139 S. Ct. 2228 (2019).

[134] *Foster*, 578 U.S. at 513–14; *Flowers*, 139 S. Ct. at 2235.

[135] Petition for Writ of Certiorari at i, *Foster*, 578 U.S. 488 (2016) (No. 14–8349) (asking whether the courts below had failed to recognize a *Batson* violation); Petition for Writ of Certiorari at i, *Flowers*, 139 S. Ct. 2228 (2019) (No. 17–9572) (asking "[w]hether a prosecutor's history of adjudicated purposeful race discrimination may be dismissed as irrelevant when assessing the credibility of his proffered explanations for peremptory strikes against minority prospective jurors").

[136] Wash. St. Sup. Ct. Gen. R. 37(f) (2018) (containing Washington's new standard).

[137] *Id.*

[138] *Id.* at 37(e).

[139] *Id.* at 37(h).

with this rule to date.[140] Since GR37 came into effect on April 24, 2018, there have been at least two cases in which the trial court disallowed the peremptory challenge because an objective observer would view it as revealing an implicit bias.[141]

Other states have begun to follow Washington's lead. California took a similar approach to Washington, but used legislation rather than a judicial rule.[142] The California Legislature passed a statute that amended its *Code of Civil Procedure* by expanding the groups that are protected from discriminatory peremptory challenges, switching to an "objectively reasonable person" standard in determining whether a peremptory challenge is discriminatory, recognizing that bias could be implicit or explicit, and identifying a number of presumptively invalid reasons for a peremptory challenge, even though lawyers had used these reasons in the past and judges had accepted them.[143] Other states, such as Oregon[144] and Connecticut, are considering moving in the direction taken by Washington. Connecticut established a Task Force to consider how the state should proceed[145] and the Task Force issued a report on December 31, 2020.[146] One of the report's recommendations was to have the Connecticut Supreme Court undertake a rule change similar to GR37 in Washington, which would include an "objective observer's standard," an assessment based on the "totality of circumstances," and a list of "presumptively invalid" reasons for exercising a peremptory challenge, including reasons that had been acceptable in the past.[147]

[140] A Westlaw search for cases in the State of Washington that mentioned GR37 from the time the rule became effective (Apr. 24, 2018) until the date of the search (May 20, 2020), yielded only eight cases.

[141] *See, e.g.*, State v. Pierce, 455 P.3d 647, 654 (Wash. 2020) (applying GR37 to the peremptory challenge exercised against Juror 6 by the State and finding the reasons for the strike "presumptively invalid" under GR37); State v. Omar, 460 P.3d 225, 229 (Wash. Ct. App. 2020) (holding that the reasons given by defendant Omar for the exercise of a peremptory challenge against Juror 16 were "nebulous" and that an "objective observer could view race as a factor in the challenge"; thus, the trial court properly denied the peremptory challenge).

[142] *See, e.g.*, People v. Bryant, 253 Cal. Rptr. 3d 289, 295 (Ct. App. 2019).

[143] AB 3070, Juries: peremptory challenges (Sept. 30, 2020) (amending CAL. CIV. PROC. CODE § 231.7).

[144] *See, e.g.*, State v. Curry, 447 P.3d 7, 14 (Or. Ct. App. 2019).

[145] *See* e-mail from Neal Feigenson, Professor of L., Quinnipiac Univ. Sch. of L., to author (July 22, 2020, 7:32 CDT) (on file with author).

[146] JURY SELECTION TASK FORCE, *supra* note 78 (Ch. 1).

[147] *Id.* at 16-17. Some lawyers in New York have urged the Court of Appeals, the highest court in New York, to create a similar Task Force that would explore *Batson* reforms in New York. *See, e.g.*, Barbara Zolot, Commentary, *How New York State Can Fix Broken Promises of 'Batson,'* N. Y. L.J. (Apr. 1, 2021), https://www.law.com/newyorklawjournal/2021/04/01/how-new-york-state-can-fix-broken-promises-of-batson/ [https://perma.cc/33L4-E87E].

States may indeed lead the way in trying to make it more difficult for lawyers to engage in discriminatory peremptory challenges, just as they did with discriminatory peremptory challenges based on race and gender. Before the US Supreme Court's decision in *Batson* v. *Kentucky*,[148] states such as California and Massachusetts had found that race-based peremptory challenges violated their state constitutions.[149] Before the Supreme Court held gender-based peremptory challenges to be unconstitutional in *J.E.B.* v. *Alabama* ex rel. *T.B.*,[150] eleven states had held that they were impermissible.[151] It might be that the Supreme Court will be moved to alter or eliminate the *Batson* test only after there are sufficient circuit and state court splits, just as the Court waited to revisit race-based peremptory challenges until state and federal courts had addressed the issue and reached different conclusions.[152]

However, as long as *Batson* depends on lawyers to give reasons for their peremptories when challenged, and on judges to assess those reasons, even the states with more objective *Batson* tests might still provide a cover for discrimination. Washington's revised test makes it easier to show that the peremptory is being exercised in a discriminatory manner because the discrimination no longer has to be purposeful. That is a step in the right direction. However, lawyers and judges can still evade the test, though just not as often as they now evade *Batson*. In addition, the Supreme Court's *Batson* test and Washington's more objective version of it only attempt to uncover discriminatory peremptory challenges; they do not seek to eliminate other peremptory challenges. As long as

148 476 U.S. 79 (1986).

149 *See id.* at 82 n.1 (providing cases).

150 511 U.S. 127 (1994).

151 Nancy S. Marder, *Beyond Gender: Peremptory Challenges and the Roles of the Jury*, 73 TEX. L. REV. 1041, 1050 (1995) (noting that Arizona, California, Hawaii, Illinois, Maryland, Massachusetts, New Jersey, New Mexico, New York, North Dakota, and Washington had found gender-based peremptory challenges to be impermissible).

152 *See* McCray v. New York, 461 U.S. 961, 963 (1983). Justice Stevens, joined by Justices Harry A. Blackmun and Lewis F. Powell, Jr., wrote a brief opinion "respecting the denial of the petitions for writs of certiorari" in which he explained his vote to deny the petitions. *Id.* at 961. He wrote that although the issue of race-based peremptory challenges is an important one, it was wise to let the state and federal courts consider the issue before the Court did. *Id.* at 963. Justice Stevens' opinion was useful because it indicated to future litigators that there were five justices (three as part of his opinion and Justices Thurgood Marshall and William J. Brennan, Jr., who dissented in a separate opinion), who thought the issue should ultimately be addressed. By waiting until *Batson v. Kentucky*, the Court had not only the benefit of the lower courts' reasoning, but also a case that challenged race-based peremptory challenges on Sixth and Fourteenth Amendment grounds (unlike *McCray*, which raised only a Sixth Amendment violation). The Court ended up finding a Fourteenth Amendment violation in *Batson*, 476 U.S. 79 (1986), whereas the Sixth Amendment proved to be a dead end. *See* Holland v. Illinois, 493 U.S. 474 (1990).

idiosyncratic peremptory challenges are permitted, as indeed both tests permit, then qualified prospective jurors will continue to be excluded from serving on a jury.

One alternative that North Carolina experimented with, albeit for a limited amount of time, was taking death off the table as a possible sentence in a capital case if a criminal defendant could show that race was a "significant factor" in jury selection or sentencing. The legislature in North Carolina passed a statute, the North Carolina Racial Justice Act of 2009 (RJA),[153] and the governor signed it into law. The statute provided that the death penalty could not be considered in a capital case if the defense was able to show that the prosecutor had exercised a peremptory challenge based on race. Although this statute led to several criminal defendants being sentenced to life in prison without parole rather than to death,[154] after only four years the legislature repealed the statute once the majority of the legislature became heavily Republican, and the Democratic governor was replaced by a Republican governor.[155] Although this remedy showed promise, it was short-lived, limited to capital cases, and subject to change based on which party was in control of the state legislature and the executive branch.

## OTHER MINIMAL LIMITATIONS ON WHO CAN SERVE SHOULD BE MAINTAINED

Although peremptory challenges should be eliminated because they keep qualified citizens from serving on juries, other limitations on who can serve, such as juror qualifications and for cause challenges, should be maintained as long as they are minimal and reexamined periodically. Juror qualifications ensure that jurors have the basic skills to serve, and for cause challenges ensure that a prospective juror who says he or she cannot be impartial or cannot satisfy the appearance of impartiality will not serve in a particular case.

[153] 2009 N.C. Sess. Laws § 15A-2011(b)(2) (codified as amended at N.C. GEN. STAT. § 15A-2011(b)(2) (2012)) (repealed 2013).

[154] *See, e.g.*, Barbara O'Brien & Catherine M. Grosso, *Beyond* Batson's *Scrutiny: A Preliminary Look at Racial Disparities in Prosecutorial Peremptory Strikes Following the Passage of the North Carolina Racial Justice Act*, 46 U.C. DAVIS L. REV. 1623, 1652–54 (2013) (finding that the RJA had helped more white capital defendants than black capital defendants, but the authors remained optimistic that it would change prosecutors' behavior over time).

[155] Matt Smith, *'Racial Justice Act' Repealed in North Carolina*, CNN (June 21, 2013, 3:48 AM), https://www.cnn.com/2013/06/20/justice/north-carolina-death-penalty/index.html.

## Juror Qualifications

To serve as a juror in federal district court, a person must satisfy certain statutory qualifications.[156] Currently, those who are eligible to serve must be citizens of the United States who are at least eighteen years old and have resided in the judicial district for at least one year.[157] They also need to be able to read, write, and speak in English.[158] Finally, they need to be free of mental or physical infirmities that would prevent them from serving,[159] and cannot have a charge pending or have been convicted of a crime that is punishable by more than one year in prison.[160]

Admittedly, these qualifications limit who can serve as jurors, and some states, which typically have state qualifications that follow the federal qualifications, have begun to question some of them. For example, New Mexico permits citizens who speak Spanish rather than only English to serve as jurors.[161] It is the only state to do so. In California, the California Assembly wanted to make jury service available to noncitizens.[162] However, Jerry Brown, California's governor at the time, vetoed the bill.[163] Some scholars have urged that convicted felons should be permitted to serve as jurors.[164] Maine is the only state

[156] *See* 28 U.S.C. § 1865(b). State courts typically follow a similar set of requirements. *See, e.g.*, 705 ILCS 305/2 (providing that jurors in Illinois must be inhabitants of the county, over eighteen years old, free from "all legal exception," citizens of the United States, and able to understand English).

[157] 28 U.S.C. § 1865(b)(1). I have described the qualifications necessary to be a juror in the affirmative, though the statute actually describes them in the negative. For example, the statute provides that a person is qualified to serve "unless" he or she "is not a citizen of the United States." *Id.*

[158] *Id.* § 1865(b)(2)–(3).

[159] Disabilities, such as lack of sight or hearing, do not preclude a person from serving on a jury. For example, states such as Illinois provide hearing-impaired jurors with an interpreter and the interpreter can accompany the juror into the jury room during deliberations, even though jurors are usually the only ones allowed to be present in the jury room when the jury deliberates. *See, e.g.*, IPI, *supra* note 88 (Ch. 2), § 1.07.

[160] 28 U.S.C. § 1865(b)(4)–(5).

[161] *See* N.M. Const. art. VII, § 3 (providing that citizens cannot be deprived of their right to serve as jurors because of an inability to speak, read, or write in English).

[162] *See California: Bill Would Allow Noncitizen Jurors*, N.Y. Times, Aug. 23, 2013, at A16 ("California would become the first state to allow noncitizens who are in the country legally to be jurors under a bill that cleared the Assembly on Thursday [Aug. 22, 2013] and heads to Gov. Jerry Brown's desk.").

[163] *See* Patrick McGreevy & Melanie Mason, *Brown Vetoes Bill for Noncitizens to Serve on Juries; Move Runs Counter to Governor's Recent Decisions That Expand Immigrant Rights*, L.A. Times, Oct. 8, 2013, at A1 ("Gov. Jerry Brown on Monday [Oct. 7, 2013] vetoed legislation that would have made California the first state in the nation to allow legal immigrants who are not citizens to serve on juries.").

[164] *See, e.g.*, James M. Binnall, Twenty Million Angry Men: The Case for Including Convicted Felons in Jury Service (2021).

that currently permits this without restrictions,[165] but New York[166] and Illinois[167] are considering whether to follow Maine's lead and open up jury service to convicted felons, and Maryland had considered it before its legislative session adjourned.[168]

The federal and state juror qualifications remain fairly minimal. The qualifications require basic skills that are useful for jurors to have, such as reading, writing, and understanding English so that they can follow the trial and communicate with each other. The summons that citizens receive in the mail (described in Chapter 1) informs them of these qualifications. For example, the summons for jury duty in Cook County, Illinois includes a box that asks whether the recipient is a citizen of the United States, a resident of Cook County, and understands the English language.[169] These are modest requirements. If the recipient responds "no" to any of these questions, he or she is instructed to call the Office of Jury Administration and the telephone number is provided.[170]

Even minimal qualifications, however, should not be seen as fixed in stone. They should be reexamined to ensure that they still perform a useful function. For example, one scholar, James Binnall, has recently urged that convicted felons should be permitted to serve as jurors.[171] He has undertaken empirical studies and a survey and has found that convicted felons are not predisposed against the government, as has long thought to be the case,[172] and that jury service, like voting, could be "transformative"[173] in helping convicted felons to reintegrate back into the community.[174] In addition, with mass incarceration so prevalent, Binnall believes that it is particularly important that this large group of citizens should not be automatically excluded from jury service; it would benefit them, the parties, and the community if they were

[165] *See id.* at 93 (identifying Maine as "the only jurisdiction to place no restrictions on a convicted felon's opportunity to serve as a juror").

[166] *See* NAT'L CTR. FOR STATE CTS., JUR-E BULLETIN (Feb. 22, 2019), https://www.ncsc.org/newsroom/jure/2019/feb-22 [https://perma.cc/3NG6-EDCX].

[167] *See* O'Sullivan, *supra* note 103 ("A pending bill in Illinois would allow those with criminal convictions to be considered for jury service . . . ." ).

[168] *Id.* ("[S]imilar legislation [allowing those with criminal convictions to be considered for jury service] was under consideration in Maryland before the legislative session adjourned.").

[169] Summons To Appear, *supra* note 6 (Ch. 1).

[170] *Id.*

[171] BINNALL, *supra* note 164, at 8.

[172] *See id.* at 83 ("[F]elon-jurors do not approach deliberations from a fixed, pro-defendant position.").

[173] *Id.* at 94.

[174] *Id.* at 93–106; *see also id.* at 106 (using Maine, where convicted felons can serve on juries, the author found that the "jury's formative or reformative power is nondiscriminatory, in that inclusion fosters prosocial change among all who take part").

permitted to serve as jurors.[175] They have important insights to contribute to the jury's deliberations.[176]

Even if citizens meet the qualifications, they have only cleared the first hurdle for jury duty. They can still be excused for hardship, but they must raise this themselves and the judge must decide whether to grant it. In any case, an excuse for hardship is not necessarily a barrier to jury service, but an escape hatch for those who have immediate medical, family, or work responsibilities that preclude them from serving at a particular time. Prospective jurors who do not have a hardship excuse can still be excluded for cause; however, for cause challenges are decided by the judge, who announces the reason in open court and on the record.

## For Cause Challenges

Those prospective jurors who meet the qualifications for jury service must still clear the hurdle of for cause challenges. As explained earlier,[177] these are challenges for which a reason must be given in open court. The judge decides whether to grant a for cause challenge and there is no set number. Judges are usually restrained about granting for cause challenges, though this may be because they know that lawyers can still exercise peremptory challenges. However, a recent study suggests that race might play a role in judges' decisions about for cause challenges, at least in Louisiana and Mississippi.[178] Although for cause challenges might need closer scrutiny, they are still essential because they provide a way to remove prospective jurors who say outright that they cannot be fair to the defendant. Prospective jurors who hold such a strong view, which they recognize and share with the court, cannot serve on that particular jury. They need to be removed to ensure that the parties receive a fair trial.

[175] *See id.* at 143 ("Today, millions of Americans bear the mark of a felony conviction, and in certain communities, they comprise a critical mass of citizens who ought to be eligible for jury service.").

[176] *Id.* at 104–05 (finding that those with a felony conviction "bring something unique and valuable to the jury process"; they are "more accurate judges of a criminal defendant's credibility" and recognize the importance of "empathy").

[177] *See supra* text accompanying notes 11–13 (Ch. 2) (describing for cause challenges).

[178] *See* Thomas Ward Frampton, *For Cause: Rethinking Racial Exclusion and the American Jury*, 118 MICH. L. REV. 785, 794, 796–97 (2020) (finding, based on trial records, that in Louisiana, prosecutors raised for cause challenges against African-American prospective jurors more often than against white prospective jurors and judges acceded to those challenges; and, in Mississippi, judges initiated for cause challenges against African-American prospective jurors more often than white prospective jurors and prosecutors did not object).

Typically, judges grant for cause challenges in limited instances. For example, they grant a for cause challenge if there is a familial connection between the prospective juror and one of the participants in the trial, if the prospective juror has a financial stake in the outcome of the case, or if the prospective juror says he or she cannot be impartial.[179] The US Supreme Court has identified these and other limited instances, but judges are free to grant for cause challenges for other reasons as well. For example, a judge is likely to grant a for cause challenge if a prospective juror has been the victim of the same kind of crime for which the defendant is being tried.[180] Even if the prospective juror says he or she can be impartial, the prospective juror is unlikely to satisfy the appearance of impartiality. Another instance in which a judge should grant a for cause challenge is when the prospective juror is uncertain about whether he or she can be impartial. This occurred in *United States v. Martinez-Salazar*,[181] and although the trial judge attempted to rehabilitate the prospective juror who had gone back and forth about whether he could be impartial, nine Supreme Court Justices disagreed with the trial judge's denial of a for cause challenge in that instance.[182]

For cause challenges are yet another hurdle that prospective jurors must overcome before they can serve as jurors, yet this is an appropriate hurdle because for cause challenges exclude those who say in open court that they cannot be impartial or satisfy the appearance of impartiality. Although most citizens are open to being transformed into responsible jurors, not all citizens are. There will be some who hold extreme views and acknowledge those views in open court. There needs to be some mechanism for removing them and the for cause challenge is such a mechanism.

For cause challenges allow for the elimination of those citizens who, through their own self-assessments or their familial or financial connections to the parties or other trial participants, make clear that they are not open to being transformed. For example, in the criminal trial of Martin Shkreli, a CEO of a drug company that dramatically increased the

[179] *See* Hopt v. Utah, 120 U.S. 430, 433 (1887).

[180] *See, e.g.*, Mize, *supra* note 36 (Ch. 2), at 12 & nn.9–11 (granting for cause challenges to prospective jurors who had relatives who had been victims of guns or drugs, both of which were germane to the case at hand).

[181] United States v. Martinez-Salazar, 528 U.S. 304 (2000) (holding that the defendant was not denied his full allotment of peremptory challenges even though he had to use one of his peremptory challenges to strike a prospective juror who should have been removed for cause).

[182] *Id.* at 309 (describing the district court judge's decision to deny defendant's for cause challenge as erroneous).

price of its drugs, and who was charged with eight counts of securities and wire fraud, the judge needed to rely on for cause challenges to remove many prospective jurors who had already decided that the defendant was guilty. These prospective jurors' comments included the following: "I'm aware of the defendant and I hate him"; "When I walked in here today I looked at [the defendant], and in my head, that's a snake . . ."; "Your Honor, totally he is guilty and in no way can I let him slide out of anything . . . ."[183] If there were no means of removing the prospective juror who says that he or she cannot be impartial, then the requirements of due process, including an impartial decision-maker, and the requirements of a fair trial, including an impartial jury, could not be met. Similarly, if there were no way of removing the prospective juror who was related to one of the parties or who stood to gain or lose financially based on the jury's verdict, then once again, the parties would be denied an impartial decision-maker and a fair trial.

Although juror qualifications and for cause challenges limit who can serve as jurors, they do so in minimal ways. Moreover, they are both carried out in open court and for all to see. Prospective jurors learn about juror qualifications from their summons, from the Jury Administrator, and from the judge. They also learn about for cause challenges from the judge. Any prospective juror who is removed by a for cause challenge hears the judge give the reason in open court, as do all the other participants and observers in the courtroom, and the reason becomes part of the court record. A criminal defendant, if convicted, can appeal a trial judge's denial of a for cause challenge, assuming that the defendant had objected at the time and had not removed the prospective juror in question with a peremptory challenge.[184] As for cause challenges are carried out in public with reasons stated by the judge that are on the record and, under certain conditions, subject to appellate review, there are a number of protections built into the for cause challenge.

183 Dominic Rushe, *'I Hate Him': Martin Shkreli Court Transcript Reveals Struggle for Impartial Jurors*, GUARDIAN (Aug. 17, 2017), https://www.theguardian.com/us-news/2017/aug/17/martin-shkreli-trial-jurors-wu-tang-clan [https://perma.cc/6CEN-DJS2].

184 In *United States v. Martinez-Salazar*, 528 U.S. 304 (2000), the Supreme Court held that a criminal defendant's Fifth Amendment right to due process was not violated when the trial judge denied him for a cause challenge, even though the trial judge should have granted it. The reason was that the defendant removed the prospective juror in question using a peremptory challenge. Thus, the prospective juror, though he should have been removed for cause, did not end up sitting on the jury and so there was no prejudice to the defendant.

## SUMMARY

Peremptory challenges exclude prospective jurors from jury service, including those who have met the juror qualifications, appeared in court, said they could be impartial, and withstood challenges for cause, and their removal is cloaked in secrecy. When prospective jurors are struck with a peremptory challenge they do not typically learn why they have been removed. Sometimes they are removed for lawyers' idiosyncratic reasons and sometimes they are removed for lawyers' discriminatory reasons. Either case results in their removal from the petit jury. Discriminatory peremptory challenges do even more harm than idiosyncratic peremptory challenges because they signal to prospective jurors that they are not worthy of serving and the discrimination takes place in open court where it is clear to those in the courtroom what is happening. Whether peremptory challenges are motivated by the idiosyncratic or discriminatory views of lawyers, they should be eliminated. Peremptory challenges are not needed to perform the traditional purpose of identifying prospective jurors' subtle biases not only because they cannot do so effectively, but also because the jury process will transform these citizens into jurors.

Peremptory challenges are antithetical to the transformation of citizens into jurors because they lead to the removal of citizens who, though qualified to serve, are nevertheless removed because of lawyers' idiosyncratic or discriminatory exercise of their peremptory challenges. As a result, peremptory challenges interfere with the creation of diverse juries. Less diverse juries create several harms; they exclude jurors of different races, genders, and ethnicities, who are likely to have different life experiences and points of view that they could bring to the jury's deliberations. Such jurors can challenge each other's assumptions and interpretations of the evidence. Discriminatory peremptory challenges also undermine the integrity of the jury system and the legitimacy of the jury's verdict. Peremptory challenges do not succeed in removing prospective jurors with subtle biases, which everyone has, because lawyers are not able to identify such biases; even if they were, there is no evidence that such subtle biases come into play during the deliberations. The transformation view recognizes that it is important to have a diverse jury if the trial evidence is to be examined critically. Peremptory challenges stand in the way of producing diverse juries that random selection, tempered only by minimal juror qualifications and for cause challenges, will otherwise produce.

4

# JURY INSTRUCTIONS: REINFORCING GROUP IDENTITY AND MAKING INSTRUCTIONS ACCESSIBLE TO JURORS

At the end of the trial, after the jurors have heard all the evidence and arguments, they hear the jury instructions. The judge reads them aloud in open court, taking as much time as is needed to read them in their entirety. The judge explains in the instructions that the jurors' task is to apply the law as the judge gives it to them to the facts as the jurors find them. The instructions also include a number of key concepts, such as the elements of the crime or civil claim, burden of proof, types of evidence, and the need to assess witness credibility. After the judge reads the instructions aloud, the jurors leave the courtroom and enter the jury room, where they will deliberate.

The traditional view of jury instructions is that the instructions mainly provide jurors with the law to apply and that jurors will understand the instructions and know how to use them when they enter the jury room. The traditional view assumes juror understanding, even though the instructions can be lengthy, written in legal jargon, and delivered as a lecture by the judge. To the extent that jurors have trouble understanding the instructions, the traditional view has accepted the need for modest adjustments, such as having jury instruction committees try to draft instructions in plain language, giving jurors some preliminary instructions, and providing them with a written copy of the instructions. In general, however, the traditional view is that jurors understand the instructions once they have heard them read aloud by the judge.[1]

[1] For example, although the Supreme Court was able to parse the jury instructions in *Arthur Andersen LLP v. United States*, 544 U.S. 696 (2005), as it tried to decide whether the addition or subtraction of particular words had shifted the burdens established by Congress, the jurors might

Jury instructions help transform jurors' behaviors and attitudes so that they become responsible jurors. One way that instructions do this is by having jurors hear the instructions when they are seated together in the jury box in front of the parties, the public, and the press. The jury box reminds jurors that they are part of a group endeavor. The public reading by the judge reinforces the seriousness of what the jurors are being asked to do when they enter the jury room. As the jurors listen to the instructions, they see the parties before them, which is yet another visual reminder of the consequences of their task. Although having jury instructions read aloud by the judge is not the best way to convey the law, it is particularly effective in helping jurors to take their role as jurors seriously and to understand their individual responsibility in this group endeavor.

The transformation view recognizes that the performance in the courtroom – of the judge intoning the instructions for however long the instructions take – is an important part of imbuing the jurors with a sense of what is required of them when they enter the jury room. The fact that the judge engages in this public reading of the instructions, during which everyone in the courtroom remains silent and attentive, signals that great care is required with how the jurors will proceed in the jury room. The jurors' task, though a difficult and important one, is a group task and their burden will be shared by all the jurors alike. The reading in open court also reassures the parties and the public that the jurors have heard the instructions from start to finish.

However, the instructions, communicated as a lengthy lecture at the end of the trial, will not necessarily reach a diverse group of citizens with different learning styles. For instructions to contribute to citizens' transformation into jurors, the jurors also need to understand the substance of the instructions. Although the judge's reading of the instructions in open court is important so that the jurors take their group task seriously, this mode of communication does not necessarily convey the substance of the instructions to all of the jurors. To ensure that the jurors understand the instructions, the judge needs to take a number of additional steps, such as giving the jurors preliminary and as-needed instructions, providing them with a written copy of the instructions, permitting them to take notes, and giving them an opportunity to submit questions about the instructions. These steps will

not even be able to remember if particular words had been used unless they were given a written copy of the instructions to which they could refer during their deliberations.

enable jurors to understand the substance of the instructions so that they will be guided by them during their deliberations. The instructions need to be accessible to all the jurors so that they enter the deliberations with a shared understanding of the tasks that they must perform and the procedures they must follow and so that they can deliberate as equals in the jury room.

## HOW JURY INSTRUCTIONS WORK

The judge gives the jury final instructions at the close of the trial and prior to the jury deliberations.[2] The instructions provide the jurors with the law that is relevant to the case they have heard. The judge will usually say to the jurors that their job is to apply the law as the judge has given it to them to the facts as they have found them.[3] The instructions will also explain many basic concepts about the trial, such as the different types of evidence (direct or circumstantial), the need to assess witness credibility, and the need to decide whether the party that has the burden of proof has met its burden. In a criminal case, for example, the judge instructs the jury on the charges against the defendant and the elements that the prosecution is required to prove "beyond a reasonable doubt," as well as on the "presumption of innocence" to which the defendant is entitled.

Typically, the instructions contain many basic concepts, and it would be useful for the jury to have knowledge of some of these at the start of or during the trial. Thus, in some courtrooms, the judge will give jurors several preliminary instructions, so that they have a framework from which to view the trial, and he or she will give other instructions as they become relevant during the trial. The final instructions at the end of the trial can remind the jury of some of the earlier instructions and provide other instructions for the first time.

When judges deliver instructions, they usually work from pattern jury instructions. These are boilerplate instructions that have been written by a jury instruction committee, usually consisting of lawyers and/or judges. Often one committee writes the civil jury instructions

[2] Some courts will also provide preliminary instructions at the start of the trial and other instructions throughout the trial as they are needed. *See infra* text accompanying notes 24–25, 95–100.

[3] Judges typically instruct the jury as to its role as follows: "Your job is to decide all of the factual questions in this case . . . . I will decide all of the legal questions in this case . . . ." 1A KEVIN F. O'MALLEY ET AL., FEDERAL JURY PRACTICE AND INSTRUCTIONS § 10.01 (Westlaw 6th ed. Jan. 2022 update).

while another committee writes the criminal jury instructions.[4] These committees write pattern instructions that lawyers and judges in a particular case can then tailor to that case. Each committee tries to work carefully from the case law and statutes to create instructions that it believes state the law accurately. In some states, the pattern instructions will have been approved by the highest court of the state.[5] In other states, the pattern instructions will not have been approved by the highest court of the state in advance, but they provide the best source for reliable instructions in that state.[6] In other words, if trial judges use these pattern instructions, they are less likely to be reversed on appeal on the instructions than those judges who draft their own instructions. The judge and lawyers in any given case use the pattern instructions and adjust them according to the particulars of that case. However, jurors have trouble understanding these instructions. They tend to be written in a wooden style for the general case and laden with legal terms that are likely to sound like foreign words to the jurors.[7]

## THE TRADITIONAL VIEW OF WHAT JURY INSTRUCTIONS ARE SUPPOSED TO ACCOMPLISH

The traditional view of jury instructions assumes that each juror who has been selected to serve is unbiased and understands his or her role from the outset, and only needs to be given final instructions with the relevant law at the end of the trial. At that point, according to the

4 For example, in Illinois there are two committees, the Illinois Supreme Court Committee on Pattern Instructions in Civil Cases and the Illinois Supreme Court Committee on Pattern Instructions in Criminal Cases, that write the jury instructions in their respective areas. Similarly, in California, when the Judicial Council appointed a task force to rewrite its jury instructions, the task force was divided into two subcommittees: one to rewrite the civil jury instructions and the other to rewrite the criminal jury instructions. *See, e.g.*, James D. Ward, *Jury Practice: The New Civil Jury Instructions*, CAL. LAW., Feb. 2004, at 38, 38.

5 For example, before the Task Force in California rewrote its instructions, there were two books of approved pattern instructions – one known as the *Book of Approved Jury Instructions (BAJI)* and the other known as *California Jury Instructions: Criminal (CALJIC)*. *See* CIVIL COMM. ON CAL. JURY INSTRUCTIONS, CALIFORNIA JURY INSTRUCTIONS – CIVIL (BAJI) (2005); COMM. ON STANDARD JURY INSTRUCTIONS, CRIMINAL, OF THE SUPER. CT. OF L.A. CNTY., CAL., CALIFORNIA JURY INSTRUCTIONS – CRIMINAL (CALJIC) (7th ed. 2003).

6 *See, e.g.*, Leonard Post, *Spelling It out in Plain English*, NAT'L L.J., Nov. 8, 2004, at 1, 19 (noting that in Michigan, where adherence to pattern instructions is "voluntary" because the Michigan Supreme Court never formally adopted them, "everyone uses them because of the fear of being reversed") (quoting Michigan Circuit Judge William Caprathe, who chaired the drafting committee for the criminal jury instructions).

7 *See, e.g.*, Nancy S. Marder, *Bringing Jury Instructions into the Twenty-First Century*, 81 NOTRE DAME L. REV. 449, 461 (2006) ("When faced with the choice of simplifying the language but risking reversal or using the legal language, the legal language prevails.").

traditional view, the judge just needs to read the jury instructions aloud to the jurors from start to finish, and no matter how lengthy or complicated they are, the jurors will absorb them like sponges absorb water. Judges have long delivered jury instructions in accordance with this view.[8]

The traditional view also assumes that jurors know how to work together as a group without being told anything more about the process or receiving any additional guidance from the judge. In fact, the judge is not supposed to provide any guidance at all about how jurors should proceed in the jury room because it is up to the jurors to structure their deliberations. If the jurors have any questions about the instructions, they have to wait until after they have begun their deliberations to get answers – either by consulting their fellow jurors or by sending a note to the judge.

Some judges leave jurors more in the dark than the traditional view requires by failing to provide jurors with any information even when they ask for it. For example, one jury felt not only that the judge failed to provide any assistance when the jurors requested it, but also that he went out of his way to keep the jury from understanding anything.[9] The foreperson described the judge as having an antagonistic relationship with the jury and with everyone else who came into contact with him.[10] The foreperson observed that the judge kept the jury "as out of it as possible" and provided little guidance, especially when the jury felt most in need of it.[11] The judge denied the jury's request for a written copy of the instructions,[12] and instead, the judge responded simply by

[8] *See* B. Michael Dann, *"Learning Lessons" and "Speaking Rights": Creating Educated and Democratic Juries*, 68 IND. L.J. 1229, 1239–41 (1993).

[9] BURNETT, *supra* note 39 (Ch. 1), at 81.

[10] *Id.* at 57 ("This was the judge who had browbeaten everyone who had spoken to him throughout the trial, who had been magnificently impolite at every opportunity.").

[11] *Id.* at 81.

[12] New York does not permit jurors to be given a written copy of the instructions over the defendant's objection. *See, e.g.*, People v. Baker, 926 N.E.2d 240, 245 (N.Y. 2010) (noting that the prosecutor's slides with legal definitions were not given to the jury during its deliberations because "a jury cannot be given only certain portions of final instructions in writing over the defendant's objection"); People v. Johnson, 615 N.E.2d 1009–10 (N.Y. 1993) ("During jury deliberations the trial court, over the defendant's objections, complied with a jury request for a written copy of the court's entire charge. The Appellate Division concluded this was error, reversed the judgment of conviction and ordered a new trial . . . . We affirm the order of the Appellate Division."); People v. Owens, 509 N.E.2d 314, 318 (N.Y. 1987) ("[T]he distribution of written instructions to the jury is not expressly authorized by law, and error in such submissions cannot be deemed harmless."). The judge presiding over the case in which Burnett was the foreperson could have explained this to the jury, but according to Burnett's recollection, the judge simply denied the jury's request. *See* BURNETT, *supra* note 39 (Ch. 1), at 90.

rereading the instructions in their entirety.[13] The jury did not find this response to be the least bit helpful.[14]

However, other judges who take the traditional view of jury instructions try to provide jurors with instructions that will give them the basic information they need to understand their task. In some courts, judges allow jurors to take notes, including during the reading of the instructions. Some courts provide jurors with a written copy of the instructions that they can follow as the judge reads the instructions aloud. They can also take their written copy into the jury room and use it as a reference during the deliberations. Even when judges do not give jurors individual copies of the written instructions, they might give jurors a single copy when they go into the jury room so that jurors do not have to rely wholly upon their memory. Some states have even rewritten their pattern instructions to try to make them more accessible to a lay person. Thus, even with the traditional view, some courts have taken some steps, albeit with great reticence, because they recognize that not all jurors will be able to listen to a single reading of the jury instructions and understand and retain the substance of it for use during the deliberations. However, these practices have not become widespread, except perhaps for note-taking,[15] mainly because the traditional view requires only the judge's reading of the final instructions at the end of the trial.

## THE LIMITATIONS OF THE TRADITIONAL VIEW OF JURY INSTRUCTIONS

The traditional view of jury instructions is that jurors know their job from the time they are selected and mainly need to know the relevant law, which the judge provides through his or her final instructions. According to this view, the judge just needs to read the jury instructions aloud at the end of the trial. The judge will then have given the jurors all the information they need to proceed with their jury deliberations.

Jury instructions, as currently provided, have flaws recognized even by the traditional view. For example, it is clear that jurors do not always understand the instructions.[16] One reason they have trouble understanding the instructions is because the language is largely geared

[13] BURNETT, *supra* note 39 (Ch. 1), at 90–91.
[14] *Id.* at 91.
[15] *See infra* notes 50–55 and accompanying text (describing how note-taking has become a widely accepted practice).
[16] *See, e.g.*, Marder, *supra* note 7, at 454–58 (citing empirical studies).

toward lawyers and judges. Jury instruction committees, typically consisting of lawyers and judges, write the instructions and want to make sure that they state the law accurately. They essentially write the instructions for appellate judges who will review them on appeal. Thus, these committees tend to use language from statutes or case law or employ terms of art. Such language is not necessarily understandable by lay people.[17] There are myriad empirical studies conducted over the past fifty years showing that jurors have long had difficulty understanding the language of jury instructions.[18] Numerous studies over the years also show that using plain language helps jurors to understand the instructions.[19] Some states, such as California, Arizona, and Delaware, have tried to rewrite their instructions using plain language.[20] Yet, the move toward plain language jury instructions, which received attention from a number of states in the late 1990s and early 2000s[21] seems to have lost some of its momentum.

Another difficulty with jury instructions that satisfy the traditional view is that they do not include a road map that indicates to jurors how these disparate instructions fit together.[22] The jury instruction committees that write the instructions, and the lawyers and trial judges who tailor the instructions for the individual case, have a road map. They have headings that go with each instruction and they understand how the instructions fit together in a book of instructions. The jurors, who lack legal training and instruction headings, are without a road map. Thus jurors, who have the least amount of training and are most in need of assistance, are denied headings or any other indicia of how these instructions relate to each other. One recent study demonstrated that even when jurors understand the language of the instructions, without a road map they have trouble understanding the instructions.[23]

[17] *See, e.g.*, *id.* at 454 & nn. 9–11 (providing empirical studies).

[18] *See, e.g.*, *id.* at 454–58.

[19] *See, e.g.*, Peter Tiersma, *Asking Jurors to Do the Impossible*, 5 TENN. J.L. & POL'Y 105, 142–45, 146 (2009) [hereinafter Tiersma, *Asking Jurors*]; Peter Tiersma, *The Rocky Road to Legal Reform: Improving the Language of Jury Instructions*, 66 BROOK. L. REV. 1081, 1100 (2001).

[20] *See, e.g.*, Marder, *supra* note 7, at 475–76 (describing California's efforts to rewrite its jury instructions in plain language); James D. Wascher, *The Long March Toward Plain English Jury Instructions*, CBA REC., Feb.–Mar. 2005, at 50, 51 (describing various states' efforts to rewrite their instructions in plain language, including Alaska, Delaware, Michigan, Minnesota, Missouri, and North Dakota).

[21] *See supra* note 20.

[22] *See* Shari Seidman Diamond, Beth Murphy & Mary R. Rose, "*The Kettleful of Law*" *in Real Jury Deliberations: Successes, Failures, and Next Steps*, 106 NW. U. L. REV. 1537, 1597–98 (2012) (describing jurors' need for a road map of the instructions).

[23] *Id.*

Yet another difficulty with instructions that satisfy the traditional view is that the judge typically instructs the jurors at the end of the trial. If the judge does not provide preliminary instructions at the start of the trial, the jurors sit through the trial uncertain about what they are seeing. Preliminary instructions give jurors a framework. Such instructions tell jurors what the case is about, how the trial will proceed, and what they will need to decide at the end of the trial. Even if preliminary instructions are later included as part of the final instructions, they help jurors to understand what they are about to see. Similarly, jurors benefit from hearing instructions throughout the trial, especially at moments when the instructions are about to come into play, such as hearing an instruction about the need for jurors to assess witness credibility right before hearing witnesses testify.

The traditional view, in which the judge instructs only at the end of the trial, fails to give jurors the framework they need to make sense of the trial and their role in it. As one juror who served during the first criminal trial of former Illinois Governor Rod Blagojevich complained, the jurors felt like they were told, "Here's a manual, go fly the space shuttle."[24] They found that the instructions, which were more than 100 pages in length, failed to prepare them for their task.[25] Moreover, jurors have trouble understanding lengthy instructions delivered only at the end of the trial, rather than preliminary and as-needed instructions delivered throughout the trial and summarized again at the end.

## HOW JURY INSTRUCTIONS HELP TRANSFORM CITIZENS INTO JURORS

Even if some of the shortcomings of jury instructions that are accepted by the traditional view could be corrected, this view nevertheless misses an essential, but unacknowledged, role of jury instructions: to transform citizens into jurors. Jury instructions are not only a means of giving jurors the law to follow, but also a way to create a shared group responsibility for the deliberations. Jurors hear the instructions while seated together in the jury box; and the jury box, which keeps jurors together and apart from everyone else in the courtroom, reminds jurors of the group task they will soon undertake. The jurors hear the instructions directly from the judge, who reads the instructions slowly,

[24] Monica Davey & Susan Saulny, *Jurors Fault Complexity of the Blagojevich Trial*, N.Y. TIMES, Aug. 19, 2010, at A1 (quoting Juror Steve Wlodek).

[25] *Id.*

carefully, and in their entirety, while everyone else in the courtroom remains silent. This public reading reinforces the seriousness of what the jurors are being asked to do when they go into the jury room to reach a verdict. As the jurors listen to the instructions, they also see the parties before them, which is yet another visual reminder of the consequences of their task. The jurors' work is out of the ordinary and requires their utmost care and attention, but they do not perform it alone. No individual juror shoulders all of the responsibility of decision-making; rather, all twelve jurors must come to see themselves as equal participants who need to contribute to the collective knowledge and endeavor once they begin their deliberations.

Although the judge's public reading of the instructions is important to the transformation view because it conveys to jurors the seriousness of the group task they are about to undertake, it is also important to the transformation view that the jurors understand the substance of the instructions. The instructions will help to anchor the deliberations so that the jurors reach a verdict based on the law as provided by the judge and the facts as found by the jury. A diverse jury, like any diverse group, will have different styles of learning; thus, it is important that the instructions are conveyed in a variety of ways. Some jurors will absorb the instructions by hearing them read aloud; others will need to hear the reading while taking notes; still others will need to be able to review a written version after listening to the instructions read aloud; and all jurors will benefit by knowing that they can ask questions at the end of the instructions and by hearing relevant portions of the instructions throughout the trial and then repeated at the end of the trial. The judge needs to provide jury instructions in a variety of ways to take account of jurors' different learning styles. The judge is more likely to reach all of the jurors with their disparate learning styles if he or she provides preliminary instructions, as-needed instructions, individual written copies of the instructions, paper and pen for note-taking during the instructions, and an opportunity for jurors to ask questions immediately after the judge has read the instructions aloud.

### Sitting in the Jury Box

The jurors sit together in the jury box as the judge reads the final instructions aloud to them. Having the jurors sit together helps them to think of themselves as a jury. They sit together with their fellow jurors and apart from everyone else in the courtroom. Of course, they have been sitting together in the jury box throughout the entire trial.

But it is important that they sit together for the reading of the final charge. The task they are about to undertake, difficult though it may be, will be done as a group. They will have each other to turn to for a variety of perspectives, recollections, and assessments.

As the jurors sit together in the jury box listening to the instructions, they are reminded that they have a group responsibility to reach a verdict. They are being charged by the judge with this group task. They are being told, as a group, that their job is to apply the law that the judge has given them to the facts as they find them. Reaching a judgment – whether by a judge or a jury – is a difficult experience.[26] The jurors are about to undertake this arduous task, but they will do so as a group. By sitting together in the jury box as the judge reads their final instructions, they are reminded that they will perform this difficult task as a group, not as individuals. Thus, the responsibility falls equally on all their shoulders. They can look around at fellow jurors seated next to them and in front of them and they are reminded that they will not perform this task alone.

The jurors are reminded of the awesome responsibility they face as they see the parties before them. The jurors listen to the instructions read by the judge and know that their verdict will have serious repercussions for the parties. The parties are physically present before them; they are not an abstract idea. The jurors hear the instructions read aloud as they face the parties whose fate they will decide. They cannot help but feel the enormous responsibility that they have to these parties to do their job as responsibly as possible.

As the jurors sit in the jury box listening to the judge read the instructions everyone else in the courtroom can observe them. The jurors know they are being observed and they try to remain attentive and impassive, as they have throughout the trial.[27] It is important that everyone in the courtroom can observe the jurors in the jury box listening to the instructions. The press, the public, and particularly the parties, can see that the jurors have heard the instructions from start to finish. Those in the courtroom are able to witness this act in a way

[26] *Cf.* Robert M. Cover, *Violence and the Word*, 95 YALE L.J. 1601, 1609 (1986) ("[J]udges deal pain and death.").

[27] *See, e.g.*, JURY TRIAL INNOVATIONS, *supra* note 50 (Ch. 2), at 305 (app. 13) ("Additionally, you are immediately aware that you are very much part of the 'show' as you are watched by the principals in the case while being scrutinized by the attorneys so they can get a 'read' on how their case is being accepted, so you try to be neutral in your responses, which effectively eliminates all avenues of expression since we are not permitted to discuss it.") (quoting a juror in a high-profile capital case).

that they could not have done if the jurors simply took a written copy of the instructions and read them on their own in the jury room. By having the jurors sit in the jury box during the reading of the instructions, everyone in the courtroom is reassured that the jurors have heard the instructions in their entirety.

### Having the Judge Read the Instructions Aloud

As the jurors sit together in the jury box, the judge reads the instructions aloud. The judge's reading of the instructions adds to the solemnity of the experience and reinforces what is at stake for the parties. The reading can take several hours or more, and during this time everyone in the courtroom is silent except for the judge. It is an experience akin to a clergyman delivering a sermon, but rather than delivering the sermon with fervor, the judge tries to deliver his or her instructions with a calm, dispassionate voice.[28]

Jurors often look to the judge as the authority figure in the courtroom.[29] They recognize that the lawyers are advocates for their respective clients, but the judge is supposed to be a neutral, impartial figure. Having the judge read the instructions aloud to the jury means that the jurors hear the instructions from a source they have grown to trust. They want to do the best job they can in trying to understand and follow the instructions and in trying to take their responsibility seriously.

The formal language of the instructions conveys to the jurors that they are to take the instructions seriously. Although the lawyers and judges on jury instruction committees have attempted to make the instructions understandable and to rewrite them in plain language, they still incorporate statutory language and terms of art. This language is unfamiliar to most jurors, who are not usually trained in the law. Although the language is an obstacle to easy comprehension, it gives

[28] *See* Terry A. Maroney, *(What We Talk About When We Talk About) Judicial Temperament*, 61 B.C. L. REV. 2085, 2100 n.62 (2020) (quoting FED. JUD. CTR., COMPETENCIES FOR UNITED STATES JUDGES 33 (2018) (describing judicial temperament as including the extent to which a judge "[e]xhibits an even tone, a calm voice, and appropriate body language under pressure")).

[29] *See, e.g.*, GROVE, *supra* note 32 (Ch. 1), at 96 ("[O]ne could sense a determination on the jury's behalf that this trial should come out well in the eyes of everyone in court, and most particularly the judge's."); TOCQUEVILLE, *supra* note 3 (Intro.), at 296–97 (describing the civil jury trial in which the judge's "influence over [the jurors] is almost unlimited" and even after the trial, the judge "continues to influence the habits of thought, and even the characters, of those who acted with him in his official capacity"); Blanck, Rosenthal & Cordell, *supra* note 48 (Ch. 2), at 133–36 (finding that jurors are influenced not only by what a judge says but also by the way in which he or she says it).

a formality to the reading and it signals to the jurors that what they are hearing is weighty, out of the ordinary, and requires their full attention. Indeed, for the jurors to try to understand this formal language, they need to pay close attention to it.

The amount of time that the judge spends reading the instructions aloud also signals to jurors that their task is serious and they must see it in that light. The judge reads the instructions for however long it takes, and it can take hours. As the judge reads the instructions aloud the court reporter takes down every word while everyone else in the courtroom remains silent. The jurors remain silent too, but they also know that they have an obligation to remain attentive. After all, they know that everyone in the courtroom is watching them and trying to discern from their expressions their response to the instructions.

The judge's reading of the instructions also signals to the jury and to those in the courtroom that the jury is to be guided by the instructions. The jury wields enormous power insofar as it has been summoned to decide this dispute for the community. As one former juror recognized: "It was we twelve [jurors] who had ultimate power in this court."[30] The jury is supposed to follow the law and to decide the facts based on the evidence.[31] The instructions will serve as an anchor for the jury's deliberations. The jurors, like the judge, are not "knight[s]-errant roaming at will in pursuit of [their] own ideal of beauty or goodness."[32] They are supposed to follow the instructions. Although the jury has the power to nullify – in other words, not to follow the law[33] – that power should be exercised only in rare instances.[34] Juries do not nullify often, though there are few empirical studies that have examined this question.[35] The jurors listen to the instructions as carefully as they can because they know that the instructions will provide them with whatever guidance they are going to receive.

[30] Grove, *supra* note 32 (Ch. 1), at 34 (quoting former juror Trevor Grove, who served as the foreperson).

[31] 1A O'Malley et al., *supra* note 3, § 10.01.

[32] Benjamin N. Cardozo, The Nature of the Judicial Process 141 (1921).

[33] *See, e.g.*, United States v. Dougherty, 473 F.2d 1113, 1130 (D.C. Cir. 1972).

[34] The nullifying jury, like the hung jury, should occur only in rare instances. Professor Hans Zeisel has described the hung jury as a "treasured, paradoxical phenomenon." Hans Zeisel, *. . . And Then There Were None: The Diminution of the Federal Jury*, 38 U. Chi. L. Rev. 710, 719 (1971). He explained that it is "treasured because it represents the legal system's respect for the minority viewpoint that is held strongly enough to thwart the will of the majority," and it is paradoxical because the hung jury can only be tolerated in "moderation." *Id.* at 719 n.42. If it occurs too often, hung juries "would impede the effective functioning of the courts." *Id.*

[35] *Cf.* Paula L. Hannaford-Agor, Valerie P. Hans, Nicole L. Mott & G. Thomas Munsterman, Are Hung Juries a Problem? (2002) (studying hung juries).

It is also important that the judge reads the instructions aloud to the jurors so that they have all heard the instructions from beginning to end. Even if this is an ineffective way for some jurors to absorb the information, it means that all of the jurors have at least heard the same instructions in their entirety. They might not understand all the parts of all of the instructions, but they heard them. If they were left on their own to read the instructions when they entered the jury room, they might not all read them from start to finish. One juror in the first criminal trial of former Illinois Governor Rod Blagojevich lamented the enormity of the task: "I'm supposed to judge a man's life and read 105 pages of law? . . . To me that was completely ridiculous and not fair."[36] All of the jurors, by virtue of having had the instructions read aloud to them, have heard them. They enter the jury room with equal exposure and with no juror having had exclusive control over the instructions, as could have happened if they were just given a single written copy. Thus, during the deliberations they can all participate and no juror can claim to be the sole expert as to the meaning of the instructions.

Finally, as they are read aloud by the judge in open court, the instructions are taken down by the court reporter and preserved as part of the record for any challenges a party might raise on appeal. The reading aloud by the judge also gives him or her one last opportunity to ensure that the instructions are correct, at least insofar as the judge can tell at that moment. As the judge reads, he or she can make any last-minute corrections so that the jurors hear the most accurate version that is available, as does the court reporter.

## Instructing Jurors to Be Self-Policing

Several of the instructions that the judge will read aloud to the jurors tell them, as well as others in the courtroom, that the jurors need to self-police during their deliberations. For example, if one juror sees another juror doing online research or posting online about the trial, that juror must alert the court.[37] Each juror has to take responsibility for the group

[36] Bob Secter & Stacy St. Clair, *Blagojevich Jury's Advice: Keep It Simple*, CHI. TRIB., Aug. 28, 2010, https://www.chicagotribune.com/news/ct-xpm-2010-08-28-ct-met-blagojevich-jury-08 29-20100828-story.html [https://perma.cc/A6ML-FNKF] (quoting juror Ashlee Moore); *see* Erin Emery, *The Jury That Couldn't: Scenes from a Mistrial in Teller County*, DENV. POST, July 3, 2003, at 1A (quoting a juror in a first-degree murder trial who said: "It was really frustrating because we were not getting any help on how do you go about this, how do you approach the situation . . . . You're supposed to decide the outcome of a man's life—blind—and that's not acceptable.").

[37] *See, e.g.*, IPI, *supra* note 88 (Ch. 2), § 1.01(A)[6]–[12] (Cautionary Instructions (Prior to Opening)).

and be protective of the group deliberations. Each juror has an obligation to ensure that the rest of the jurors act in accordance with the instructions. The group is central to the deliberations, and the judge, by reading the instructions aloud to the jurors, who are seated together in the jury box, reinforces this message.

Several of the instructions that the judge provides at this juncture tell the jurors that they must take responsibility for each other's behavior. Such instructions put the jurors on notice that they must look after the group. Once they enter the jury room, they will be beyond the watch of the judge, as well as the public, the press, and the parties; they will be on their own. They will need to take charge of how they conduct themselves. The instructions read aloud by the judge in this public setting inform the jurors of their responsibility and inform others in the courtroom as well. The jurors' status is about to shift. They will move from being under the watch of others to being on their own. The instructions read aloud by the judge impart this information to the jurors as well as to all who have observed the trial.

**The Timing of the Instructions**

The judge reads the final instructions at the end of the trial but before the jury begins its deliberations.[38] The rationale for this timing is that the instructions are the last words that the jurors hear before they go into the jury room to deliberate. Therefore, the instructions will be fresh in their minds. In some courts, the judge will read the jury instructions before closing argument; in other courts, the judge will read the instructions immediately after closing argument.[39] But whether the instructions are given before or after closing argument, they provide a transition for the jurors. Up until this point, the jurors have observed the trial and been observed by others in the courtroom. When they enter the jury room, where they will deliberate in secret, they will no longer be observed by others. In addition, they will no longer be observers; rather, they will be active participants in their own deliberations. They will decide how to organize their deliberations, how to ensure participation, and how to complete the task that they have been assigned. The judge's instructions, read aloud in the public setting of the courtroom, signal to jurors the seriousness of their task. However, once they begin their deliberations, they will transition from being told

[38] In some courtrooms, the judge also will have given jurors preliminary instructions as well as instructions on a need-to-know basis.

[39] *See, e.g.*, IPI, *supra* note 88 (Ch. 2), § 1.01(C) (Cautionary Instructions (After Closing)).

what to do by the judge to deciding for themselves how best to proceed. Thus, they also need to understand the substance of the instructions.

## STEPS JUDGES CAN TAKE TO ENSURE THAT INSTRUCTIONS HELP TRANSFORM CITIZENS INTO JURORS

The transformation view recognizes that jurors sit together in the jury box listening to the judge read the instructions aloud to prepare them to perform a group task for which they will share responsibility as members of the group. As the jurors hear the instructions from the judge, they see before them the parties who will be affected by their verdict. The parties' presence makes the jurors acutely aware of the enormity of the task that awaits them when they enter the jury room and begin their deliberations.

The instructions, read aloud in this public manner, convey an important message about the group endeavor, but this lengthy lecture is unlikely to be the best way to communicate complicated information to a diverse group of citizens who are likely to have a wide range of learning styles. Given that jurors are drawn from different backgrounds and have different learning styles, they do not all enter the courtroom knowing the nature of their task. Jury instructions need to convey substantive information to jurors who have different ways of learning.

For instructions to contribute to citizens' transformation into jurors, the judge needs to take a number of steps in addition to reading the instructions aloud to the jury as a group at the end of the trial. The judge needs to impart this information in different ways, such as by providing preliminary instructions that give a framework for the trial, individual written copies of the instructions that jurors can read while the judge reads the instructions aloud, paper and pen so that jurors can write down their questions or confusions, and the opportunity for jurors to ask questions after the judge has read the instructions aloud. If jurors can ask questions immediately after the public reading and in a group setting, they are more likely to have a shared understanding of the instructions. These steps are not written in stone; different ways of reaching jurors are likely to change as modes of presenting information change. The key point is that instructions need to be accessible to all the jurors so that they enter the deliberations with an understanding of the task they must perform and the procedures they must follow. Armed with this knowledge, they can deliberate as equals and make sure that their perspectives are available for group consideration.

### Ensuring That Jurors Understand the Substance of the Instructions

In order to reach all the jurors with their different learning styles, judges need to present the instructions in a variety of ways. Michael Dann, a former trial court judge in Maricopa County, Arizona, drew from modern theories of education to explain that jurors, like all people, are likely to have different styles of learning[40] and the more they can engage with the new material, the more readily they can absorb it.[41] Researchers in other disciplines have long noted that human memory does not work like a tape recorder.[42] One cannot simply hear something once and play it back with perfect recall. Instead, one has to engage with the material in order to understand it. When applied to jury instructions, some jurors learn by listening to the judge read the instructions aloud in the courtroom,[43] while others understand the material if they can listen to the instructions and follow along with a written copy; still others prefer to listen to the instructions read aloud, to take notes, and to review the written instructions and their notes after the reading. The judge needs to read the instructions aloud, for the reasons described in this chapter, but he or she also needs to make the instructions accessible to jurors with a variety of learning styles. Judge Dann and the Arizona Supreme Court,[44] as well as reformers in other states,[45] have identified a number of ways to offer jury instructions so that they reach jurors who learn in different ways.

[40] *See* Dann, *supra* note 8, at 1241–42.

[41] *See id.*

[42] *See, e.g.*, Buckhout, *supra* note 53 (Ch. 2), at 23 (describing how memory does not work like a tape recorder, and suggesting that such a view, though widely held in the nineteenth century, is a "fallacy" that needs to be rejected because "[h]uman perception is a more complex information-processing mechanism").

[43] One judge dreaded the reading of the instructions because she knew that most jurors' "eyes would glaze over" as she began her reading. Jacqueline Connor, *Jurors Need to Have Their Own Copies of Instructions*, L.A. DAILY J., Feb. 25, 2004, at 7.

[44] Judge Dann was not the only jury reformer in Arizona. In 1993, the Arizona Supreme Court established a jury reform committee that issued fifty-five recommendations, many of which were adopted by the Arizona Supreme Court. *See* B. Michael Dann & George Logan III, *Jury Reform: The Arizona Experience*, 79 JUDICATURE 280, 282 (1996).

[45] *See, e.g.*, Marder, *supra* note 7, at 475–85 (describing jury reforms led by Chief Justice Ronald M. George in California, Chief Justice Stanley Feldman in Arizona, and Chief Judge Judith Kaye in New York).

*Individual Written Copies of the Instructions*

As the judge reads the jury instructions aloud at the end of the trial, each juror should have a written copy of the final instructions. Some jurors might choose to follow the written copy as the judge reads the instructions aloud. If there are words that jurors are unsure of as the judge reads the instructions, they can see the words on the page and they might recognize them. If they just want to listen to the reading of the instructions, they can choose to proceed in that way. Whether by listening or by listening and reading, jurors will have different ways to grasp the information presented in the instructions.[46] Some people learn best by listening to a presentation, some by reading the words on the page, and some by reviewing the written words later on.

An individual written copy of the instructions gives jurors additional options. One judge, who has given each juror a written copy for many years, described a written copy as "wildly successful" and "an inexpensive, effective way to virtually guarantee juror understanding of the law."[47] After jurors have followed their individual written copy of the instructions as the judge read the instructions aloud, they can then take their individual copy into the jury room. This gives each juror easy access to the instructions and helps them to keep their deliberations grounded in the law. It also means that they can refer back to the instructions and do not have to rely on their memory.

*Note-Taking during the Instructions*

Another way that some jurors learn is by taking notes during the reading of the instructions, and ideally throughout the trial. Note-taking is a basic learning tool, as any student knows.[48] The court has only to provide jurors with paper and pens to make this option available,[49] though it could be updated with an iPad for jurors who feel more comfortable typing notes and reading them on a screen. In 1992, the American Bar Association and the Brookings Institution

[46] *See, e.g.*, JURY TRIAL INNOVATIONS, *supra* note 50 (Ch. 2), at 19 ("[M]aterial is better remembered when it is presented in several different forms than in a single form. Having the jurors both listen to and read the instructions should capitalize on this effect.").

[47] Connor, *supra* note 43, at 7.

[48] *See* Videotape: Order in the Classroom (Institute of the International Association of Defense Counsel (IADC) 1998) (depicting how students in a classroom would be befuddled if they had to learn according to the rules that jurors have to follow in the courtroom).

[49] Gregory E. Mize & Paula Hannaford-Agor, *Jury Trial Innovations Across America: How We Are Teaching and Learning from Each Other*, 1 J. CT. INNOVATION 189, 211 (2008) (noting that in more than two-thirds of state and federal trials, jurors are permitted to take notes and that "in the vast majority of those trials jurors were provided with writing materials").

wrote a joint report in which they described juror note-taking throughout the trial as "the most widely suggested reform for enhancing juror comprehension."[50] Although the report noted that note-taking was "far from universal,"[51] five years later a book on jury innovations described juror note-taking as "a widespread technique."[52] Note-taking went from a tool that judges and lawyers initially resisted until they had experience with it,[53] to a tool that became commonplace in many courtrooms.[54] By 2008, more than two-thirds of both state and federal trial courts permitted juror note-taking, and the vast majority of courts even provided jurors with the requisite writing materials.[55] Note-taking helps jurors to absorb complicated material,[56] such as jury instructions. It allows them to organize information, to think critically about it, to make connections, and to record thoughts and questions. An added benefit is that jurors who are permitted to take notes feel greater satisfaction with their jury service.[57]

Allowing jurors to take notes during the reading of the instructions helps some of them to understand the substance of the instructions. If jurors have an individual written copy of the instructions, they can take notes on that copy as the judge reads the instructions aloud. In this way, jurors can listen to the judge read the instructions aloud, see the words on the page, and make notes in the margins of their written copies.

Even if jurors do not have an individual written copy of the instructions, they should still be permitted to take notes during the reading of

[50] ABA/Brookings Symposium, Charting a Future for the Civil Jury System 18 (1992).
[51] *Id.* at 19.
[52] Jury Trial Innovations, *supra* note 50 (Ch. 2), at 141.
[53] *See, e.g.*, Larry Heuer & Steven Penrod, *Juror Notetaking and Question Asking During Trials: A National Field Experiment*, 18 Law & Hum. Behav. 121, 140 (1994) ("Both judges and attorneys were significantly more enthusiastic about notetaking if they had experience with jurors taking notes."); Leonard B. Sand & Steven Alan Reiss, *A Report on Seven Experiments Conducted by District Court Judges in the Second Circuit*, 60 N.Y.U. L. Rev. 423, 446–52 (1985) (reporting generally favorable reactions by judges and lawyers to juror note-taking).
[54] *See, e.g.*, Jury Trial Innovations, *supra* note 50 (Ch. 2), at 141 (observing in 1997 that "[i]n most jurisdictions, the trial judge has discretion to permit jurors to take notes").
[55] Mize & Hannaford-Agor, *supra* note 49, at 211.
[56] Jury Trial Innovations (2d ed.), *supra* note 93 (Ch. 1), at 127 ("The process of notetaking keeps jurors alert and interested in the trial . . . ."). According to some studies, handwriting, rather than typing, notes leads to more effective learning. *See, e.g.*, Perri Klass, *Writing to Learn*, N.Y. Times, June 21, 2016, at D6 ("[T]here is a growing body of research on what the normally developing brain learns by forming letters on the page, in printed or manuscript format as well as in cursive."); Maria Konnikova, *What's Lost As Handwriting Fades*, N.Y. Times, June 3, 2014, at D1 ("For adults, typing may be a fast and efficient alternative to longhand, but that very efficiency may diminish our ability to process new information.").
[57] Jury Trial Innovations (2d ed.), *supra* note 93 (Ch. 1), at 127.

the instructions. Note-taking at this juncture allows jurors to write down the main points contained in the instructions. They also can write down questions they may have, words they do not understand, or concepts they think the jury needs to focus on as soon as it begins its deliberations. In this way, jurors will not have to rely wholly on their memory. They will have their notes as a reminder of the judge's instructions.

Note-taking during the instructions has the same benefits as note-taking throughout the trial. It helps jurors to listen attentively,[58] to identify what they think is most important and to write it down, and to jot down their questions so that they can discuss them with their fellow jurors during deliberations. Some people learn by listening to a lecture, but only if they can take notes at the same time. Jurors are no exception. A recent study found that the act of taking notes by hand, rather than by typing, enhances the learning process.[59] The physical act of writing requires critical thought, selection, and organization in a way that typing does not. For some jurors, then, taking notes can be essential for understanding the information conveyed in the jury instructions.

### *A Notebook with Vocabulary and a Road Map*

Another way that jurors can master the substance of the instructions is with a notebook that contains legal terms used in the instructions as well as a road map or table of contents for the instructions. Arizona, for example, adopted a reform that allows judges to provide jurors with notebooks that contain information useful for understanding the case;[60] these notebooks could also contain a list of words that are useful for understanding the instructions. The notebooks used in Arizona courtrooms typically contain basic information, such as a list of the parties, lawyers, and witnesses, copies of key exhibits, preliminary jury instructions, and a seating chart for the courtroom identifying the participants.[61] The notebook is similar to the "jury bundle" given to jurors at the Old Bailey Criminal Court in London, England.[62] The jury bundle in a criminal case typically includes the indictment, any stipulations, and all of the exhibits, including photos, maps, records, emails,

[58] *Id.*
[59] Konnikova, *supra* note 56, at D1.
[60] *See, e.g.*, ARIZ. R. CIV. P. 40(f) (authorizing the use of juror notebooks); ARIZ. R. CRIM. P. 18.6(d)(2) (giving courts discretion to provide notebooks in criminal trials).
[61] *See* JURY TRIAL INNOVATIONS, *supra* note 50 (Ch. 2), at 110 (suggesting contents of notebooks); THE POWER OF 12, *supra* note 17 (Ch. 1), at 78–79 (same).
[62] *See* Marder, *supra* note 113 (Ch. 3), at 539–42 (describing jury bundles).

and transcripts.[63] It is useful for jurors in the United States, just as for jurors in England and Wales, to have basic information in one place. Before the judge reads the final instructions, he or she could add a page that contains legal terms used in the instructions as well as a road map or table of contents that shows the organizational structure of the instructions, which jurors could add to their notebook.[64] These basic additions to the juror notebooks would help jurors understand the instructions.

*An Audio or Video Recording of the Judge Reading the Instructions*

An audio or video version of the judge reading the instructions is also useful for the jury during its deliberations. Although a written copy of the instructions goes a long way toward reducing the number of juror questions about the instructions during the deliberations,[65] an audio or video recording can help jurors answer their own questions without interrupting their deliberations. Should a question about the instructions arise during the deliberations, the jurors can simply replay that portion of the judge's reading. They can stop the audio or video and discuss the instruction.

One reason that an audio or video is useful is that information is conveyed not just from words on the page, but also through intonation, facial expressions, and other body language.[66] Thus, jurors could glean much of this information from an audio or video of the judge reading the instructions aloud. The traditional way of answering a jury's question during deliberations is for the jury to send a note to the judge, for the judge to call everyone back into the courtroom, and for the judge to reread the relevant instruction. One of the problems with this practice is that it does not usually answer the jury's question.[67] Another problem is that it takes time and interrupts the jury in the midst of its deliberations and can deter the jury from asking other questions.[68] As one juror explained: "[E]very time we asked a question, we had to file into

[63] *See id.*

[64] *See* Diamond, Murphy & Rose, *supra* note 22, at 1597–98 (describing jurors' need for a road map of the instructions).

[65] *See* Connor, *supra* note 43, at 7.

[66] *See, e.g.*, Blanck, Rosenthal & Cordell, *supra* note 48 (Ch. 2), at 133–36 (describing the importance of a judge's body language and the messages it might convey).

[67] *See* BURNETT, *supra* note 39 (Ch. 1), at 91 (describing the judge's rereading of the instructions after the jury had sent him a note with questions as "answer[ing] exactly none of our questions").

[68] *See* SCOTT E. SUNDBY, A LIFE AND DEATH DECISION: A JURY WEIGHS THE DEATH PENALTY 49–50 (2005).

the courtroom, they brought in the defendant, they'd call in all the attorneys, it caused such a big deal, we just tried to resolve any further disputes on our own."[69] With a video or audio, the jury has the benefit of the judge's presentation, with all the subtle information conveyed by body language and tone of voice, without disrupting its deliberations. Some lawyers and judges have worried that jurors might give too much weight to this one particular instruction, but this is just as likely to happen whether the jury replays the particular instruction in the jury room or the judge rereads the particular instruction in the courtroom.

These different ways of presenting the instructions, in addition to having the jury listen to the judge read the instructions aloud, take into account that jurors have different styles of learning and will absorb the information in different ways. If jurors listen to the reading of the instructions, but also have the opportunity to follow a written copy of the instructions, to take notes as the instructions are being read, to review their notes and written copy during the deliberations, and to have an audio or video of the judge reading the instructions aloud that they can take into the jury room, they are more likely to understand the substance of the instructions.

*Juror Questions*

Another way to help jurors understand the substance of the instructions is to permit them to ask questions after the judge has read the final instructions aloud and to have the judge answer jurors' questions, to the extent the judge is permitted to do so. If jurors can get answers to their questions, they will not have to speculate or make up answers during deliberations. With juror questions about the instructions, like questions during *voir dire*, it is useful for jurors to hear each other's questions and for all the jurors to hear the judge's answers. The jurors' group questioning of the judge will help to ensure that they have a shared understanding of the instructions. Having the judge answer jurors' questions about the instructions, though admittedly a practice that most judges have eschewed, would help citizens in their transformation into jurors because it would give them confidence that they understand the substance of the instructions. It would allow them to enter the jury room as equals insofar as they have heard each other's questions and the judge's responses to them.

[69] *Id.* at 50 (quoting a juror).

Almost thirty years ago, Judge Michael Dann suggested that jurors should be permitted to ask questions about the instructions after the judge read them aloud.[70] Some academics have recommended this practice as well.[71] So far, however, few judges have been willing to adopt this practice. When he was a federal district court judge, Judge Stanley Sporkin adhered to pattern instructions and was reluctant to deviate from the words on the page. At one conference, he explained that if he gave the instructions in his own words, Chief Judge Abner Mikva, who then sat on the Court of Appeals for the District of Columbia, would reverse him.[72] One judge who always gave jurors "a complete set of jury instructions in writing, with a table of contents to each juror before opening statements" was Judge Mark W. Bennett, a former United States District Court Judge for the Northern District of Iowa.[73] He was a federal judge for twenty-five years and permitted jurors to ask questions about the instructions without encountering any problems.

The practice of permitting jurors to ask questions about the instructions right after they have heard them is likely to be embraced by jurors, even though most judges and lawyers resist it. There are myriad empirical studies conducted over more than fifty years showing that jurors have long had difficulty understanding jury instructions.[74] Indeed, one empirical study involving former jurors found that they understood the instructions on the law less than half the time.[75] However, jurors who requested help from the judge performed better than jurors who did not.[76] One finding from this study was that "[w]hen the judge responded by providing supplemental information, either in the form of written instructions or by explaining the instructions in their own words, the jurors' understanding of the instructions reached fairly high levels (up to 67%)."[77]

70 Dann, *supra* note 8, at 1260.
71 *See, e.g.*, Diamond, Murphy & Rose, *supra* note 22, at 1607; Marder, *supra* note 7, at 501–02; Tiersma, *Asking Jurors*, *supra* note 19, at 146–47.
72 Fred H. Cate & Newton N. Minow, *Communicating with Juries*, 68 IND. L.J. 1101, 1111 (1993).
73 E-mail from Mark W. Bennett, U.S. Dist. Ct. Judge, N. Dist. of Iowa, to author (May 10, 2017, 07:06 CDT) (on file with author).
74 *See, e.g.*, Marder, *supra* note 7, at 454–58.
75 *See* Alan Reifman et al., *Real Jurors' Understanding of the Law in Real Cases*, 16 LAW & HUM. BEHAV. 539, 550 (1992).
76 *Id.* at 551.
77 *Id.*

In a related area, some courts allow jurors to submit written questions for witnesses via the judge.[78] Jurors appreciate the opportunity to submit written questions to witnesses, even if they do not have many questions.[79] Jurors are likely to feel the same way about having the opportunity to ask questions about the instructions. Interestingly, lawyers and judges often oppose the idea of having jurors submit written questions to witnesses, but once they have experience with the practice, they usually like it.[80] The same is likely to be the case when judges and lawyers have experience with jurors asking questions about the instructions.

One prosecutor described that moment in the trial after the instructions have been read aloud but before the jury begins its deliberations as "dangerous" because the trial participants have gone through the trial but the jury has not yet reached a verdict.[81] Judges and lawyers do not want to take any risks at that particular time. However, if the jurors submitted their questions about the instructions in writing to the judge, just as they do for witnesses, then there would be less risk in permitting jurors' questions about the instructions. The judge would have a chance to review the questions about the instructions and to consult with the lawyers before deciding how to respond, just as the judge does with jurors' questions for the witnesses.

One issue that lawyers and judges often worry about with respect to jurors submitting written questions to a witness is that jurors might not understand if the judge cannot ask the witness one of the questions that a juror has submitted.[82] However, judges typically instruct jurors beforehand that there might be some questions that the judge cannot answer because of certain legal constraints, and jurors understand that instruction.[83] If lawyers and judges have the same concern with respect to jurors' questions about the instructions, the judge can explain that the question is not one that the law permits him or her to answer. Jurors

[78] *See* Nancy S. Marder, *Answering Jurors' Questions: Next Steps in Illinois*, 41 LOY. U. CHI. L.J. 727, 727 n.1 (2010) (citing surveys of states that permit jurors to submit written questions to witnesses).

[79] *Id.* at 744.

[80] When lawyers and judges in Colorado and New Jersey had experience with the practice of jurors submitting written questions to witnesses through the judge, they usually had a positive response to the practice. *See id.* at 747–48.

[81] Marie Comiskey, Discussant, Panel on Cutting-Edge Developments in Juries and Lay Participation in Law, Law & Soc'y Annual Meeting (May 28, 2021).

[82] Marder, *supra* note 78, at 740.

[83] *Id.* ("Various studies, including an empirical study, pilot program, and interviews with jurors after the trial, suggest that jurors understand this instruction and follow it.") (citations omitted).

are likely to accept that explanation for why the judge cannot answer a particular question about the instructions, just as they do when the judge explains that he or she cannot ask a particular question of a witness. Indeed, Chief Judge Holderman, who was a federal district court judge in the Northern District of Illinois, participated in a pilot program in which one of the practices he tried was permitting jurors to submit written questions to witnesses via the judge.[84] He continued the practice after the pilot program had ended because he found there were many benefits,[85] and in his experience, jurors always understood if he could not ask the witness one of their questions because it sought inadmissible evidence.[86]

Judges are also reluctant to have jurors ask questions because they worry that any deviation from the pattern instructions might lead them to say something that could result in a reversal on appeal.[87] Trial judges' concerns are reinforced by appellate courts that continue to review jury instructions by parsing each individual written word, rather than by considering jury instructions from the jurors' perspective. An example of this approach is a jury instruction given by Seventh Circuit Judge Richard A. Posner in a jury trial in which he sat by designation as a trial judge.[88] He omitted the word "corruptly" in a jury instruction because he thought it was "surplusage."[89] During a pretrial conference, Judge Posner had rejected the government's instructions because he thought they contained "too much 'legal jargon.'"[90] With respect to "corruptly," he told the lawyers: "No one knows what 'corruptly' means. Then there's a definition, a person acts corruptly if he or she acts with the purpose of wrongfully impeding the due administration of justice. Well that doesn't help. You don't need 'corruptly.'"[91] Judge Posner was attentive to what a jury might understand; however, a panel of his colleagues from the Seventh Circuit, focusing on what the Supreme Court had said about the need for the word "corruptly" in *Arthur Andersen LLP* v. *United States*,[92] disagreed and reversed him

[84] Holderman, *supra* note 107 (Ch. 2), at 786.
[85] *Id.* at 787.
[86] *Id.* at 788.
[87] *See supra* text accompanying note 72 (providing an exchange between Judge Sporkin and Chief Judge Mikva).
[88] *See* United States v. Edwards, 184 F. Supp.3d 635 (N.D. Ill. 2016).
[89] *Id.* at 643.
[90] United States v. Edwards, 869 F.3d 490, 497 (2017).
[91] *Id.*
[92] Arthur Andersen LLP v. United States, 544 U.S. 696 (2005).

on appeal.[93] The Seventh Circuit explained that even if a trial judge thinks "an element may be confusing, ambiguous, or difficult to describe in terms that jurors will understand," the trial judge "must ensure that the instructions convey each element of the charged crime[, and t]he instructions here did not."[94]

Appeals courts need to review jury instructions from the perspective of the jurors. They need to remember that in some trial courts, jurors are not even given a written copy of the instructions, so they are unlikely to remember the particular words that are used in the instructions, including the words that are being challenged on appeal. In other courts, jurors are made to share one written copy of the instructions during deliberations. Whichever juror has the copy is likely to have more influence over how the jury interprets the words than the other jurors.

Even when jurors receive individual written copies of the instructions, they will not necessarily understand all the words. However, jurors, unlike judges, are not permitted to consult dictionaries. If they do not know the meaning of a word, they can send a note to the judge. The judge might not respond, or might reread the definition provided in the instruction (the one that the jurors said they did not understand!), or the judge might try to explain in his or her own words the term in question, but then the judge runs a risk on appeal. Appeals courts need to review instructions from the jurors' perspective and they should consider which tools the jurors had at their disposal; otherwise, jury instruction committees and trial judges will continue to write jury instructions that are geared to appellate judges rather than to juries consisting of lay people.

Permitting jurors to ask questions about the instructions also helps them in their transformation from citizens into jurors. If jurors are able to ask questions immediately after the judge reads the instructions or submit them in writing, they will be able to proceed to the jury room for their deliberations with confidence that they have understood the instructions. They might still find that as deliberations proceed, they think of new questions (which they can submit to the judge by sending a note from the foreperson), but at least they would have had their initial questions answered. The exchange between the jurors with questions and the judge with answers also means that all of the jurors hear all of the questions and all of the judge's responses. They will all

[93] *Edwards*, 869 F.3d at 500.
[94] *Id.*

have the same information about the instructions and will begin their deliberations on an equal footing.

## HOW INSTRUCTIONS ENHANCE THE JUDGE–JURY RELATIONSHIP

The judge can help citizens in their transformation into jurors, and instructions are one means by which the judge provides citizens with the knowledge needed to be a juror. Jurors eventually understand their role by observing the judge and by listening to his or her instructions. Although the judge and jury have separate roles to play, they need to work together and to understand that they are engaged in a partnership. The traditional view of this partnership is that the judge is all-knowing and the jurors are kept in the dark until the end of the trial when the judge instructs them before their deliberations. However, the judge and jury need to work together from the outset if citizens are to be transformed into jurors by the time they enter the jury room for their deliberations.

One way to view the judge–jury relationship is as an ongoing dialogue.[95] This relationship helps the jury achieve the necessary understanding to deliberate effectively and impartially. *Voir dire* lays the foundation for the judge–jury relationship by beginning the dialogue between judge and jury, as described in Chapter 2. Jury instructions can foster or impede the judge–jury relationship, depending on how they are given.

If jury instructions are to be part of an ongoing dialogue between judge and jury, they need to be structured differently than the traditional view provides. To begin with, instructions need to be given in a way that allows for more of an ongoing exchange between judge and jury than the usual practice. Rather than having the judge instruct the jury only at the end of the trial, he or she needs to provide preliminary instructions at the beginning of the trial so that jurors have a framework in which to place what they observe during the trial. The judge's preliminary instructions could also provide jurors with information about their role, the case, and the law. Empirical studies have found that instructions at the beginning and end of a trial help jurors to focus

[95] Dann & Logan, *supra* note 44, at 283.

on relevant evidence and remember it,[96] to follow the law,[97] and to feel more satisfied with their jury experience.[98]

During the trial, the judge should give other instructions as they are needed so that jurors hear the instruction and immediately understand its relevance. For example, before a police officer is about to testify, the judge should instruct the jury that the police officer's testimony is not entitled to any more or less weight because of his or her job. The police officer is to be regarded like any other witness, and it is the jury's task to decide how credible that police officer's testimony is.[99] The American Bar Association's *Principles for Juries and Jury Trials* suggests that courts should move in this direction. It calls for judges to instruct "[w]hen necessary to the jurors' proper understanding of the proceedings."[100]

When the judge reads the final instructions at the end of the trial, he or she should provide jurors with alternative ways to absorb the instructions, as described earlier, including an individual written copy of the instructions,[101] note-taking, a notebook page with vocabulary, a road map showing how the instructions are organized, an audio or video of the judge reading the final instructions, and the opportunity to ask questions after the reading of the instructions.

The ongoing instructions throughout the trial, as well as the final instructions at the end, supplemented by written copies, note-taking, and road maps and legal terms, will leave jurors feeling that the judge has kept them informed throughout the process. Jurors will appreciate the judge's efforts and they will try to follow the judge's instructions. They will do this even when they disagree with any of the individual instructions. The judge will have built up a reservoir of good will and the jurors will try to perform their job as responsibly as possible.

[96] *See, e.g.*, Amiram Elwork, Bruce D. Sales & James J. Alfini, *Juridic Decisions: In Ignorance of the Law or in Light of It?*, 1 LAW & HUM. BEHAV. 163, 177 (1977) (finding that instructions at the beginning of the trial helped jurors to focus on relevant evidence and to remember it).

[97] *See, e.g.*, Larry Heuer & Steven D. Penrod, *Instructing Jurors: A Field Experiment with Written and Preliminary Instructions*, 13 LAW & HUM. BEHAV. 409, 425–26 (1989) (finding that preliminary instructions helped jurors to follow the law); Saul M. Kassin & Lawrence S. Wrightsman, *On the Requirements of Proof: The Timing of Judicial Instruction and Mock Juror Verdicts*, 37 J. PERSONALITY & SOC. PSYCH. 1877, 1881, 1884–85 (1979) (finding that mock jurors who were given preliminary instructions were less likely to view the defendant as guilty than those who received no instructions or who received instructions only at the end of trial).

[98] *See, e.g.*, Heuer & Penrod, *supra* note 97, at 426 (finding that preliminary instructions increased juror satisfaction).

[99] *See, e.g.*, 1 LEONARD B. SAND ET AL., MODERN FEDERAL JURY INSTRUCTIONS: CRIMINAL § 7–16 (2021) (Law Enforcement Witness).

[100] AM. B. ASS'N, *supra* note 14 (Ch. 3), at 17.

[101] Diamond, Murphy & Rose, *supra* note 22, at 1594–95 tbl.6.

## USING THE JUDGE–JURY RELATIONSHIP TO PERSUADE JURORS TO FOLLOW INSTRUCTIONS THEY MIGHT OTHERWISE RESIST

Even when jurors understand the instructions, they might resist following them, but the judge–jury relationship, begun during *voir dire* and developed by ongoing instructions throughout the trial, might ultimately persuade jurors to follow them. They will have trust in the judge and will understand that judge and jury each have a role to play. They will try to fulfill their role because of what they have learned by watching and listening to the judge.

One example of jurors following an instruction because of their respect for the judge, even though they might disagree with the instruction, is the instruction that jurors must refrain from using the Internet and social media to do online research about the trial or to communicate about it online. Jurors, especially young jurors, use the Internet and social media around the clock. They might have difficulty accepting that they cannot do research or communicate online about the trial while they are serving as a juror.

### Instructing Jurors to Avoid the Internet and Social Media

A number of states and the federal courts have rewritten their instructions, taking care to be specific about the online communications that jurors must refrain from during the trial, and why.[102] These revised instructions are likely to be more effective than the earlier instructions, which simply told jurors not to seek information about the trial from any outside sources, such as newspapers, magazines, television, and radio; not to talk to anyone about the trial, including family and friends; and not to do any outside research about the trial.[103] Judges thought that these earlier cautionary instructions were broad enough to encompass online communications and online research about the trial, but jurors did not always see them that way. They did not necessarily know that doing a Google search or finding information on Wikipedia constituted outside research.[104] They did not

102 Meghan Dunn, Fed. Jud. Ctr., Jurors' Use of Social Media During Trials and Deliberations: A Report to the Judicial Conference Committee on Court Administration and Case Management (2011), https://www.fjc.gov/sites/default/files/2012/DunnJuror.pdf [https://perma.cc/5J6L-ULQ4].

103 *See* Grant Amey, *Social Media and the Legal System: Analyzing Various Responses to Using Technology from the Jury Box*, 35 J. Legal Pro. 111, 122–23 (2010).

104 *See, e.g.*, Andrea F. Siegel, *Judges Confounded by Jury's Access to Cyberspace*, Balt. Sun (Dec. 13, 2009), https://baltimoresun.com/maryland/anne-arundel/bs-xpm-2009-12-13-bal-md-ar-tmi13dec13-story.html [https://perma.cc/7V48-3GFE].

view an online search from a smartphone or laptop as doing outside research. After all, they were not going to a library or consulting an expert.[105] Rather, they were simply turning to Google or Wikipedia, which is what they do whenever they have a question in their private or professional lives, and what they assumed they could do as jurors.[106] Similarly, when a juror shared his or her views about the trial on Facebook or Twitter, they were not "discuss[ing]" the case with friends or family;[107] they were simply updating their friends and family about their day's activities on Facebook or sharing their impressions with their followers on Twitter.

A growing number of media stories recounting instances of jurors' improper use of the Internet and social media made it clear to some judges that the language typically found in the earlier cautionary instructions did not convey to jurors what judges thought it did. A number of state pattern jury instruction committees,[108] as well as the federal jury instruction committee,[109] rewrote their cautionary instructions to be more specific than they had been in the past. The state and federal committees revised their respective instructions so that the instructions mention the Internet and social media explicitly and give examples, such as Google, Wikipedia, and Twitter, of sources that cannot be turned to for information or an exchange of views.[110] For example, in January 2011, the Illinois Supreme Court Committee on Jury Instructions in Civil Cases revised its preliminary cautionary instruction so that it was more specific and included several examples:

> For example, you must not use the Internet, [including Google,] [Wikipedia,] [(insert current examples)], or any other sources that you might use every day, to search for any information about the case, or the

[105] *See also id.* ("But information that a decade ago was inconvenient for inquisitive jurors to learn is now at their fingertips . . . .").

[106] *See* John Schwartz, *As Jurors Turn to Web, Mistrials Are Popping Up*, N.Y. TIMES, Mar. 18, 2009, at A1.

[107] ILL. SUP. CT. COMM. ON JURY INSTRUCTIONS IN CIVIL CASES, ILLINOIS PATTERN JURY INSTRUCTIONS—CIVIL § 1.01[8] (2011 ed.) [hereinafter 2011 IPI] (prohibiting jurors from discussing the case with anyone).

[108] Some of the states that were quick to revise their jury instructions to address social media and the Internet included California, Connecticut, New York, Pennsylvania, Utah, and Washington. *See* e-mail from Jeannine Turgeon, Judge, Dauphin Cnty. Ct. of Common Pleas, Pa. to Pattern Jury Instruction List [PJILIST] (Nov. 21, 2011) (on file with author).

[109] *See* Jud. Conf. Comm. on Ct. Admin. & Case Mgmt., *Proposed Model Jury Instructions: The Use of Electronic Technology to Conduct Research on or Communicate About a Case*, U.S. COURTS (Dec. 2009), https://www.uscourts.gov/sites/default/files/jury-instructions.pdf [https://perma.cc/GH8Q-JGXX].

[110] *Committee Suggests Guidelines for Juror Use of Electronic Communication Technologies*, THIRD BRANCH, Apr. 2010, at 3.

> law which applies to the case, or the people involved in the case, including the parties, witnesses, lawyers, and judge.[111]

In general, the revised pattern cautionary instructions typically include a list of sources that are intended to be illustrative, not exhaustive, and advise judges that they should update the list based on new developments in technology and communication.[112] The instructions also try to explain to jurors *why* it is so important for them to refrain from online communication about the trial.[113] As social science research has demonstrated, "compliance can be measurably increased by simply adding the word 'because' and some type of explanation."[114]

The timing of this instruction to refrain from engaging in online research or communication is also important. This instruction needs to be given at the beginning and end of the trial as well as every time there is a recess throughout the trial and deliberations. Typically, the cautionary instruction was given at the beginning of the trial *or* at the end of the trial before the jurors began their deliberations.[115] However, if the judge simply gives this instruction at the end, the jurors might have been going online throughout the trial. If the judge only gives this instruction at the beginning of the trial, the jurors are likely to forget the admonition at some point during the trial, particularly if it is a lengthy trial. However, if the judge gives the instruction at the beginning and at the end of the trial, as well as before and after any recesses, the juror cannot say he or she was unaware of it or forgot about it.

Repetition of the instruction to avoid the Internet and social media is critical. One federal district court judge even went so far as to ask the jurors every time they returned from a recess whether they continued to abide by the instruction.[116] Moreover, he asked for a show of hands – an affirmative act by the jurors – indicating that they continued to adhere

[111] *See, e.g.*, 2011 IPI, *supra* note 107, § 1.01 [7]. The judge can decide which material to include if it appears in brackets. This instruction also contains a bracket with a note to the judge to add current examples. In the interest of full disclosure, I serve as the Professor/Reporter for this Committee, and have held this position since October 2003.

[112] *See Committee Suggests Guidelines for Juror Use of Electronic Communication Technologies*, *supra* note 110.

[113] *See, e.g.*, Susan MacPherson & Beth Bonora, *The Wired Juror, Unplugged*, TRIAL, Nov. 2010, at 40, 42.

[114] *Id.* at 42.

[115] *See* Dann & Logan, *supra* note 44, at 281.

[116] Then Chief Judge James F. Holderman, from the Northern District of Illinois, explained at the Allerton Conference that this was his practice and that he found it to be effective. *See* Panel Discussion, Social Media and Internet Use by Jurors During Civil Trials, Allerton Conference (Apr. 12, 2013) (notes on file with author) [hereinafter Panel Discussion on Social Media].

to the instruction during the break.[117] This is a useful approach and one that other judges should emulate. Repetition and a show of hands mean that the jurors know that they will have to respond in public before everyone in the courtroom. This act, similar to the earlier oath they took when they were impaneled as jurors, calls for a public display that they will adhere to the instructions, including the instruction that they are to decide the case only on the law and the evidence that they hear in the courtroom, and not on untested information that might be available on the Internet or on social media.

Some courts have reinforced this cautionary instruction by using visual displays, such as posters, brochures, notices, or cards, as reminders. This approach is similar to having judges reinforce the reading of the instructions by giving jurors an individual written copy, permitting note-taking, providing notebooks, and giving the jury an audio or video recording of the reading. A poster in the jury room, where jurors spend a lot of time, is one way to convey a message through words and images. One poster, commissioned by the Washington State Judiciary and later adopted by some federal district courts, is an example of images and words that reinforce each other and remind jurors to avoid communicating about the trial using the Internet and social media.[118] The poster, measuring twenty by twenty-four inches, is in the shape of a giant cell phone.[119] Although this poster includes more text than is desirable, it does at least highlight, by the use of font size, capital letters, and color, three rules for jurors: "Do not talk to anyone, or let anyone talk to you about the case"; "Do not receive or send electronic communications about the case"; and "Avoid outside information from the internet or other sources."[120] Another visual reminder that courts in England considered using was a card containing jurors' rights and responsibilities, including their responsibility to avoid the Internet and social media.[121] The idea was that jurors could carry this laminated card in their pocket, alongside their cell phone, so that they would have a tangible reminder. Although the card

117 *Id.*

118 Gabriell Butler, *Federal Judges, Courtroom Posters Say "No" to Social Media*, 95 JUDICATURE 240, 240 (2012).

119 *See* e-mail from Rick Neidhardt, Reporter, Wash. Pattern Jury Instruction Comm. to Pattern Jury Instruction List [PJILIST] (Nov. 21, 2011) (on file with author) (providing .pdf of poster).

120 *Id.*

121 *See* Thomas, *supra* note 111 (Ch. 2), at 50 (suggesting that courts in England and Wales provide jurors with written juror guidelines that they keep with them throughout the trial and that include instructions on why they must not use the Internet to seek or share information about the trial).

has not yet been put into use, some English judges distribute a jury notice that performs a similar function.[122]

## An Example of the Judge–Jury Relationship

The judge–jury relationship also motivates jurors to heed instructions. For example, jurors might follow the instruction to refrain from online communications about the trial, not just because it is repeated throughout the trial and reinforced through different mediums, but also because the judge has established a good working relationship with the jury and the jury has come to respect the judge. With such a relationship between judge and jury, the jurors are willing to abide by the instructions, including the instruction that tells them to avoid online communication and research about the trial. Jurors might not like the instruction, and might not be truly convinced that it is necessary, but they are likely to follow it because the judge has said that it is important and he or she has developed a good working relationship with the jury.

In 2012, Judge Amy St. Eve, then a United States District Court Judge in the Northern District of Illinois, along with her law clerk, and United States District Court Judge Matthew Kennelly, did an "informal survey" to ascertain whether jurors in their two courtrooms appeared to follow the instruction to refrain from engaging in online research and communication about the trial.[123] Over the course of 16 months, these two federal judges had 140 actual jurors complete a short survey after their jury service.[124] The central finding was that only 6 out of 140 jurors reported any temptation to communicate about the case using social media, and all 6 claimed not to have succumbed to the temptation.[125] The lesson the authors drew from this study was the importance of repeatedly instructing jurors not to communicate online or do online research about the trial.[126] They concluded that the survey showed that jurors will follow the judge's instructions.[127]

In 2014, Judge St. Eve, along with her former law clerk, worked with Judge Charles Burns, a judge in the Circuit Court of Cook County, Illinois Criminal Division, to expand and to update the

122 Att'y Gen. v. Davey, [2013] EWHC 2317 (Admin) 2317, Q.B. 348 [11], [13], [59] (Eng.).
123 Amy J. St. Eve & Michael A. Zuckerman, *Ensuring an Impartial Jury in the Age of Social Media*, 11 Duke L. & Tech. Rev. 1, 21 (2012).
124 *Id.* at 20–21.
125 *Id.* at 21.
126 *Id.* at 24–25.
127 *Id.*

2012 survey.[128] They were able to add 443 responses to the 140 responses collected in the earlier study.[129] Both judges used a model social media instruction during opening and closing instructions, and at various points throughout the trial in some of the longer trials. From the 583 juror responses from both studies, they found that the overwhelming number of jurors (520 or 89.19 percent) were "not tempted" and did not use social media to do research about the trial or to discuss their views of the trial on social media.[130] Of the small number of jurors (forty-seven or 8.06 percent) who were tempted to use social media, forty-five said that they had not succumbed to temptation, and the other two did not respond.[131]

The authors found from the juror comments that jurors refrained from using social media to discuss the trial – whether or not they had been tempted to do so – mainly because of the judge's instructions.[132] However, the judges also included in their article "the voices of actual jurors" and the reasons they gave for their behavior.[133] These reasons supported the view that most jurors take their responsibilities seriously and try to do a good job. The reasons also supported the view that the jurors did what they were supposed to do because of the judge. The judge had told them not to go online and they were following what the judge had told them. They kept referring to the judge as part of their explanations as to why they had not succumbed to temptation. They refrained from discussing the trial on social media because of the judge, or in their words: "[The] judge told us not to communicate," "The request of the judge," and "The Judge saying not to."[134] The two judges took these comments to mean that the jurors followed the instruction. However, another interpretation is that these jurors followed the judge. A number of the jurors involved in the studies were tempted to go online, but felt that they had to do what the judge asked them to do because the judge wanted to make sure that the trial was fair ("I respect the process") and that the jurors remained impartial ("I did not want to sway my opinion"; "Afraid I would be bias[ed]").[135] As one juror

[128] Amy J. St. Eve, Charles P. Burns & Michael A. Zuckerman, *More from the #Jury Box: The Latest on Juries and Social Media*, 12 Duke L. & Tech. Rev. 64 (2014).
[129] *Id.* at 78.
[130] *Id.* at 79.
[131] *Id.* at 79–80.
[132] *Id.* at 80, 83.
[133] *Id.* at 66.
[134] *Id.* at 80.
[135] *Id.* at 82.

explained, it is part of the role of the juror: "I was tempted, but my respect for the privilege of service as a juror to our Court System prevented me from doing so."[136]

Judge St. Eve and her coauthors were undoubtedly correct that instructing the jurors clearly and continuously on the issue of refraining from social media helped jurors to do what their role required, but judges also need to recognize the role that they play in helping jurors to act as responsible jurors. These judges spoke to the jurors throughout the trial on the importance of this instruction. They gave reasons for the instruction; they provided the instruction on an ongoing basis; and they explained to the jurors what was at stake for the parties.[137] In the end, the jurors responded by acting in accordance with the instruction, as well as with the judges' repeated requests that they abide by it.

The jurors' respect for the judge is important not just because it might inspire them to follow jury instructions with which they disagree, but also because the judge–jury relationship spans the entire trial. One prescient juror noted that the judge was "one key element to the successful melding of a group of strangers into a resonant orchestra."[138] This same juror observed that the trial judge in their case had "[a] genuine interest in, and immediate responses to [the jury's] needs and requests."[139] The juror appreciated the "complicated role the judge plays in simultaneously balancing all aspects of the trial so we can have the optimum climate to do our respective tasks well."[140] As to the judge–jury relationship, one judge wisely observed: "It has been my experience that jurors take their cues from the judge. If the judge conveys a feeling of genuine concern for the trial, as well as for the welfare and comfort of the jurors, the jurors respond with their finest effort to achieve the goal of true justice, regardless of the verdict."[141]

136 *Id.*

137 For example, Virginia Kendall, a federal district court judge in the Northern District of Illinois, explained to judges at a conference that she spoke to jurors throughout the trial about the need to abide by the instructions, including the instruction to refrain from discussing or researching the trial online or on social media. She told jurors that she, too, as a judge, had to resist those same temptations that she was asking them to resist. *See* Kendall, *supra* note 82 (Ch. 2).

138 JURY TRIAL INNOVATIONS, *supra* note 50 (Ch. 2), at 306 (app. 13) (Letter from a Juror in a High-Profile Case).

139 *Id.*

140 *Id.*

141 Takasugi, *supra* note 40 (Ch. 2), at 840.

## SUMMARY

The judge reads the final instructions aloud to the jurors sitting in the jury box, while everyone else in the courtroom listens; in this way, the instructions play an integral role in transforming citizens into jurors. The public reading helps jurors to recognize that they are members of a group and will have to reach a group decision. The public reading also ensures that all of the jurors have heard the instructions and have had equal exposure to them. A public reading of the instructions, during which the jurors see the parties before them, makes vivid the connection between the verdict they will reach and the real-world consequences it will have for the parties. As the public reading proceeds, and for as much time as it takes, everyone in the courtroom is silent except for the judge. The jurors know they are being observed and must sit impassively and attentively throughout the public reading. The jurors know that they must look attentive, and this might actually help them to be attentive. At the same time, the public reading builds support for the verdict – whichever way it goes – because the parties and the public see that all of the jurors hear the instructions from start to finish.

Although it is important that the judge read the instructions aloud, it is also important that he or she presents the instructions in a variety of ways so that all of the jurors with their different learning styles can grasp the substance. The judge can reach jurors with different learning styles by giving jurors an individual written copy of the instructions, the opportunity to take notes (either by hand or by typing on an iPad), a notebook page with vocabulary that the jurors will hear in the instructions along with a road map that indicates the organization of the instructions, and an audio or video of the judge reading the instructions that the jurors can take with them into the jury room. These supplementary ways of conveying the instructions are likely to change as new modes of presentation develop. The judge also needs to provide jurors with a group opportunity to ask questions about the instructions following the reading. This practice will ensure that jurors understand the instructions and will enter the jury room with confidence because they have all been able to ask their questions and to hear the judge's responses.

The jury instructions are also a key way for the judge to communicate with the jury throughout the trial in order to develop the judge–jury relationship and to provide jurors with an understanding of the trial so that by the time they reach the jury room they will be prepared to deliberate. The judge needs to give the jurors preliminary instructions so that they have a framework for what they will see, as-needed instructions to explain particular moments during the trial, and final instructions read aloud by the judge but also presented in a variety of other ways. These instructions throughout the trial will allow the jurors to feel that they understand what is happening during the trial and will help to build the judge–jury relationship. The jurors come to view the judge as a source they can turn to in understanding their role. When jurors encounter instructions they do not necessarily agree with, such as the need to forgo communicating or doing research about the trial online, they might nevertheless be willing to follow them because of the relationship that the judge has tried to foster between judge and jury throughout the trial.

By listening to the judge read the instructions to them as a group as they sit in the jury box and by having the instructions presented to them in a variety of ways so that they grasp the substance, the jurors start to develop a common understanding of the instructions as a group. The jurors will also begin to understand their role as jurors through their relationship with the judge. The jurors want to perform their job responsibly, and the judge wants them to do this as well. As one juror explained: "[O]ne could sense a determination on the jury's behalf that this trial should come out well in the eyes of everyone in court, and most particularly the judge's."[142]

[142] GROVE, *supra* note 32 (Ch. 1), at 96 (quoting former juror and foreperson Trevor Grove).

5

# JURY DELIBERATIONS: PERFORMING THE JURY'S MAIN TASK WITH SOME ASSISTANCE FROM THE JUDGE

After the judge has read the final instructions aloud, the jurors then leave the courtroom and enter the jury room, where they will conduct their deliberations. The jurors take on the challenge of deliberations as a group. They are supposed to apply the law that the judge has given them to the facts as they find them in an effort to reach a verdict.

The traditional view of jury deliberations is that it is up to the jurors to structure their deliberations as they see fit, and the judge must not intrude in *any* way. The traditional view assumes that the individuals selected for the jury were ready from the outset to undertake deliberations. According to this view, they know how to work together as a group to achieve a unanimous decision and they need little help from the judge. Although jurors do not always know how to begin their deliberations or what to do if they cannot reach a verdict, the traditional view, for the most part, leaves jurors to figure this out on their own.

According to the transformation view, citizens have, for the most part, been transformed into jurors by the time they are called upon to deliberate. Several structural features of the jury room help to complete this transformation, including that jurors deliberate in isolation, their deliberations are protected by the secrecy of the jury room, and, in certain cases, jurors are sequestered. These structural features, not found in everyday business meetings, help jurors to recognize that their deliberations are an out-of-the-ordinary experience that demands a strong commitment to the group endeavor. The unanimity requirement, which depends on jurors giving reasons for their views and requires each juror to vote and all jurors to agree eventually on the verdict, demands a level of group effort that most ordinary group decisions do not entail. In addition, the instructions help to transform citizens into jurors by trying to focus them on the evidence and the law, by ensuring that all jurors have this knowledge, and by making jurors aware of their need to self-regulate for the sake of the group.

The transformation view recognizes that when individual jurors are impaneled, they have unconscious biases (as all people do), that they might not view their task with the seriousness it requires, and that they might not know how to work well with the strangers who constitute their jury. However, the stages of the jury process, including deliberations, help to transform these citizens into jurors who perform their task responsibly. The setting of the jury room and the very design of the deliberations contribute to this transformation.

The transformation view also recognizes that the judge can play a role in assisting these citizens in their transformation into jurors without compromising the independence of the jury. Judges can give instructions that provide some guidance as to how jurors might begin their deliberations and what tasks the foreperson might perform, even while explaining that these instructions are meant as suggestions that the jurors are free to follow or to reject. The main point is that the jurors should not be left bereft of guidance when they walk into the jury room. The judge can easily dispel their initial fears. Similarly, if the jurors reach an impasse, the judge can invite the attorneys to present additional arguments on the sticking point for the jury, rather than delivering a charge that tells the jurors to go back and deliberate some more and that usually puts pressure on the holdouts to conform with the majority. Finally, if the jury indicates it has reached an impasse, the judge can also deliver an instruction on nullification so that the jury understands its power. Under the transformation view, the jurors need to understand the full extent of the jury's power, in contrast to the traditional view where the judge keeps this information from the jury.

## WHAT JURY DELIBERATIONS ENTAIL

After the jurors enter the jury room, the door is closed and they proceed on their own. Typically, there is a bailiff outside the door or nearby who is available to convey any notes from the jury to the judge, such as the jury's requests for exhibits or recesses or any questions the jury has for the judge.

The jurors are supposed to deliberate, vote, and reach a verdict. The vote and the verdict are the end result, but the mainstay of their work is the deliberation. In all civil and criminal cases in federal court,[1] and in all serious criminal cases in state courts, the jury must reach a unanimous verdict.[2] The requirement of unanimity makes jury deliberations central to the jury's task. In many cases, jurors will not be able to reach unanimity without engaging in careful, thorough deliberations.

After observing mock jury deliberations, social scientists have identified two styles of jury deliberations. One style, "verdict-driven" deliberation, is when the jurors walk into the jury room and take an initial vote.[3] As a result of the initial vote, two coalitions form, and jurors contribute facts or arguments to support only the side with which they voted. This style can lead to acrimonious deliberations as jurors try to support the position with which they initially voted. The jurors in the film *12 Angry Men* followed this style of deliberation, and their deliberations were, indeed, acrimonious.[4] The other style of deliberation, "evidence-driven," is when the jury delays an initial vote and instead goes around the table with each juror having the chance to contribute his or her recollections and points of view.[5] This style is likely to lead to more harmonious deliberations as well as to more facts and recollections being available for group consideration than in verdict-driven deliberations. This style also leads to everyone having participated, at least initially. Although a vote is eventually taken, it is only taken after all the jurors have offered their recollections and made them available for group consideration.

During deliberations, whether evidence-driven or verdict-driven, there is little structure that is imposed explicitly by the judge on the

[1] *See* Fed. R. Civ. P. 48; Fed. R. Crim. P. 31.

[2] *See* Ramos v. Louisiana, 140 S. Ct. 1390, 1397 (2020).

[3] Reid Hastie, Steven D. Penrod & Nancy Pennington, Inside the Jury 163–65 (1983).

[4] 12 Angry Men, *supra* note 1 (Intro.). After engaging in a verdict-driven style of deliberation, the jurors tried to switch to an evidence-driven style. They began to go around the table and have each juror give his reasons in an effort to convince Juror #8 why he should switch his vote and join the majority. However, they quickly started to interrupt each other and had to abandon their attempt to engage in an evidence-driven style of deliberation. Having begun with a verdict-driven style, it was too late to adopt an evidence-driven style of deliberation.

[5] Hastie, Penrod & Pennington, *supra* note 3, at 163–65; *see* Charles Hawkins, Interactions and Coalition Realignments in Consensus-Seeking Groups: A Study of Experimental Jury Deliberations 106–09 (Aug. 17, 1960) (unpublished doctoral dissertation, University of Chicago) (identifying two styles of deliberation, but labeling them "deliberating in unity" and "deliberating in factions").

jurors other than that they need a foreperson. In some courtrooms, the first juror seated in the jury box automatically becomes the foreperson. In others, the judge instructs the jurors to select a foreperson before they begin their deliberations. The jurors can use any method they want to select their foreperson. The foreperson does not receive any additional instructions as to his or her duties and must decide how best to carry out the role.

Another requirement is that the jury's deliberations are protected by the secrecy of the jury room; jurors cannot talk with anyone outside the jury room during their deliberations. One explanation for the secrecy of the deliberations is that it enables jurors to be candid with each other.[6] They can take a stance that might be unpopular with the public but that seems justified to them based on the evidence they heard in the courtroom and the instructions they are supposed to follow in reaching their verdict. They are not supposed to be swayed by popular opinion or to take into account information that was not admitted into evidence and tested through cross-examination in the courtroom in front of all of the jurors.

The secrecy of the jury room also protects jurors from outside influence or even jury tampering. There is a wall that exists between the jurors and the outside world when the jurors deliberate. The goal is for jurors to reach their own verdict and not be influenced by any outsiders. They are kept apart from all others while they deliberate. In some cases, the jury is sequestered, which means that the jurors are kept together overnight rather than going home. The court arranges for a sequestered jury to be transported from the courthouse to a hotel, where the jurors have their meals and sleep, and arranges for them to return to the courthouse the next day to resume their deliberations. At the hotel, they are under the supervision of the bailiff (or a federal marshal if the case is in federal court), who ensures that the jurors are not exposed to any media coverage of the trial.

## THE TRADITIONAL VIEW OF JURY DELIBERATIONS

The traditional view of jury deliberations is that the jurors enter the jury room and know what to do. They have observed the trial and the judge has instructed them on the law. They are then escorted to the jury

[6] *See, e.g.*, United States v. Thomas, 116 F.3d 606, 608, 618 (2d Cir. 1997) (describing the importance of the secrecy of the jury room).

room by the bailiff. The bailiff usually tells the jurors that if they need anything they should let him or her know; the bailiff will be sitting outside the jury room or will, at least, be nearby. The bailiff then closes the door to the jury room and the jurors proceed on their own.

In most courtrooms, the jurors will not have been told anything about how to conduct their deliberations.[7] The traditional view of deliberations is that it is up to the jurors to structure their deliberations as they see fit, and that the judge must not intrude in any way. The jury will be told to select a foreperson as soon as they enter the jury room (if they are in a courtroom that leaves this decision up to the jury). This will be the jurors' first act as a deliberating jury. Other than the requirement that they have a foreperson, the judge usually says little about the deliberations. The traditional view is that the deliberations are the province of the jurors and the judge must respect the jury's independence at this stage.[8]

The traditional view assumes that individual citizens are ready to deliberate without any guidance from the court. This is consistent with the traditional view of *voir dire*, which is that once the lawyers have weeded out the prospective jurors who they believe are biased or about whom they have doubts, those who are seated on the jury are ready to go. They are supposed to know what to do because the traditional view of jurors is that they are found, not made. This is also consistent with the traditional view of jury instructions, which is that jurors just need to hear them once at the end of the trial and they will understand them and be able to apply them during the deliberations. When it comes to deliberations, the traditional view is that jurors can perform their tasks of deliberating and reaching a unanimous verdict without any guidance from the judge on how to proceed when they enter the jury room.

If the jurors need anything from the court during the deliberations, the foreperson can send a note to the judge with their request. For example, if the jurors want to examine an exhibit that was presented during the trial, the foreperson can send a note to the judge and if there is no objection to the jury having the exhibit, the bailiff will bring the exhibit to the jurors in the jury room. Thus, even under the traditional view of deliberations, there can be some back and forth between judge and jury, but it is quite limited. It typically includes requests for exhibits or recesses, though the jury can also send questions to the judge. For

[7] *See infra* Chapter 5 (Giving Jurors Guidance on How to Begin Deliberations).
[8] *See, e.g.*, *Thomas*, 116 F.3d at 619 ("It is the historic duty of a trial judge to safeguard the secrecy of the deliberative process that lies at the heart of our system of justice . . . .").

example, if the jury has a question about one of the instructions, the typical response by a judge is to bring everyone back to the courtroom and for the judge to reread the particular instruction about which the jury has a question. The judge is careful not to stray from the words of the instruction because he or she does not want to say anything that might be cause for reversal on appeal.

## THE LIMITATIONS OF THE TRADITIONAL VIEW OF DELIBERATIONS

Although the traditional view of jury deliberations as the sole province of the jury ensures jury independence, it has serious limitations because there are times when the jury would benefit from judicial guidance. With all the instructions that a judge typically gives, he or she does not usually give jurors any instructions on what to do when they enter the jury room, other than to select a foreperson. Judges typically do not instruct jurors on how to deliberate; they do not even make suggestions. Even though this is the moment when jurors might feel uncertain about how to proceed, the judge, in accordance with the traditional view, does not offer jurors any guidance. From the jurors' perspective, then, the traditional view of deliberations leaves them woefully unprepared for how to begin their deliberations.

Similarly, judges are reticent to respond to any questions the jury has once it has begun its deliberations. The jury is permitted to send a note to the judge whenever it has a question even though the judge does not typically instruct the jury that it can do this. The jury might have a question about something that occurred during the trial, such as an instruction, the testimony of a witness, or some procedure that it observed. The jurors would have discussed the question among themselves during the deliberations and then found that they could not resolve it. They were instructed not to consult outside sources, including friends and family, and not to do their own research, including going online or using books or other outside sources.[9] Some judges resist answering the jury's questions.[10] Others respond by calling everyone

[9] *See, e.g.*, IPI, *supra* note 88 (Ch. 2), § 1.01(A) [6], [7] & [8] ("You should not do any independent investigation or research on any subject relating to this case . . . . For example, you must not use the Internet, [including Google,] [Wikipedia,] . . . or any other sources that you might use every day, to search for any information about the case . . . .").

[10] *See, e.g.*, SUNDBY, *supra* note 68 (Ch. 4), at 167 ("Adding insult to injury from the jurors' perspective, judges sometimes would appear to turn a cold shoulder when the jury asked them to clarify instructions or define terms such as 'mitigating.'"); Simon Romero et al., *Scrushy Jury*

back into the courtroom and simply rereading the relevant portion of the instruction or testimony, though such a rereading, as one juror observed, "answered exactly none of our questions."[11]

If jurors reach an impasse during their deliberations, the judge's response, in accordance with the traditional view, is again very limited. At this point, a jury will typically send a note to the judge and tell him or her that they cannot agree; they see no route to reaching a unanimous verdict, and they are not sure what to do next. In federal court, the judge typically delivers what is called an *Allen* charge.[12] States usually have their own version of this charge.[13] Essentially, an *Allen* charge tells jurors to go back to the jury room and to deliberate some more.

The *Allen* charge has been nicknamed the "dynamite charge" because it often leads jurors to reach a verdict.[14] It functions like a stick of dynamite and blows up the logjam. It might function in this way because it is hard to remain a holdout – a juror who votes contrary to the majority. Social scientists have found that when there is just one holdout or even two, the holdouts usually succumb to group pressure.[15] It is only when there are three or four such jurors that they have sufficient support to remain holdouts and perhaps to produce a hung jury.[16] Only in fictional accounts of deliberations, such as *12 Angry*

*in Deadlock; Judge Says Keep Trying*, N.Y. TIMES, June 4, 2005, at C1 (reporting that "the jury sent a note on Wednesday, asking that a portion of the trial transcript be read back to them," but it was "a request the judge denied").

11 BURNETT, *supra* note 39 (Ch. 1), at 91.

12 In *Allen v. United States*, 164 U.S. 492 (1896), the Court approved an instruction in which the trial judge "remind[s the jurors] of the nature of their duty and the time and expense of a trial, and urg[es] them to try again to reach a verdict." United States v. Anderton, 679 F.2d 1199, 1203 (5th Cir. 1982) (citations omitted). One scholar has called for the elimination of the *Allen* charge because it tries to produce a unanimous verdict when a hung jury would be the appropriate result. *See* SONALI CHAKRAVARTI, RADICAL ENFRANCHISEMENT IN THE JURY ROOM AND PUBLIC LIFE 39–59 (2019).

13 *See, e.g.*, People v. Prim, 289 N.E.2d 601, 607 (Ill.1972) (providing the language to be used by a judge in Illinois when a jury has reached an impasse).

14 For criticism of the *Allen* charge because it encourages holdout jurors to succumb to the views of the other jurors or because it fails to serve any useful purpose, see Huffman v. United States, 297 F.2d 754, 759 (5th Cir. 1962) (Brown, J., concurring and dissenting). For more recent academic criticism, see CHAKRAVARTI, *supra* note 12, at 39–59.

15 HANS & VIDMAR, *supra* note 65 (Ch. 3), at 110 ("Pressures to conform to the group are strong."); KASSIN & WRIGHTSMAN, *supra* note 9 (Ch. 2), at 182 ("The majority almost always wins."); Rita J. Simon, *Jury Nullification, or Prejudice and Ignorance in the Marion Barry Trial*, 20 J. CRIM. JUST. 261, 263 (1992) ("There were no instances [in the data from the University of Chicago Experimental Jury Project] in which one juror or even two held out against the other ten or eleven and then succeeded in persuading them to adopt their position.").

16 HANS & VIDMAR, *supra* note 65 (Ch. 3), at 110 ("It is only when a minority juror has initial support, in the form of other jurors with similar views, that the probability that a juror will sway the majority or hang the jury improves."); Simon, *supra* note 15, at 263.

*Men*, can one juror manage to turn around eleven other jurors to his or her point of view.[17]

Another point at which the traditional view limits what the jury can know is when a jury considers nullification during its deliberations, though few juries actually end up considering, much less engaging in, jury nullification.[18] Jurors might not use the word "nullification," but they might have reached a point in their deliberations when they feel compelled not to follow the law, even though the judge had instructed them that they must follow the law and the prosecutor would have made that point in closing argument.[19] Juries have the power not to follow the law, though the judge will not have told them this. In fact, in all federal circuits[20] and almost all state courts,[21] judges do not instruct juries on their power to nullify. In the Second Circuit, if any juror urges nullification during deliberations, the other jurors are supposed to know that they should send a note to the judge alerting him or her to this development; the judge can potentially remove that juror from the jury.[22] Of course, if the jurors are in agreement about nullification, this will not come to the attention of the judge, even in the Second Circuit.

However, if the jurors are uncertain about their power, and would like the judge to confirm this power, they will not receive such confirmation. Typically, a judge will tell them that their job is to find the

[17] HANS & VIDMAR, *supra* note 65 (Ch. 3), at 110 ("[*12 Angry Men*'s plot, in which one juror persuades the other eleven to change their vote,] makes for a gripping movie, but outcomes like this one almost never occur in real life.").

[18] *See* Andrew D. Leipold, *Rethinking Jury Nullification*, 82 VA. L. REV. 253, 259 (1996) (suggesting that the jury's power to nullify is "rarely exercised"); Nancy S. Marder, *The Myth of the Nullifying Jury*, 93 NW. U. L. REV. 877, 946 n.318 (1999) (same). It is difficult to conduct empirical studies on nullifying juries. The best approximation has been to examine the rate of hung juries, and infer that nullifying juries would constitute a subset of hung juries. Kalven and Zeisel found that hung juries occurred in only 5.5% of the cases in their study. *See* HARRY KALVEN, JR. & HANS ZEISEL, THE AMERICAN JURY 56 (1966). More recently, Hannaford-Agor et al. found that the average hung jury rate for the thirty jurisdictions in their study was 6.2%. *See* HANNAFORD-AGOR ET AL., *supra* note 35 (Ch. 4), at 25.

[19] *See, e.g., Frontline: Inside the Jury Room* (WGBH broadcast Apr. 8, 1986) (transcript at 7) [hereinafter *Inside the Jury Room* transcript]. In the case of Leroy Reed, which took place in Wisconsin, the trial judge did not instruct jurors as to nullification, but he did permit defense counsel to make the point in closing argument that the jury had the power to acquit even if it concluded that the defendant had violated the law. Defense counsel did not use the word "nullification" in his closing argument. *Id.*

[20] *See* Nancy S. Marder, *The Interplay of Race and False Claims of Jury Nullification*, 32 U. MICH. J. L. REFORM 285, 310 n.116 (1999) (providing cases).

[21] Only two states, Indiana and Maryland, permit judges to instruct jurors that they can determine the law and facts. *See* JEFFREY ABRAMSON, WE, THE JURY: THE JURY SYSTEM AND THE IDEAL OF DEMOCRACY 62 (1994). Although their state constitutions provide for this right, their judiciaries have narrowed this right through case law. *See* Marder, *supra* note 20, at 310 n.116 (providing cases).

[22] United States v. Thomas, 116 F.3d 606, 617-18 (2d Cir. 1997).

facts and apply the law as the judge has given it to them; their job is not to question the law. The judge might also remind them of the oath they took to follow the law. Although jurors do take such an oath and the judge does instruct them that they must follow the law, and does not tell them about the jury's power to nullify, juries do in fact have this power. They just have to know about it from some source other than the judge.

The traditional view of deliberations leaves jurors in the dark in a number of ways, and this can lead them to feel frustration. Jurors do not receive any instructions on how to begin their deliberations or what the role of the foreperson is. When they have a question and send a note to the judge, he or she does not always answer their question or explain when the law does not permit him or her to answer it. Sometimes the judge simply does not respond; other times, the judge just rereads the very instruction that the jury said it did not understand. Jurors do not receive much guidance when they reach an impasse, other than being told to return to the jury room and continue their deliberations. If they struggle because they are not sure about the extent of their power as a jury, the judge does not instruct them on nullification. These omissions, which are part of the traditional view of deliberations, leave jurors struggling when judicial guidance would be useful.

## HOW JURY DELIBERATIONS TRANSFORM CITIZENS INTO JURORS

Jury deliberations have certain structural features that help transform citizens into jurors who are able to work together as a jury. For most jurors, deliberations are unlike any previous decision-making experience they have had. However, the structural features of the deliberations help jurors to work together as a group, to take their task seriously, to scrutinize the evidence carefully, to listen closely to each other, and to try hard to reach a unanimous verdict based on reasons that they articulate to the group.

One structural feature that helps jurors to see themselves as part of a group is the jury's isolation. The jurors are kept together in the jury room throughout their deliberations and are kept apart from everyone else. This isolation reinforces the jurors' group identity. Moreover, the jurors constitute an unusual kind of group insofar as they are supposed to speak to each other candidly. Everything they say during their deliberations is protected by the secrecy of the jury room. Their isolation in a jury room helps them to maintain their focus; they are to do nothing else but deliberate. It also protects them from outside influences and distractions. Their isolation can be even more complete if the jury is sequestered, meaning that the jurors do not return to their homes and families at night. This added isolation is necessary in some cases so that the jury will not be influenced by outside views, including those of the media covering a high-profile trial or of any others who seek to influence the verdict.

There are also several structural features that ensure that the jury engages in a careful and thorough deliberation. One such feature is that the jury must have a foreperson. Although the foreperson does not receive any guidance as to how to perform this role, a foreperson who considers the group dynamics and tries to ensure that everyone has a chance to speak and that everyone listens to what the others say will serve as a model for the other jurors as to how to put the needs of the group first.

Another structural feature is that the jurors have instructions to follow. They might not understand all of the instructions, but they know that their deliberations are to be grounded in the instructions. The instructions anchor their deliberations. The instructions also ensure that the jurors start their deliberations as equals in that they have all heard the instructions read aloud by the judge in open court.

Yet another structural feature is that the jurors need to engage in a particular type of deliberation in which they give reasons for their views. It is not enough simply to announce their views; they need to explain them, particularly if they want to persuade other jurors to see the evidence the way they do. In addition, they must cast a vote whenever a vote is called for by the foreperson. The unanimity requirement imposes a formidable structure on the deliberations. The jurors need to listen to each other, particularly to those jurors who do not agree with the majority. If the majority ignores any dissenting jurors, it is unlikely that the jury will reach a unanimous verdict; instead, it will become a hung jury.

These structural features, which encourage certain behaviors in the jurors, help them to understand that they are being called upon to make a decision that is quite out of the ordinary. It is a decision that can have momentous consequences for the parties and the community. The structural features also slow down their deliberations. Having to reach a unanimous verdict means that they must listen to dissenting jurors and try to persuade them to see the case in a different way. Having a diverse jury might also slow down the deliberations because it means that people from different backgrounds, experiences, and perspectives, who might start out from different positions, still need to come together and reach the same result in the case. Although these structural features might lengthen the deliberations, they help to ensure that jurors listen to each other and give careful consideration to an array of points of view.

### The Isolation and Secrecy of the Jury Room

The isolation of the jury room signals to the jurors that they must work together as a group. They leave the public courtroom at the end of the trial and go into the privacy of the jury room where they will conduct their deliberations. When they enter the jury room, the bailiff accompanies them. The bailiff makes sure that all the jurors are present, explains that if they need anything they should let the bailiff know, and then the bailiff leaves, closing the door behind him or her. This isolation of the jurors in the jury room is made more dramatic when the bailiff locks the door, as is done at the Old Bailey Criminal Court in London,[23] or as was done in the film *12 Angry Men*.[24]

It is significant that the jurors have their own room apart from everyone else in the courtroom in which to conduct their deliberations. They have only each other to turn to as they begin. The physical isolation that the jury room affords them also signals that they will have to depend on each other as they try to figure out how to proceed. On the one hand, how to begin seems like a daunting task. On the other hand, it means that they will finally have the opportunity to discuss the case. They have sat through the trial together, and yet, the judge had instructed them not to discuss the case with anyone, including their fellow jurors. With the beginning of the deliberations, however, they are finally at liberty to discuss the case with each other.

The isolation and the starkness of the jury room also ensure that when the jurors are in that room, they focus entirely on their deliberations. No other distractions are available or permissible. The jury room typically consists of a table and chairs for the jurors. There might be water, paper and pens, and an adjoining restroom, but otherwise not much else. The claustrophobic jury room in *12 Angry Men* provides a typical example, though that jury room at least had windows (though

[23] Grove, *supra* note 32 (Ch. 1), at 176 ("We ... were led back to our cheerless jury room.... Then the ushers [who look after the jury] withdrew and locked the door.").

[24] Rose, *supra* note 65 (Ch. 2), at 165 ("[The guard] exits, closing the door .... We hear the lock click.").

they were hard to open) and a rickety fan that did not provide much relief from the heat of a summer day in New York City.[25] If deliberating jurors need a break, they must send a note to the judge with their request. Even if jurors are accustomed to attending meetings or collaborating in groups as part of their work lives, it is rare to have the kind of isolation that jurors experience during their deliberations. There are no colleagues or computer screens competing for their attention. They can focus, without interruption, on their deliberations. Unlike work meetings that have a set amount of time, they will deliberate until they are done. Their task is so important that there is no predetermined end point.

The jury room, unlike other rooms where a work meeting might take place, is also protected by secrecy. While jurors are deliberating, they are not allowed to discuss what is said in the jury room with anyone outside the jury room, including family and friends. What is said in the jury room stays in the jury room, at least until the jury is dismissed, and even longer in some states.[26] The secrecy of the jury room means that jurors are free to express their views candidly with each other. They do not have to worry about how their views will be received outside because their views are to remain inside the jury room. Thus, the secrecy of the jury room allows jurors to engage in a candid exchange that is rare in other settings.

During deliberations, the secrecy of the jury room not only protects what jurors say to each other, but also protects them from outside influences. The jurors are not allowed to reveal what they or any other jurors said in the jury room and they are not permitted to speak about the case to anyone outside the jury room. The isolation of the jury room and the secrecy of the jury deliberations are intended to allow the jurors to deliberate freely and to keep the jurors beyond the reach of outsiders who might seek to influence their views or their votes.

Isolated in the jury room and protected by its secrecy, jurors are with fellow jurors about whom they know something, but not that much. They are a group of disparate individuals brought together to perform one extremely important task. The isolation and secrecy of the jury room might also enable them to speak freely and not have to worry about conforming to certain expectations that they would encounter if they were deliberating with friends or acquaintances. They do not

[25] 12 ANGRY MEN, *supra* note 1 (Intro.).

[26] *See, e.g.*, CONN. FED. LOC. CT. R. 83.5(1)(b) ("Jurors may only speak or write about their own participation in the trial. [They] may not discuss the deliberations of the jury, votes of the jury, or the actions or comments of any other juror.").

know each other very well, and much like people who are seated next to each other on an airplane and are able to speak freely because they will not see each other again, the jurors come together to perform one task and will then go their separate ways.

**Reinforced Isolation through Sequestration**

When a case is high profile and therefore likely to attract a lot of media coverage, or if there are concerns that outsiders might try to influence the jury's verdict, the judge can have the jury sequestered. As explained earlier, this means that the jury remains under the supervision of the court. Sequestered jurors stay together in a hotel for the duration of a trial, rather than returning to their homes and families every night after the trial. They are taken by bus or van from the courthouse to a hotel, where they are kept under the watchful eye of a bailiff or marshal. They might room with other jurors and they have their meals together. The main justification for sequestering a jury is so that the jurors will not be influenced by media coverage of the trial or by friends, family members, or any other outsiders.[27]

This enforced group experience helps to transform citizens into jurors by focusing the jurors' attention on the trial, keeping them away from distracting or corrupting outside information, and reinforcing the idea that they are performing a unique role as a jury. Indeed, their role is so important that the state will pay for them to be housed and fed and looked after by an official of the court for the duration of the trial.[28]

Sequestration provides jurors with additional time together, outside of the courthouse, and helps them to get to know each other better, which in turn, can affect their deliberations. One sequestered jury in a high-profile case included a juror who had a lot of resources and connections in New York City, where the trial took place.[29] He was

[27] New York, which used to require all felony criminal juries to be sequestered, had a unique reason for sequestration. The court officers had lobbied the legislature to codify that requirement because they received overtime pay for supervising sequestered juries. The statute was finally amended when Chief Judge Judith Kaye sought a change so that sequestration could be limited to the trials that really needed it. *See* Sengupta, *supra* note 90 (Ch. 1), at A1 ("The principal opposition [to reform] came from unions representing court officers. Their overtime pay accounts for nearly two-thirds of the $2.5 million spent every year when jurors are put up for the night.").

[28] *See id.* (describing the costs of having court officials look after sequestered juries while they are at a hotel and being transported to and from the courthouse).

[29] *See* Kassin & Wrightsman, *supra* note 9 (Ch. 2), at 170–71 (describing the "social director" role of Juror Andrew Choa in the trial of John Mitchell and Maurice Stans on charges that they had conspired to obstruct a Securities and Exchange Commission investigation of President Nixon's reelection campaign funds).

able to arrange special events for the jurors.[30] He eased their feelings of dislocation and homesickness during a time when they could not be with their families. His informal role looking after the social well-being of the jurors gave him outsized influence when it came to the jury deliberations.[31]

In another high-profile jury trial, several social scientists served as early jury consultants and aided the defense lawyers who represented several religious leaders and activists, charged with conspiring to raid draft boards, destroy records, kidnap Presidential Adviser Henry Kissinger, and blow up heating tunnels in Washington, DC.[32] One of the consultants' roles was to assist the defense attorneys during jury selection. The consultants were worried that the defendants, who were being tried in Harrisburg, Pennsylvania – a conservative city – would not receive a fair trial. The government had significant resources and the defendants did not. In addition, the defense lawyers and consultants worried that the local community would not be open-minded when it came to protesting the Vietnam War, as the defendants were alleged to have done.[33]

The consultants advised the defense attorneys to consider which jurors might become friends during the long trial during which the jury would be sequestered.[34] The jury consultants were right that some of the young women of similar age would seek each other out during meals and their time at the hotel.[35] However, some of the consultants' predictions about which jurors would be open-minded toward the defendants proved to be erroneous.[36] In the end, several jurors became so vociferous in their views that the jury became a hung jury, and the judge declared a mistrial.[37] However, the government opted not to retry the defendants. In this case, the sequestration of the jury exacerbated the ill will that had developed among some of the jurors during the deliberations.

Thus, sequestration, which intensifies the group experience, can help jurors to reach agreement or to become fixed in their views. But either way, as difficult as it is for the jurors to be away from their

[30] *See id.* at 171 (same).
[31] *See id.* (same).
[32] Schulman et al., *supra* note 40 (Ch. 3), at 37.
[33] *Id.* at 39, 84.
[34] *Id.* at 44.
[35] *Id.*
[36] *Id.* at 43–44.
[37] *Id.* at 79.

families,[38] sequestration reminds them every day and evening that they are performing a very special task. They are to be kept apart from their families and friends so that they can focus on their task without any distractions. They are also to be kept apart from everyone except their fellow jurors so that they are not subject to outside influences. They are to reach their verdict based only on the evidence that was presented at the trial and are not to consider media coverage of the trial or the views of any outsiders, including family, friends, or those who wish to tamper with the jury. Indeed, seven of the jurors who were interviewed in the antiwar protesters' trial mentioned above believed that "sequestration was essential to their being conscientious jurors."[39]

**The Foreperson as a Catalyst for the Other Jurors' Transformation**

The foreperson is the first person who has to step into the role of juror during deliberations and he or she can set an example for the other jurors. The foreperson has to start the deliberations and to figure out how best to proceed. All courts require juries to have a foreperson. At the very least, it means there will be one person who takes care of the jury's administrative matters, from sending notes to the judge, to suggesting when to vote, to recording the votes. In addition to performing administrative tasks, the foreperson on some juries will become an influential juror who uses his or her position to make clear his or her point of view.[40] On other juries, however, the foreperson will try to take a more neutral stance and use the role to make sure that the jurors deliberate in an organized manner and stay focused on their task.[41] The foreperson who uses his or her role to ensure that other jurors participate in the deliberations and listen respectfully to each other will help the jurors to become engaged in the task of the group.

The foreperson can be selected in different ways. In some courtrooms, the foreperson is the first juror who was seated on

[38] As an example of how difficult jurors find sequestration, in the trial of organized crime boss John Gotti, the anonymous and sequestered jurors asked the federal judge if they could have conjugal visits, and the judge, after consulting with other judges, agreed that they could. *How Courts Care for Jurors in High Profile Cases*, *supra* note 34 (Ch. 1). The judge understood that sequestration imposes additional hardships on jurors: "They are removed from their families and jobs and are unable to share their experiences with anyone, until their obligations at the courthouse have been fulfilled." *Id.* (quoting U.S. District Judge I. Leo Glasser).

[39] Schulman, *supra* note 40 (Ch. 3), at 83.

[40] *See, e.g.*, KASSIN & WRIGHTSMAN, *supra* note 9 (Ch. 2), at 178–79 (providing examples).

[41] *See, e.g.*, *Inside the Jury Room* transcript, *supra* note 19, at 3 ("All the foreperson does is put[] his name on a document.") (quoting foreperson James Pepper).

the jury.[42] In other courtrooms, the jury selects its own foreperson, which is its first order of business when the jurors enter the jury room to begin their deliberations.[43] If the jury selects its own foreperson, it is more likely to choose a white man with status because those characteristics fit a common perception of a leader.[44] If the first juror seated in the jury box becomes the foreperson then that is likely to challenge stereotypes about who a leader can be. However, there is also the chance that the person selected will not want to be the leader or have the skills necessary to be a good leader; but there remains the possibility that the selected juror, in spite of his or her initial reservations, will rise to the occasion and fulfill the role well.

In an actual jury deliberation in Wisconsin, filmed by WGBH and broadcast on public television in 1986 as *Inside the Jury Room*, a male juror who sat at the head of the table (even though a female juror sat at the head of the table too) asked who wanted to be the foreperson, and the other jurors said that he should be the foreperson.[45] The person who sits at the head of the table and asks "Who wants to be the foreperson?" is usually asked to take on the role.[46] In *Inside the Jury Room*, the man who was asked by the others to assume the role of foreperson readily agreed. He said that the foreperson had a limited function; he mainly handled administrative matters.[47] However, this foreperson, though he did not dominate the deliberations, did make the initial suggestion that the jurors go around the table and give their views rather than voting right away.[48] Thus, he led this jury to adopt an evidence-driven style of deliberation, which set a respectful tone for the deliberations that ensued. With an evidence-driven style, the jurors might not always agree with each other, but they are more likely to disagree in a respectful manner than with a verdict-driven style of deliberation in which two coalitions form and jurors align themselves with one coalition or the other based on their initial vote.

[42] This was the practice of Judge Leonard B. Sand, a federal district court judge in the Southern District of New York, for whom I had the privilege of clerking in 1988–89.

[43] *See, e.g.*, *Inside the Jury Room* transcript, *supra* note 19, at 3 ("Let's choose a foreperson before we do any reading or whatever.") (quoting James Pepper, who became the foreperson).

[44] *See, e.g.*, KASSIN & WRIGHTSMAN, *supra* note 9 (Ch. 2), at 178; Marder, *supra* note 99 (Ch. 1), at 595 & nn.9–10 (citing studies).

[45] *Inside the Jury Room* transcript, *supra* note 19, at 3.

[46] *See, e.g.*, KASSIN & WRIGHTSMAN, *supra* note 9 (Ch. 2), at 178.

[47] *Inside the Jury Room* transcript, *supra* note 19, at 3.

[48] *Id.* at 8.

In general, the foreperson holds a unique position on the jury and is able to influence the dynamics of the jury deliberations. The foreperson can make sure that everyone participates. If there are jurors who dominate the discussion and others who do not contribute, the foreperson can remind everyone of the need to participate and the need to listen to each other. The foreperson also can suggest ways to ensure that the jurors have equal opportunities to express their views. The foreperson might also need to step in when the discussion becomes heated. Although the judge does not usually give the foreperson this information, except in general terms, the foreperson could discover this role, especially if he or she is accustomed to leading groups in his or her work life. If the foreperson does not play this role and some jurors dominate and prevent others from speaking, the jury will not have the benefit of twelve jurors' points of view. In addition, the jury experience is likely to be an unpleasant one for all the jurors. The jurors might still accomplish their task and reach a verdict, but they will leave having had a frustrating deliberation.[49]

Thus, the foreperson is the first juror who has to assume his or her role during the deliberations and ensure that the jury engages in a careful and thoughtful deliberation. The foreperson has to play this role even if he or she has qualms about performing it well. A foreperson who is organized and attuned to group dynamics can help the jury function as a group by keeping it on task and by thinking about all of the jurors and whether they are engaged in the deliberations. The foreperson has to put the needs of the jury above his or her own needs. All of the jurors will have to learn to do this, but the foreperson has to do it from the outset of the deliberations, and if the foreperson does this well, he or she can serve as a model for the other jurors.

### Instructions as a Constraint on Deliberations

Juries are constrained during deliberations by their instructions. They are supposed to conduct their deliberations in accordance with the law and other instructions that the judge has read aloud to them in open

[49] *See, e.g.*, *Female Jurors Assert Sexism Hurt Menendez Deliberations*, N.Y. TIMES, Jan. 31, 1994, at A13, https://www.nytimes.com/1994/01/31/us/female-jurors-assert-sexism-hurt-menendez-deliberations.html [https://perma.cc/43YF-NJUH] ("It was hostile in there .... There were insults, sexual comments. They [the male jurors] tried to outshout us.") (quoting Tracy Miller, a female juror in the trial of Erik and Lyle Menendez); *Woman Juror: Men Bullied Her to Convict*, L.A. DAILY J., Jan. 4, 1994, at 3 ("A female juror who voted to convict a man of bank robbery now contends she was bullied by nine male jurors into changing her position in a case of alleged gender bias.").

court. They have to decide the case based on the evidence presented in the courtroom and they have to convince each other based on reasons that they articulate during their deliberations. In some courtrooms, jurors are given individual written copies of the instructions;[50] in other courtrooms, they are given one written copy of the instructions to share among all the jurors;[51] and in still other courtrooms, they are not given a written copy at all.[52] In all courtrooms, however, the instructions can help transform citizens into jurors by providing them with the law that grounds their deliberations. Although jurors are most likely to be reminded of this constraint when they have their own individual written copies, the instructions help to anchor jury deliberations, to give jurors equal access to the law, and to help jurors self-police in the jury room at a time when they are beyond the watch of the judge or any other court officer.

*Instructions as an Anchor*

When jurors enter the jury room, particularly when they have individual written copies of the instructions, they are reminded that they must use these instructions to anchor their deliberations. In open court, the judge instructed them on the law. They need to follow the law and the other instructions as guideposts throughout their deliberations. For example, they need to consider the different elements in a criminal case and decide whether the government has proven each element beyond a reasonable doubt. They need to look at the evidence that the prosecution has provided and decide whether they find it credible and whether it provides enough factual basis to support each element of the crime. Their deliberations do not proceed willy-nilly, but rather, they are grounded in what the government needs to prove; what support the government has provided; and whether the government has proven its case beyond a reasonable doubt.

[50] Arizona, for example, provides a written copy of the jury instructions to every juror so that each can follow as the judge reads the instructions aloud to the jury. *See, e.g.*, ARIZ. R. CIV. P. 51(b)(1); ARIZ. R. CRIM. P. 21.3(d).

[51] As late as 2005, Illinois had provided the jury with only one written copy of the instructions to refer to during its deliberations. *See* ILL. SUP. CT. COMM. ON JURY INSTRUCTIONS IN CIVIL CASES, ILLINOIS PATTERN JURY INSTRUCTIONS—CIVIL 7 (2005 ed.) [hereinafter 2005 IPI].

[52] In some states, such as New York, courts do not provide the jury with even a single written copy of the jury instructions. *See, e.g.*, Terry Carter, *The Verdict on Juries*, A.B.A. J., Apr. 2005, at 41, 42 (reporting on New York's pilot studies, including giving jurors copies of the written instructions, and noting that these practices have been tried on an experimental basis but have not yet been adopted as accepted practices).

Even if jurors have different interpretations of the instructions, they understand, for the most part, that the instructions need to anchor their deliberations. All of the jurors need to make arguments that are grounded in the instructions. They cannot just offer personal preferences. They need to give reasons during deliberations, similar to judges' reasons in their opinions.

One study of an actual jury deliberation found that most of the jurors tried to use the instructions to make sure that all of the jurors made arguments, rather than arguments that were outside of the law that the judge had given them.[53] The study focused on a jury deliberation that was filmed by CBS and broadcast on television in 1997.[54] The case involved defendant Modesta Solano, who was tried for possessing and transporting drugs; the man with whom she had traveled had reached a plea agreement and had testified against her.[55] Ms. Solano claimed that she had not packed the suitcases for their travels and did not know that they contained drugs. Ms. Solano's case was heard by an eight-person jury in an Arizona trial court.[56] The jury took its first vote after forty-one minutes of deliberations; six jurors voted to convict and two jurors voted to acquit.[57]

Interestingly, the two jurors who voted to acquit had different reasons for their votes. One gave a legal reason; he said the government had not established Ms. Solano's guilt beyond a reasonable doubt.[58] The other juror, named Joe, voted to acquit because he did not think that Ms. Solano should go to jail while her partner went free. As Joe explained: "I was not going to do something that was against my beliefs and conscience and logic that would make me regret what I had done for the rest of my life."[59] The other jurors pointed to the instructions to try to convince Joe to give reasons that were consistent with the law. They did not accept that Joe wanted to go outside the law and consider fairness or his conscience. The majority insisted that Joe was free to disagree with the view of the majority, as the other dissenting juror did, but that he had to make arguments that were consistent with the law

53 *See* Matthew P. Fox, *Legal Consciousness in Action: Lay People and Accountability in the Jury Room*, 43 QUALITATIVE SOCIO. 111, 122–23, 128 (2019).

54 *CBS Reports: Enter the Jury Room* (CBS broadcast Apr. 16, 1997) (transcript at 31–58) [hereinafter *Enter the Jury Room* transcript].

55 *Id.* at 33–34.

56 *Id.* at 44.

57 Fox, *supra* note 53, at 133.

58 *Id.* at 118 (describing Juror 5's vote to acquit as based on the prosecution not having proven its case beyond a reasonable doubt).

59 *Enter the Jury Room* transcript, *supra* note 54, at 49.

that the judge had given them.[60] The majority kept trying to persuade Joe to reframe his argument. At one point, Joe appeared to do so, albeit reluctantly.[61] The majority was willing to accept his reason when it was based on reasonable doubt, but not when it was based on opposition to a minimum mandatory sentence.[62] At that point, the majority was willing to have the foreperson send a note to the judge indicating that the jurors had reached an impasse and could go no further.

After twelve hours of deliberations, the jury was declared to be a hung jury.[63] It is surprising that this jury became a hung jury, not only because there were only two dissenting jurors and it is hard for two jurors to hold out, but also because the two dissenting jurors had different reasons for their votes. One dissenting juror gave a legal argument, while Joe made an argument based on fairness. The other jurors were unwilling to accept Joe's reason until he rephrased it as an argument that was consistent with the law the judge had provided in the instructions. Thus, the dissenting jurors were not even able to stand together in terms of their reasons and to give support to each other. Yet, they were able to withstand group pressure and to remain as holdouts. Ms. Solano was tried a second time and the second jury convicted her after a mere forty-five minutes of deliberation.[64]

This actual jury deliberation from Arizona, though only one jury, nevertheless provides some insight into how jurors can use the instructions to anchor their deliberations. The majority in this case insisted that jurors give arguments that were supported by the law as provided in the jury instructions. Of course, not every jury adheres so closely to the jury instructions.

In *Inside the Jury Room*, an actual jury deliberation in Wisconsin, filmed by WGBH and broadcast on public television in 1986, the jurors began by focusing on the law as the judge had instructed the jury on it, but by the end of the deliberations eleven out of twelve jurors were framing their arguments according to broader concerns such as the role of the jury and the need to do justice.[65] Only one juror, a fireman, insisted that the jury needed to follow the instructions to the letter of the law. In the end, when he became the lone holdout, he succumbed to group pressure. He understood the other jurors' arguments, but he did

60 Fox, *supra* note 53, at 129.
61 *Id.* at 132.
62 *Id.*
63 *Enter the Jury Room* transcript, *supra* note 54, at 57.
64 *Id.*
65 *See Inside the Jury Room* transcript, *supra* note 19, at 23–24.

not agree with them. However, he did not feel that he could continue to challenge them. He said that he would not stand in the way of the eleven jurors who felt so strongly about their views.[66] He changed his vote, but not his view about how the law should be understood. He explained: "I will change and vote along with you to make a unanimous vote. But I will never feel right about it."[67] The instructions were the starting point for this jury's deliberations, but not the end point, whereas for the fireman, the instructions were the starting point and the end point.

The instructions remind the jurors that they are engaged in an unusual form of deliberation. They are to decide whether the party with the burden of proof has met its burden. The instructions are a reminder – a tangible reminder when jurors are given written copies of the instructions – that the deliberations need to be grounded in the law. Jurors might view the instructions differently, but all the jurors on the Wisconsin jury began with the instructions. Some jurors, like the fireman, thought a literal reading of the instructions was appropriate. The other jurors thought a broader reading of the instructions was consistent with their role, but even they began with the instructions and then started thinking more broadly about larger issues like justice. Even those jurors who considered the larger issues of juries and justice did not think that they had abandoned the instructions. Rather, they had started with the instructions and then considered larger issues that developed from their discussion of the instructions.

### *Instructions as an Equalizer*

Another way that the instructions help transform citizens into jurors is that they provide all the jurors with equal access to the law and remind all of them that they have an equal role to play as jurors during the deliberations. Jurors come from different backgrounds, with different life experiences as well as levels of achievement and education. Nevertheless, when they walk into the jury room, they are all supposed to be equal as jurors. They each have one vote and they are each expected to participate in the deliberations. Most are lay people who are unfamiliar with the law. The foreperson has a role that could be used to exert more influence, but, oftentimes, the foreperson regards the role as simply entailing several administrative tasks. When these twelve

[66] *Id.* at 24 ("I will not hold out to hold up 11 people that are very strong in their feelings.") (quoting Juror Karl Buetow).

[67] *Id.*

citizens, drawn from different walks of life, enter the jury room they are supposed to assume their role as jurors on a level playing field. The instructions can be used to maintain that level playing field throughout the deliberations.

The instructions reinforce the jurors' equality in the jury room. Each juror has only to turn to the instructions to buttress his or her argument.[68] Even if the jurors do not have a written copy of the instructions in the jury room, they can still use the instructions, which the judge has read aloud to them in open court, to support their arguments during deliberations.[69]

In *Inside the Jury Room*, the fireman acknowledged that he did not have the education that several of the other jurors had, such as the English professor, the doctor, the computer programmer, and the psychologist.[70] Yet, he was able to maintain his stance, which was contrary to the view of the other jurors, and to use the instructions to defend his position, at least for a while. He was able to do this in spite of the other jurors' education and oratory. The judge had instructed the jurors that there were three elements that the government had to satisfy and one had already been agreed upon by stipulation. Once those three elements were met, according to the fireman, the prosecution had met its burden and the jury should convict. It seemed like a straightforward case. Indeed, all the jurors ultimately agreed that the prosecution had met the three elements. The fireman proposed a literal reading of the statute that the judge had instructed them on, but the other jurors thought a broader reading was more appropriate in this particular case. They recognized that defendant Leroy Reed, a convicted felon, was a man of limited intelligence who had wanted to find meaningful work and to contribute to society by purchasing a handgun and becoming a private detective, as he had seen advertised in a magazine. When the sheriff had stopped him outside the courthouse and told him to go home and bring back the handgun he had recently purchased, he fully cooperated. In addition, the jurors agreed that the law, which provided that a convicted felon

[68] *See, e.g.*, Refo, *supra* note 94 (Ch. 1), at 6 ("When there was a question about the law, someone would go back to the language in the instructions—we each had a copy—and find an answer.").

[69] Fox, *supra* note 53, at 124 (noting that "all [jurors] have equal epistemic rights to invoke this information").

[70] *See Inside the Jury Room* transcript, *supra* note 19, at 21 ("I don't have the education and the training to put myself into your class as far as being able to understand the human mind and how it works . . . .") (quoting Juror Karl Buetow).

should not possess a handgun, was "a good law,"[71] but eleven jurors thought it should not apply in Reed's case. They were guided by other considerations beyond the law contained in the judge's instructions.

Jury instructions also can serve as an equalizer because they require that all the jurors participate in order to make sense of them. Jury instructions are often difficult to understand.[72] They are typically written in legal language, and while they might make sense to lawyers and judges, they oftentimes make little sense to people without legal training. All of the jurors are needed to try to decipher the meaning of the instructions. The jurors need to work together, as part of a group effort, to figure them out. Different jurors might offer different interpretations and the jury needs to decide which interpretation is correct.

The instructions, then, allow citizens who entered the jury room as lay people, unfamiliar with the law, to work together as jurors, to parse the language of this seemingly opaque document, and to reach a new understanding of the instructions as a group. They decide on the meaning of the instructions and their applicability to the case before them through their participation in the jury room.

### *Instructions as an Aid to Jury Self-Policing*

Instructions also help the jurors to constrain each other's behavior for the sake of the jury when the jurors are beyond the watch of the judge. When the jurors leave the courtroom, they enter the jury room where they will deliberate. The bailiff closes the door behind them, and they proceed as they see fit. Neither judge nor bailiff can observe what they do. Several of the judge's instructions require the jurors to police themselves throughout their deliberations. For example, one instruction typically tells jurors not to do research or communicate about the case online and urges jurors to let the judge know if another juror violates this instruction.[73] Another instruction that some judges give explains to jurors that everyone – including judges and jurors – has implicit biases and jurors need to recognize these in themselves and try to resist them, and they also need to help other jurors to do the same.[74]

71 *Id.* at 22 (quoting Juror John Boly).

72 *See, e.g.*, Marder, *supra* note 7 (Ch. 4), at 454 (citing empirical studies showing that jurors have difficulty understanding jury instructions).

73 *See, e.g.*, IPI, *supra* note 88 (Ch. 2), § 1.01(B)[6] & (C)[11] ("If you become aware of any violation of these instructions, it is your legal duty to report this to me immediately.").

74 For Illinois' version of this instruction in civil cases, see *id.* § 1.08 (Implicit Bias) ("You must carefully evaluate the evidence and resist, and help each other to resist, any urge to reach a verdict that is influenced by bias for or against any party or witness."). California and

These and similar instructions that call for jurors to self-police during deliberations help to transform citizens into jurors – even when jurors are no longer under the watchful eye of the judge. Such instructions give jurors the responsibility to look after each other and to take action on behalf of the group even at the expense of individual jurors.

*Instruction to Avoid Social Media*

One of the ways that federal and state courts try to help jurors stay offline during their jury service is by giving instructions repeatedly about the need to avoid communicating and doing research about the trial on the Internet and social media, and asking jurors to report any juror who disobeys this instruction. Once jurors begin their deliberations, they are on their own. Thus, many judges will give this instruction before the jurors deliberate, every time there is a break in the deliberations, and when the jurors leave the deliberations at the end of each day.[75]

The court faces a particular challenge when jurors begin their deliberations. The jurors are in the jury room, and the judge is not. Will the jurors continue to abide by the instruction that asks them to refrain from discussing the case online or doing any research about the case on the Internet or on social media? Some states' instructions ask any juror (not just the foreperson) to send a note to the judge if they see another juror violating this instruction.[76] A number of judges who have participated in empirical studies that try to assess the extent to which jurors communicate or do research about the trial on the Internet or social media report that the main way they learned about jurors' use of online research or communication was when other jurors sent a note to the judge letting him or her know.[77]

The instruction to avoid social media, which calls on jurors to report any violations that they might see during their deliberations, alerts

Washington also have instructions to make jurors aware of the harms of implicit bias. *See, e.g.*, JUD. COUNCIL OF CAL., CALIFORNIA CIVIL JURY INSTRUCTIONS (CACI) 113 (2021) (Bias); W. Dist. of Wash., *supra* note 84 (Ch. 2).

75 *See* Holderman, *supra* note 107 (Ch. 2), at 788 ("It is my practice to remind the jurors at the beginning of every trial day and again at the end of every trial day about the need for them to comply with their individual responsibilities – to be fair jurors and not to seek or obtain outside information to help them reach their verdict. No juror, to my knowledge, has ever let me down.").

76 *See supra* note 73 (providing the version of this instruction used in civil cases in Illinois).

77 *See, e.g.*, DUNN, *supra* note 102 (Ch. 4), at 4 (acknowledging that 13 judges out of 508 judges who responded to an online questionnaire said it was difficult to observe jurors using social media and that they learned jurors had used social media mainly from other jurors' reports).

jurors to the problem and provides them with a step they can take if they see any violation. Although individuals use the Internet and social media in their daily lives to share what they are doing, to get answers to quotidian questions, and to do research whenever they have a question, jurors are not permitted to use the Internet or social media in any of these ways to get information pertaining to the trial. A practice that is commonplace in their daily life becomes forbidden in the courtroom and jury room. Jurors have to put aside their everyday attitudes toward the Internet and social media and follow the court's prohibitions.

Jurors need to assume their role as jurors, and this instruction, which they have heard throughout the trial and still might hear before and after every recess while they deliberate, reminds them of their role as jurors. Although the lure of the Internet and social media is strong, the instruction helps them to maintain their resolve and to make sure that their fellow jurors maintain their resolve as well.

This instruction reminds jurors throughout their deliberations that their verdict must be based only on the evidence that was presented in court and tested through cross-examination. Although most decisions do not require this level of care, a jury's verdict does. For this reason, jurors need to refrain from looking at the Internet and social media for information about the trial. They need to reach their verdict based only on the most reliable form of information available, which is information that has been admitted into evidence and tested through cross-examination. This admonition to eschew outside information and to rely only on evidence presented in the courtroom reminds them of the nature of the jury's task, which is to render a verdict that will affect the parties' lives in significant ways.

*Instruction to Recognize and Resist Implicit Biases*

Another instruction that asks jurors to self-police for the sake of the group pertains to implicit biases. Everyone has them, including judges and jurors. They are the shortcut judgments, based on stereotypes, that people make in their daily lives and of which they are unaware. However, in daily life the ramifications of shortcuts in decision-making are not as significant as they are in the jury room. If jurors decide cases based on their implicit biases, then defendants will be denied a fair trial. If judges do not provide jurors with any information about implicit biases, then jurors might be unaware of them.[78] If judges

[78] *See, e.g.*, *Understanding the Effects of Unconscious Bias*, *supra* note 103 (Ch. 1) ("Understanding that [implicit bias] can happen is an important first step in preventing it from tainting your decision-making process during a trial.") (quoting attorney Annette Hayes).

instruct jurors on implicit biases, it is unclear whether the instructions will change jurors' behavior. Results from empirical studies have been mixed.[79] It is also unclear whether jurors are willing to challenge each other on their implicit biases. Even in the face of uncertainty, some courts have responded by instructing jurors on implicit biases.[80] Other courts have coupled the instruction with a juror orientation film on implicit bias so that jurors hear the message in more than one way and at different points in the jury process.[81] Meanwhile, some courts have decided not to instruct on the issue at all.

In courts that instruct jurors about implicit biases, the instruction is typically given at the start of the trial and before the jurors begin their deliberations. In some courts, the instruction tells jurors to try to recognize and resist these biases in themselves and to help other jurors to recognize and resist them during the deliberations.[82]

An implicit bias instruction is another example of an instruction that helps citizens to be transformed into jurors. It asks jurors to challenge each other for the sake of the group. Of course, it is not easy to recognize an unconscious bias in oneself, much less to recognize it in another and to bring it to that person's attention. If courts do not raise the subject, then jurors might not know anything about it. Or some jurors might know about implicit bias and other jurors might not. An implicit bias instruction provides information to all the jurors. In this way, jurors can enter the jury room as equals, with the knowledge they need to conduct a fair and impartial deliberation. Even if all jurors do not make use of this information, some jurors can help lead the way. The instruction provides jurors with knowledge about human behavior that they might not otherwise have,[83] and gives them permission to broach this difficult subject during their deliberations. Jurors can use the instruction to make sure that all jurors try hard to avoid implicit biases. A juror

79 *See, e.g.*, Jennifer K. Elek & Paula Hannaford-Agor, *Implicit Bias and the American Juror*, 51 CT. REV. 116 (2015) [hereinafter Elek & Hannaford-Agor, *Implicit Bias*]; Jennifer K. Elek & Paula Hannaford-Agor, *First, Do No Harm: On Addressing the Problem of Implicit Bias in Juror Decision Making*, 49 CT. REV. 190 (2013) [hereinafter Elek & Hannaford-Agor, *First, Do No Harm*].

80 *See supra* note 74 (noting that Illinois, California, and Washington provide instructions on implicit bias).

81 *See, e.g.*, *Understanding the Effects of Unconscious Bias*, *supra* note 103 (Ch. 1) (providing Washington's film on implicit bias); W. Dist. of Wash. *supra* note 84 (Ch. 2) (providing Washington's instruction on implicit bias).

82 *See, e.g.*, IPI, *supra* note 88 (Ch. 2), § 1.08 (Implicit Bias).

83 *See, e.g.*, Jerry Kang, Nat'l Ctr. for State Cts., *Implicit Bias: A Primer for Courts* (2009); Elek & Hannaford-Agor, *Implicit Bias*, *supra* note 79, at 116; Elek & Hannaford-Agor, *First, Do No Harm*, *supra* note 79, at 190.

might not recognize an implicit bias in himself or herself, but another juror might, and might be able to point it out as constructively as possible.

The instruction on implicit bias reinforces my argument that jurors are made, not found. They must strive to be impartial throughout the trial and the deliberations. It is an ongoing process. Even though one is never free of implicit biases, there is the possibility that one can become aware of such biases in oneself during deliberations, particularly with the assistance of one's fellow jurors.

**Giving Reasons to Fellow Jurors**

Deliberations help to transform citizens into jurors by requiring them to give reasons for their view of the case. It is not enough just to have a view; one has to be able to explain and justify it. Jurors must engage in a deliberation that requires giving reasons. They must focus only on the case before them and they must give reasons to justify their views. Their reasons either persuade their fellow jurors or they do not. If they do not, they must look for other reasons or be willing to change their own view of the case.

Thus, this group endeavor can lead jurors to hold different views in the end than they held at the beginning. They can be changed by the group deliberative process. They might think of arguments that they never would have thought of if they were just deciding the case on their own. Or, they might still see the case the way that they did at the start, but through the group deliberation they recognize that there are other ways to view the case. The process of deliberating, and in particular of having to give reasons for one's own view and listening to reasons for others' views, can indeed lead to a transformation in how one sees the case and how one understands one's own role as a juror.

Deliberations can lead jurors to a new understanding of their role. In the actual jury deliberation filmed for *Inside the Jury Room*, one juror, a doctor, raised the issue of the role of the juror.[84] The judge had instructed the jurors that they were to "follow the judge's instructions and to reach a unanimous verdict."[85] At first glance, the case seemed cut-and-dried. The government had established that Leroy Reed had satisfied all three elements of the statute. Yet, as the jurors discussed the case further, the doctor raised the question whether the role of the juror

[84] *Inside the Jury Room* transcript, *supra* note 19, at 11.
[85] *Id.* at 3.

was really so limited.[86] Did the jurors just have to look at those three elements and interpret them in a literal way? Or should they give thought to the role they were supposed to play in deciding the case and whether it was part of their task to make sure that Leroy Reed was treated fairly and justly? As the doctor put it: "Has justice been done?"[87]

The fact that twelve jurors had to discuss the case as a group meant that the doctor could raise this issue, and say that he did not believe the role of the juror was to be a computer or an automaton.[88] If that were the juror's role, then why turn to thinking, reasoning people? Why not turn to machines? Several of the other jurors, including an English professor, a naturalist, and a computer programmer, started to see the juror's role with this broader understanding and to support the doctor's position.[89] Eventually, all the other members of the jury, with the exception of the fireman, saw the role of the juror and the role of justice as overriding questions for the group to consider.[90] The doctor, who had initially expressed his position with some caution, soon found that it was embraced by almost all the other jurors. Finally, the fireman too began to understand what the other jurors were saying, though he did not truly accept their point of view.[91] He voted with them, but still had reservations.[92] However, the group discussion had moved the fireman from someone who saw his role in a very limited way to a juror who now understood the juror's role in a broader sense, though he was still reluctant to embrace that broader understanding of the role. If the fireman had been deciding Leroy Reed's case on his own, rather than as part of a group, he would never have conceived of the role of the juror in this way. Similarly, the other jurors might not have reached this broader view of the juror's role, which they ultimately embraced, if they had not come into contact with the doctor who was willing to give voice to it during the group's deliberations. Even the doctor, who first questioned the role of the juror, might not have come to this broader conception of the juror's role if the other jurors had not added their support in response to his initial question.

The group deliberation allows jurors to reach insights that they would not have reached on their own. It also allows them to do far

[86] *Id.* at 15 (quoting doctor).
[87] *Id.*
[88] *Id.* at 11.
[89] *Id.* at 16 (quoting English professor).
[90] *Id.* at 23, 25 (quoting naturalist).
[91] *Id.* at 22.
[92] *Id.* at 24, 26.

more testing of their ideas than if they were making decisions on their own. One juror can make an argument, but other jurors can question it or raise a counterargument. In addition, jurors need to give reasons to each other and defend their point of view. When they can no longer give reasons, they consider changing their vote, as the fireman did on the jury considering the charges against Leroy Reed,[93] and as Juror #3 (played by Lee J. Cobb) did in *12 Angry Men* when he became the only remaining juror in favor of conviction.[94]

**The Unanimity Requirement**

The requirement that a jury reach a unanimous verdict, which is a requirement in all civil and criminal cases in federal courts[95] and in serious criminal cases in all state courts[96] also helps citizens to step into their role as jurors. Every juror has to accept responsibility for his or her vote and for the verdict that the jury reaches. In fact, in criminal cases in federal court, either party can request that the judge poll the jurors after the verdict has been announced so that each juror must say in open court that the verdict represents his or her vote.[97] Some states have this practice as well.[98]

In jurors' daily lives, decisions do not typically require everyone's agreement. In some work settings, for example, a manager decides. The manager might seek input from workers but still makes the ultimate decision. In other workplaces, a majority might be able to make decisions or set policies. In a classroom, the teacher usually decides. The teacher decides when assignments are due or how the course will be structured. Even in voluntary associations, such as charitable or religious work, there is oftentimes a hierarchy and not everyone gets an equal say. However, with a jury, this is not the case. Every juror gets an equal vote and every juror must agree with the outcome or else there is

93 *Id.* at 24.

94 12 Angry Men, *supra* note 1 (Intro.).

95 *See* Fed. R. Civ. P. 48(b) (providing that "the verdict must be unanimous"); Fed. R. Crim. P. 31(a) ("The verdict must be unanimous.").

96 *See* Ramos v. Louisiana, 140 S. Ct. 1390 (2020) (holding that the unanimity requirement in criminal jury trials is fundamental to the Sixth Amendment and applies to criminal trials in state courts by virtue of the Fourteenth Amendment to the U.S. Constitution).

97 *See* Fed. R. Crim. P. 31(d) (Jury Poll).

98 For example, in the jury trial in Chicago, Illinois, in which former police officer Jason Van Dyke was found guilty of second-degree murder and sixteen counts of aggravated battery with a firearm after he shot and killed Laquan McDonald, the polling of the jury was a dramatic moment in the courtroom. *See infra* text accompanying notes 101–04.

a hung jury. Since every juror must agree, every juror must be persuaded. No juror can be discounted or ignored.

The unanimity requirement means that jurors cannot just dismiss what other jurors say during deliberations because every juror's vote will be needed in order to reach a unanimous verdict. If jurors enter the jury room and take an initial vote, thus engaging in a verdict-driven style of deliberation, the jurors' work could be over if all jurors vote in the same way. However, with the unanimity requirement, if there is even one juror who votes differently, the jurors must engage in further deliberations until they all agree. The film *12 Angry Men* illustrates jurors' eagerness to vote and to complete their task, but in that film one juror, Juror #8 (played by Henry Fonda), voted in a way that was contrary to the other eleven jurors, which meant that the jury had to continue to deliberate. If a jury cannot reach a unanimous verdict, then there is no verdict at all. The judge will declare the jury to be a hung jury and the prosecutor will decide whether to retry the defendant before another jury.

The unanimity requirement means that all jurors must listen to each other and address every argument that is raised until they reach a consensus. A majority cannot dismiss a minority simply because there are fewer of them. Rather, the majority must engage the minority and listen to their reasons. The majority must offer their own reasons and try to persuade the minority to see the case their way. Every juror is integral to the jury's task. Having to reach a unanimous verdict with a group of strangers on an issue of grave consequence to the parties makes clear to the jurors that this is no ordinary deliberation. This is a deliberation in which the stakes are extraordinarily high and the jurors must take care with their reasons and their votes in a way that is not required in daily life. They need to give their reasons and persuade others or be persuaded by them.

No juror can be ignored because a unanimous verdict requires every juror's vote. It is significant that the jurors must vote, and not just say that they agree. When one has to affirmatively raise one's hand or write down one's vote on a piece of paper, an additional step is required; it is more than just expressing agreement or even remaining silent while others say they agree. Before there can be a verdict, there must be an actual vote.

This need for the jury to act as a single voice and to reach a unanimous verdict based on a unanimous vote means that citizens who serve as jurors cannot evade responsibility for the votes they cast.

They cannot blame the jury's verdict on someone else, as they might do in their daily lives. Jurors have to take responsibility for the jury's verdict in a way that they might be unfamiliar with in their work or personal lives. As a result, serving as a juror can be a difficult experience. After all, other people's lives are in the balance. As the mother of one young juror said, her daughter "had never before been forced to make difficult decisions like this."[99]

Once the jurors reach a unanimous verdict and return to the courtroom where the verdict will be announced, the judge can poll them individually to ensure that the verdict represents their vote. Even though the jury verdict is a group decision and the jurors do not have to give reasons for the verdict except to each other during their deliberations, they might have to say in open court that the verdict represents their vote. In federal court in criminal cases, the judge typically polls the jurors individually to make sure that they are in accord with the verdict.[100] The polling of jurors can also take place in state court.

The polling of jurors, who are seated in the jury box, takes place in open court before the judge, the parties, the public, and the press. It requires each juror to take responsibility for his or her vote and for the verdict in this public setting. This can be a dramatic and tense moment in the courtroom, as it was in a jury trial in Illinois involving Jason Van Dyke, a white police officer, who had killed an African-American man named Laquan McDonald.[101] The jury found Van Dyke guilty of second-degree murder and sixteen counts of aggravated battery with a firearm for each of the sixteen bullets he had fired.[102] It is "rare" in general for American police officers to be convicted in deadly shootings,[103] and it was rare for a jury in Chicago to convict a police officer of a criminal shooting, particularly when the police officer was white and the victim black,[104] but it happened in this case. During the

[99] Seth Mydans, *Juror in Denny Case Recounts Stress and an Obsession with Detail*, N.Y. TIMES, Oct. 27, 1993, at A18 (describing the daunting challenge faced by one young juror in the case involving the beating of Reginald Denny).

[100] *See* FED. R. CRIM. P. 31(d) (Jury Poll).

[101] WBBM, a local radio news station in Chicago, provided listeners with coverage of the courtroom when the verdict was announced and the jurors were polled.

[102] Mitch Smith & Julie Bosman, *Jason Van Dyke Sentenced to Nearly 7 Years for Murdering Laquan McDonald*, N.Y. TIMES (Jan. 18, 2019), https://www.nytimes.com/2019/01/18/us/jason-van-dyke-sentencing-html [https://perma.cc/AQM9-B76N].

[103] *Id.*

[104] *See, e.g.*, Megan Crepeau et al., *The Trial of Officer Jason Van Dyke; A Historic Murder Conviction*, CHI. TRIB., Oct. 7, 2018, at C1 ("The verdict marked the first time in more

polling of the jurors, everyone listened with bated breath. The tension and suspense in the courtroom were palpable. There was great relief once the polling had been completed and the judge thanked the jurors for their service and dismissed them.

The unanimity requirement reinforces the enormity of the jury's task and the contribution that every juror must make. The jury is charged with making a decision that has serious repercussions for the parties. The jurors cannot take this decision lightly. Every juror must vote for the verdict and be willing to announce in open court that he or she voted in accordance with the verdict. This public display of the juror's role puts pressure on each juror to think carefully whether he or she agrees with the verdict. Even when a juror votes with the other jurors in the jury room, the public polling gives the jurors another chance to make sure that they are in agreement with the verdict. There have been instances in which jurors have voted with the other jurors in the jury room, only to realize when they have to announce their vote in open court that they cannot support the verdict.[105]

Jurors have to vote in the jury room and reach a unanimous verdict and then they have to be willing to go into the courtroom and announce their individual agreement with the verdict in open court. The unanimity requirement, which comes into play in the jury room and is then repeated in the courtroom, reminds jurors that their task is an extraordinary one and their level of certainty and agreement exceeds what is required for ordinary, everyday decisions. Jurors know when they enter the jury room that they will have to reach a unanimous verdict and that they might be called upon to announce their agreement with the verdict in open court. These requirements of the deliberation – giving reasons, voting, reaching a unanimous verdict, announcing votes in open court – all help jurors to recognize that the deliberation they are about to embark on when they enter the jury room will call for a level of responsibility,

than 50 years that a Chicago police officer has been convicted of murder for an on-duty incident.").

[105] *See, e.g.*, Callaham v. United States, No. 19-CF-167, 2022 D.C. App. LEXIS 45, at *11–12, *15–16, *19–21 (Feb. 3, 2022) (describing a jury that had reached a unanimous verdict but during polling one juror disagreed; the appellate court held that additional anti-deadlock instructions were coercive in this case); Crowder v. United States, 383 A.2d 336 (D.C. 1978) (polling of jurors revealed that the twelfth juror dissented; because the identity and numerical division became known, as well as the assertiveness of the dissenting juror, the trial judge abused his discretion by not discharging the jury).

seriousness, and care that they might never have given any decision-making in the past, but that they must now give as jurors.

**Having Diverse Juries**

Diverse juries might make reaching unanimity more difficult, but having jurors from different backgrounds means that the jury has a broad array of perspectives from which to view the case. If jurors start out with different assumptions, and have to convince each other of their point of view, this can produce more thorough deliberations. It also means that jurors can learn a lot from each other. Although jurors' different perspectives might make it more difficult for them to reach a consensus, though the empirical evidence suggests otherwise,[106] at the very least, it can reassure the community outside the jury room that the jury reached a well-considered verdict.

When jurors come from different backgrounds, perspectives, and life experiences, they are likely to bring into the deliberation room different ways of viewing the case.[107] Such diversity can enhance the deliberations and lead to new group insights. The jurors, each with their different perspectives, might focus on different facts and pieces of evidence,[108] correct each other's mistaken notions,[109] broaden each other's perspectives, and suggest different ways of looking at the evidence. A diversity of viewpoints can lead to a more thorough, well-considered deliberation than if everyone agrees from the start. Yet, during the deliberations, the jurors must also try to reach a common understanding. They will have to challenge each other and be willing to rethink their own views. For a diverse jury to agree on a verdict means that the evidence was strong enough that jurors came to view

[106] *See* Valerie P. Hans, Challenges to Achieving Fairness in Civil Jury Selection, 2021 Forum for State Appellate Court Judges, Pound Civil Justice Institute, July 17, 2021, at 4 (describing a study of hung juries in criminal cases in state courts that found that "the jury's diversity bore *no* relationship to the likelihood of a hung jury").

[107] *See, e.g.*, HANS & VIDMAR, *supra* note 65 (Ch. 3), at 50 ("[A] jury composed of individuals with a wide range of experiences, backgrounds, and knowledge is more likely to perceive the facts from different perspectives and thus engage in a vigorous and thorough debate.").

[108] *See, e.g.*, HASTIE, PENROD & PENNINGTON, *supra* note 3, at 236 ("The group memory advantage over the typical or even the exceptional individual is one of the major determinants of the superiority of the jury as a legal decision mechanism."); *id.* at 81 (describing the impressive collective memory of a jury and noting that jurors remember 90% of the evidence and 80% of the judge's instructions).

[109] *See, e.g.*, Ballew v. Georgia, 435 U.S. 223, 233 (1978) ("When individual and group decisionmaking were compared, it was seen that groups performed better because prejudices of individuals were frequently counterbalanced . . . ."); HANS & VIDMAR, *supra* note 65 (Ch. 3), at 50 ("The jury's heterogeneous makeup may also lessen the power of prejudice.").

the case in the same way even though they might have started out with very different positions.

A racially diverse jury allows jurors to challenge each other's biases, and can even lead white jurors to engage in more thorough and careful deliberations than they would on a homogeneous jury by being more willing to discuss race-related issues. Psychologist Samuel Sommers has conducted a number of empirical studies examining the effects of race on jury deliberations.[110] In one study using mock jurors, he found that white jurors on racially diverse juries discussed more facts, made fewer inaccurate statements, and considered more race-related topics than white jurors on homogeneous juries.[111]

A jury that is diverse by gender also allows jurors to draw from different experiences to contribute in different ways to the jury deliberations. In the 1950s, there were a number of studies that showed that men and women played different roles on the jury, with men being more oriented toward the task and women being more oriented toward the social dynamics of the jury.[112] Of course, these studies were done in an era when many women were expected to stay at home and raise a family and men were expected to be breadwinners. These restrictive gender roles, though not as pervasive as they once were, have not disappeared altogether, nor have pay gaps – even when men and women perform the same jobs.[113] Even as women continue to gain entry to workplaces that were once closed to them,[114] they continue to contribute points of view that might be different from those offered by their male peers because of different life experiences. There have been a number of studies (not limited to juries) showing that groups that are diverse by gender engage in more thorough deliberations and broaden

110 *See, e.g.*, Sommers, *supra* note 67 (Ch. 3), at 597; Sommers & Ellsworth, *supra* note 67 (Ch. 3), at 1025.

111 Sommers, *supra* note 67 (Ch. 3), at 605–06.

112 *See, e.g.*, Fred L. Strodtbeck & Richard D. Mann, *Sex Role Differentiation in Jury Deliberations*, 19 SOCIOMETRY 3, 5 (1956) (observing that in mock juries consisting of men and women, men focused more on accomplishing the task set out for them, whereas women tended to be more concerned with the social dynamics of the group).

113 *See, e.g.*, Emma Goldberg, *Salary Transparency Fails to Fix the Gender Pay Gap*, N.Y. TIMES, July 4, 2021, at 5 (finding that "even when women and men work the exact same jobs, men earn more" and making salary information public has not fixed the "gender wage gap").

114 *See, e.g.*, Phillips, *supra* note 57 (Ch. 3), at A16 (noting the growing number of African-American women in the U.S. military); Clay Risen, *At More Distilleries, Women Call the Shots*, N.Y. TIMES, July 7, 2021, at D1 (observing that women are attaining positions of authority in the whiskey business, but they are still encountering sexism).

the perspectives available to the group.[115] In a study that I conducted in 1999, I found that actual jurors, who completed a survey after their juries had reached a verdict, believed they had more thorough deliberations and expressed greater satisfaction with their jury experience when they served on juries that were diverse by gender (meaning closer to an equal number of men and women) than jurors who served on juries that consisted primarily of male jurors or primarily of female jurors.[116] Similar findings have been shown with boards of corporations and groups of investors.[117]

The US Supreme Court has recognized the importance of drawing jurors from venires that represent a fair cross section of the community. Although the Court has not extended this requirement to petit juries,[118] it has recognized the importance of having women and African Americans on the venire. Both these groups had been traditionally excluded from jury service. The Court has not been able to identify exactly what difference it makes to have panels that are diverse by gender or race, but it has alluded to the benefits. In 1946, in *Ballard* v. *United States*, Justice Douglas wrote:

> It is said . . . that an all male panel drawn from the various groups within a community will be as truly representative as if women were included. The thought is that the factors which tend to influence the action of women are the same as those which influence the action of men – personality, background, economic status – and not sex. Yet it is not enough to say that women when sitting as jurors neither act nor tend to act as a class. Men likewise do not act as a class. But, if the shoe were on the other foot, who would claim that a jury was truly representative of the community if all men were intentionally and systematically excluded from the panel? The truth is that the two sexes are not fungible; a community made up exclusively of one is different from a community composed of both; the subtle interplay of influence one on the other is among the imponderables. To insulate the courtroom from either may not in a given case make an iota of difference. Yet a flavor, a distinct quality is lost if either sex is excluded.[119]

115 *See* Marder, *supra* note 99 (Ch. 1), at 600–06 (describing studies).
116 Nancy S. Marder, *Juries, Justice & Multiculturalism*, 75 S. CAL. L. REV. 659, 700, 703, 706–07 (2002).
117 *See id.* at 695–98 (citing studies involving groups of investors and companies).
118 *See* Taylor v. Louisiana, 419 U.S. 522, 538 (1975) ("It should also be emphasized that in holding that petit juries must be drawn from a source fairly representative of the community we impose no requirement that petit juries actually chosen must mirror the community and reflect the various distinctive groups in the population.").
119 329 U.S. 187, 193–94 (1946).

Twenty years later, in *Peters* v. *Kiff*, Justice Marshall offered a similar explanation:

> When any large and identifiable segment of the community is excluded from jury service, the effect is to remove from the jury room qualities of human nature and varieties of human experience, the range of which is unknown and perhaps unknowable. It is not necessary to assume that the excluded group will consistently vote as a class in order to conclude, as we do, that its exclusion deprives the jury of a perspective on human events that may have unsuspected importance in any case that may be presented.[120]

Juries that are diverse by race, gender, and a variety of other characteristics are likely to produce more thorough and well-considered deliberations, even if reaching agreement might take more time and effort. A diverse jury helps to transform citizens into jurors by ensuring that they have a wide swath of perspectives to consider during their deliberations. By listening to each other and challenging each other, a disparate group of individuals can be transformed into a group of jurors who are open to different points of view. By assessing each other's arguments and finding points of overlap, they can arrive at a unanimous verdict, even if they started out far apart from each other.

The parties also benefit from a diverse jury's thorough jury deliberation, as does the larger community. Both need to believe in the legitimacy of the jury to make this important decision. A jury that "looks like America" is more likely to inspire public and party confidence in the jury and to elicit acceptance for its verdict even if some disagree with the verdict.

## STEPS JUDGES CAN TAKE TO ENSURE THAT JURY DELIBERATIONS TRANSFORM CITIZENS INTO JURORS

Although jurors have to conduct their own deliberations, there are steps that judges can take that will aid jurors at moments when they need assistance and will enable jury deliberations to be more effective than they currently are at helping citizens to be transformed into jurors. Judges need to provide guidance about how jurors can begin their deliberations. They can explain that they want to give jurors a starting point based on what has worked well for juries in the past. However, judges can add that every jury is free to decide for itself how

[120] Peters v. Kiff, 407 U.S. 493, 503–04 (1972).

to begin its deliberations. Judges also need to inform jurors about what to do if they have questions during their deliberations or reach an impasse, and what the full power of the jury entails, including the power to nullify. This information will help all the jurors to begin their deliberations with full knowledge about how to proceed. They will understand that they can turn to the judge for help at various points during their deliberations. These steps will give jurors the knowledge they need about their role and enable them to deliberate more effectively as a group, especially when they encounter hurdles along the way.

### Giving Jurors Guidance on How to Begin Deliberations

With few exceptions, judges do not instruct jurors on how they should begin their deliberations; but this is one point at which jurors have expressed the need for some guidance. Judges have shown restraint, for fear of intruding in decisions that are supposed to rest entirely with the jury. However, judges could offer jurors guidance on how to begin deliberations and what the foreperson does, while being clear that the jurors decide how to proceed. This information from the judge will make the start of deliberations less daunting for jurors.

Jurors enter the jury room to begin their deliberations and are sometimes at a loss about how to begin. As one female juror lamented in a first-degree murder trial: "'It was really frustrating because we were not getting any help on how do you go about this, how do you approach the situation,' she said. 'You're supposed to decide the outcome of a man's life – blind – and that's not acceptable.'"[121] In some courtrooms, jurors are told to select a foreperson, but after they have done that, then what do they do? One jury foreperson, Graham Burnett, who wrote a book about his jury experience, expressed frustration that the court did not provide any instructions on how the jurors should proceed with their deliberations.[122] Federal District Court Judge Kane, who read Burnett's book, was so moved by Burnett's plea for guidance that he drafted a deliberation instruction that he routinely gives to juries in his courtroom.[123]

Judge Kane's deliberation instruction provides juries with basic information on how to begin their deliberations, including a brief

[121] Emery, *supra* note 36 (Ch. 4), at 1A.

[122] *See* BURNETT, *supra* note 39 (Ch. 1), at 79–85.

[123] John L. Kane, *Giving Trials a Second Look*, JUDGES' J., Fall 2004, at 29, 30–31 (providing instruction).

description of actions the foreperson can take, the need for jurors to listen carefully to each other, the inadvisability of an early vote, a caution that there may be differences among jurors and even points of impasse, but that patience, hard work, and respect will go a long way toward overcoming these potential hurdles.[124] Judge Kane is careful to tell jurors that he is just offering suggestions, and that the jurors are free to structure their deliberations as they see fit. Judge Kane explains to the jurors: "I am not directing you how to proceed, but I offer the following suggestions that other juries have found helpful so that you can proceed in an orderly fashion, allowing full participation by each juror, and arrive at a verdict that is satisfactory to each of you."[125] Indeed, Judge Kane's instruction provides jurors with extremely helpful information.

The American Judicature Society (AJS), like Judge Kane, has tried to fill the gap and has created a deliberation instruction in the form of a pamphlet, *Behind Closed Doors: A Guide for Jury Deliberations*, that it encourages judges to share with juries.[126] If a judge were reticent about instructing the jury on how to begin its deliberations, he or she could simply give each juror a copy of the AJS pamphlet. The pamphlet tells jurors that they are free to structure their deliberations however they want,[127] but it offers some suggestions that they might find useful, like waiting before they take a vote and giving every juror a chance to speak. The pamphlet also explains some basics, such as the role of the foreperson and the qualities and skills to look for when selecting a foreperson.[128] The pamphlet offers responses to the jurors' most basic questions, especially: "How do we start?"[129] Finally, it provides information that judges might think jurors know, but that they probably do not know, such as how they can communicate with the judge during their deliberations and that they might be polled individually in open court after they have reached their verdict.[130]

Both the AJS pamphlet and Judge Kane's instruction on deliberations advise jurors to wait before taking a vote. Although neither the pamphlet nor the instruction refers to the two styles of deliberation

124 *Id.*
125 *Id.* at 30.
126 *See* AM. JUDICATURE SOC'Y, BEHIND CLOSED DOORS: A GUIDE FOR JURY DELIBERATIONS (1999) (providing general information about jury deliberations).
127 *Id.* at 3 ("You are free to deliberate in any way you wish.").
128 *Id.* at 4.
129 *Id.*
130 *Id.* at 8–9.

("evidence-driven" and "verdict-driven") that social scientists have identified, both the pamphlet and Judge Kane recommend that jurors listen to each other first and wait before taking a vote.[131] In essence, Judge Kane and the AJS pamphlet recommend an evidence-driven style of deliberation, in which the jurors go around the table giving every juror a chance to speak[132] and refrain from taking a vote until later in the process, after there has been sufficient discussion. Of course, both the pamphlet and Judge Kane are careful to mention that jurors can decide for themselves which approach to take, but they both advise waiting to vote. The pamphlet tells jurors that they "will probably feel more confident and satisfied with [their] eventual verdict than if [they] rush things."[133] Judge Kane tells jurors that "[e]xperience has also shown that such early votes frequently lead to disruptive, unnecessarily lengthy, inefficient debate and ineffective decision making."[134] With respect to both the pamphlet and the instruction, jurors are likely to appreciate the guidance, even if they decide not to follow it.

Some states, such as Michigan, provide a bare-bones instruction on deliberations, which does not give jurors much information.[135] In civil jury trials in Michigan, the judge instructs juries to conduct their deliberations in "a businesslike manner."[136] Although this does not tell jurors much, and certainly not as much as the AJS pamphlet or Judge Kane's instruction, it does at least remind jurors that they can draw on their work experience and consider how they would conduct a meeting in their workplace. It reminds them that although they are new to the role of juror, they can use skills that they have developed in their work lives. The instruction also gives jurors a starting point; it tells them they need to select a foreperson before they do anything else.[137]

131 *See id.* at 7; Kane, *supra* note 123, at 30.

132 The U.S. Supreme Court illustrates how structure can change participation – whether for Justices or jurors. When the COVID-19 pandemic struck in the spring of 2020 and the Justices could no longer meet for oral argument in the courtroom, they held oral argument by telephone. In doing so, they moved from a free-form style of questioning the lawyers in the courtroom to a limited (but equal) amount of time for each Justice to ask questions of the lawyers. The Justices proceeded in order of seniority. One result of this change in structure was that every Justice participated equally in asking questions, including Justice Thomas, who had long been known for not asking any questions during oral argument. If jurors followed an evidence-driven style, in which everyone contributed their views and recollections at least at the beginning of the deliberations, then every juror would provide their input, just as Justice Thomas now contributes his questions.

133 Am. Judicature Soc'y, *supra* note 126, at 7.

134 Kane, *supra* note 123, at 30.

135 *See* M Civ JI 60.01 (Jury Deliberations), Mich. B.J., Jan. 2018, at 70.

136 *Id.*

137 *Id.* ("You should first select a foreperson.").

One problem with the Michigan instruction is that it offers very general advice. For example, the instruction tells jurors that they should "weigh the evidence with an open mind and consideration for each other's opinions" and they should resolve differences by discussing them "in a spirit of fairness and frankness."[138] Arguably, it is better for the instruction to speak in generalities than not to speak at all, but it is hard to put generalities into effect. It is even harder to put generalities into effect when they are seemingly contradictory: "[D]o not hesitate to reexamine your own views and change your opinion if you are convinced that it is wrong. However, none of you should surrender your honest conviction ... solely because of the opinion of your fellow jurors or for the mere purpose of returning a verdict."[139] The Michigan instruction does at least provide jurors with one specific piece of information: It tells jurors that they can contact the judge by sending a note to the bailiff.[140] This instruction on deliberations, even though it is limited and general, is still better than no instruction at all.[141]

**Responding to Jurors' Questions**

Judges are reticent to respond to any questions the jury has once it has begun its deliberations, but this is another point when the jury turns to the judge for guidance and it is helpful to jurors for the judge to provide it. If the judge answers the jurors' question or explains why he or she cannot, the jurors will feel that they can perform their role as jurors as ably and responsibly as possible.

Currently, once the jury begins its deliberations, it can send a note to the judge whenever it has a question. The jurors have been instructed not to consult outside sources, such as friends or family, and not to do their own research, whether online or with books.[142] They can, however, turn to the judge for guidance. Jurors need to know in advance that they can send a note to the judge, as the AJS pamphlet informs them, and judges need to answer their questions to the extent that they can.

138 *Id.*
139 *Id.*
140 *Id.*
141 Illinois, for example, does not provide jurors in civil cases with an instruction on deliberations.
142 *See, e.g.*, IPI, *supra* note 88 (Ch. 2), § 1.01(A)[6]–[12] (Cautionary Instructions (Prior to Opening)), § 1.01(B)[1]–[6] (Cautionary Instructions (During Trial)), § 1.01(C)[6]–[12] (Cautionary Instructions (After Closing)).

For example, jurors might have a question about the instructions. Presumably, the jurors have already discussed the particular instruction among themselves and found that they did not understand a word or phrase or that they disagreed as to the meaning of that word or phrase. When the jury sends a note to the judge with its question, some judges resist answering it.[143] Other judges respond to a question about the instructions by calling everyone back into the courtroom and simply rereading the relevant portion of the instruction or all of the instructions. However, such a rereading, as one juror remarked "answered exactly none of our questions."[144] Instead, the judge needs to try to answer the jury's questions about the instructions. The jurors want to understand the instructions so that they can perform their role as jurors as responsibly as possible. The judge should also want the jurors to understand the instructions; they need to work together.

Admittedly, the judge is reluctant to say anything in his or her own words because that would entail deviating from the pattern instructions, which might provide grounds for reversal on appeal.[145] In addition, there is always the possibility that a second reading might actually answer the jury's question. During a second reading of the instruction, jurors are likely to focus on the word or phrase they did not understand. However, in one judge's experience a rereading was unlikely to provide clarification: "When jurors would send out questions asking about the meaning of a concept or term, the custom was always to reread the instruction, as if the jurors would understand a second recital with the renewed dulcet tones of the judicial officer."[146]

If the rereading does not help, as a number of jurors have pointed out,[147] then the judge needs to answer the question in his or her own words. After all, the judge and jury are engaged in a common endeavor.

[143] *See, e.g.*, SUNDBY, *supra* note 68 (Ch. 4), at 167 ("Adding insult to injury from the jurors' perspective, judges sometimes would appear to turn a cold shoulder when the jury asked them to clarify instructions or define terms such as 'mitigating.'"); Romero et al., *supra* note 10, at C1 (reporting that "the jury sent a note on Wednesday [June 1, 2005], asking that a portion of the trial transcript be read back to them," but it was "a request the judge denied").

[144] BURNETT, *supra* note 39 (Ch. 1), at 91.

[145] *See, e.g.*, Wascher, *supra* note 20 (Ch. 4), at 52, 54 (describing the response of Cook County Circuit Court Judge Stuart A. Nudelman, a past president of the Illinois Judges' Association, to a jury's question on the instructions: "[H]e declined to answer the jury's question both because he was not entirely sure how to answer and because any answer might well have been 'a guarantee of the appellate court saying that, as the trial judge, I went too far and that it's the jury's job to interpret instructions.'").

[146] Connor, *supra* note 43 (Ch. 4), at 7.

[147] *See, e.g.*, BURNETT, *supra* note 39 (Ch. 1), at 91; SUNDBY, *supra* note 68 (Ch. 4), at 49–50 (describing jurors who felt intimidated by the process of having to return to the courtroom to

It is critical for both judge and jury that the jurors understand the instructions. The jury, if left without an answer to its question, might simply make up its own answer. The jurors do not want to do this, particularly because they take seriously their responsibility and want to perform their task as best they can, but the judge who declines to answer the jury's question, or answers only by rereading the instruction, places the jury in this untenable position. If the jury asks a question that the judge is not permitted by law to answer, then the judge can explain this. Jurors will at least feel that they tried to get as much information as they could and they will usually be understanding if the judge tells them that he or she cannot respond. Jurors have shown such understanding when they have requested the judge to ask a particular question of a witness and the judge did not feel that he or she was permitted by law to ask the question.[148] As social scientists have observed, an explanation can go a long way toward satisfying jurors (even if it is not the explanation that the jurors wanted).[149]

**Engaging in a Judge–Jury Dialogue When Jurors Reach an Impasse**

Whereas the traditional view leaves jurors to their own devices, even when they reach an impasse, or at most permits the judge simply to instruct the jurors to continue their deliberations, the transformation view sees the judge as being able to help juries achieve a better process for their deliberations without interfering with the verdict the jury ultimately reaches. One step the judge can take to help jurors when they reach an impasse is to have the attorneys provide additional argument on whatever the sticking point is for the jury. In this way, all jurors will receive additional information that could change their point of view and allow the jury to reach a unanimous verdict.

In all federal criminal and civil jury trials,[150] and in serious state criminal jury trials,[151] the jurors need to reach a unanimous verdict, but sometimes they reach an impasse that they cannot resolve for themselves. The typical response in federal or in state court is for the judge to

hear the judge reread portions of the instructions anytime the jury submitted a question to the judge).

148 *See, e.g.*, Marder, *supra* note 78 (Ch. 4), at 751 & n.123.

149 *See, e.g.*, MacPherson & Bonora, *supra* note 113 (Ch. 4), at 42 ("[C]ompliance can be measurably increased by simply adding the word 'because' and some type of explanation.").

150 *See* Fed. R. Crim. P. 31(a); Fed. R. Civ. P. 48(b).

151 *See* Ramos v. Louisiana, 140 S. Ct. 1390 (2020) (holding that the Sixth Amendment's right to a unanimous jury trial in serious criminal cases applies to the states via the Fourteenth Amendment).

tell the jurors to continue to deliberate. The judge usually instructs the jurors to listen to the other side's view, but not to give in if they feel strongly about their position. The instruction might not sound as though the judge is putting pressure on the holdout jurors to conform to the larger group's view, but that is oftentimes the result. In federal court, the judge's instruction is known as an *Allen* charge.[152] In state courts, the judge usually gives a similar charge, though it has a different name.[153] Some states, however, prohibit such a charge.[154] The effect of the charge is to break the impasse, which is why it is colloquially known as the "dynamite charge." One reason it might have this effect is because it is hard for holdout jurors to maintain their stance, particularly when under pressure, albeit indirectly, from the judge.

Judges can play a more constructive role than delivering a dynamite charge when a jury reaches an impasse and seeks help from the judge. They can find out what the sticking point is for the jurors and have the attorneys present additional argument on that issue. Judges should help the jurors – all of the jurors, including the holdout jurors – to fulfill their role as jurors as satisfactorily as possible. Of course, it might not be possible for all jurors to be satisfied all of the time with the verdicts reached by their juries. Telling jurors to listen to each other is, in general, good advice, but not when the effect is to put pressure primarily on the holdout jurors in order to produce a verdict. If the holdout jurors succumb to group pressure after hearing an *Allen* charge, they might regret their verdict afterward and have negative views about their jury experience.

An alternative is for judges to resume their dialogue with the jury at the point at which the jury signals to the judge that it has reached an impasse and sees no route to unanimity. When Judge Dann was still a trial judge in Superior Court in Maricopa County, Arizona, he urged trial judges to forgo the dynamite charge at this juncture and, instead, to meet with the jury to find out what the problem was.[155] Arizona rules now permit this practice,[156] and instructions give guidance to the

152 *See* Allen v. United States, 164 U.S. 492, 501 (1896); United States v. Anderton, 679 F.2d 1199, 1203 (5th Cir. 1982). For additional discussion of the *Allen* charge, see *supra* notes 12–16 in this chapter and accompanying text.

153 For example, Illinois' version of the *Allen* charge is provided in *People v. Prim*, 289 N.E.2d 601 (Ill. 1972).

154 California, for example, prohibits an *Allen* charge. *See, e.g.*, People v. Gainer, 566 P.2d 997, 1006 (Cal. 1977) (en banc).

155 *See* Dann & Logan, *supra* note 44 (Ch. 4), at 283; *see also* THE POWER OF 12, *supra* note 17 (Ch. 1), at 120–24.

156 ARIZ. R. CIV. P. 40(j); ARIZ. R. CRIM. P. 22.4.

jurors.[157] Judge Dann described the judge's role at this point as engaging in "a dialogue" with the jury.[158] Once the judge learns from the jury the point of disagreement, he or she can have the lawyers engage in additional argument on that point.[159]

The additional argument by the lawyers might help the jury to resolve its disagreement, though it might not happen in every case. It could be that the jury remains divided and that the judge will ultimately have to declare the jury to be a hung jury. However, it could be that the jury is able to reach a verdict. With either outcome, the advantage of a dialogue with the judge compared to an *Allen* charge by the judge is that the dialogue does not put pressure predominantly on the holdout jurors. The additional information can give either side – the majority of jurors or the holdout jurors – new insights about the case. The burden will not necessarily fall on the holdout jurors to go along with the majority. It might be that the majority sees that it was wrong.

The additional argument by the attorneys allows all of the jurors to rethink their positions. It gives all of them new information to consider. Two psychologists, Saul Kassin and Lawrence S. Wrightsman, Jr., offer two explanations for why jurors change their vote after the jury has reached an impasse: They can acquire new information that leads them to change their vote ("informational influence") or they can succumb to group pressure ("normative influence") and change their vote.[160] Kassin and Wrightsman make clear that informational influence leads to a change in point of view, whereas normative influence does not, which is why they describe "the ideal deliberation as one in which the informational influences are strong and the normative influences are weak."[161]

When a jury reaches an impasse, the judge has a key role to play in helping the jurors to resolve that impasse, without making some of the jurors feel that they are under pressure to vote in a way that is contrary to the views they hold about the case. This is important so that the jurors can vote in a way that reflects their true views and so that they leave the jury room satisfied with how they have fulfilled their role as jurors.

157 ARIZ. R. CIV. P. 40(j) cmt; ARIZ. R. CIV. P. 22.4 cmt.
158 Dann & Logan, *supra* note 44 (Ch. 4), at 283.
159 *Id.* at 283 n.6.
160 KASSIN & WRIGHTSMAN, *supra* note 9 (Ch. 2), at 185.
161 *Id.*

Admittedly, a jury that fails to reach a unanimous verdict and is declared to be a hung jury might feel that it has failed in its task. Sometimes jurors on a hung jury have expressed their disappointment when they speak to the press after the verdict. After all, they have failed to reach a verdict, which is the task they were supposed to accomplish. For example, the foreperson in the first criminal trial of former Illinois Governor Rod Blagojevich felt this way after his jury was declared a hung jury and he expressed his view when he spoke to the press[162] and at an academic conference after the trial.[163] However, he also explained that all the jurors respected the holdout juror. Although the other jurors did not share her view of the case, they recognized that it was her right to vote according to her strongly held view.

Professors Harry Kalven and Hans Zeisel recognized these competing responses to a hung jury when they noted that although a hung jury has failed to deliver a verdict, it is also a "valued assurance of integrity, since it can serve to protect the dissent of a minority."[164] The foreperson in the Blagojevich jury trial understood this point at an intellectual level, but he still felt disappointed that his jury had not reached a verdict.[165] In contrast, when a holdout changes his or her vote to go along with the majority, the holdout can feel bad even if the rest of the jury feels that it has accomplished its task. The lone holdout juror in the criminal jury trial in *Inside the Jury Room* felt bad when he did not stand his ground.[166] In fact, he told his fellow jurors that he would regret his capitulation for the rest of his life: "I will change and vote along with you to make a unanimous vote. But I will never feel right about it."[167]

It may not be possible for all the jurors to feel good about their vote, but if the judge puts a finger on the scale by giving an *Allen* charge it is likely to leave the holdout jurors feeling dissatisfied. Undoubtedly,

[162] *See* Davey & Saulny, *supra* note 24 (Ch. 4), at A1 ("'It was kind of a bittersweet thing,' Mr. Matsumoto said, . . . 'relief that the trial is over, but frustration that we didn't accomplish what we set out to do.'") (quoting James Matsumoto, foreperson in the first criminal trial of former Illinois Governor Rod Blagojevich).

[163] *See, e.g.*, Marder & Hans, *supra* note 2 (Intro.), at 814 & n.141 ("I failed to convince [the holdout juror] of the truth I saw; it was not my fault, but we [the jury] failed.") (quoting former foreperson James Matsumoto) (notes on file with authors).

[164] KALVEN & ZEISEL, *supra* note 18, at 453.

[165] Marder & Hans, *supra* note 2 (Intro.), at 814–15 ("Although this former juror recognized that a hung jury is an accepted part of the American jury system, he still felt that his jury had failed because it had been unable to reach a verdict on all counts.") (footnote omitted).

[166] *Inside the Jury Room* transcript, *supra* note 19, at 24.

[167] *Id.*

judges want juries to reach a verdict.[168] Indeed, jurors want juries to reach a verdict.[169] However, jurors want to do the right thing and to cast a vote that is consistent with their strongly and sincerely held views. Judges should not try to tip the scales; rather, they should respond in a way that helps all the jurors to rethink their positions. Allowing additional argument on the point that is causing the impasse seems a route that is more likely to respect all the jurors than the *Allen* charge, which puts more pressure on the holdouts than on the jurors who are in the majority. This might be because it is harder to be a holdout juror than a juror in the majority. In fact, social scientists have observed that it is hard for just one or two jurors to remain as holdouts; usually three or four jurors are needed for them to withstand the pressure to go along with the majority.[170]

### Instructing Jurors on Nullification

Another step that judges can take so that citizens are transformed into jurors who know the full extent of their power is to instruct them on nullification. Currently, judges do not instruct jurors on nullification before or during their deliberations, even though jurors need to know about it to understand fully their role as jurors. If the judge does not instruct the jury on nullification, some jurors might know about the jury's power to nullify and others might not; thus, they will enter the jury room without the same knowledge of the jury's power. In addition, if jurors do not learn about nullification until after their verdict, they are likely to feel misled by the judge, regretful about their verdict, and dissatisfied with their experience as jurors. The judge needs to trust jurors and to give them all the information they need, including information about nullification so that they can perform their role with as much understanding as possible

Jury nullification is when the jury decides not to follow the law. This is different from mistake, which is when the jury misunderstands the law. Nullification is when the jury understands the law, but decides not

[168] Of course, if hung juries were a frequent occurrence, the jury system would collapse. Professor Hans Zeisel recognized this paradox about the hung jury. He noted that the hung jury is "treasured because it represents the legal system's respect for the minority viewpoint that is held strongly enough to thwart the will of the majority," but it is "paradox[ical]" because the hung jury can only be tolerated in "moderation" – "too many hung juries would impede the effective functioning of the courts." Zeisel, *supra* note 34 (Ch. 4), at 719 n.42.

[169] *See, e.g.*, HANS & VIDMAR, *supra* note 65 (Ch. 3), at 111 ("There is quite possibly no more demoralizing experience for jurors than the inability to reach a verdict, particularly after a lengthy and tiring trial."); Marder & Hans, *supra* note 2 (Intro.), at 814–15 & nn.141–43.

[170] *See, e.g.*, HANS & VIDMAR, *supra* note 65 (Ch. 3), at 110.

to follow it. Although nullification can occur in civil as well as in criminal cases, the judge can intervene in civil cases[171] and in criminal cases in which the evidence is insufficient or the jury convicts.[172] However, in criminal cases in which the jury acquits, the judge cannot take action and the verdict cannot be appealed. Thus, in criminal cases in which the jury acquits, the acquittal stands regardless of the reason, including when the jury acquits based on nullification.

Juries have the power to nullify because of a confluence of practices and principles, including the general verdict, the secrecy of the jury room, and the Double Jeopardy Clause. In criminal cases, the jury renders a general verdict in which it has to decide whether the criminal defendant is guilty or not guilty.[173] Jurors can have different reasons for their vote, but they only have to give reasons to each other, not to anyone outside the jury room. Only the vote of guilty or not guilty is communicated to those outside the jury room.[174] Thus, no one outside the jury room knows whether the jury reached its general verdict based on nullification or some other reason. In addition, the jury deliberates in secret.[175] No one else is permitted in the jury room while the jury deliberates; this ensures that outsiders do not know the reasons for the jury's verdict. In addition, once a defendant has been acquitted, he or she cannot be retried by the same sovereign for the same crime;[176] to do so would violate the Double Jeopardy Clause of the Fifth Amendment to the US Constitution.[177] Even if the judge disagrees with the

[171] In civil cases in federal court, a judge can grant a motion for judgment as a matter of law before the case goes to the jury, *see* FED. R. CIV. P. 50(a), or a renewed motion for judgment as a matter of law after the verdict. *See* FED. R. CIV. P. 50(b).

[172] In criminal cases in federal court, a judge can grant a motion for judgment of acquittal after the close of all the evidence if the judge believes that the evidence is insufficient to support a conviction. *See* FED. R. CRIM. P. 29(a). The judge can also grant a motion for judgment of acquittal before the case is submitted to the jury or after the jury returns a verdict of guilty. *See* FED. R. CRIM. P. 29(b) & (c).

[173] FED. R. CRIM. P. 31.

[174] There are a few exceptions to the general verdict in criminal cases. According to *United States v. Spock*, 416 F.2d 165, 182 n.41 (1st Cir. 1969), courts have employed questions in two specific contexts in criminal cases: sentencing and treason trials. In addition, courts have also found questions acceptable in extremely complex criminal trials when they are used to reduce juror confusion. *See* United States v. Palmeri, 630 F.2d 192, 203 (3d Cir. 1980).

[175] In *United States v. Thomas*, 116 F.3d 606, 618 (2d Cir. 1997), the Second Circuit described the secrecy of jury deliberations as "the cornerstone of the modern Anglo-American jury system."

[176] However, a criminal defendant can be prosecuted by different sovereigns (such as a state and federal sovereign) for the same conduct. *See* Gamble v. United States, 139 S. Ct. 1960 (2019) (reaffirming the longstanding "separate sovereigns" doctrine, which permits federal and state governments to bring a separate criminal prosecution against the same person for the same conduct).

[177] The Fifth Amendment provides: "nor shall any person be subject for the same offence to be twice put in jeopardy of life or limb." U.S. CONST. amend. V.

acquittal, case law, beginning with *Bushel's Case*,[178] has long recognized that only those in the jury room can understand what motivated the jury to reach its verdict, and others, including the judge, cannot put themselves in the jurors' shoes. Thus, the secrecy of the deliberations and the opacity of a general verdict mean that the jury can reach its verdict without any scrutiny, even by the judge. The Double Jeopardy Clause precludes an appeal of an acquittal so the acquittal stands. As long as these principles and practices are followed, juries have the power to nullify.

Even though the jury has the power to nullify, it does not always know about this power. In all federal circuits,[179] and almost all state courts,[180] judges cannot instruct juries on nullification. Jurors have to acquire knowledge about nullification on their own. Some jurors might know about it (even if they do not know the word) from movies or books in popular culture. Other jurors might know about it from nullification advocates. Paul Butler, an academic and former prosecutor, wants African-American jurors to engage in race-based nullification and to acquit African-American defendants charged with victimless drug crimes.[181] He hopes that African-American communities will learn about this power through grassroots organizing and word of mouth. Members of the Fully Informed Jury Association (FIJA) stand on the courthouse steps distributing leaflets so that potential jurors know about their power to nullify, particularly in drug cases and other laws with which FIJA members disagree.[182] However, these efforts can be hit-or-miss and not all jurors will know about their power to nullify. In some cases, defense lawyers are permitted to lay the groundwork for the jury to nullify (without actually mentioning the word "nullification") in their closing argument, but jurors might dismiss the lawyers' arguments as zealous advocacy and remain doubtful about whether they can nullify unless they hear it from the judge.

Judges usually explain that jurors should not be instructed on nullification because although juries have the power to nullify, they do not

178 Bushel's Case (1670), 124 Eng. Rep. 1006 (C.P.).

179 Marder, *supra* note 20, at 310 n.116 (providing citations that show that the federal circuits do not permit an instruction on nullification).

180 Only two states, Indiana and Maryland, permit judges to instruct jurors that they can determine the law and the facts. Although their state constitutions provide for this right, their judiciaries have narrowed this right through case law. *See id.*

181 Paul Butler, *Racially Based Jury Nullification: Black Power in the Criminal Justice System*, 105 YALE L.J. 677, 679 (1995).

182 Joe Lambe, *Bill Would Let Juries Decide Law in Cases; Legal Establishment Reacts to Measure with Shock, Dread*, KAN. CITY STAR, Apr. 8, 1996, at A1.

have the right, and an instruction would encourage "lawless" behavior. Judges typically view nullification as contrary to the rule of law and they do not want to encourage this lawless behavior.[183] After all, judges and jurors took an oath to follow the law.[184] In addition, judges instruct jurors that they are to find the facts and apply the law as the judge gives it to them.[185] Judges resist the idea of telling jurors that their role entails more discretion than this instruction suggests. They worry about juries overstepping their role and intruding into legislators' or judges' roles. Thus, the danger of telling jurors about nullification is that it will lead to "anarchy" and "chaos."[186]

Some judges have explained that an instruction on nullification will lead jurors to engage in it more often, which they fear will undermine the legal system. Judge Leventhal, writing for the majority in *United States* v. *Dougherty*,[187] explained that informing jurors about nullification was like eliminating speed limits. If there are speed limits, drivers might exceed them by a few miles and that does not cause havoc on the roads, but if there were no speed limits and every driver could choose his or her own speed, that would produce chaos.[188] Judge Leventhal's view, which reflects the traditional view, is that jurors have the power to nullify, and they do it occasionally, but if judges told them they could nullify, it would be like removing all speed limits for drivers. If judges instructed jurors on nullification, then jurors would stop following the law and the law would become whatever any jury decides it should be. So, the traditional view leaves it up to jurors to discover nullification on their own if the case they must decide seems to call for it.

Some judges and academics have tried to draft an instruction that tells jurors that they have the power to nullify, but they should use it

183 *See, e.g.*, United States v. Thomas, 116 F.3d 606, 616 (2d Cir. 1997); United States v. Perez, 86 F.3d 735, 736 (7th Cir. 1996) ("An unreasonable jury verdict, although unreviewable if it is an acquittal, is lawless, and the defendant has no right to invite the jury to act lawlessly."); United States v. Washington, 705 F.2d 489, 494 (D.C. Cir. 1983) (per curiam).

184 *Compare* 28 U.S.C. § 453 (2018) (a federal judge's oath: "I, ___ ___, do solemnly swear (or affirm) that I will administer justice without respect to persons, and do equal right to the poor and to the rich, and that I will faithfully and impartially discharge and perform all the duties incumbent upon me as ___ under the Constitution and laws of the United States. So help me God.") *with* CALIFORNIA SUPERIOR COURT CRIMINAL TRIAL JUDGES' DESKBOOK, *supra* note 77 (Ch. 2), at 356 (a juror's oath in California: "You and each of you, do solemnly swear that you will well and truly try the cause now pending before this Court, and a true verdict render therein, according to the evidence and the instructions of the Court, so help you God?").

185 *See supra* note 3 (Ch. 4) (providing typical instruction).

186 United States v. Dougherty, 473 F.2d 1113, 1133–34 (D.C. Cir. 1972).

187 *Id.* at 1116.

188 *Id.* at 1134.

sparingly. Although it is not an easy instruction to draft, this does not mean that it cannot be done. One possibility would be for the judge to borrow from the language of John Adams and instruct jurors as follows: "It is not only [a juror's] right, but his [or her] duty . . . to find the verdict according to his [or her] own best understanding, judgment and conscience."[189] Another possibility is to use Judge Dann's formulation, which is, in part: "If you determine that the defendant has been proven guilty beyond a reasonable doubt, but you cannot in good conscience support a guilty verdict, you cannot be required to do so. However, you should exercise with great caution your power to find not guilty a defendant whose legal guilt has been proven."[190] If judges provide either instruction it will mean that each juror will be educated as to nullification (even without using the word). Judge Dann's version also makes the point that nullification should be reserved for rare instances. If properly instructed, jurors will then understand the full power of the jury, and will not have regrets afterward that the judge had withheld important information from them.

It is important for the judge to be candid with jurors – the success of the judge–jury relationship depends on it. Moreover, the current instruction that judges typically give juries to follow the law presents an incomplete picture and does a disservice to the judge and to the jury. It does not inform the jury of the full range of its powers and it puts the judge in the uncomfortable position of not being completely honest with the jury.

*Trusting Jurors with a Nullification Instruction*

At the core of the nullification instruction is a judge's trust in jurors. Trust is essential to the judge–jury relationship. The jury needs to be able to trust the judge and trust that the judge will give it the information it needs to perform its role fully. Conversely, the judge needs to be able to trust the jury and to give it all the information it needs, including information about nullification, so that it can perform its role with as much understanding as possible. Although judges might trust jurors in many ways, including making life or death decisions

[189] Mark DeWolfe Howe, *Juries as Judges of Criminal Law*, 52 HARV. L. REV. 582, 605 (1939) (quoting 2 LIFE AND WORKS OF JOHN ADAMS 253–55 (C. F. Adams ed., 1856)); Marder, *supra* note 18, at 957.

[190] B. Michael Dann, *The Constitutional and Ethical Implications of 'Must-Find-the-Defendant-Guilty' Jury Instructions*, *in* JURY ETHICS: JUROR CONDUCT AND JURY DYNAMICS 107, 107 (John Kleinig & James P. Levine eds., 2016).

about defendants in some criminal cases, they seem to pull back when it comes to instructing jurors on nullification.

The typical view of nullification, though it prevails in all federal and state courts and is widely held by most judges, is not held by *all* judges. Chief Judge Bazelon, dissenting as to instructing on nullification in *United States* v. *Dougherty*, explained that judges need to trust jurors, be candid with them, and assume that they will behave responsibly even if they are instructed on nullification.[191] He trusted jurors to understand and abide by such an instruction. He thought it far more harmful to keep this information about nullification from jurors than to instruct them on it. If jurors learned about their power to nullify after their jury service they would feel that the judge had deceived them.

Chief Judge Bazelon also pointed out that judges view jurors as representing the judgment of the community and so they should be able to vote according to their conscience when they think the case requires it.[192] To have judges instruct them that they must follow the law, when in fact they can follow their conscience, does not give them a complete understanding of their role and might lead them to vote in a way that they would not have done if they had been given full information. This lack of knowledge could lead them to have regrets long after their jury service has ended.[193]

Indeed, Chief Judge Bazelon's concerns for jurors who were not instructed on nullification came to pass with the Wisconsin jury that heard the case of Leroy Reed. The jury reached a verdict based on nullification without the instruction, so the lack of instruction did not affect their verdict in this case (though that will not always be true in other cases). However, the jury had to struggle a lot more than was necessary in order to figure out the information that the judge had failed to impart to them. Even worse, the instruction that the judge had given suggested a limited role for the jury.[194] The judge instructed the jury just to apply

191 United States v. Dougherty, 473 F.2d 1113, 1142 (D.C. Cir. 1972) (Bazelon, C.J., concurring in part and dissenting in part) (explaining why judges should instruct juries about nullification).

192 *Id.* at 1139, 1142.

193 *See, e.g.*, *Enter the Jury Room* transcript, *supra* note 54, at 49 ("I was not going to do something that was against my beliefs, and conscience and logic that would make me regret what I had done for the rest of my life.") (quoting Juror "Joe"); *Inside the Jury Room* transcript, *supra* note 19, at 24 ("I will change and vote along with you to make a unanimous vote. But I will never feel right about it.") (quoting Juror Karl Buetow, a fireman).

194 This is a standard instruction that is given to jurors. *See, e.g.*, 1A O'Malley et al., *supra* note 81 (Ch. 2), § 10.01 ("I instruct you that the law as given by the Court in these and other instructions constitute the only law for your guidance. It is your duty to accept and to follow the law as I give it to you even though you may disagree with the law."); Judicial Council of California Criminal Jury Instructions (CALCRIM) § 101 (2020)

the law as the judge had given it to them to the facts as they found them. The jurors' oath reinforced that message.[195] The nullification instruction would make the deliberations less agonizing in certain cases, such as the case of Leroy Reed, and would have made the deliberations far less agonizing for particular jurors, such as the holdout juror.

A nullification instruction would transform citizens into jurors who understood the full extent of their power as jurors. It would allow jurors to avoid *The Wizard of Oz* misconception. In *The Wizard of Oz*, Dorothy struggled mightily to get to the Emerald City because she thought she needed the help of a wizard in order to return home. When she reached the Emerald City, however, and met the wizard, she discovered that he was just a man, not a wizard, and that she had always had the power to go home on her own. The jury struggles with nullification because it has not been instructed on it – in fact, it has been instructed in a contrary way – only to discover after the verdict that it had the power to nullify all along.

### *How a Nullification Instruction Transforms Citizens into Jurors during Deliberations*

A nullification instruction transforms citizens into jurors by giving them knowledge about the full extent of the jury's power, which includes the power to nullify. Professor Zeisel's observation about hung juries[196] is equally applicable to nullifying juries: If juries nullify all the time, the system will collapse. However, if juries nullify in the rare cases that call for it, then they will be able to vote according to their conscience without bringing about the collapse of the jury system. A nullification instruction would tell jurors that their role includes an awesome power to nullify but that it should be invoked only in the rarest of cases.

In most criminal cases, if the government has proven all the elements of the crime beyond a reasonable doubt, the jury should and will convict. However, in rare cases,[197] the jury does not think justice will

(Cautionary Admonitions) ("Your verdict must be based only on the evidence presented during trial in this court and the law as I provide it to you.").

195 A typical juror's oath is: "You and each of you, do solemnly swear that you will well and truly try the cause now pending before this Court, and a true verdict render therein, according to the evidence and the instructions of the Court, so help you God?" CALIFORNIA SUPERIOR COURT CRIMINAL TRIAL JUDGES' DESKBOOK, *supra* note 77 (Ch. 2), at 356. The ending could be modified slightly to read: "according to your best judgment of the evidence and the instructions of the Court, so help you God?"

196 *See supra* note 168 and accompanying text.

197 Paula L. Hannaford-Agor & Valerie P. Hans, *Nullification at Work? A Glimpse from the National Center for State Courts Study of Hung Juries*, 78 CHI.-KENT L. REV. 1249, 1277 (2003)

be done by a literal application of the statute to the defendant's case. The jurors struggle to reconcile their sense of what justice requires in the particular case, and what their role as juror entails, with what the judge has instructed them to do, which is to apply the law as the judge has given it to them to the facts as they have found them. They are to apply the law whether they agree with it or not and regardless of whether they think it should be applied to the defendant. At some point in their deliberations, they face a conundrum. Do they follow the judge's instruction to apply the law or do they follow what they believe is their broader calling to do justice in this particular case? An instruction on nullification would transform them as deliberating jurors so that they could follow the broader calling to do justice and not feel that they were disobeying their oath or the judge's instructions.

*Inside the Jury Room* provides a rare glimpse of the role that a nullification instruction would have played and how a jury had to struggle to figure out its broader role in the absence of such an instruction.[198] The case, as described earlier,[199] involved Leroy Reed, a convicted felon who was charged with possession of a handgun. Reed, a man of limited mental ability, saw a magazine advertisement that said he could become a private investigator if he sent away for a badge and purchased a handgun. Since he was in need of employment, he sent away for the mail-order badge and purchased a handgun. He then went to the local courthouse wearing his badge and looking for clients. A sheriff eventually questioned him and asked him to go home and return with the handgun, which Reed did. The sheriff then arrested him and charged him with being a convicted felon in possession of a handgun.

Reed was tried by a Wisconsin jury and the deliberations were filmed and aired on television.[200] Although the judge refused to instruct the jury on nullification, he did permit Reed's attorney to allude to it, albeit indirectly, in his closing argument. The jurors began their deliberations by working within the confines of the three elements of the statute. According to the statute, Reed had to be a convicted felon (which had been stipulated), possess a handgun, and have knowledge that he possessed a handgun while being a convicted felon. Some of the jurors, working with the three

(finding it "unlikely that juries are frequently nullifying the law strictly on preconceived personal notions of justice").

198 *See supra* note 19.

199 *See supra* Chapter 5 (Giving Reasons to Fellow Jurors).

200 *See supra* note 19.

elements of the statute, thought that Reed might not have knowledge that he had violated the statute because of his limited mental capacity. As one juror asked: "I wonder if we could find room in the law . . . that perhaps [Reed] didn't, in [the] full sense of the word, 'know' he was a felon, and didn't, in the full sense of the word, 'know' that he possessed a firearm."[201] To several of the jurors, it seemed likely that Reed was unable to understand all the elements of the statute and put them together. He could know that he was a convicted felon and that he was not supposed to have a handgun, but he had obtained a handgun so that he could be a private investigator. They reasoned that he might not understand that possession of a handgun by a convicted felon was a violation of the statute, even if his purpose – to support himself as a private investigator – was well-meaning.

Several of the jurors began to resist such a narrow role for the jury. They did not think they had been summoned as jurors simply to look at three elements of the statute, find that they had been met, and convict. As one juror, a doctor, asked: If such a cut-and-dried application of the statute were all that was required, then why summon a jury? The court could just as easily have turned to a computer for that purpose. In the words of the doctor: "I am not a computer, and I will not accept everything [that] I'm told . . . just because I am told that . . . it is true. I can't do that as a thinking, breathing, human being."[202] He explained that the role of juror demanded more than being a computer; it demanded that the jurors ask the following: "Has justice been done? And in my mind, I'm still trying to decide that. And that's my basic point. That's what we're here to do. It's not to just say, 'The law says this.' The judge says that, but I don't think that's what he means."[203]

Eventually, the jurors moved from the role of the jury to the question of justice. They reached this point after one hour and four minutes of deliberations and one vote in which nine jurors voted not guilty and three voted guilty.[204] Immediately after that vote, one juror who had voted guilty changed his vote to not guilty.[205] The vote was then ten to two for a not-guilty verdict. Those who had voted not guilty tried to

[201] *Inside the Jury Room* transcript, *supra* note 19, at 14 (quoting Juror Barbara Bornstein). Although other jurors pointed out to her that the statute did not require Reed to "know" that he was a convicted felon, it did require him to "know" that he possessed a handgun. Therefore, other jurors focused their comments on whether Reed knew that he possessed a handgun.

[202] *Id.* at 11.

[203] *Id.* at 15 (quoting Juror Lester Sauvage).

[204] *Id.* at 16 (describing the initial ballot).

[205] *Id.* (same).

help those who had voted guilty to see the case from the broader perspective of doing justice. As one juror in the majority explained: "I'm having a lot of trouble with that larger frame, too. I'm starting to ask some of these bigger questions about: where is justice; who is being served; even, why was this case brought?"[206] The jurors also returned to a more detailed discussion of the facts, including what Reed knew when he purchased the gun. One interpretation of these facts was that Reed was purchasing a gun, not as a weapon, but merely as one of the accoutrements, like the badge, that was needed to assume the role of private investigator as delineated in the magazine advertisement.[207]

After two hours of deliberation, and a second ballot, there was one juror, a fireman, who continued to view the case in a literal manner and to vote guilty. He worried that the other jurors were delving too deeply into what Reed knew or did not know. Although the fireman acknowledged that there could be exceptions to the law,[208] he thought the other jurors seemed to pick and choose what Reed knew or did not know. He was able to agree with the other jurors that even though the law is "a good law,"[209] the case should not have been brought by the prosecutor and the prosecution of such a case seemed, in the words of another juror, "grotesque and unreasonable."[210] However, the fireman thought the statute should be applied, in another juror's words, on "a very concrete level."[211] Ultimately, the fireman agreed that he would not "hold out to hold up 11 people that are very strong in their feelings."[212] However, at that point, he was close to tears and said that he did not feel good about going along with the others and that this decision would haunt him for the rest of his life. One juror, the only African-American man on the jury, quickly moved to take a vote, whereas another juror, a naturalist, wanted to make the fireman feel better about his decision. She was not comfortable with accepting his change of vote, if he would regret it for the rest of his life. She explained her reasoning to him, in an effort to make him feel more comfortable with his change of vote:

> I was aware of the weight that's on each one of us as a juror, and I thought, hey, this guy's guilty . . . . Could I live with my writing 'guilty'

[206] *Id.* (quoting Juror John Boly).
[207] *Id.* at 16–19.
[208] *Id.* at 21 (acquiescing that there are exceptions to the law).
[209] *Id.* at 22 (quoting Juror John Boly).
[210] *Id.* at 24 (quoting Juror Barbara Bornstein).
[211] *Id.*
[212] *Id.* (quoting Juror Karl Buetow).

> for this particular person. Boy, I mashed around with that for a while and I said, 'If there's any justice, really, it's in drawing attention to this man's personal situation or limitations.' . . . But judging him 'not guilty[,'] then I can believe in 'jury.'[213]

Thus, this jury moved from consideration of the statute and trying to interpret its meaning, particularly terms that the jurors thought were ambiguous, to a consideration of the role of the jury and what justice required in this case. Although the jury reached a decision to nullify, it came to this decision only after a full and careful consideration of the law and the facts. It achieved a result that those taking a traditional view would label as law-disregarding insofar as it did not engage in a literal application of the statute; but the jury reached its decision through a process that was law-regarding insofar as it tried to interpret the statute's terms and reconcile them with the broader purposes of the law and the jury.

What would have happened if the judge had given this jury a nullification instruction? The result would have been the same, but the jurors would have been less torn throughout their deliberations. Although almost all the jurors ultimately concluded that the jury could go beyond the literal elements of the statute and consider the role of the jury and its obligation to do justice, several jurors struggled with whether these broader issues were beyond consideration by the jury. They felt that the judge's instructions constrained them to determine whether the government had proven the three elements of the statute beyond a reasonable doubt and that they should not go beyond that limited task. They were persuaded by their fellow jurors to consider these larger issues but they also thought that they were disobeying the judge's instructions. The fireman was so reluctant to consider anything beyond the three elements of the statute that he thought he would regret his change of vote for the rest of his life. He felt great reluctance to do what the others thought they could do as jurors. If the judge had instructed the jury on nullification, the fireman would not have struggled so mightily. He would have understood that he did not have to stop at a literal interpretation if this were one of those rare cases that required nullification. Indeed, all the jurors felt that the court had deceived them when they learned about nullification after the fact. The jurors felt that if they had been instructed on nullification, they

[213] *Id.* at 25 (quoting Juror Roberta Bass).

could have reached the same verdict in less time and with far less anguish.

If the jurors had followed the instruction the judge had given them and not nullified, all of them (with the exception of the fireman) would likely have regretted their votes for the rest of their lives. Without a nullification instruction, some juries struggle with their verdict, but decide not to nullify. They feel bound to adhere to the judge's instruction to follow the law, yet they have a case before them that they think cries out for a different verdict – namely, doing justice even if it means not following the law literally. In those rare cases, the jurors need to know that the power of the jury includes the power to nullify; thus, the judge needs to instruct the jury on this power. Even if the judge does not instruct on nullification in every case, he or she should instruct on it when the jury sends a note to the judge describing its situation.[214] The judge should give a nullification instruction so that the jurors understand the jury's power and can act in accordance with it. In this way, they will not have to regret their verdict for the rest of their lives.

## SUMMARY

Before and sometimes during deliberations, the jury needs guidance from the judge, yet this is when the traditional view keeps the judge from providing any instructions at all. If judges instructed jurors on how to begin their deliberations, what qualities to look for in a foreperson, how to get their questions answered, what to do when they reach an impasse, and what the full extent of their power is – including the power to nullify – the judge will help to transform citizens into jurors during their deliberations. Some juries will figure out how to proceed without the judge's assistance at these difficult points in the deliberations, but other juries will not. If judges provide this information as a matter of course, then all jurors will enter the jury room armed with what they need to know to perform their role as responsible jurors.

[214] I realize that my position is contrary to what the Second Circuit has said when the jury sends a note to the judge indicating that one of its jurors intends to nullify. The Second Circuit has explained that the judge can interview that juror and find out whether he or she intends to nullify, and if that is the case, the judge can dismiss that juror from the jury. The Second Circuit reasoned that a judge need not stand by and refrain from taking action when informed by the jury that there is a nullifying juror. Although the Second Circuit views such a note as reason to interview and possibly dismiss the juror, *see* Thomas v. United States, 116 F.3d 606, 622 (2d Cir. 1997), I see such a note as the basis for an instruction to the jury about its power to nullify.

Although judges have not typically instructed juries on issues pertaining to their deliberations, they can do so and still make clear that it is up to the jury how to use this information. The jury is still the master of its deliberations. A judge can suggest to jurors that they wait to take a vote, but that it is still their decision. A judge can also suggest qualities that are useful for a foreperson to have and first steps that the foreperson should take, but it is entirely up to the jury whether to follow that advice. Similarly, a judge can try to answer the jury's question when the foreperson sends a note, but the judge also needs to explain that there might be instances when he or she cannot answer the jury's question. Judges can have the lawyers conduct additional argument when jurors reach an impasse rather than simply delivering a dynamite charge and telling jurors to keep deliberating. Finally, the judge can instruct jurors on their power to nullify, but make clear that it is a power that should be exercised only in rare cases. If judges take these steps, then jurors will be able to deliberate as fully informed jurors who understand the full extent of their role and can be trusted to exercise their power responsibly.

**Summary of the Jury Process**

Every stage of the jury process – from the summons to the deliberations – helps to transform citizens, who might not have wanted to serve initially, into jurors who serve responsibly. The summons, which arrives in the mail and indicates official business, alerts the recipient to the out-of-the-ordinary nature of jury duty. The setting of the courthouse and the courtroom also suggest that serious decisions are made within these formal buildings and rooms. *Voir dire*, in which prospective jurors are seated in the jury box and questioned as a group, set apart from everyone else in the courtroom and yet observed by everyone present, signals to prospective jurors that they will be asked to exercise unusual power if they are selected to serve. As prospective jurors hear those before them say that they can serve and be impartial, they start to think that they too can serve and be impartial. They might have begun *voir dire* thinking about their excuses, but in the midst of the questioning by the judge, they experience a change and start to think about why they *can* serve. The judge, through his or her questioning during *voir dire* and instructions throughout the trial, continues to develop a relationship with the jurors that helps them to understand the enormity of their task.

When the judge delivers the final instructions to the jurors before they enter the jury room for their deliberations, the public reading of the instructions reminds the jurors of the serious task that awaits them. The jurors absorb this lesson as they sit together in the jury box, with the parties before them, and listen to the judge who slowly and carefully reads the instructions that will guide them during their deliberations. The public reading conveys to jurors the seriousness of the task that lies before them.

When the jurors enter the jury room, they are isolated from all others and able to speak freely with each other. The isolation and the secrecy of the jury room protect their deliberations and allow them to focus in a way they cannot do in their daily lives. The unanimity requirement in federal courts, and in serious criminal cases in state courts, ensures that jurors will listen to each other and have to respond. No juror's point of view can be ignored. Everyone's view and vote is needed for unanimity, which is appropriate for a decision of this magnitude. Each juror must vote and the vote must be unanimous. Furthermore, jurors are often called upon to announce their vote in open court. Most citizens have never been required to make a decision that requires such attention and care.

Jury deliberations are not only the pinnacle of the transformation of citizens into jurors that every stage in the jury process has helped lead to, but also jury deliberations are the key stage that ensures that the transformation is complete. The structural features of the deliberations, including that the jurors deliberate as a group with no one else present and that their deliberations are protected by the secrecy of the jury room, help to reinforce the group nature of their work. The need to reach unanimity helps to ensure that the jurors listen and respond to each other. The unanimity requirement also helps to ensure that biases are acknowledged and resisted. The fact that the jurors are placed in a room until they, and they alone, make a decision that will have enormous consequences for the parties, whom they have observed throughout the trial, helps to ensure that jurors treat the case with a level of care that they might well not have been able to do when they were first impaneled as jurors.

The experience that citizens, as jurors, go through at every stage of the jury process helps them to behave in a remarkable way. They need to be able to work with a diverse group of strangers and come to a unanimous decision by applying complex laws to difficult-to-interpret facts to produce a verdict that is critical to the lives of fellow citizens whom they do not know. And jurors need to do this in a way that is respected and accepted by members of the community because they trust the jurors and they trust the process. Peremptory challenges, which impede the diversity of the jury and interfere with the community's trust, stand in the way of the transformation that the jury process otherwise brings about; accordingly, peremptory challenges should be eliminated.

Once jurors are done with their service, they go through a different transformation. They leave their public role as jurors and return to their private lives as citizens. There is one more stage of the jury process that can help with this transformation and that is the post-verdict interview in which the judge meets with jurors, thanks them for their service, answers their questions, and gives them information that can help them in their transformation from jurors into engaged citizens.

Judges do not always meet with jurors for a post-verdict interview, but it is an important step in jurors' transformation into engaged citizens. The post-verdict interview can also ensure that jurors return to their community as emissaries for the jury system and that judges acquire information about the jury experience from every group of jurors as this will help them to improve the experience for the next group of jurors.

# 6

# THE POST-VERDICT INTERVIEW: HOW JUDGES CAN HELP JURORS IN THEIR TRANSFORMATION FROM JURORS INTO ENGAGED CITIZENS

After the verdict has been announced in open court, the judge dismisses the jurors so that they can resume their lives as private citizens. Often that dismissal is considered the last step in the role of a juror. However, there can be a final stage of the jury process, which is the judge's post-verdict interview with the jury. A judge can conduct a post-verdict interview to thank jurors for their service, to inform them about additional proceedings in the case, to tell them that the lawyers and media might want to interview them, and to inform them about resources that are available to them should they experience stress arising from their jury service. The judge can also use the post-verdict interview to learn about the jurors' experience, to answer any questions they have, and to ask them to complete exit questionnaires that will help the judge improve jury service for future jurors. A post-verdict interview might also encourage jurors – who typically have a good jury experience – to heed their summons when they are called again, to convince their family, friends, and members of the public to serve, and perhaps to become more engaged citizens when they return to their daily lives after jury duty.

The traditional view of the post-verdict interview is that it is not an essential stage of the jury process. Although some judges hold a post-verdict interview, many judges do not. It is left to the individual judge to decide. Just as the traditional view of citizens is that they are ready to serve from the moment they enter the courthouse, the traditional view of jurors is that they are able to return to their private lives with little or no help from the judge. The traditional view essentially sees the jurors' role as over once the verdict has been announced in open court and the jurors have been polled.

According to the transformation view, however, citizens are transformed into responsible jurors through every stage of the jury process. Every stage – from summons through deliberations – helps them to become responsible jurors who understand the seriousness of the jury's task. Although the responsibility of being a juror reaches its height during the deliberations, there is still a role for jurors to play when they communicate about the trial with attorneys, the media, the public, their family, and their friends after their jury service has ended. In interviews or conversations, they need to convey that they performed their role responsibly and took their task seriously. They become emissaries for the jury system and their observations will inspire others to heed their summons and the community to accept the jury's verdict. A post-verdict interview with the judge can help them in the performance of this role.

A post-verdict interview with the judge can inform jurors that lawyers and media might want to interview them and that they should think carefully about what they want to say about how the jury went about its task. What jurors say about their jury experience in their interviews with lawyers and the media and in conversations with their friends and family will shape how other citizens respond to their summons when they receive it in the mail. What jurors say about their jury experience will also affect whether the community accepts the verdict. Jurors, who took their role seriously and deliberated carefully and impartially, need to be able to convey this to others. The post-verdict interview with the judge gives jurors notice and opportunity to think about how they want to describe their role as jurors to others.

In the group setting of the post-verdict interview, jurors can also acquire information that can help them integrate their jury experience into their own private lives. The post-verdict interview with the judge can give jurors information about what happens next in the case, what the judge's role will be, and what resources are available if they need help. There is also some evidence that those who serve as jurors might become more engaged citizens, willing to vote and to participate in community activities, after their jury service.

## WHAT THE POST-VERDICT INTERVIEW ENTAILS

The judge's post-verdict interview with the jury is the least routinized stage of the jury process. Some judges conduct such an interview, and some do not. Those judges who do conduct a post-verdict interview meet with jurors as a group after they have been dismissed and are free to leave. The meeting can take place in the courtroom, after everyone else has left it, or in the jury room or the judge's robing room, both of which are usually near the courtroom.

Judges who meet with jurors for a post-verdict interview usually start by thanking the jurors for their service. They also ask the jurors if they have any questions, other than whether the jury has reached the correct verdict. Some judges use the interview to tell jurors what the next stage in the case will be and to invite them to return and observe it. For example, in a criminal case in which the jury has convicted the defendant, jurors could return to observe the sentencing. In a particularly difficult case, the judge can tell jurors about available services, including professionals who can help jurors cope with any stress they may experience. In other cases, particularly high-profile cases, the judge can tell jurors that the media and lawyers might seek to interview them, so that they can think about what they might want to say about their jury experience. Finally, some judges use the post-verdict interview as an opportunity to ask jurors to complete a brief exit questionnaire so that judges can learn about the jurors' experience and the court can make improvements for future jurors.

## THE TRADITIONAL VIEW OF THE JUDGE'S POST-VERDICT INTERVIEW WITH JURORS

The traditional view of the judge's post-verdict interview with jurors is that once jurors have concluded their task of applying the law to the facts, have reached a verdict, and have been dismissed, there is no further role for these citizens. From this perspective, post-verdict interviews are not an essential step in the jury process. There is no rule that requires a post-verdict interview. The traditional view assumes that jurors will figure out anything they need to know about returning to their private lives. For example, if they need help coping with stress after the trial, they will find it on their own. From a judge's perspective, a post-verdict interview could present several challenges, which leads some judges to avoid an interview.

One reason that some judges might forgo a post-verdict interview is that they know that jurors are eager to leave the court and return home after their jury service. Judges typically thank jurors for their service in open court and then dismiss them. Some judges might think that any additional meeting, no matter how brief, will detain jurors when they are eager to leave the court and so they refrain from a post-verdict interview.

Another reason that some judges might decide not to meet with jurors after a verdict is because they worry that the jurors might ask them questions they are not permitted to answer. The question that is probably foremost in the jurors' mind is: Did they reach the correct verdict? However, this is the one question that the judge definitely cannot answer.[1]

Yet another reason judges might decide not to meet with jurors after a verdict is because they do not want to learn anything that might put the verdict in jeopardy. If any of the jurors' questions or comments raise an issue that the judge then needs to pursue, such as whether particular conduct on the part of any of the jurors constituted misconduct, that would threaten the verdict. This might be a case of the judge following the adage "what I don't know, can't hurt me." If the judge does not meet with jurors, then jurors will not have a convenient opportunity to raise an issue that might require further examination by the judge. A juror might still raise an issue with the judge later on if he or she continues to remain troubled by it, but it would require a little more initiative on the juror's part than a meeting with the judge right after the verdict.

## THE LIMITATIONS OF THE TRADITIONAL VIEW OF THE POST-VERDICT INTERVIEW

The traditional view of post-verdict interviews leaves the decision whether to conduct such an interview up to individual judges. Currently, some judges hold these interviews and others do not. This means that some jurors miss out on important information about what comes next for them. The traditional view assumes that jurors will acquire this information on their own if they need it, but not all jurors manage to do so.

[1] MODEL CODE OF JUD. CONDUCT Canon 2, r. 2.8(C) (AM. BAR ASS'N 2020) ("A judge shall not commend or criticize jurors for their verdict other than in a court order or opinion in a proceeding."); JURY TRIAL INNOVATIONS (2d ed.), *supra* note 93 (Ch. 1), at 170 ("[The judge] may explain that judges are not permitted to comment on the verdict but are permitted to answer general questions about the trial process."); AM. BAR ASS'N, *supra* note 14 (Ch. 3), at 127 ("Under no circumstances should the court praise or criticize the verdict or state or imply an opinion on the merits of the case . . . .").

The traditional view also fails to recognize that judges will find post-verdict interviews useful. These interviews give judges the opportunity to hear about jurors' experiences and their suggestions for improvements. In addition, if the post-verdict interview becomes an established practice, then judges can share what they learn with each other. The exit questionnaires, in particular, will yield more useful data and insights if many judges collect the same type of information.

## HOW POST-VERDICT INTERVIEWS HELP TRANSFORM JURORS INTO ENGAGED CITIZENS

Although the jury process until this point has helped transform citizens into jurors, the post-verdict interview with the judge helps by transforming jurors back into private citizens, and perhaps into more engaged citizens than they were before their jury service. The post-verdict interview can also provide jurors with an opportunity to inform the judge about how the jury experience can be improved for future jurors.

Jurors must integrate their jury experience into their private lives. Although in many cases this might be easy, in all cases there is the potential for this to be challenging due to the responsibility jurors feel about the role they played in meting out justice. The post-verdict interview aids jurors by making them feel appreciated, giving them the opportunity to speak to the judge about their experiences as jurors, and providing them with much-needed information about what happens next. Judges can use the post-verdict interview to provide jurors with information that can help them to understand the ways in which the case may proceed now that the jury has reached its verdict, whether and when they need to speak with attorneys and the media so that they can figure out what they want to say, and what to do if they feel stress or have questions or problems in the days ahead.

The interview can leave jurors feeling good about their jury service, which will lead them to be responsive when they are summoned again. The interview might even help them to become goodwill ambassadors for the jury system and encourage their friends and family to respond when they are summoned to serve. Some researchers have even observed a connection between citizens who serve as jurors and who afterward become more engaged citizens willing to perform other tasks of citizenship, such as voting.

The post-verdict interview also gives jurors an opportunity to share with the judge their experiences as jurors. In this way, jurors help to educate the judge about improvements that would benefit future jurors. Judges can use the post-verdict interview to ask jurors to complete an exit questionnaire. The information judges collect can help them to improve the jury process for future jurors.

### Meeting as a Group One Last Time

After the judge has formally thanked the jurors in the courtroom and dismissed them, he or she can informally meet with them in the jury room, the judge's robing room, or even in the empty courtroom for a post-verdict interview.[2] The judge conducts the post-verdict interview with the jurors as a group. Just as the jurors have been treated as a group from the time they first entered the courtroom, they will be treated as a group one last time by the judge. Meeting as a group ensures that the jurors hear the same information, just as they did when the judge asked them questions during *voir dire* and instructed them before their deliberations. It also means that the judge will be a less intimidating figure because the jurors, though they are now face-to-face with the judge, do not have to meet with the judge on their own. Moreover, each juror can gain confidence to ask his or her own questions by hearing the questions that other jurors ask.

### Having the Judge Show Appreciation

Most importantly, the post-verdict interview gives the judge an opportunity to thank jurors personally for their service. The interview, particularly if it is held in the more intimate setting of the jury room or robing room, means that the thanks can be given in a more personal way than in open court. But even if the interview takes place in the courtroom, the judge can add a personal touch. For example, one judge stands at the jury box as the jurors return to the courtroom and "shakes

[2] The ABA's *Principles for Juries and Jury Trials* recommends that judges meet with jurors in the presence of the parties and the lawyers. AM. BAR ASS'N, *supra* note 14 (Ch. 3), at 127 (Principle 18A). *Jury Trial Innovations* recommends that judges meet informally with just the jurors, unless the judge only feels comfortable meeting with the jurors in the presence of the parties and lawyers. JURY TRIAL INNOVATIONS (2d ed.), *supra* note 93 (Ch. 1), at 170 ("Typically, the parties and their attorneys are not invited to participate in these meetings, although some judges favor their participation in the interest of the attorneys' education."). This source notes that most judges who use the post-verdict interview meet informally with the jurors. This seems the better course, especially if the goal is to give jurors a chance to get information they need to resume their role as private citizens, including their right to say no to interviews with attorneys.

each juror's hand, looks them in the eye, and thanks them by name for their help."[3]

Since jurors tend to remember their jury experience vividly – even years later – it is important for the judge to thank jurors for their service and to emphasize that their participation is truly appreciated. This appreciation goes a long way. It leaves jurors feeling that the sacrifices they made to perform their civic duty were recognized by the judge. Some judges give jurors a certificate of appreciation, particularly during Juror Appreciation Week.[4] Although this is a nice gesture, even a simple "Thank you" makes them feel appreciated. Jurors do not receive much compensation for their jury service,[5] so the judge's gratitude becomes their recompense.

Appreciation leaves jurors feeling good about their jury service. Even though the act of judging is difficult (and judges have experience with the difficulty of judging and can allude to that shared experience),[6] appreciation from the judge acknowledges the difficulty of the jurors' task. Appreciation might also help the jurors to feel good about the hard work they did and to return more easily to their private lives. It might also inspire them to serve as emissaries for the jury system and to encourage future prospective jurors to heed their summons.

### Providing Information to Create Fully Informed Jurors

The post-verdict interview provides jurors with information that will help them to leave their public role as jurors and to return to their private lives as citizens. The judge can use the post-verdict interview to answer any remaining questions that jurors have about the trial, to explain how to handle media and attorney requests for interviews, to mention next steps in the case and how the jurors can follow the case on appeal, to provide information about resources for dealing with any stress they might feel in response to their jury service, and to give them a basic

[3] Jury Trial Innovations, *supra* note 50 (Ch. 2), at 297 (app. 12).

[4] *See, e.g.*, Nora Jones, *New York State Celebrates Juror Appreciation Week*, Daily Rec. Rochester (N.Y.) (Nov. 20, 2002), https://plus.lexis.com/api/permalink/023cc117-9c95-45f5-b4f1-2f2a5ec53039/?context=1530671 ("We are giving out certificates of appreciation to each juror called in this week.") (quoting Chuck Perreaud, New York Commissioner of Jurors for the Seventh Judicial District).

[5] For example, jurors receive $17.20 per day for their jury service in Chicago, Illinois. *See Frequently Asked Questions*, State of Ill., Cir. Ct. of Cook Cnty., www.cookcountycourt.org/For-jurors/Frequently-Asked-Questions [https://perma.cc/Q5RA-C6M6].

[6] *See, e.g.*, Cover, *supra* note 26 (Ch. 4), at 1609 ("[J]udges deal pain and death.").

understanding of juror misconduct in case they have any concerns about their deliberations.

All of this information, conveyed by the judge during the post-verdict interview, will ensure that jurors are fully informed about issues that might arise once they leave the courtroom. Just as the judge has given them information about their role throughout the trial and during any moments of difficulty in their deliberations, so too the judge should equip them to deal with issues that might arise once they leave the courtroom and leave their role as jurors behind. If jurors have this information, they will know how to respond and their preparedness will help them resume their private lives more seamlessly. The judge, by keeping jurors fully informed at this stage, just as he or she did throughout the trial, can reinforce the jurors' respect and help them to maintain the positive feelings they have developed throughout their jury experience. As one former law clerk explained: "The jurors love the chance to speak with the judge."[7]

### Giving Jurors the Opportunity to Tell the Judge about Their Jury Experience

The post-verdict interview also gives jurors an opportunity to speak about their experience as jurors. Some judges ask jurors how the judge could improve the jury experience. Thus, they give jurors a chance to reflect on their experience and to make suggestions during the post-verdict interview. Other judges ask jurors to complete a brief exit questionnaire, which gives jurors another opportunity to express their views.

The experience of serving on a jury makes a lasting impression on most jurors. They can usually recall it in great detail even many years later. The post-verdict interview is one way to help jurors talk about the experience, see it in a positive light, and share it with others afterward so that future prospective jurors will heed their summons when it arrives in the mail. Some research has even suggested that when jurors have a good experience, they return to their communities as more engaged citizens, willing to vote,[8] or possibly be more involved in

[7] Kirk W. Schuler, *In the Vanguard of the American Jury: A Case Study of Juror Innovations in the Northern District of Iowa*, 28 N. ILL. U. L. REV. 453, 483 (2008).

[8] *See, e.g.*, JOHN GASTIL, E. PIERRE DEESS, PHILIP J. WEISER & CINDY SIMMONS, THE JURY AND DEMOCRACY: HOW JURY DELIBERATION PROMOTES CIVIC ENGAGEMENT AND POLITICAL PARTICIPATION 45–46 (2010) (finding that jury service in criminal trials increased voting among low-frequency voters); Valerie P. Hans, John Gastil & Traci Feller, *Deliberative Democracy and the American Civil Jury*, 11 J. EMPIRICAL LEGAL STUD. 697 (2014) (finding that jury service in civil trials increased voting, depending on jury size, unanimity rule, defendant identity, and case type).

community activities. Similarly, perhaps these jurors, once they reenter their communities, will also be goodwill ambassadors for the jury system and change other citizens' minds about their willingness to serve.

## STEPS JUDGES CAN TAKE TO HELP JURORS IN THEIR TRANSFORMATION FROM JURORS INTO ENGAGED CITIZENS

For jurors to make the transition from jurors to private citizens, they need to be fully informed about the issues they are likely to face. Some judges will be new to post-verdict interviews and others might only address some issues but not others. However, there are a number of issues that judges can attend to in their post-verdict interviews to ensure that jurors' transformation from juror back to private citizen is a smooth one. If judges use the post-verdict interview to give jurors all the information they need to handle their return back to being private citizens, they might even become engaged citizens following their jury service.

### Answering Jurors' Questions

Post-verdict interviews need to give jurors an opportunity to ask the judge questions they have about the trial that have not yet been answered. For example, jurors could have questions about some procedure they saw in the courtroom during the trial or some procedure that is likely to follow the trial, such as sentencing. Of course, the judge will have to make clear that he or she cannot answer any questions pertaining to the verdict, and cannot say anything about whether he or she thinks the verdict is correct.[9] The judge can, however, address other questions and if there is a question that the judge thinks is inappropriate to answer, he or she can explain why, and the jurors will usually understand.

Indeed, in courtrooms in which jurors are permitted to submit written questions to witnesses via the judge, the judge explains that he or she cannot ask certain questions of the witnesses. Jurors understand this and nevertheless appreciate the opportunity to submit written questions to witnesses.[10] Courtrooms that permit juror questions to

[9] *See supra* note 1 and accompanying text.

[10] *See, e.g.*, Marder, *supra* note 78 (Ch. 4), at 740 ("Various studies, including an empirical study, pilot program, and interviews with jurors after the trial, suggest that jurors understand this instruction and follow it.") (footnotes omitted).

witnesses have produced positive responses from jurors. For example, the jurors in one trial in which jurors' questions to witnesses were permitted wrote an unsolicited letter to the judge in which they expressed their appreciation for the practice: "We sincerely hope this practice is continued and encourage its expansion to other courtrooms as well."[11]

Just as jurors appreciate the opportunity to have their questions to witnesses answered during the trial, they are likely to appreciate the opportunity to have any remaining questions answered by the judge after the trial. Although there have been no empirical studies testing this, it might be that in courts that permit jurors to ask questions of witnesses via the judge, jurors will have fewer questions to ask the judge during the post-verdict interview. So far, there is empirical and anecdotal evidence that in courts that permit jurors to ask questions of witnesses via the judge, the jurors appreciate the opportunity to ask questions,[12] even if they do not actually ask any questions.[13] The same is likely to be the case with juror questions during the post-verdict interview with the judge, though there is still a need for empirical studies to be done on this.

### Informing Jurors about Interviews with Attorneys

During the post-verdict interview, the judge should also tell jurors that the attorneys in the case might try to interview them and that it is up to the jurors to decide whether or not they want to be interviewed.[14] Different jurisdictions have different local rules and the judge should

11 Warren D. Wolfson, *An Experiment in Juror Interrogation of Witnesses*, CBA REC., Feb. 1987, at 12, 17 (quoting unsolicited letter from jurors).

12 *See, e.g.*, Larry Heuer & Steven Penrod, *Increasing Juror Participation in Trials Through Note Taking and Question Asking*, 79 JUDICATURE 256, 261 (1996) ("First, it is clear that jurors are in favor of the opportunity to ask questions and take notes."); Eugene A. Lucci, *The Case for Allowing Jurors to Submit Written Questions*, 89 JUDICATURE 16, 17 (2005) ("[J]urors universally approve of and appreciate the ability to clear up confusion by asking questions . . . ."); Wolfson, *supra* note 11, at 17 ("After each of the five cases, I asked jurors what they thought of the question-asking procedure. Each time the verdict was quick and unanimous: they were pleased and appreciative."); Patrick S. Pemberton, *Out of the Mouths of Jurors. In Los Angeles They're Letting the Jurors Quiz Witnesses*, CAL. LAW., Nov. 2000, at 18 ("[T]he judges who participated in the [L.A.] pilot program were generally pleased with the results. And so were a large majority of the participating jurors, according to a poll that was done.").

13 *See, e.g.*, Rachel M. Zahorsky, *James Holderman: Jury Duties*, A.B.A. J., Nov. 9, 2009, http://abajournal.com/legalrebels/article/james_holderman_jury_duties [https://perma.cc/8MS3-88HD] ("The mere fact that [jurors] have been invited to participate in the proceedings is enough to keep their focus.") (quoting Judge Holderman).

14 *See, e.g.*, Takasugi, *supra* note 40 (Ch. 2), at 840 ("After the verdict, the court met with the jurors to inform them of what they could expect from the newspeople and the attorneys who tried the case [in *United States v. DeLorean*].").

inform the jurors of the relevant local rules in their jurisdiction. Some local rules require the attorneys to seek the permission of the judge first and limit the subjects about which the lawyers can question jurors. If judges provide jurors with this information, then jurors can decide whether to speak to the attorneys. This knowledge is likely to make it easier for the jurors to resume their lives as private citizens. They can decide to forgo the interview with attorneys and return to their private lives immediately.

If jurors agree to be interviewed by the attorneys at least they will have had a chance to collect their thoughts beforehand and decide what they are willing to discuss. If they are forewarned by the judge about the possibility of interviews with the attorneys, they will not be caught off-guard and might have even more positive things to say about a jury system that prepares them for all kinds of interviews, including those with attorneys. If jurors know that attorneys might interview them and they agree to be interviewed, they can think carefully about what they want to say about their jury experience and how best to convey the care with which their jury undertook its task.

Attorneys have many different reasons for seeking to interview jurors after a trial. Some want to find out which of their arguments were persuasive and which ones were not. Some want to learn whether jurors found their communication or presentation skills effective or what the jurors liked or disliked about their performance or presence in the courtroom. Other times, attorneys want to discover whether there are any grounds for a claim of juror misconduct.

Jurors have responded to attorney requests for interviews in different ways. Sometimes they agree to be interviewed individually; other times, they agree to meet with the attorney as a group.[15] In some cases, jurors have prepared a statement that they do not want to discuss the trial with anyone, including the attorneys. Attorney interviews with jurors can take place by phone or in person.[16]

The key point is that the judge should tell jurors during the post-verdict interview that the attorneys might ask to interview them and that they need to know that they can decline the request. They should also know what the limitations are in their jurisdiction. In some states, such as Colorado, Idaho, and Texas, judges instruct jurors after the verdict that they are free to discuss the case with whomever they want,

[15] JURY TRIAL INNOVATIONS (2d ed.), *supra* note 93 (Ch. 1), at 174.
[16] *Id.*

but they are also free to decline all inquiries.[17] Federal courts in Louisiana and Wyoming take a similar approach, as delineated in their local rules.[18] In federal district courts in the Ninth Circuit, judges tell jurors: "[Y]ou do not *have* to talk to anyone about the case if you do not want to."[19] In federal district courts in Connecticut, there is a local rule that advises jurors that they do not have to discuss the case with anyone after the verdict.[20] Jurors are also told that they "may only speak or write about their own participation in the trial. [They] may not discuss the deliberations of the jury, votes of the jury, or the actions or comments of any other juror."[21] Lawyers and parties are prohibited from asking jurors about the jury's deliberations, votes, or the comments of other jurors.[22] Finally, there is a provision that tells jurors "no person may contact, communicate with or interview any juror in any manner which subjects the juror to harassment, misrepresentation, duress or coercion."[23] Jurors need to know that they can just say no if they do not want to talk to the attorneys. They also need to know that they can report any harassment, but if the judge does not give them this information, they might not know it. The Connecticut rules afford more protection to jury deliberations and juror privacy than do local rules for federal courts in most other states, but they are less protective of juror privacy than they once were. In the past, the *Connecticut Federal Local Court Rule* provided: "No juror shall respond to *any* inquiry as to the deliberations or vote of the jury or of any other individual juror, except on leave of Court."[24]

[17] *See, e.g.*, Colo. Sup. Ct. Comm. on Pattern Civ. Jury Instructions, Pattern Civil Jury Instructions § 1:18 (2021) ("You may now talk to anyone, including the attorneys and parties, about the case. Whether you do so is entirely up to you."); 1 Idaho Sup. Ct. Civ. Jury Instructions Comm., Idaho Jury Instructions (IDJI) 1.17, at 45 (2003) ("You many now discuss this case with the attorneys or with anyone else. For your guidance, I instruct you that whether you talk to the attorneys, or to anyone else, is entirely your own decision."); Tex. R. Civ. P. 226a ("I now release you from jury duty. Now you may discuss the case with anyone. But you may also choose not to discuss the case; that is your right.").

[18] *See* La. Loc. Ct. R. (E.D., W.D.) 47.5 ("A juror has no obligation to speak to any person about any case and may refuse all interviews or requests for comments."); Wyo. Fed. Loc. Ct. R. 47.2(b) ("No juror has any obligation to speak to any person about any case and may refuse all interviews and comments.").

[19] Jury Trial Innovations, *supra* note 50 (Ch. 2), at 293 (app. 11). The judge can provide this information in open court or during a post-verdict interview with the jury.

[20] *See* Conn. Fed. Loc. Ct. R. 83.5(1)(b).

[21] *Id.*

[22] *See id.* at 83.5(c).

[23] *Id.* at 83.5(d).

[24] Conn. Fed. Loc. Ct. R. 12 (f)(1) (1992) (emphasis added). In some countries, such as England and Wales, nobody is allowed to ask jurors about their jury deliberations. This

**Informing Jurors about Interviews with the Media**

Judges should also use the post-verdict interview with jurors to give them information about speaking to the media so that they know that they do not have to answer questions but, if they choose to do so, they can think ahead about how they want to respond. The goal of judges should be to help jurors understand what the media is likely to request so that jurors can return to their daily lives with as few interruptions and regrets as possible. In ordinary cases, the media is unlikely to be interested in interviewing jurors. However, in a high-profile case there is likely to be a lot of media interest and members of the media will probably seek out jurors in order to interview them about the trial.

The media is likely to seek out jurors for interviews from the moment the jurors appear on the courthouse steps so judges need to provide guidance so that they can return to their private lives as quickly as possible. Jurors should not have to figure out how to deal with the media without any information; otherwise, they might have regrets about what they said and how they handled the interview. At the very least, jurors should be told, as they are in some states and federal district courts, that they do not have to respond to any media requests for interviews or comments. Of course, those jurors who would like to discuss their jury experience with the media are free to do so, within the limits set by the state or federal local court rules.

A judge can also mention to jurors that if they choose to speak to the media, there are different ways they can do this. A juror can talk to a member of the media one-on-one; jurors can meet with members of the media as a group; the jurors can have one juror speak on behalf of the jury; or the jurors can prepare a written statement that they give to the media as their sole communication.[25] Although this is a decision that the jurors must all make together if they want to communicate as a group with the media, it is useful to have the judge

prohibition applies not only to lawyers and members of the press, but also to academics and researchers. *See* Contempt of Court Act, 1981 § 8(1) (Eng.) (providing that "it is a contempt of court to obtain, disclose or solicit any particulars of statements made, opinions expressed, arguments advanced or votes cast by members of a jury in the course of their deliberations in any legal proceedings").

[25] For example, after a jury acquitted Damian Williams and Henry Watson of the most serious charges in the beating of truck driver Reginald Denny during the Los Angeles riots and convicted them on several reduced charges, the foreperson arranged a meeting with the press so that she could read a statement from the jury. *See* Seth Mydans, *Leader Denies Bias or Fear on Riot Jury*, N.Y. TIMES, Oct. 26, 1993, at A16. The jury's statement explained: "The verdicts were decided according to the law, not from intimidation, fear of another riot, nor were the verdicts based on black versus white." *Id.* (quoting the jury foreperson).

lay out the possible ways of communicating with the media so that the jurors are aware of their options.

Judges can also take steps so that jurors' interaction with the media will not overwhelm them immediately. Many jurors, even those who are willing to talk to members of the media, do not feel ready to talk to them the moment the trial has ended. Deliberations can be difficult and rendering judgment in a case can be emotionally taxing. Some jurors might need a little time to recover and to consider what they want to say about their jury experience, whereas others might want to be interviewed right away so that they can then leave the public role of juror behind and return to their private role as citizen more readily. Judges also can help jurors to cope with media interviews in practical ways. In addition to alerting jurors that the media might try to interview them as soon as they step outside the courthouse, judges can arrange for jurors to exit the courthouse from a side entrance so that they can avoid an interview on the spot and have some time to prepare what they would like to say.

In high-profile cases in which jurors have been seated anonymously and their names and addresses have been withheld from the judge, the parties, the media, and the public during the trial, the jurors' identifying information can be withheld several hours or even several days after the verdict so that jurors have a little more time to recover from the trial and to consider how they want to respond to media inquiries. Even a brief delay would be useful for jurors because it would give them distance from the pressures of deliberations, and yet the postponement would only be temporary. Appellate courts have upheld limited delays in the past because the information is made public soon after.[26] After one jury trial involving multiple defendants who believed they were separate from the United States, not subject to its authority, and who occupied the Malheur National Wildlife refuge and were armed, a federal district court judge maintained the anonymity of the jurors during the trial and then took the unusual step of appointing "a pro bono attorney to represent those [jurors] interested in remaining anonymous following the trial."[27]

Jurors need some assistance from the judge so that they can avoid the limelight if they prefer and resume their private lives as soon as possible

[26] *See, e.g.*, United States v. Doherty, 675 F. Supp. 719, 723–24 (D. Mass. 1987) (withholding jurors' names and restricting the press from seeking interviews with jurors for a week following the verdict, in response to the jurors' request that their names and addresses not be released at all), *aff'd in part, rev'd in part on other grounds*, 867 F.2d 47 (1st Cir. 1989).

[27] *How Courts Care for Jurors in High Profile Cases*, *supra* note 34 (Ch. 1).

after jury service. Without such protections, citizens might become even more reluctant than they are now to heed their jury summons. Judge Zagel, who presided over the first and second criminal trials of former Illinois Governor Rod Blagojevich, noted after the first trial that the news media had become "rapacious" and that "the dogged pursuit of jurors after a verdict will deter people from wanting to serve" as jurors.[28] He suggested that the immediate release of jurors' names after the first Blagojevich trial, which had ended in a hung jury, led to incidents that could have been avoided by a short delay in releasing jurors' names. In the second trial, he decided to delay the release of jurors' names until 9 a.m. on the morning after the verdict was read, and at least twelve hours from the reading of the verdict.[29] He concluded that this brief delay was necessary to give the jurors time to figure out what they wanted to tell the media and to decide how best to protect their own privacy.[30]

Jurors also need to know that they can return to the judge for assistance if they are under siege by the media. Some state and federal courts have rules that provide that jurors are not to be harassed or intimidated by anyone after they have completed their jury service, and that includes the media. Federal district courts in Connecticut, for example, follow such a rule.[31] That way, the juror who feels that he or she is being "hounded" by the media or the juror who returns home and finds that his or her premises are surrounded by members of the media can return to court and seek the judge's assistance. State and federal district courts should move in the direction of Connecticut in terms of protecting jurors from harassment by the media.

In state or federal district courts without this kind of protection, jurors must fend for themselves. One juror fled to the Caribbean after serving as a juror in a high-profile trial, while another moved temporarily to another house.[32] After the first trial of former Illinois Governor Blagojevich, Judge Zagel said that he was "troubled" by instances in

[28] Annie Sweeney, *Blagojevich Judge Fears Media Frenzy*, CHI. TRIB., Feb. 25, 2011, at 8.

[29] United States v. Blagojevich, No. 08 CR 888-1, 2011 U.S. Dist. LEXIS 19722, at *11 (N.D. Ill. Feb. 28, 2011).

[30] *Id.*

[31] *See supra* note 23 and accompanying text.

[32] *See, e.g.*, Nancy S. Marder, *Deliberations and Disclosures: A Study of Post-Verdict Interviews of Jurors*, 82 IOWA L. REV. 465, 488–89 (1997) (providing examples of jurors who felt hounded by the press and took different approaches to escape the press – from boarding a plane to Jamaica to moving temporarily to another house); David E. Rosenbaum, *Prayer Was the Turning Point, a Juror Says*, N.Y. TIMES, May 5, 1989, at A19 (citing the experience of Juror Tara Leigh King).

which jurors had been "hounded by reporters in the hours and days following their verdict."[33] According to Judge Zagel, one juror reported that "[a] helicopter hovered" over the juror's home and another juror "complained that the same reporter rang the doorbell every half an hour."[34] After the first trial in the Blagojevich case, the holdout juror was not identified by name initially.[35] However, after the media continued to pursue her, she eventually agreed to reveal her name and to answer their questions.

Judge Zagel expressed concern that the unrelenting pursuit of jurors after a verdict will deter future jurors from being willing to serve. His concern needs to be addressed. After all, jurors do not volunteer to serve as jurors; they are summoned to serve. After they perform their role as jurors, they need to return to their lives as private citizens. If they are prevented from doing so by media camped out in front of their homes, leading them to be interviewed even though they had not wanted to be, then jurors who are summoned for the next trial are less likely to heed their summons, knowing that it can entail harassment and intimidation afterward. Jurors who are harassed by the media might be left with a bad ending to their jury experience, which would also leave them less inclined to serve as goodwill ambassadors for the jury system.

If jurors have a post-verdict interview with the judge and are forewarned about media interviews, they will have the chance to consider whether they want to be interviewed, the format they prefer for the interview, and what they want to convey about their jury experience in the interview. Jurors who agree to media interviews, whether individually or in a group, have the opportunity to convey to the public that they took their task seriously; they engaged in careful and impartial deliberation; and they arrived at their verdict only after thoughtful deliberation. Such observations about their experience are likely to help the wider community to accept the verdict whether they agree with it or not.

33 Sweeney, *supra* note 28, at 8.

34 *Id.*

35 *Compare What Went Down; Juror Stood Fast, Held out on Charge that Blagojevich Tried to Sell Obama's Senate Seat*, CHI. TRIB. (RedEye ed.), Aug. 19, 2010, at 6 (describing the holdout as "the lone holdout"), *with Blago Juror Speaks*, CHI. TRIB. (RedEye ed.), Aug. 28, 2010, at 5 ("Who is the holdout juror . . .? Her name is JoAnn Chiakulas . . . ."), *and* Stacy St. Clair, *The Holdout Juror; For the 1st Time, Suburban Woman Explains Her Vote*, CHI. TRIB., Aug. 27, 2010, at 1 ("Chiakulas and two other jurors broke their silence in an interview Wednesday night [Aug. 25, 2010] and offered their account of the deliberations and the trial's aftermath.").

### Explaining the Judge's Post-Verdict Role to the Jury

Judges also can use the post-verdict interview to explain to jurors that judges and juries work in a partnership in which they perform different tasks and that the jurors have done their part in reaching a verdict and now the judge must do his or her part. The jurors need to understand that the judge has a separate role to play after the jury has reached a verdict, and he or she is not just unraveling the work that the jury has done. The judge needs to explain to jurors about post-verdict motions, *additur* and *remittitur* in civil cases, and sentencing in criminal cases. If jurors do not know about these aspects of the judge's job, they might think that they have wasted their time if the judge is just going to modify or reject their work. They might regret their jury service, which they would not do if they had a better understanding of the interplay between the judge's and the jury's respective roles.

Although the judge does not need to go into great detail about post-verdict motions, he or she should explain briefly that in either a civil or a criminal case, the losing party can file a motion after the verdict asking the judge to review it, except if the jury acquits the defendant in a criminal case. Even if the trial judge grants one of these motions, it does not mean that the jury erred. For example, in a civil case in federal court, the losing party can file a motion for judgment as a matter of law.[36] In other words, the party argues that the judge should grant the motion because "a reasonable jury would not have a legally sufficient evidentiary basis" to find for the party on that issue.[37] In a criminal case in federal court, the defendant who has been convicted can ask the judge to grant a motion for judgment of acquittal.[38] In the criminal context, the defendant argues that the government's evidence was "insufficient to sustain a conviction."[39] In both contexts, these motions can be made before the case is submitted to the jury[40] and then renewed after the jury has returned a verdict.[41] State courts provide for similar motions. Jurors need to understand that the granting of such a motion does not mean that the jury made a mistake; it could mean that the judge wanted to wait until all the evidence was in before ruling on whether the evidence was sufficient to support the legal claim or charge. Jurors also need to understand that there are several points for

36 *See* FED. R. CIV. P. 50(a).
37 *Id.* at 50(a)(1).
38 *See* FED. R. CRIM. P. 29(b) & (c).
39 *Id.* at 29(a).
40 *See* FED. R. CIV. P. 50(a)(1) & (2); FED. R. CRIM. P. 29(a).
41 *See* FED. R. CIV. P. 50(b); FED. R. CRIM. P. 29(b) & (c).

review built into the judicial process because a verdict has such a great impact, whether in a civil or a criminal case.

In a civil case in which the jury decides liability and then damages, the judge should use the post-verdict interview with jurors to explain briefly about *remittitur* and *additur*. Otherwise, if the jurors learn that the judge decreased or increased the damages they awarded, they will wonder why they were needed at all. *Remittitur* allows a judge to reduce the damage award that the jury has reached,[42] whereas *additur* allows a judge to increase the award.[43] In other words, the jury's damage award is not the final word. The judge also has a role to play in this process. Often the judge will reduce the damage award for reasons the jury could not have been aware of, such as the need to adhere to a state statute that mandates a cap on damage awards for noneconomic injury, such as pain and suffering. In such a case, the judge's reduction of the jury's damage award does not mean that the jury "got it wrong," but rather, that the jury was not given all the information to which the judge was privy. Therefore, the judge should explain to the jury that the award of damages is a two-step process that involves both jury and judge. The jury does its part when it decides a damage award; it is then the judge's job to review that award. Otherwise, jurors might simply feel that their work was unnecessary; this was the case with some jurors who struggled with a punitive damage award, which was then reduced by the judge due to a statutory cap in that state.[44]

In one of the most well-known civil cases,[45] the so-called "McDonald's coffee cup case,"[46] a jury awarded Stella Liebeck a punitive damage award of $2.7 million for the injuries she suffered when she was severely burned

[42] Remittitur, "[t]he power to reduce damages ... is recognized by virtually all judicial systems." JACK H. FRIEDENTHAL, MARY KAY KANE & ARTHUR R. MILLER, CIVIL PROCEDURE § 12.4, at 564 (5th ed. 2015).

[43] Additur, "the power to increase damages ... has not been accepted in all courts," *id.*, largely because it did not exist under common law, leading the Supreme Court to hold in *Dimick v. Schiedt*, 293 U.S. 474 (1935), that additur violated the Seventh Amendment. *Id.* However, some state courts have upheld its constitutionality under state law. *See* FRIEDENTHAL, KANE & MILLER, *supra* note 42, at 564.

[44] *See, e.g.*, Mark Curriden, *Jury Awards Fall Under Weight of Obscure Law; Sometimes, Jurors Desire to Mete out Justice Is Outweighed by State's Limits on Amounts*, DALL. MORNING NEWS, May 7, 2000, at 1A (quoting a juror who felt that the jury's struggle to award punitive damages was unnecessary, given the judge's decision to reduce the award due to a statutory cap).

[45] Rick Lempert has described the McDonald's coffee cup case as the case "known around the world." Richard Lempert, *The American Jury System: A Synthetic Overview*, 90 CHI.-KENT L. REV. 825, 840 (2015).

[46] Liebeck v. McDonald's Rests., P.T.S., Inc., No. CV-93–02419, 1995 WL360309, at *1 (D.N. M. Aug. 18, 1994).

by a cup of McDonald's coffee.[47] The jurors did not understand why the judge reduced their punitive damages award to $480,000, particularly because Stella Liebeck had been severely injured and McDonald's had known about the problem of its exceptionally hot coffee but had declined to warn consumers or to change the temperature at which it served its coffee. The jury's award received a lot of media coverage,[48] but the judge's *remittitur* received little attention.[49] It is not surprising, then, that the jurors and public alike do not understand that the jury's damage award does not mark the end of the process, but that the award must still be reviewed by the judge. The judge can use the post-verdict interview to explain to jurors that the damage award entails a joint effort on the part of the judge and the jury.

In criminal cases, if the jury decides that the defendant is guilty, then it remains for the judge to determine the sentence, and the judge should explain this process to jurors during the post-verdict interview. With the exception of capital sentencing schemes in some states, where juries are asked in a separate penalty phase of the trial to recommend either the death penalty or a life sentence,[50] the jury has not traditionally played a role in sentencing. In both federal and state courts, that task has been left to the judge. Although juries in some states used to play a role in sentencing, that has not been the practice throughout most of American history.[51] In federal court, the judge decides the sentence and can look to, but is no longer bound by, the *United States Sentencing Guidelines*.[52] However, if the judge relies on any facts to increase the defendant's sentence, these facts need to be found by the jury. The jury's enhanced fact-finding role in sentencing was developed in a line of US Supreme Court cases.[53] Once again, both judge and jury have different, but connected, roles to play in sentencing. In the case of a conviction, the judge determines the sentence, but if the judge wants

[47] *Id.*

[48] *See, e.g.*, Nancy S. Marder, *Juries and Damages: A Commentary*, 48 DePaul L. Rev. 427, 427–28 nn.2–4 (1998).

[49] *See, e.g.*, Maura Dolan, *Huge Jury Awards Seldom Live up to Their Billing; Lawsuits: Plaintiffs Often Pocket Far Less, Study Finds*, L.A. Times, Nov. 26, 1996, at A1.

[50] *See* Marder, *supra* note 18 (Ch. 5), at 891 n.62 (providing examples of states that have capital juries decide whether to impose a life or a death sentence).

[51] *See, e.g.*, Nancy J. King, *The Origins of Felony Jury Sentencing in the United States*, 78 Chi.-Kent L. Rev. 937, 937–38 (2003).

[52] U.S. Sent'g Comm'n, Guidelines Manual (1998) [hereinafter Sentencing Guidelines].

[53] *See, e.g.*, United States v. Booker, 543 U.S. 220 (2005); Blakely v. Washington, 542 U.S. 296 (2004); Ring v. Arizona, 536 U.S. 584 (2002); Apprendi v. United States, 530 U.S. 466 (2000).

to include any enhancement, he or she can only do so if the jury has found the facts to support that enhancement.

Judges should use the post-verdict interview to provide jurors with a brief explanation of both the judge's and the jury's distinct roles in sentencing and to invite jurors to attend the sentencing if they would find it helpful.[54] In one case, the foreperson attended the sentencing because he felt that someone from the jury should be present.[55] Another judge developed the practice of sending a post-verdict letter to inform jurors about the progress of the case for which they had served as jurors.[56] In a criminal case, such an update might include the sentence the judge imposed. In a civil case, it can include whether the judge granted any motions.

Jurors might want to know what happened to their case upon sentencing or review of the verdict or damage award. This is a way of treating jurors with respect and appreciation, as well as contributing to their understanding of their role. For some jurors, this information might help them to return to their lives as private citizens, knowing that they were not the sole decision-makers but worked in tandem with the judge. Other jurors might not want to know anything more about the case, so they can put it behind them. One juror suggested in a letter to the judge that jurors might not be able to absorb everything that a judge says during a post-verdict interview because they are feeling "numb and so deeply emotionally exhausted, [they] don't hear much."[57] That same juror suggested that judges provide written information that jurors "can take with them to read at their leisure."[58]

## Explaining the Appellate Process

Just as the jury does not have the last word on the verdict or damage award, the trial judge does not have the last word either. After the jury has rendered its verdict, and the judge has acted on any motions for judgment as a matter of law (in civil cases) or judgment of acquittal (in criminal cases) as well as motions to decrease or increase the damage

[54] JURY TRIAL INNOVATIONS, *supra* note 50 (Ch. 2), at 299 (app. 12) ("For some jurors, attendance at the sentencing provides important closure.").

[55] *See, e.g.*, Marder, *supra* note 113 (Ch. 3), at 574 n.168 (mentioning a foreperson who attended the sentencing of a defendant who had been convicted of raping his stepdaughter).

[56] Donald E. Shelton, New Jury System Ideas, Jury Summit 2001, New York (Feb. 3, 2001). I thank Judge Shelton for telling me about this practice that he instituted in his courtroom in Ann Arbor, Michigan.

[57] JURY TRIAL INNOVATIONS, *supra* note 50 (Ch. 2), at 303, 306 (app. 13) (Letter from a Juror in a High-Profile Case).

[58] *Id.*

award (in civil cases) or for a new trial (in civil and criminal cases), the losing party can appeal from the final judgment as a matter of right, meaning that the appellate court has to hear the case; its review is not a matter of discretion. The only exception is if the jury acquits the defendant in a criminal case. The prosecutor cannot appeal the acquittal and the acquittal stands.

Although the jury verdict and damage award in a civil case are subject to review by the appellate court, the standard that the appellate court uses is highly deferential to the jury. The appellate court applies a deferential standard to any factual findings the jury has made, as indicated in a special verdict[59] or interrogatories.[60] The appellate court will accept a jury's factual findings unless they are "clearly erroneous."[61] In contrast, the appellate court is less deferential to the trial judge's instructions and legal conclusions, which the appellate court will review "*de novo*."[62] One reason for the difference in standards is that the appellate court can judge the law from the record and is in as good a position as the trial judge, if not better due to its distance from the trial proceedings, to render a judgment as to the correct law. However, it is much harder for an appellate court to put itself in the position of a jury that has sat through a trial and made certain credibility determinations in the course of its deliberations in order to reach factual findings as a jury.[63] Therefore, although the jury's factual findings are subject to review by trial and appellate judges, they are reviewed according to a deferential standard.

In a criminal case, the jury returns a general verdict of either guilty or not guilty. If the latter, then there is no further review by an appellate court; the jury's verdict is final. If the former, the appellate court can review it, but because it is a general verdict,[64] there are no factual

[59] *See* FED. R. CIV. P. 49(a) (Special Verdict).

[60] *See id.* at 49(b) (General Verdict with Answers to Written Questions).

[61] *See, e.g.*, Cooper Indus. v. Leatherman Tool Group, Inc., 532 U.S. 424, 440 n.14 (2001) ("While we have determined that the Court of Appeals must review the District Court's application of the *Gore* test *de novo*, it of course remains true that the Court of Appeals should defer to the District Court's findings of fact unless they are clearly erroneous.").

[62] *See, e.g.*, United States v. Edwards, 869 F.3d 490, 496 (7th Cir. 2017) ("We review *de novo* whether jury instructions accurately summarize the law, but give the district court substantial discretion to formulate the instructions provided that the instructions represent a complete and correct statement of the law.") (citations omitted); *id.* at 501 ("We review *de novo* the district court's legal conclusion regarding the constitutionality of 18 U.S.C. § 1512(b)(3).").

[63] *See* Bushel's Case (1670), 124 Eng. Rep. 1006, 1012 (C.P.) ("A man cannot see by another[']s eye, nor hear by another[']s ear, no more can a man conclude or infer the thing to be resolved by another[']s understanding or reasoning . . . ." ) (quoting Chief Justice Vaughan).

[64] *See, e.g.*, United States v. Spock, 416 F.2d 165 (1st Cir. 1969) (reversing a conviction of conspiracy to counsel draft evasion because the trial court had put to the jury ten special questions in addition to a general verdict).

findings on the record. Thus, in a criminal case, a defendant who has been convicted can ask the appellate court to review the trial judge's instructions and rulings on the law. As in the civil context, the appellate court is in as good a position as the trial judge, if not better, to decide the law, and thus, the standard of review is *de novo*.

The trial judge should explain to the jurors in the post-verdict interview that the verdict in a civil case, or in a criminal case if the defendant has been convicted, will be reviewed by the appellate court. Jurors should not feel that they are being second-guessed or that their work is being questioned. Rather, they should understand that the judicial system has multiple levels of review, and their work is part of a larger process. As one jury scholar has described it: "The jury system is a system, and both the judge and jury are key components."[65] The jurors should find it reassuring to learn that their verdict is part of a broader judicial system, and that their work, though essential to the process, does not stand alone. This knowledge might help them to shoulder their responsibility and lessen any doubts that plague them. It might help them to leave behind their role as jurors and return to their role as private citizens.

### Helping Jurors Cope with Stress

For those jurors who have trouble coping with the stress caused by their role, there are several steps that the judge can take during the post-verdict interview to aid them. Without the assistance of the judge or the court, some jurors might have difficulty leaving their jury experience behind them and resuming their daily life. Extreme juror stress is more likely to arise in cases that involve unusual circumstances, but some jurors might experience stress even in more run-of-the-mill cases.

In cases that involve gruesome evidence or issues likely to provoke a strong emotional response, the court can hire a psychologist, psychiatrist, or social worker to "debrief" the jurors after the verdict. One suggestion is that the professional hired to lead this debriefing session should have training in post-traumatic stress disorder (PTSD).[66] After the post-verdict interview, the judge can invite any jurors who are interested to attend this debriefing session led by a professional counselor (not by the judge).[67] The session should also be open to the alternate jurors and the trial judge because they would have been

[65] Lempert, *supra* note 45, at 839–40.
[66] *See* JURY TRIAL INNOVATIONS (2d ed.), *supra* note 93 (Ch. 1), at 172–73.
[67] *Id.* at 173.

exposed to the same evidence or issues.[68] In federal court, judges can authorize free counseling for jurors who served in a traumatic trial through an interagency agreement with the Federal Occupational Health Employee Assistance Program.[69]

In the case of Jeffrey Dahmer, the court made two psychiatrists available to jurors. Dahmer had been charged with the murder of a number of young boys, and the jurors had been subjected to testimony about cannibalism and sex with corpses. After the trial, the judge advised jurors that two psychiatrists would be available to talk to them. He explained that this would give jurors the opportunity to "talk, cry or vent rage."[70] The Dahmer trial exposed jurors to deeply disturbing evidence, but other cases could also result in stress, such as those that entail a lot of media attention, sequestration of jurors, lengthy trials, or the death penalty.

After the trial of mass murderer Dylann Roof in the District Court of South Carolina, jurors were offered counseling services.[71] During the trial, the jurors heard graphic details about how Dylann Roof had opened fire at close range on members of the Emanuel African Methodist Episcopal Church during their Bible study. The jurors also watched a video of the defendant laughing as he confessed to the killings in an interview with law enforcement. Finally, the jurors saw the defendant's mother collapse in the courtroom with a heart attack, after a day of hearing emotional testimony. After this traumatic trial ended, the judge and Jury Administrator made a counseling service available to all the jurors because "[j]urors aren't especially equipped to listen to or watch graphic and disturbing material."[72]

For less traumatic cases, the judge or court can provide jurors with information about possible reactions they might have and resources to turn to if their symptoms persist. For example, in Maricopa County, Arizona, the Superior Court provides a brochure called *Tips for Coping after Jury Duty*.[73] This brochure lets jurors know that some might feel stress after being a juror, and others might not. The brochure describes some of the symptoms, such as "anxiety, sleep or appetite changes, moodiness, physical problems . . . second guessing your verdict, feeling guilty, fear, trouble dealing with issues or topics related to the case" so

68 *Id.*
69 *See How Courts Care for Jurors in High Profile Cases*, *supra* note 34 (Ch. 1).
70 Dirk Johnson, *Dahmer Jurors Tell of Emotional Impact*, N.Y. TIMES, Feb. 17, 1992, at A11.
71 *How Courts Care for Jurors in High Profile Cases*, *supra* note 34 (Ch. 1).
72 *Id.* (quoting Jury Administrator Jeff Cargile).
73 JURY TRIAL INNOVATIONS, *supra* note 50 (Ch. 2), at 309–10 (app. 14).

that jurors know what they might experience.[74] The brochure provides several commonsense remedies, such as talking to friends or family members or contacting fellow jurors. Jurors who continue to experience such reactions can call any of the mental health organizations listed in the brochure and receive further assistance.

One juror, in a letter to the judge, suggested telling jurors what is "'normal'" to feel and providing jurors with literature that they can take with them after the post-verdict interview with the judge.[75] This juror pointed out that it "takes a few weeks for some reactions to surface" so jurors should have information they can read at a later point.[76] This juror also noted that "[a]ll coping skills are not equal, and if the state can ask people to make the sacrifices [jurors] must make to serve, then it seems appropriate that they have something in place to assist those who don't carry the burden as well as others."[77]

One of the messages that the trial judge needs to convey to jurors is that it is important for them to resume their everyday lives. As the Maricopa County, Arizona brochure advises: "The case is now over and it is important for you to get on with your life."[78] Although the judge cannot provide mental health counseling, he or she can provide valuable information that will aid jurors in their transition back to their private lives. This information can include letting jurors know that they might experience stress, and that in the case of unusual stress, they should seek the assistance of a professional. Some courts have tried to ease jurors' return to their daily lives by producing a brochure that gives jurors information about and resources for dealing with stress that they might need in a few days or weeks.

Juror stress can also arise from a case that involved a violent crime; after the verdict jurors are concerned about their safety or the safety of their families. Some judges address these concerns during the post-verdict interview. They explain that threats to jurors' personal safety are rare, but if a threat does occur then the juror should contact the court. Juror anxiety about their safety can cause stress, just like juror responses to the trial; in either case, the judge needs to address the problem. As one writer observed: "This discussion can help ease such concerns and enhance jurors' sense that the court is concerned about

[74] *Id.* at 310 (app. 14).
[75] *Id.* at 306 (app. 13).
[76] *Id.*
[77] *Id.*
[78] *Id.* at 309 (app. 14).

their well-being."[79] Jurors might be able to return to their daily lives more readily knowing that the judge cares and is prepared to assist them should a threat arise.

Every so often, however, there is a juror who is plagued by regrets and who is unable to move beyond the experience. Although many jurors might feel "changed" by their experience as jurors,[80] particularly in capital cases, a very few might feel so profoundly changed that they are unable to accept the vote they cast and return to their daily lives. A documentary, *Lindy Lou, Juror Number 2*, describes the experience of Lindy Lou, who was a juror in a capital case twenty years ago.[81] She, along with the other jurors, voted for a death sentence. Lindy Lou has had regrets about her vote ever since. Soon after the verdict and sentence, Lindy Lou befriended the defendant and asked for his forgiveness, which he gave her prior to his execution.

Twenty years later, Lindy Lou still has trouble accepting that she voted for the death sentence. The documentary shows her taking a journey to visit the other jurors, or at least those who are willing to meet with her, and hearing their recollections of the case. She also revisits the courtroom where the trial was held and the Mississippi State Penitentiary where the defendant was imprisoned until his execution. The other jurors have a range of reactions, from one who claims not to remember the case, to another who was unaware that the defendant had been executed, to several who are quite confident that they reached the correct result (as to the guilty verdict and the death sentence).

Lindy Lou is not sure what this journey will bring her, but she hopes it will allow her to put the trial behind her. Ever since her vote in favor of a death sentence, she has been asking herself why she voted that way. Perhaps she hopes to find answers from the other jurors. As one resource suggests, "[s]ometimes it is helpful to talk to people who went through the experience with you."[82] Lindy Lou does not emerge from her journey with any answers, but she finds solace in the idea that questioning the death penalty, even twenty years after the fact, might have a ripple effect, not just with her fellow jurors but perhaps with their children. So one possibility is that her questions, her journey, and the

79 *Id.* at 302 (app. 12).
80 *Id.* at 305 (app. 13).
81 Lindy Lou, Juror Number 2 (Public Broadcasting System 2018).
82 Jury Trial Innovations, *supra* note 50 (Ch. 2), at 310 (app. 14) (Arizona Superior Court's *Tips for Coping After Jury Duty*).

record of her journey will help future generations to rethink the death penalty.

**Grappling with Juror Misconduct**

The judge can also use the post-verdict interview to explain to jurors the term "juror misconduct" because it can arise in their interview with the attorneys or when any juror chooses to raise it with the judge after the verdict. Of course, the judge needs to proceed carefully on this topic because most cases will not involve juror misconduct and the topic might add to jurors' stress and make it more difficult for them to put their jury service behind them and to return to their daily lives. Nevertheless, it is useful for the judge to raise the issue so that the jurors know what the term means and that they can turn to the judge if they think that juror misconduct played a role in their deliberations.

One reason that attorneys might want to interview jurors after the verdict is to see if juror misconduct played any role in the case. Attorneys are not supposed to use their interviews with the jurors as fishing expeditions to see if there is any basis for challenging the verdict, but some attorneys do use the interview in this manner. Therefore, it is important for the judge to alert jurors to this possibility. If the judge briefly explains what constitutes juror misconduct and mentions that some attorneys will ask about it during their post-verdict meeting with jurors, the jurors can go into that meeting well informed. They will know from the judge, who is a neutral and authoritative source, what constitutes juror misconduct and so they will not be caught off guard by an attorney who asks them about it.

The judge also needs to inform jurors about juror misconduct in case any jurors think that juror misconduct occurred during their deliberations. Juror misconduct can arise during the trial or deliberations, but if any jurors alert the judge at the time of the conduct – whether during the trial or the deliberations – then the judge can make the necessary inquiries. For example, in *United States v. Thomas*,[83] several of the jurors complained that Juror #5 was disturbing them during the trial and so the judge interviewed all of the jurors to learn more about Juror #5's behavior.[84] The judge did not find it to be juror misconduct. However, during the deliberations, jurors wrote

[83] United States v. Thomas, 116 F.3d 606 (2d Cir. 1997) (involving several defendants convicted of violations of federal narcotics laws who appealed on the ground that the district court judge abused his discretion by removing one of the jurors pursuant to FED. R. CRIM. P. 23(b)).

[84] *Id.* at 610.

to the judge indicating that Juror #5 disagreed with the law and was not open to argument or reason.[85] The judge again interviewed all of the jurors. He wanted to learn whether Juror #5 was attempting to nullify or simply thought the prosecution had not proven its case beyond a reasonable doubt. The trial judge concluded that Juror #5 would not convict regardless of the evidence.[86] At this point, the judge removed Juror #5 and replaced him with an alternate.

After the jury convicted the defendants in *Thomas*, several of the defendants raised the issue of the removal of Juror #5 on appeal. The Second Circuit reversed, indicating that the trial judge should have engaged in further inquiry to determine if Juror #5 had met the high threshold needed to remove a juror who was in the midst of deliberations. The Second Circuit concluded that it is the task of the trial judge to dismiss for "just cause" a juror who is intent on nullifying, but that a trial judge must make sufficient inquiry to determine if that is really the juror's intent, and that the trial judge in this case had not done so.[87]

If the alleged juror misconduct comes to light after a verdict has been reached, there are narrow circumstances in which further inquiry by the judge can take place. In federal court, and in most state courts, the judge will consider juror misconduct only if the juror or jurors introduced extraneous prejudicial information or if any jurors were subjected to outside influence. *Federal Rule of Evidence* 606(b), or its state rule equivalents, limit what the judge can inquire about the jurors' deliberations. The reasons for this are to protect the finality of the verdict and the secrecy of the jury room so as to encourage candid deliberation among jurors. Judges cannot inquire into the jurors' reasoning or their "mental processes" during their deliberations.[88] However, the US Supreme Court, in *Peña-Rodriguez* v. *Colorado*, carved out an exception when the allegations were that a juror expressed racial bias against a party during jury deliberations.[89]

[85] *Id.* at 611.

[86] The trial judge concluded that Juror #5 refused to convict based on "preconceived, fixed, cultural, economic, [or] social ... reasons that are totally improper and impermissible." *Id.* at 612 (quoting trial judge).

[87] *Id.* at 617–18.

[88] FED. R. EVID. 606(b).

[89] Peña-Rodriguez v. Colorado, 137 S. Ct. 855, 869 (2017) (holding "that where a juror makes a clear statement that indicates he or she relied on racial stereotypes or animus to convict a criminal defendant, the Sixth Amendment requires that the no-impeachment rule give way in order to permit the trial court to consider the evidence of the juror's statement and any resulting denial of the jury trial guarantee").

Even before *Peña-Rodriguez*, some trial courts found racial bias during deliberations to be a form of juror misconduct that had to be addressed, and if substantiated, would require a new trial. For example, in a New York civil case, *Lam* v. *Cheng*, which involved an action for defamation and intentional infliction of emotional harm, the jury found in a 5 to 1 vote that there was not defamation by some of the defendants, that there was defamation by one defendant but not with reckless disregard of the statement's falsity, and that the one defendant who had made such a statement with reckless disregard had not caused harm to the plaintiff's reputation or standing in the community.[90]

After the verdict in *Lam* v. *Cheng*, the jury foreperson, a white man, testified that he had been verbally abused by four jurors – three African-American women and one Latina. He claimed that the four jurors expressed racial hostility toward him during the deliberations, accused him of having a homosexual encounter with the plaintiff's lawyer in the courthouse bathroom, and castigated him for reporting their racist statements to the judge. Another juror, an African-American man, agreed with the foreperson's account of the racial animus expressed during the deliberations. The four jurors continued to express racial animus toward the foreperson and the juror who had disagreed with them, in spite of the judge's admonition that race should play no part in the deliberations.

The trial judge, after observing that jury verdicts should only be disturbed in exceptional circumstances, found such circumstances in *Lam* v. *Cheng*.[91] The racial prejudice of the four jurors undermined the jury's ability to assess the evidence impartially. The court said that the affidavits of the two jurors, as well as their earlier complaints to the judge of racist behavior in the jury room, were not mere afterthoughts raised by disaffected jurors but attested to bias by the four jurors and that such bias constituted juror misconduct. The court set aside the verdict, which it found irrational and motivated by racial animus and pressure, and granted plaintiff's motion for a new trial based on juror misconduct. Although the trial judge's ruling was initially affirmed on appeal by the New York Appellate Term,[92] it was subsequently reversed by the New York Appellate Division.[93]

90 *See Jury Verdict Is Rejected as "Irrational," "Tainted by Racial Animus"*; *Lam v. Cheng*, 226 N.Y. L.J. 25 (2001).
91 2001 N.Y. Misc. LEXIS 1272 (Civ. Ct. Aug. 31, 2001).
92 762 N.Y.S.2d 759 (App. Term 2003) (per curiam).
93 773 N.Y.S.2d 303 (App. Div. 2004) (order).

Although juror misconduct does not arise very often, when it does arise jurors need to know that they can turn to the judge. If the judge briefly describes what juror misconduct is and that the jurors can alert the judge to it even after the verdict, that should make it easier for the jurors to leave behind their role as jurors and to resume their role as private citizens. They need not agonize over what to do; they need not wonder if they should take action. They know that they can turn to the judge and share their concerns about behavior during deliberations that they think might constitute juror misconduct. If jurors do not know about this outlet, they might end up keeping instances of juror misconduct to themselves and having regrets about it for years afterward. At least if they can share their concerns with the judge, he or she can either act upon them or dispel them, thus freeing jurors from these concerns and allowing them to return to their private lives more readily.

## HELPING THE JUDGE TO IMPROVE THE JURY EXPERIENCE FOR FUTURE JURORS

The post-verdict interview with jurors can also provide the judge with valuable information about how to make the juror's role more satisfying for future jurors. The judge can acquire this knowledge through his or her informal discussion with the jurors after the verdict. The judge can also acquire this knowledge more systematically by giving jurors a brief exit questionnaire at the end of the post-verdict interview. Thus, the post-verdict interview should be seen not only as a way for jurors to acquire information from the judge that will ease their return back to being private citizens, but also as a means for judges to acquire information both on an impressionistic and a systematic basis that will improve the jury experience for future jurors.

The post-verdict meeting between judge and jurors gives the judge an opportunity to hear from jurors firsthand about their jury experience and their suggestions as to how the judge could improve the experience for jurors. One suggestion is that judges use the post-verdict interview to ask jurors about their perceptions of jury service and their suggestions for improving it.[94] In particular, the judge could ask jurors "whether there were specific parts of jury service that they found particularly confusing or irritating."[95] Trial judges who do this have reported that

[94] *See* Jury Trial Innovations, *supra* note 50 (Ch. 2), at 201.
[95] *Id.*

"they learn a great deal from jurors during these meetings" and that jurors "appreciate the personal touch from the judge."[96] Another writer noted that jurors will complain about "delays and breaks in the proceedings" and wonder why they occurred and why the trial took so long.[97] These questions allow the judge to explain the gaps and to "reassure jurors that their time was not being wasted unnecessarily."[98] Some judges also ask jurors what the court could do differently to make jury service a more positive experience.[99] The judge's interest in and responsiveness to jurors help "affirm for the jurors the importance of their role and their contribution."[100]

Some judges, in addition to holding a post-verdict interview with jurors, also ask them to complete a brief exit questionnaire before they leave. Judges who use exit questionnaires are interested in getting juror feedback that will help them to make improvements in the jury experience.[101]

There are several advantages to collecting information from jurors in a consistent and systematic way over time. One benefit is that it gives judges some insights into jurors' experiences and how those experiences might vary based on demographic characteristics. For example, do court personnel treat jurors differently because of their race, gender, age, or socioeconomic status? By collecting questionnaires over time, judges can also see if any patterns change. If jurors indicate that their impression of jury service is more favorable after they have served, but that response then lessens over time, what are the possible explanations and what steps can courts take to return to the earlier pattern?

Some courts, such as the US District Court for the Western District of Tennessee, located in Memphis, Tennessee, commission exit surveys

[96] *Id.*
[97] *Id.* at 298 (app. 12).
[98] *Id.*
[99] *Id.* at 299.
[100] *Id.*
[101] *See, e.g.*, Mark W. Bennett, *Reinvigorating and Enhancing Jury Trials Through an Overdue Juror Bill of Rights: A Federal Trial Judge's View*, 48 ARIZ. ST. L.J. 481, 518 (2016) ("In every jury trial in my quarter century as a federal trial court judge, I have sought written input about the trial from the jurors after their verdict. . . . It is hard for me to imagine why a trial judge would not want, seek, and benefit from such feedback."); Marder, *supra* note 116 (Ch. 5), at 705 & n.202 (noting that Judges Schwartz and Chotiner in Los Angeles Municipal Court have distributed questionnaires to jurors for years); Schuler, *supra* note 7, at 483–84 (noting that Judge Mark Bennett, when he was a federal district court judge in the Northern District of Iowa, not only met with jurors after the verdict in order to get their feedback, but also provided them with a voluntary posttrial questionnaire).

of jurors several times a year.[102] Exit surveys from one judge, for example, revealed that the jurors' experiences "were almost uniformly positive."[103] Jurors said that they "had apprehensions going in, but had a fairly positive experience."[104] The most negative comments usually pertained to minor services that did not work properly, such as a water fountain, an eating facility, or a call-in system.[105] The Memphis court analyzes its surveys so that it has information about the demographic characteristics of jurors, the length of the case for which they served, the time they spent waiting, and their initial attitudes toward service when they received their jury summons.[106]

Although some of the exit questionnaires include questions that lead to quantitative results, other questions allow for jurors to write their own suggestions and comments.[107] The free-form response enables jurors who have just gone through the experience to speak from that experience and to share with the court their ideas about what would improve the experience for future jurors. Yet another benefit of an exit questionnaire is that it gives all jurors an equal voice. Some jurors express themselves best in conversation, whereas others feel more comfortable in writing.[108] The questionnaire provides a vehicle for those jurors who prefer to respond in writing.

The post-verdict interview, coupled with the exit questionnaire, allows the court to hear from all jurors and to hear from them in the medium through which they prefer to express themselves. Although one potential problem is that jurors who dominated the deliberations might dominate the post-verdict interview,[109] that is less of a concern in courtrooms in which the judge also distributes an exit questionnaire. If all jurors have a chance to express their views, whether in the post-verdict interview or the exit questionnaire, they are likely to feel that they have been heard by the judge. They have served as jurors and reflected on their experience and are now ready to return to their private lives.

102 BOATRIGHT, *supra* note 7 (Ch. 1), at 108–09.
103 *Id.* at 109.
104 *Id.*
105 *Id.*
106 *Id.*
107 For sample exit questionnaires, see JURY TRIAL INNOVATIONS, *supra* note 50 (Ch. 2), at 313–18 (app. 15); JURY TRIAL INNOVATIONS (2d ed.), *supra* note 93 (Ch. 1), at 215–16 (app. 7).
108 *See, e.g.*, CAIN, *supra* note 42 (Ch. 2), at 11 (noting that introverts "often feel as if they express themselves better in writing than in conversation").
109 *See, e.g.*, JURY INNOVATIONS, *supra* note 50 (Ch. 1), at 298 (app. 12).

Some judges have used the exit questionnaire to study a particular problem that they have noted in the courtroom and want to address by getting feedback directly from actual jurors. An example is the questionnaire that Judge Amy St. Eve, along with Judge Matthew Kennelly, gave to 140 jurors who had served as jurors in their two courtrooms.[110] They created a questionnaire to help them learn whether jurors used social media to discuss the trial or do research, even though these two federal district court judges had instructed jurors, multiple times throughout the trial, not to do so. In a follow-up study, Judge St. Eve, working with Judge Charles Burns, a judge in the Circuit Court of Cook County, Criminal Division, expanded and updated the earlier survey.[111] The two studies, which produced 583 completed juror questionnaires, led the authors to conclude that jurors were following the instruction to refrain from using social media to discuss the trial, and that even the small number of jurors who reported that they had been "tempted" to communicate about the trial on social media, refrained from doing so.[112] The authors concluded that the instructions on social media were an effective way to reach jurors and to persuade them to refrain from communicating online about the trial, as long as "[c]ourts . . . instruct[ed] jurors on social media early and often."[113]

The judges and law clerk who undertook these studies asked jurors directly about their use of social media to communicate about the trial; their approach was an improvement over earlier studies that had asked judges, or other court officers, to report on what they had observed. Of course, it was hard for judges and other court officers to see whether jurors discussed the trial on social media, particularly because jurors cannot be observed by judges or other court officers when they are deliberating and when they are at home.[114] The jurors were in the best position to know about their own – and even other jurors' – usage. Thus, the authors were wise to tap into this reservoir of juror knowledge. Judges would be wise to tap into this reservoir of juror knowledge in other areas as well. The use of exit questionnaires is an example of a win–win situation for judges and jurors alike. Exit questionnaires can

[110] St. Eve & Zuckerman, *supra* note 123 (Ch. 4), at 20–21.
[111] St. Eve, Burns & Zuckerman, *supra* note 128 (Ch. 4), at 64.
[112] *Id.* at 79–80.
[113] *Id.* at 87.
[114] *See, e.g.*, DUNN, *supra* note 102 (Ch. 4), at 4; CONF. OF PUB. INFO. OFFICERS ET AL., NEW MEDIA AND THE COURTS: THE CURRENT STATUS AND A LOOK AT THE FUTURE 8–9 (2010), http://cdm16501.contentdm.oclc.org/cdm/ref/collection/ctmedia/id/23 [https://perma.cc/EFZ9-U9TT].

reveal useful information to judges about the jury experience and can give jurors an opportunity to express their views about their recent experiences.

Some judges might have reservations about using exit questionnaires because they put more demands on jurors and judges alike. An exit questionnaire requires the juror to take a little extra time at the end of the trial in order to respond. At this point, jurors are eager to leave the courthouse and return to their friends and family. Jurors might also worry about how the exit questionnaire will be used and whether they will get into trouble in any way, even though the exit questionnaire is done anonymously and the judge can encourage jurors to respond candidly.

Judges might also have concerns about an exit questionnaire. They, of course, do not want to do anything that will endanger the verdict. They might worry about an exit questionnaire, even if it is completed anonymously and asks mainly about how to improve the jury experience. The questions are unlikely to elicit information about wrongdoing on the part of jurors. Judges might also be concerned that they do not have the resources to tally the results, to store the questionnaires, and to put the information they collect to good use. However, as Judge St. Eve's studies have shown, judges can look to assistance from their law clerks. Moreover, the information gleaned from a survey can be put to good use quite easily. One former magistrate in Chicago developed a short questionnaire that magistrate judges completed whenever they presided over a case that settled.[115] This questionnaire allowed magistrate judges to learn which types of cases settled and for how much, and this information was used to guide future litigants who were engaged in settlement talks.[116] Thus, a short questionnaire, which took the magistrate judges just a few minutes to complete, provided guidance that could save future litigants a lot of time and anguish when trying to settle a case.

As long as exit questionnaires are short and can be completed anonymously by jurors, they provide useful feedback and remain a valuable tool for judges and jurors alike. They might be the quickest way for judges to learn about jurors' experience, including what jurors are unwilling to say directly to a judge. They are also a way for jurors to

[115] Morton Denlow & Jennifer E. Shack, *Judicial Settlement Databases: Development and Uses*, JUDGES' J., Winter 2004, at 2–3.

[116] *Id.* (describing the form that magistrates can complete when they settle a case, which includes information about the type of case, the settlement amount and other terms, and the settlement conference dates, but no party names or case numbers).

reflect, if only briefly, on their jury experience and to share their views with the judge about what courts do well in their treatment of jurors and where improvements still need to be made. A brief exit questionnaire also gives jurors a chance to have their say before they return to their private lives.

## SUMMARY

Post-verdict interviews need to become an established practice in all courtrooms because they help jurors in their transformation from public jurors into private citizens. Post-verdict interviews could become a uniform practice used by all judges through an addition to the local rules. A post-verdict interview allows the judge to thank the jurors for their service. The judge can also provide jurors with useful information by answering their questions about the trial, explaining their options when lawyers and members of the media want to interview them, describing post-verdict motions and appeals, and letting them know what to do in case of possible post-verdict stress or juror misconduct. A post-verdict interview also gives jurors an opportunity to speak about their experience directly with the judge. Judges who ask jurors to complete an exit questionnaire can gain valuable insights into the jury experience that can help future jurors. Exit questionnaires also give jurors another way to reflect on their experience and to give voice to it.

The post-verdict interview is also a continuation of the judge–jury partnership. It provides jurors with useful information that will make their transformation from juror back to private citizen easier. At the same time, the post-verdict interview provides judges with information they need to fine-tune the jury experience for future jurors.

Jurors who are satisfied with their jury experience, as most jurors are according to polls,[117] are likely to respond to their next summons and to serve as emissaries for the jury system. They have had the experience of being a juror; their experience was meaningful; and they are happy to repeat it, as well as to share it with anyone who asks about it. One study confirmed that "by far the most prevalent source of information about jury service was prior service as a juror or conversations with others who had served."[118] Although it is not easy to counter the negative

[117] *See, e.g.*, Marder & Hans, *supra* note 2 (Intro.), at 789 & n.5 (citing polls).
[118] Boatright, *supra* note 7 (Ch. 1), at 119; *see* Diamond, *supra* note 76 (Ch. 3), at 285–86.

portrayals of jurors and juries in popular culture, the positive experience of actual jurors is perhaps the best antidote. If jurors have a chance to reflect on their jury experience before they are interviewed by lawyers or the media, they will be able to explain how they, as jurors, took their task seriously, engaged in robust deliberations, and reached a carefully considered verdict. Their public comments about how they and their fellow jurors took their responsibility seriously can help to reassure the public about the verdict and contribute to a more positive view of the jury.

The hope is that those who have actually served as jurors will share their positive jury experiences with those who have not yet served and inspire them to heed their summons when it arrives in the mail. As some research suggests, it might also be that those who have served as jurors and had a positive jury experience are more likely to become engaged citizens, such as by voting.[119] The post-verdict interview with the judge, which can add to the jurors' positive feelings about their jury service, might help jurors to move in the direction of further citizen engagement.

[119] *See* Gastil, Deess, Weiser & Simmons, *supra* note 8, at 45–46 (observing a boost to voting by infrequent voters who served on a criminal jury); Hans, Gastil & Feller, *supra* note 8, at 712 ("[C]ivil juries *can* spark a civic awakening for jurors, depending on the context of the trial.").

# CONCLUSION

The jury has been a part of the American legal landscape for so long that we rarely reflect on how juries can possibly do what we expect them to do. How can such a difficult and important task be carried out by people who, at first blush, do not seem qualified for the task?

Jurors do not have any particular knowledge or skills that suggest that they will be able to perform their task. Individual jurors have little or no knowledge about the facts of the case that they are asked to hear. They also have little or no knowledge of the law. In addition to lacking what might seem to be critical knowledge, many jurors might not have the attributes that one would expect of a legal decision-maker, such as analytic ability, interest in the issue at hand, and the ability to focus for extended periods of time. In addition, jurors must be unusually good at communicating with each other; they need to be respectful and open-minded, and to focus on the facts and the law without being distracted by their biases or predilections. The jury, consisting of strangers with no stake in the outcome of a case, must behave more effectively as a group than groups in a workplace that are brought together through a common purpose or a shared goal.

The traditional view of the jury is that there is no significant problem in finding qualified jurors. Jurors who are up to the task can be found by screening out those who have some untoward bias or particular lack of capability. Of course, early in American history, the pool from which jurors were drawn consisted only of white men with property, and it was only many years later that the jury pool was extended to include citizens of all genders, races, and ethnicities.

The transformation view rejects the idea that jurors are found ready to serve; instead, it recognizes that jurors are made, not found. They are transformed from a group of individuals, who are strangers to each other and who have their own biases, as any group does, and who might even lack an interest in serving as jurors, at least initially. However, through the jury process, they become a group that can work together and use their collective experience and perspectives to reach unanimous agreement on a verdict. As I have argued in each chapter, each stage of the jury process contributes to creating experiences that reinforce certain behaviors that jurors will need by the time they deliberate.

The transformation view enables us to see that the various stages of the jury process – from the summons through the post-verdict interviews – are part of a single progression that brings out the necessary qualities in the jurors. If jurors are made not found and it is the stages of the jury process that transform citizens into responsible jurors, what are the implications of this new understanding of the American jury system?

One implication of the transformation view is that more citizens can serve as jurors. The traditional view is that only those who enter the courtroom as impartial can be jurors, but this is a limited view of who can serve. If, instead, the jury process is what brings about the transformation of citizens into jurors, then most citizens can serve. The only citizens who cannot serve are those who cannot survive a for cause challenge because they acknowledge that they cannot be impartial, have family members involved in the trial, or have a financial stake in the outcome of the trial.

In the United States, citizens who might have doubts about their ability to be a juror should be reassured that they can serve, and serve well. The juror who described "[e]ntering a jury box for the first time" as "entering unknown territory" does not have to worry that he finds it daunting at the outset.[1] He and other citizens do not have to walk into the courtroom knowing how to be jurors. They can be reassured that they can move from their role as private citizens to their role as jurors by virtue of the jury process. Every stage of the process will help them to step into this new role, even though "[i]t has no familiar cues and it can be an uneasy experience."[2] Yet, as this same juror recognized by the end of his jury service, "[e]xperiencing it is the only possible preparation."[3]

1 Jury Trial Innovations, *supra* note 50 (Ch. 2), at 305 (app. 13).
2 *Id.*
3 *Id.*

Another implication of the transformation view is that citizens in other countries who might have doubts about their ability to serve as jurors, particularly in countries that do not have a history of juries, should also be reassured. If the stages of their jury process track those in the United States, and their judges play a similar role as American judges, their jury process will transform their citizens into jurors as well.

There has been a resurgence of interest in citizen participation in legal decision-making around the world. In some countries, such as Spain, Russia, the Republic of Georgia, and several provinces in Argentina, this has taken the form of the jury.[4] Citizens do not have to be fearful about whether they have the capacity to serve. Indeed, when Japan first considered having citizens serve as lay judges along with professional judges on *Saiban'in seido* or collegial panels in criminal trials, one of the fears that citizens voiced was whether they had the knowledge, ability, or time to play this role.[5] The jury process in the United States, which helps to transform citizens into jurors at every stage, could serve as a model for countries that are considering or have already instituted a jury system and could assuage citizens' concerns about being unfamiliar with the role they have been asked to play.

Citizens in these countries can look to American juries and see that American citizens summoned to serve do not enter the courthouse as ready-made jurors; instead, jurors are made, not found. They might come from different walks of life and have different backgrounds, but when they enter the courtroom they share a mix of emotions including awe, fear, and even dread. Yet, the jury process works. It brings these individuals together as "a unique group,"[6] and at every stage of the jury process they understand more about what it means to be a juror so that by the time they deliberate, they can do so as an impartial jury. Of course, jurors do not go through this process alone. The judge plays an integral part. Judge and jury work together, with each performing its respective role, and through the back-and-forth between judge and jury – beginning with *voir dire* and ending with the post-verdict interview – citizens step into their role as jurors.

There is great interest around the world in the American jury system, even in countries that do not have such a system. One indication is the

[4] *See generally* JURIES, LAY JUDGES, AND MIXED COURTS: A GLOBAL PERSPECTIVE (Sanja Kutnjak Ivković, Shari Seidman Diamond, Valerie P. Hans & Nancy S. Marder eds., 2021).

[5] *See* MATTHEW J. WILSON, HIROSHI FUKURAI & TAKASHI MARUTA, JAPAN AND CIVIL JURY TRIALS: THE CONVERGENCE OF FORCES (2015).

[6] JURY TRIAL INNOVATIONS, *supra* note 50 (Ch. 2), at 305 (app. 13).

number of countries that have made their own version of the most famous American jury film, *12 Angry Men*. To date, there are foreign remakes of this iconic film in Russia, Spain, China, Japan, India (in Hindi and Tamil), the Netherlands, Germany, and Lebanon.[7] In some of these countries, the foreign version tracks the American version every step of the way; the main difference is that the jurors are played by actors from that country speaking in their own language.[8] In other versions, there are slight adjustments so that the film is more understandable to viewers in that country.[9]

In these countries' remakes of *12 Angry Men*, the central question remains the same: How can a group of ordinary citizens carry out such an important and difficult task? It is the story of twelve individuals, several of whom are ignorant, prejudiced, or indifferent, who are summoned to serve as jurors. The initial response, at least for eleven of the twelve jurors, is to make quick work of their task. The eleven vote to convict. After all, the professionals involved in the case – the lawyers and the judge – do not seem to care. However, after a vote to acquit by one juror, the other eleven jurors eventually step into their role as jurors. In the end, the jurors make as careful a decision as they can, fully recognizing that they are deciding the defendant's fate.

The film *12 Angry Men* speaks to audiences in countries across the globe, regardless of whether their government is democratic or authoritarian or whether their judicial system uses juries or does not. Unlike the United States, where most citizens accept that juries can work, many other countries are now grappling with this question. Thus, the film resonates with disparate audiences. One reason it might appeal to audiences in other countries is that it shows how a group of ordinary citizens can carry out an important and difficult task. Another reason it might be so compelling to foreign audiences is because the jury has come to symbolize the essence of democracy.

Over the centuries, the American jury trial has become one of the most powerful symbols of the judicial system both in the United States and around the world. From front-page newspaper coverage to films, a trial by jury has been the cornerstone of a system that, for all its faults, has set the standard for justice and fairness in the United States and

[7] *See* Nancy S. Marder, *What Hollywood, USA, Teaches the World (Incorrectly and Correctly) about Juries*, *in* JURIES, LAY JUDGES, AND MIXED COURTS: A GLOBAL PERSPECTIVE, *supra* note 4, at 285, 297.

[8] *Id.* at 300–01.

[9] *Id.* at 297–99.

abroad. The number of jury trials in the United States is undoubtedly decreasing,[10] but the jury continues to play an outsized role in American society. There might not be many jury trials, but those that do take place are often the subject of extensive media coverage. In addition, those who serve on the jury are deeply moved by their experience. Years afterward, they can recall their experience as a juror and describe it as if it had just taken place. However, after over two centuries of success and acceptance, the jury system is at the center of a debate in the United States and in some other countries about whether it will endure, whether it needs significant reforms, and, if so, what kinds of reforms.

One lesson that becomes clear is that reforms to the American jury system need to be made by looking at the jury process as a whole. If every stage of the process helps to transform citizens into jurors, then any reform needs to be evaluated according to how well it contributes to that transformation. The traditional view, with its focus on each stage in isolation, misses how these stages connect as a whole and misidentifies the purpose of each stage.

Every stage of the jury process needs to be reformed in line with the goal of transforming citizens into jurors. The summons, rather than being written in formal, intimidating legalese, as the traditional view finds acceptable, needs to be rewritten so that it is accessible to ordinary citizens and does not inspire fear or dread, but rather elicits a positive response that encourages citizens to heed their summons. *Voir dire*, which, according to the traditional view, focuses on determining which prospective jurors will be impartial, needs to shift from cursory questions that are unable to uncover hidden biases to questions about the role of the juror and how the ordinary citizen can draw on his or her past experience to play that role. Peremptory challenges, which provide lawyers with the opportunity to remove prospective jurors about whom they have doubts or against whom they are biased, need to be eliminated because they lead to less diverse juries. Diverse juries help in the transformation of citizens into jurors because jurors learn from each other. Jury instructions, which are delivered orally by the judge at the

[10] *See, e.g.*, THOMAS, *supra* note 104 (Ch. 2), at 147–85 (proposing an approach to halt the decline in jury trials); Shari Seidman Diamond & Jessica M. Salerno, *Reasons for the Disappearing Jury Trial: Perspectives from Attorneys and Judges*, 81 LA. L. REV. 119 (2020) (elucidating reasons for the decline in jury trials based on a survey of lawyers and judges); Mark Galanter, *A World Without Trials?*, 2006 J. DISP. RESOL. 7 (describing the precipitous decline in trials); Mark Galanter, *The Vanishing Trial: An Examination of Trials and Related Matters in Federal and State Courts*, 1 J. EMPIRICAL LEGAL STUD. 459 (2004).

end of the trial in open court still need to be delivered in that manner to remind jurors what is at stake, but the substance also needs to be conveyed in a variety of ways to meet jurors' different learning styles, including providing jurors with an individual written copy of the instructions, allowing jurors to take notes, and giving jurors the opportunity to ask questions about the instructions.

The deliberations mark the culmination of the transformation of citizens into jurors. By the time jurors reach this stage of the jury process, they need to be ready to deliberate on their own, beyond the watch of the judge and lawyers. Yet, even at this stage, they need not be left entirely adrift, as the traditional view suggests. Rather, deliberations need to be reformed so that the judge gives jurors some guidance about how to begin their deliberations, even if, in the end, jurors choose not to follow that advice. Deliberations also need further involvement by the judge if the jury reaches an impasse. The judge, rather than issuing the typical instruction to the jury to keep deliberating, needs to see if additional argument by the lawyers would be useful.

The post-verdict interview, which some judges provide and others do not, needs to become incorporated into the jury process. These interviews provide judges with a unique opportunity to guide jurors from their role as jurors back to their role as private citizens by giving them critical information, such as whether and in what form they should speak to lawyers and the media after the trial and whom to contact if they experience post-trial stress or suspect juror misconduct. A post-verdict interview with the judge can help jurors to return to their private lives more easily because it gives them information they might need. Post-verdict interviews, in which the judge thanks the jurors for their service and answers their remaining questions, can also add to jurors' satisfaction with their jury experience. The judge's appreciation for the task that jurors have performed is likely to enhance their experience and might even encourage them to urge their friends and families to serve whenever they are summoned.

The reforms that are likely to aid in the transformation of citizens into jurors would benefit from empirical testing beforehand. Researchers could examine summonses, described in Chapter 1, and how they could be redesigned so that they are easier to read and less likely to intimidate recipients. Researchers could collect summonses from all US states, develop metrics to evaluate which ones are accessible to lay people and which ones are off-putting. State courts could incorporate the design elements from the most successful states' summonses into their own summonses or just adopt the summons that does best in the testing because it conveys the relevant information most effectively. The summons from Massachusetts, which researcher Robert Boatright identified as a model for other states to follow over twenty years ago, might or might not be the best model for states today.[11] Testing could shed light on this question.

In this digital era when images and visual depictions are so essential to how information is conveyed, a summons that contains only words might not be the best way to reach people. State courts could work with design schools to develop summonses, consisting of words and images that are easy to understand and capture people's attention. Even if the summons still consists only of words, these could be placed on the page in ways that make them clear and easy to grasp.[12] Just as over time airlines have become more creative with the videos they have developed to familiarize travelers with an airplane's features and safety procedures, so too, courts could break free from the common practice of attempting to squeeze as many words as possible on a page and try a mix of words and images so that each reinforces the message of the other.

A reform raised in Chapter 2 is whether citizens would be aided in their transformation into jurors if they donned plain black robes, much like judges wear. Some courts, assisted by jury researchers, could conduct a pilot program to see how jurors respond to wearing robes and whether the robes help them to assume their role as jurors. Although courts are usually reluctant to try pilot programs, they have done so when all of the trial participants agree in advance,[13] the state supreme court has provided for such pilot programs,[14] or the federal circuit has agreed that several federal district court judges can try a pilot program, as was done a number of years ago in the Seventh Circuit as part of the Seventh Circuit American Jury Project.[15]

[11] BOATRIGHT, *supra* note 7 (Ch. 1), at 126–28 (app. 1).

[12] *See, e.g.*, EDWARD R. TUFTE, THE VISUAL DISPLAY OF QUANTITATIVE INFORMATION 180 (1983) (observing that "words and pictures belong together" and can aid in the presentation of complicated information).

[13] *See, e.g.*, *Inside the Jury Room* transcript, *supra* note 19 (Ch. 5), at 1; *Enter the Jury Room* transcript, *supra* note 54 (Ch. 5), at 4.

[14] *See, e.g.*, Nicole L. Mott, *The Current Debate on Juror Questions: "To Ask or Not to Ask, That Is the Question,"* 78 CHI.-KENT L. REV. 1099, 1104 (2003) (describing "one pilot program during the first half of 2000, [when] the Supreme Court of New Jersey authorized juror questioning [of witnesses] for the purpose of evaluating the procedure in civil trials").

[15] *See, e.g.*, Holderman, *supra* note 107 (Ch. 2), at 786 & n.3 (describing the Seventh Circuit American Jury Project).

Another approach to determine whether it is helpful for jurors to wear robes is for researchers to use mock jurors. They could have two juries – one wearing robes and one not wearing robes – observe the same mock trial. They could then compare how the two groups experienced their role as jurors through questionnaires and interviews. They could also use benchmarks for group performance (such as whether the jury reached a unanimous verdict, and if so, how long it took) and cohesiveness (such as how many votes the jurors took during deliberations and how far apart they were in their voting until they reached unanimity) to see if the jurors wearing robes performed their role more easily than jurors who were not wearing robes. However, each type of study (mock jury or pilot program) has limitations so it is useful to try both approaches.

The elimination of peremptory challenges, a reform proposed in Chapter 3, can be studied by taking a comparative approach. Although some lawyers and judges in the United States are likely to resist the elimination of peremptory challenges, other countries' experiences might begin to assuage their concerns. England and Wales eliminated peremptory challenges in 1989, and barristers, judges, and the public remain supportive of the change.[16] One empirical study in England in 2010 found that the public still regarded jury trials as fair.[17] Another country that researchers could study is Canada. In 2019, the Parliament of Canada eliminated peremptory challenges and, in 2020, the Supreme Court of Canada upheld the change as constitutional.[18] Researchers could interview lawyers and judges in Canada to see how they are finding the new system. They could also observe jury selection in a variety of trial courts in Canada to see how it is working in practice. Although *voir dire* is different in Canada than in the United States,[19] researchers could observe what is working and what is not working as courts in Canada conduct jury selection without peremptory challenges. One result might be that jury selection goes more quickly;

[16] *See* Marder, *supra* note 113 (Ch. 3), at 553–55.

[17] *See* Thomas, *supra* note 111 (Ch. 2), at 45.

[18] *See, e.g.*, Julia Schabas, *The Abolition of Peremptory Challenges in R v Chouhan: A License for Discrimination or Safeguard for Representative Juries?*, COURT.CA (Nov. 23, 2020), http://www.thecourt.ca/the-abolition-of-peremptory-challenges-in-r-v-chouhan-a-license-for-discrimination-or-safeguard-for-representative-juries/ [https://perma.cc/HY5Q-NSLR].

[19] *See, e.g.*, Kent Roach, *A Good First Step Towards Diverse, Impartial Canadian Juries*, THE CONVERSATION (Apr. 2, 2018, 6:18 PM), https://theconversation.com/a-good-first-step-towards-diverse-impartial-canadian-juries-94257 [https://perma.cc/B7YT-SNQH].

another result might be that the petit juries are more diverse and include Indigenous people.

In the United States there are also experiments with peremptory challenges taking place at the state level that need to be studied. Recent changes in jury selection in Washington and California have tried to make it easier for a party to establish that the other side has exercised a discriminatory peremptory challenge.[20] In both states, a discriminatory peremptory challenge is one that an objective observer who "is aware that implicit, institutional, and unconscious biases, in addition to purposeful discrimination, have resulted in the unfair exclusion of potential jurors" would find discriminatory.[21] The lawyer objecting to the peremptory no longer has to establish purposeful discrimination and the typical reasons that courts have accepted in the past to justify a peremptory challenge will no longer be accepted in Washington and California. Whether by rule or legislation, Washington and California have identified a number of presumptively invalid reasons for justifying the exercise of a peremptory, such as that the prospective juror lives in a high-crime neighborhood or has family members who have had encounters with the police.

Of course, if lawyers develop ways to circumvent this new standard or to provide new reasons that are not among the prohibited reasons identified by the legislative or rule changes, Justice Thurgood Marshall will have been correct in his assessment that the only way to eliminate *discriminatory* peremptory challenges is to eliminate *all* peremptory challenges.[22] The elimination of peremptory challenges in Arizona could lead other states in the direction that Justice Marshall suggested. As researchers study the way that jury selection proceeds in Arizona without peremptory challenges,[23] they might find that juries are more diverse; jury selection is quicker than before; and lawyers and judges have adjusted to the change.

Although peremptory challenges have long been a mechanism for excluding prospective jurors based on their race, gender, or ethnicity,

[20] *See supra* text accompanying notes 132–47 (Ch. 3).

[21] WASH. ST. SUP. CT. GEN. R. 37(f) (2018); *see* CAL. CODE CIV. P. § 231.7 (d)(1) ("If the court determines there is a substantial likelihood that an objectively reasonable person would view race, ethnicity, gender, gender identity, sexual orientation, national origin, or religious affiliation, or perceived membership in any of those groups, as a factor in the use of the peremptory challenge, then the objection shall be sustained.").

[22] Batson v. Kentucky, 476 U.S. 79, 103 (1986) (Marshall, J., concurring).

[23] *See* Kanu, *supra* note 12 (Ch. 3) (describing Arizona's recent decision to eliminate peremptory challenges).

other potentially discriminatory mechanisms, such as for cause challenges or juror qualifications, also need to be the subject of empirical study. For example, it might be that for cause challenges need to be defined more narrowly so that judges' biases do not affect who gets removed by for cause challenges.[24] Similarly, juror qualifications need to be scrutinized to ensure that they are necessary and not based on stereotypical assumptions about who can serve. Jury scholars have just begun to conduct empirical studies in these areas,[25] but more work needs to be done.

Chapter 4 considered the way in which judges read the jury instructions aloud to the jurors as they are seated together in the jury box and argues that this group experience is essential for the jurors, even if this is not the best way for jurors to absorb the substance of the instructions. Because this public reading is important to the transformation of citizens into jurors who take their responsibility seriously, the judge has to rely on other ways to ensure that jurors understand the substance of the instructions. One way is to give jurors certain tools, such as an individual written copy of the instructions to follow during the reading or at least pen and paper to take notes during the reading. Another way is to give jurors the chance to ask the judge questions about the instructions after the reading. Judges usually resist this option because it could lead them to make off-the-cuff remarks that will result in reversals by appellate courts.[26]

However, judges could try the practice of permitting jurors to submit questions about the instructions as a pilot program, just as some judges did with the practice of permitting jurors to submit questions for witnesses. If judges permitted a pilot program in which jurors could submit written questions about the instructions, researchers could conduct empirical studies of the practice just as they did with the practice of permitting jurors to submit written questions to the

[24] *See, e.g.*, Frampton, *supra* note 178 (Ch. 3), at 785 (studying for cause challenges and finding that judges grant them more often when the prospective jurors are African American rather than white); Anna Offit, *Benevolent Exclusion*, 96 WASH. L. REV. 613 (2021) (examining hardship excuses and suggesting that judges' broad discretion might lead to the exclusion of poor prospective jurors even when they could actually serve as jurors).

[25] *See, e.g.*, BINNALL, *supra* note 164 (Ch. 3), at 46–92 (testing convicted felons and how they perform as jurors); Frampton, *supra* note 178 (Ch. 3), at 785 (examining for cause challenges).

[26] *See, e.g.*, Cate & Minow, *supra* note 72 (Ch. 4), at 1111 (describing one conference exchange when then Federal District Court Judge Stanley Sporkin was asked why he did not break with past practice and improve jury instructions, he looked over to then Chief Judge Abner Mikva of the United States Court of Appeals for the District of Columbia, and explained: "[Chief Judge Mikva] would overturn me.").

witnesses. In those early empirical studies of jurors' questions for witnesses, researchers looked at how many questions jurors asked of witnesses, the types of questions they asked, how much time the questions added to the trial, and how jurors felt about the opportunity to ask these questions.[27] The answers to these and other questions helped to convince lawyers and judges to adopt the practice in a number of states, and empirical studies of jurors' questions about the instructions are likely to have a similar effect.

There is also the need for empirical testing of instructions that could aid jurors in their deliberations. As described in Chapter 5, judges do not typically instruct jurors on how to begin their deliberations, even though jurors express the need for some guidance. Judges worry about intruding in the deliberations in any way because the deliberations are supposed to remain the province of the jury. The few judges who do give some guidance, such as advising jurors to avoid taking a vote right away or suggesting qualities that are useful for a foreperson to have, believe that such guidance is useful for the jury. Moreover, they take care to tell the jurors that it is up to them to decide whether to follow these suggestions. Empirical testing of such instructions would be useful. If researchers learned that jurors find such guidance useful, that they do not find it intrusive, and that they understand that they are free to depart from the judge's suggestions, other judges might be willing to provide jurors with some instructions on how to begin their deliberations.

Chapter 5 also proposed that the judge should instruct the jury on what to do if it reaches an impasse and what to do if it feels compelled not to follow the law. In the case of an impasse, the typical instruction does not provide much guidance to jurors. In the case of the jury that asks whether it has the power to nullify (even if the jury does not use that word), judges say nothing at all. There is the need for empirical testing of the kind of instruction that should be given in both of these situations. Little work has been done on the effect of an *Allen* charge, which judges give when a jury sends a note indicating it has reached an impasse. An *Allen* charge provides little direction to jurors, and yet, it seems to exert pressure on holdouts to go along with the majority.[28] Although there have been some empirical studies on instructing jurors on nullification in the past,[29] this topic has not been explored recently.

[27] *See, e.g.*, Mott, *supra* note 14, at 1111–19.

[28] *See, e.g.*, CHAKRAVARTI, *supra* note 12 (Ch. 5), at 57–58.

[29] *See, e.g.*, Irwin A. Horowitz, *Jury Nullification: The Impact of Judicial Instructions, Arguments, and Challenges on Jury Decision Making*, 12 LAW & HUM. BEHAV. 439 (1988); Irwin A. Horowitz,

Some years ago, judges concluded that an instruction on nullification would lead to "anarchy" and "chaos."[30] All federal and state courts ultimately concluded that they would not instruct on nullification, but renewed interest and study by jury researchers could reopen that question.

The post-verdict interview described in Chapter 6, in which judges meet with jurors after the verdict, is the least well-established stage of the jury process. Some judges hold such an interview, but others do not. However, it should become an accepted part of the jury process. If post-verdict interviews became widespread and judges gave jurors exit questionnaires to complete, jurors' experiences would be more widely understood.

This stage of the jury process is in much need of study. A starting point is to examine how judges use the post-verdict interview. Different judges seem to use it in different ways, and some judges ask jurors to complete an exit questionnaire. If judges used a common exit questionnaire, then a much broader picture of the jurors' experience would emerge.

The post-verdict interview could serve multiple purposes. One goal of this interview is for the judge to thank jurors for their service and to answer their questions. Another goal is to provide them with much-needed information. Yet another goal could be to encourage jurors to share their jury experience with their friends and family and urge them to heed their summons when they receive it in the mail. There might be other ways for judges to encourage jurors to become goodwill ambassadors for the jury system, and perhaps even more active citizens when they return to their private lives. The post-verdict interview remains an untapped source for obtaining juror feedback and encouraging juror engagement. Researchers could study which, if any, of these goals the post-verdict interview is able to advance.

Throughout every stage of the jury process, judges are central to the transformation of citizens into jurors yet researchers have not focused on the judge–jury relationship. Some judges are very attentive to this relationship and others are not. Are judicial courses an effective way to get judges to focus on the judge–jury relationship and to develop steps

*The Effect of Jury Nullification Instruction on Verdicts and Jury Functioning in Criminal Trials*, 9 LAW & HUM. BEHAV. 25 (1985).

[30] United States v. Dougherty, 473 F.2d 1113, 1133–34 (D.C. Cir. 1972) ("This so-called right of jury nullification is put forward in the name of liberty and democracy, but its explicit avowal risks the ultimate logic of anarchy.").

to improve this relationship, or is there a better way? A first step would be to have new judges take a course on the judge–jury relationship as part of the judicial education programs for new judges. A second step would be for researchers to figure out other junctures during the trial when the jury looks to the judge for direction or guidance and to make sure that the judge is aware of those moments and responsive to them. The post-verdict interview is an opportunity for the judge to put this question directly to the jurors and see what they recommend.

The judge can play an important role in the transformation of citizens into impartial jurors. The judge typically conducts the questioning of prospective jurors during *voir dire*, at least in federal court. The exchange between judge and jury during *voir dire* begins the judge–jury relationship. The questions the judge chooses to ask can also assist the transformation of citizens into jurors. During *voir dire*, prospective jurors shift from wanting to be excused from jury duty to wanting to serve as jurors. The exchange between judge and jury continues as the judge instructs the jury about the law. The judge's instructions need to take place throughout the trial as well as at the end so that the jurors can learn from the judge over time. The exchange needs to be two-way, with jurors being given the opportunity to ask questions about the instructions. Even though the jurors conduct their own deliberations, the judge still has an important role to play. The judge can provide jurors with some guidance at the start of their deliberations so that they do not feel adrift and overwhelmed when they enter the jury room. After the verdict, the judge needs to talk to the jurors again, not only to thank them for their service, but also to prepare them to return to their lives as private citizens. Although the jury process transforms citizens into jurors, having a judge who recognizes that he or she can assist in this transformation is extremely helpful. Otherwise, jurors have to fulfill their role in spite of the judge. They can do this, but it makes their task more difficult. As one former juror observed about an unhelpful judge: "The judge ... liked his juries as out of it as possible. This became clear early [on] ... ."[31]

Tocqueville, the French writer who visited the United States in the 1830s and wrote *Democracy in America*,[32] recognized both the power of the American jury and the unique role that the judge could play in helping jurors to fulfill their task and to become better citizens after

[31] BURNETT, *supra* note 39 (Ch. 1), at 81.
[32] TOCQUEVILLE, *supra* note 3 (Intro.).

serving as jurors. Tocqueville saw the jury as enhancing democracy in several ways. Juries taught citizens how to engage in self-governance. Ordinary citizens had to work together on the jury to reach a verdict that had legal consequences. Juries, not judges, would decide certain kinds of cases. This division of power, so central to American democracy, would also ensure that these legal decisions were widely accepted because they were made by ordinary citizens in their role as jurors rather than by professional judges.

Tocqueville also saw the jury as an opportunity for jurors to learn from the judge and to take these lessons with them and to put them into effect in their daily lives. He argued that jurors would learn from the judge how to act judiciously and they would then act judiciously in their daily lives and in business affairs. Thus, jurors would spread a judge's reasoning far beyond the courtroom.

Tocqueville was right that jurors take lessons from the judge and that the relationship between judge and juror is central to the juror's experience. He suggested that the judge–jury relationship taught jurors how to be better citizens after they had served as jurors and that they would take their newly acquired judicious thinking and apply it to their everyday lives. Although this might be true, the judge–jury relationship also helps citizens to become responsible jurors. Judges, however, do not do this alone.

When today's citizens enter the courtroom, hesitant though they may be about being there, every stage of the jury process – from the summons to the post-verdict interview – helps to transform them from ordinary citizens into responsible jurors. This is the unrecognized power of the jury. The stages of the jury process that citizens experience as jurors enable them to become jurors. The power of the American jury system is that its very structure contains the key to transforming ordinary citizens into responsible jurors.

# INDEX

CAMBRIDGE STUDIES IN LAW AND SOCIETY

*Books in the Series*

*Diseases of the Will: Alcohol and the Dilemmas of Freedom*
Mariana Valverde

*The Politics of Truth and Reconciliation in South Africa: Legitimizing the Post-Apartheid State*
Richard A. Wilson

*Modernism and the Grounds of Law*
Peter Fitzpatrick

*Unemployment and Government: Genealogies of the Social*
William Walters

*Autonomy and Ethnicity: Negotiating Competing Claims in Multi-Ethnic States*
Yash Ghai

*Constituting Democracy: Law, Globalism and South Africa's Political Reconstruction*
Heinz Klug

*The Ritual of Rights in Japan: Law, Society, and Health Policy*
Eric A. Feldman

*Governing Morals: A Social History of Moral Regulation*
Alan Hunt

*The Colonies of Law: Colonialism, Zionism and Law in Early Mandate Palestine*
Ronen Shamir

*Law and Nature*
David Delaney

*Social Citizenship and Workfare in the United States and Western Europe: The Paradox of Inclusion*
Joel F. Handler

*Law, Anthropology, and the Constitution of the Social: Making Persons and Things*
Edited by Alain Pottage and Martha Mundy

*Judicial Review and Bureaucratic Impact: International and Interdisciplinary Perspectives*
Edited by Marc Hertogh and Simon Halliday

*Immigrants at the Margins: Law, Race, and Exclusion in Southern Europe*
Kitty Calavita

*Lawyers and Regulation: The Politics of the Administrative Process*
Patrick Schmidt

*Law and Globalization from Below: Towards a Cosmopolitan Legality*
Edited by Boaventura de Sousa Santos and César A. Rodríguez-Garavito

*Public Accountability: Designs, Dilemmas and Experiences*
Edited by Michael W. Dowdle

*Law, Violence and Sovereignty among West Bank Palestinians*
Tobias Kelly

*Legal Reform and Administrative Detention Powers in China*
Sarah Biddulph

*The Practice of Human Rights: Tracking Law between the Global and the Local*
Edited by Mark Goodale and Sally Engle Merry

*Judges beyond Politics in Democracy and Dictatorship: Lessons from Chile*
Lisa Hilbink

*Paths to International Justice: Social and Legal Perspectives*
Edited by Marie-Bénédicte Dembour and Tobias Kelly

*Law and Society in Vietnam: The Transition from Socialism in Comparative Perspective*
Mark Sidel

*Constitutionalizing Economic Globalization: Investment Rules and Democracy's Promise*
David Schneiderman

*The New World Trade Organization Knowledge Agreements: Second Edition*
Christopher Arup

*Justice and Reconciliation in Post-Apartheid South Africa*
Edited by François du Bois and Antje du Bois-Pedain

*Militarization and Violence against Women in Conflict Zones in the Middle East: A Palestinian Case-Study*
Nadera Shalhoub-Kevorkian

*Child Pornography and Sexual Grooming: Legal and Societal Responses*
Suzanne Ost

*Darfur and the Crime of Genocide*
John Hagan and Wenona Rymond-Richmond

*Fictions of Justice: The International Criminal Court and the Challenge of Legal Pluralism in Sub-Saharan Africa*
Kamari Maxine Clarke

*Conducting Law and Society Research: Reflections on Methods and Practices*
Simon Halliday and Patrick Schmidt

*Planted Flags: Trees, Land, and Law in Israel/Palestine*
Irus Braverman

*Culture under Cross-Examination: International Justice and the Special Court for Sierra Leone*
Tim Kelsall

*Cultures of Legality: Judicialization and Political Activism in Latin America*
Javier Couso, Alexandra Huneeus, and Rachel Sieder

*Courting Democracy in Bosnia and Herzegovina: The Hague Tribunal's Impact in a Postwar State*
Lara J. Nettelfield

*The Gacaca Courts, Post-Genocide Justice and Reconciliation in Rwanda: Justice without Lawyers*
Phil Clark

*Law, Society, and History: Themes in the Legal Sociology and Legal History of Lawrence M. Friedman*
Edited by Robert W. Gordon and Morton J. Horwitz

*After Abu Ghraib: Exploring Human Rights in America and the Middle East*
Shadi Mokhtari

*Adjudication in Religious Family Laws: Cultural Accommodation, Legal Pluralism, and Gender Equality in India*
Gopika Solanki

*Water on Tap: Rights and Regulation in the Transnational Governance of Urban Water Services*
Bronwen Morgan

*Elements of Moral Cognition: Rawls' Linguistic Analogy and the Cognitive Science of Moral and Legal Judgment*
John Mikhail

*Mitigation and Aggravation at Sentencing*
Edited by Julian V. Roberts

*Institutional Inequality and the Mobilization of the Family and Medical Leave Act: Rights on Leave*
Catherine R. Albiston

*Authoritarian Rule of Law: Legislation, Discourse and Legitimacy in Singapore*
Jothie Rajah

*Law and Development and the Global Discourses of Legal Transfers*
Edited by John Gillespie and Pip Nicholson

*Law against the State: Ethnographic Forays into Law's Transformations*
Edited by Julia Eckert, Brian Donahoe, Christian Strümpell, and Zerrin Özlem Biner

*Transnational Legal Ordering and State Change*
Edited by Gregory C. Shaffer

*Legal Mobilization under Authoritarianism: The Case of Post-Colonial Hong Kong*
Waikeung Tam

*Complementarity in the Line of Fire: The Catalysing Effect of the International Criminal Court in Uganda and Sudan*
Sarah M. H. Nouwen

*Political and Legal Transformations of an Indonesian Polity: The Nagari from Colonisation to Decentralisation*
Franz von Benda-Beckmann and Keebet von Benda-Beckmann

*Pakistan's Experience with Formal Law: An Alien Justice*
Osama Siddique

*Human Rights under State-Enforced Religious Family Laws in Israel, Egypt, and India*
Yüksel Sezgin

*Why Prison?*
Edited by David Scott

*Law's Fragile State: Colonial, Authoritarian, and Humanitarian Legacies in Sudan*
Mark Fathi Massoud

*Rights for Others: The Slow Home-Coming of Human Rights in the Netherlands*
Barbara Oomen

*European States and Their Muslim Citizens: The Impact of Institutions on Perceptions and Boundaries*
Edited by John R. Bowen, Christophe Bertossi, Jan Willem Duyvendak, and Mona Lena Krook

*Environmental Litigation in China: A Study in Political Ambivalence*
Rachel E. Stern

*Indigeneity and Legal Pluralism in India: Claims, Histories, Meanings*
Pooja Parmar

*Paper Tiger: Law, Bureaucracy and the Developmental State in Himalayan India*
Nayanika Mathur

*Religion, Law and Society*
Russell Sandberg

*The Experiences of Face Veil Wearers in Europe and the Law*
Edited by Eva Brems

*The Contentious History of the International Bill of Human Rights*
Christopher N. J. Roberts

*Transnational Legal Orders*
Edited by Terence C. Halliday and Gregory Shaffer

*Lost in China? Law, Culture and Society in Post-1997 Hong Kong*
Carol A. G. Jones

*Security Theology, Surveillance and the Politics of Fear*
Nadera Shalhoub-Kevorkian

*Opposing the Rule of Law: How Myanmar's Courts Make Law and Order*
Nick Cheesman

*Ironies of Colonial Governance: Law, Custom and Justice in Colonial India*
James Jaffe

*The Clinic and the Court: Law, Medicine and Anthropology*
Edited by Ian Harper, Tobias Kelly, and Akshay Khanna

*The World of Indicators: The Making of Government Knowledge through Quantification*
Edited by Richard Rottenburg, Sally E. Merry, Sung-Joon Park, and Johanna Mugler

*Contesting Immigration Policy in Court: Legal Activism and Its Radiating Effects in the United States and France*
Leila Kawar

*The Quiet Power of Indicators: Measuring Governance, Corruption, and Rule of Law*
Edited by Sally Engle Merry, Kevin E. Davis, and Benedict Kingsbury

*Investing in Authoritarian Rule: Punishment and Patronage in Rwanda's Gacaca Courts for Genocide Crimes*
Anuradha Chakravarty

*Contractual Knowledge: One Hundred Years of Legal Experimentation in Global Markets*
Edited by Grégoire Mallard and Jérôme Sgard

*Iraq and the Crimes of Aggressive War: The Legal Cynicism of Criminal Militarism*
John Hagan, Joshua Kaiser, and Anna Hanson

*Culture in the Domains of Law*
Edited by René Provost

*China and Islam: The Prophet, the Party, and Law*
Matthew S. Erie

*Diversity in Practice: Race, Gender, and Class in Legal and Professional Careers*
Edited by Spencer Headworth, Robert L. Nelson, Ronit Dinovitzer, and David B. Wilkins

*A Sociology of Constitutions: Constitutions and State Legitimacy in Historical-Sociological Perspective*
Chris Thornhill

*A Sociology of Transnational Constitutions: Social Foundations of the Post-National Legal Structure*
Chris Thornhill

*Genocide Never Sleeps: Living Law at the International Criminal Tribunal for Rwanda*
Nigel Eltringham

*Shifting Legal Visions: Judicial Change and Human Rights Trials in Latin America*
Ezequiel A. González-Ocantos

*The Demographic Transformations of Citizenship*
Heli Askola

*Criminal Defense in China: The Politics of Lawyers at Work*
Sida Liu and Terence C. Halliday

*Contesting Economic and Social Rights in Ireland: Constitution, State and Society, 1848–2016*
Thomas Murray

*Buried in the Heart: Women, Complex Victimhood and the War in Northern Uganda*
Erin Baines

*Palaces of Hope: The Anthropology of Global Organizations*
Edited by Ronald Niezen and Maria Sapignoli

*The Politics of Bureaucratic Corruption in Post-Transitional Eastern Europe*
Marina Zaloznaya

*Revisiting the Law and Governance of Trafficking, Forced Labor and Modern Slavery*
Edited by Prabha Kotiswaran

*Incitement on Trial: Prosecuting International Speech Crimes*
Richard Ashby Wilson

*Criminalizing Children: Welfare and the State in Australia*
David McCallum

*Global Lawmakers: International Organizations in the Crafting of World Markets*
Susan Block-Lieb and Terence C. Halliday

*Duties to Care: Dementia, Relationality and Law*
Rosie Harding

*Insiders, Outsiders, Injuries, and Law: Revisiting "The Oven Bird's Song"*
Edited by Mary Nell Trautner

*Hunting Justice: Displacement, Law, and Activism in the Kalahari*
Maria Sapignoli

*Injury and Injustice: The Cultural Politics of Harm and Redress*
Edited by Anne Bloom, David M. Engel, and Michael McCann

*Ruling Before the Law: The Politics of Legal Regimes in China and Indonesia*
William Hurst

*The Powers of Law: A Comparative Analysis of Sociopolitical Legal Studies*
Mauricio García-Villegas

*A Sociology of Justice in Russia*
Edited by Marina Kurkchiyan and Agnieszka Kubal

*Constituting Religion: Islam, Liberal Rights, and the Malaysian State*
Tamir Moustafa

*The Invention of the Passport: Surveillance, Citizenship and the State, Second Edition*
John C. Torpey

*Law's Trials: The Performance of Legal Institutions in the US "War on Terror"*
Richard L. Abel

*Law's Wars: The Fate of the Rule of Law in the US "War on Terror"*
Richard L. Abel

*Transforming Gender Citizenship: The Irresistible Rise of Gender Quotas in Europe*
Edited by Eléonore Lépinard and Ruth Rubio-Marín

*Muslim Women's Quest for Justice: Gender, Law and Activism in India*
Mengia Hong Tschalaer

*Children as 'Risk': Sexual Exploitation and Abuse by Children and Young People*
Anne-Marie McAlinden

*The Legal Process and the Promise of Justice: Studies Inspired by the Work of Malcolm Feeley*
Jonathan Simon, Rosann Greenspan, and Hadar Aviram

*Gift Exchanges: The Transnational History of a Political Idea*
Grégoire Mallard

*Measuring Justice: Quantitative Accountability and the National Prosecuting Authority in South Africa*
Johanna Mugler

*Negotiating the Power of NGOs: Women's Legal Rights in South Africa*
Reem Wael

*Indigenous Water Rights in Law and Regulation: Lessons from Comparative Experience*
Elizabeth Jane Macpherson

*The Edge of Law: Legal Geographies of a War Crimes Court*
Alex Jeffrey

*Everyday Justice: Law, Ethnography, and Injustice*
Sandra Brunnegger

*The Uncounted: Politics of Data in Global Health*
Sara L. M. Davis

*Transnational Legal Ordering of Criminal Justice*
Gregory Shaffer and Ely Aaronson

*Five Republics and One Tradition*
Pablo Ruiz-Tagle

*The Law Multiple: Judgment and Knowledge in Practice*
Irene van Oorschot

*Health as a Human Right: The Politics and Judicialisation of Health in Brazil*
Octávio Luiz
Motta Ferraz

*Shari'a, Inshallah: Finding God in Somali Legal Politics*
Mark Fathi Massoud

*Policing for Peace: Institutions, Expectations, and Security in Divided Societies*
Matthew Nanes

*Rule of Law Intermediaries: Brokering Influence in Myanmar*
Kristina Simion

*Lactation at Work: Expressed Milk, Expressing Beliefs, and the Expressive Value of Law*
Elizabeth A. Hoffmann

*The Archival Politics of International Courts*
Henry Redwood

*Global Pro Bono: Causes, Context, and Contestation*
Edited by Scott L. Cummings, Fabio de Sa e Silva, and Louise G. Trubek

*The Practice and Problems of Transnational Counter-Terrorism*
Fiona de Londras

*Decoupling: Gender Injustice in China's Divorce Courts*
Ethan Michelson

*Anti-Constitutional Populism*
Martin Krygier, Adam Czarnota, and Wojciech Sadurski

*The Ghostwriters: Lawyers and the Politics behind the Judicial Construction of Europe*
Tommaso Pavone

*The Power of the Jury: Transforming Citizens into Jurors*
Nancy S. Marder

For EU product safety concerns, contact us at Calle de José Abascal, 56–1°,
28003 Madrid, Spain or eugpsr@cambridge.org.

www.ingramcontent.com/pod-product-compliance
Lightning Source LLC
LaVergne TN
LVHW011810200926
848484LV00005B/1133

* 9 7 8 1 1 0 8 4 8 3 3 1 5 *